THEATRUM CHEMICUM BRITANNICUM.

CONTAINING

Severall Poeticall Pieces of our Famous *English Philosophers*, who have written the *Hermetique Mysteries* in their owne Ancient Language.

Faithfully Collected into one Volume, with Annotations thereon,

By ELIAS ASHMOLE, *Esq.*

Qui est Mercuriophilus Anglicus.

THE FIRST PART.

Serpens et Bufo gradiens sup terrã, Aquila volans, est nostrũ Magisteriũ.

LONDON,

Printed by *J. Grismond* for NATH: BROOKE, at the Angel in *Cornhill.* MDCLII.

TO

All Ingeniously Elaborate Students, In the most Divine Mysteries of *Hermetique Learning*.

THe Subject *of this ensuing* Worke, *is a* Philosophicall *account of that Eminent* Secret *treasur'd up in the bosome of* Nature; *which hath been sought for of* Many, *but found by a* Few, *notwithstanding* Experienc'd Antiquity *hath afforded* faithfull (*though not* frequent) Discoveries *thereof. Past* Ages *have like* Rivers *conveied downe to us, (upon the floate,) the more* light, *and* Sophisticall *pieces of* Learning; *but what were* Profound *and* Misterious, *the weight and solidity thereof, sunke to the Bottome*; *Whence every one who attempts to dive, cannot easily fetch them up: So, that what our* Saviour *said to his* Disciples, *may (I hope without offence) be spoken to the Elected* Sons *of* Art; Unto you it is given to know the Mysteries of the Kingdome of God; but to others in Parables, that seeing they might not see, and hearing they might not understand,

Our English Philosophers *Generally*, (*like* Prophets) have received little honour (*unlesse what hath beene privately paid them*) in their owne Countrey; nor *have they* done any mighty Workes amongst us, *except in covertly administring their* Medicine *to a* few Sick, *and* healing them. (*For greater* Experiments *then what it performes in* Physick, *they never publikely made shew of.*) *Thus did* I.O. (*one of the first foure* Fellowes *of the* Fratres R. C.) *in curing the young* Earle *of* Norfolke, *of the* Leprosie; *and* Doctor B. *in carrying off the* virulency *of the* Small-pox, *twice, from* Queen Elizabeth; *insomuch that they never appeared. But in* Parts abroad *they have found more noble* Reception, *and the* world *greedy of obteyning their* Workes; *nay, (rather then want the sight thereof) contented to view them through a* Translation, *though never so imperfect. Witnesse what* Maierus, Hermannus, Combachius, Faber, *and many others have done; the first of which came out of* Germanie, *to live in* England; *purposely that he might so understand our* English Tongue, *as to Translate* Norton's Ordinall *into* Latin *verse, which most judiciously and learnedly he did: Yet (to our shame be it spoken) his* Entertainement *was too too course for so deserving a* Scholler.

How great a blemish is it then to us, that refuse to reade so Famous Authors *in our* Naturall Language, *whilst* Strangers *are necessitated, to* Reade *them in* Ours, *to understand them in their* Own, *Yet think the dignity of the* Subject, *much more deserving, then their* Paines.

If this we do but ingeniously Consider, we shall judge it more of Reason *that we looke back upon, then neglect such* pieces of Learning *as are* Natives *of our owne* Countrey, *and by this* Inquisition, *finde no* Nation *hath written more, or better, although at present (as well through our owne* Supinenesse, *as the* Decrees *of* Fate,) *few of their* Workes *can be found.* John Leland *tooke very much paines, even at the yeilding up of the* Ghost, *of our* English Learning, *to preserve its* latest *(but* weakest, *'cause almost spent)* Breath; *and from him* John Bale, *with* John Pitts *(who indeed is but* Bale's Plagiary) *hath left us a* Catalogue *of the* Writers *of this* Nation, *and that's neere all. Yet* Posterity *for this is deeply obliged. What* punishment *then did their pestilent* Malice *deserve, who rob'd us of their whole* Workes?

A Juditious Author *speaking of the* Dissolution *of our* Monasteries, *saith thus:* Many Manuscripts, guilty of no other superstition then Red letters in the Front, were condemned to the Fire; and here a principall Key of Antiquity was lost to the great prejudice of Posterity. *Indeed (such was* Learnings *misfortune, at that great Devastation of our* English Libraries, *that) where a* Red letter *or a* Mathematicall Diagram *appeared, they were sufficient to intitle the* Booke *to be* Popish *or* Diabolicall.

Our English Nation *hath ever beene happy for* Learning *and* Learned men, *and to illustrate this, I hope it will not prove distastfull.*

As first, the Druydæ *(the famous and mysterious* Druydæ) *that were* Priests, Diviners, *and* Wise men: *and took their* Originall *and* Name *from* Druys Sarronyus *the* fourth King *of the* Celts, *(styled* Sapientum & Augurum Doctor,) *who dyed Anno Mundi.* 2069.

Next

Next the Bardi, *who celebrated the* Illustrious Deeds *of* Famous Men, *which they ingeniously dispos'd in* Heroique Verse, *and sung them to the sweete* Melody *of the* Harpe : *Amongst other* Testimonies *hereof receive* Chaucer's ;

> The old gentle Brittons in her dayes
> Of divers aventures maden Layes,
> Rymed first in her Mother Tongue,
> Whych Layes, with her Instruments they songe.

These Philosophers *had their Name from* Bardus Druydus *(the* 5 King *of the* Celts,) *Who was the first* Inventor *of* Verses, *as* Berosius *tells us ; and dyed* An.Mundi 2138. *Neither of these* Sects *of* Philosophers *used any* writing (*indeed it Was not lawfull ; for,) such Was the* Policy *and* Curiosity *of* Elder Ages (*to defend their* Learning *and* Mysteries *from the Injury of* Ignorant Interpretations) *that they delivered them to* Posterity, *by* Tradition *only.*

Cæsar *testifies, (and tis a noble* Testimony) *That the* Learning *of the* Druydi, *Was first invented in* Britaine, *and thence transferr'd into* France ; *and that, in all his time , those of* France *came over hither to be Instructed.* Agricola (*in* Tacitus) *preferrs the* Britaines *before the* Students *of* France (*notwithstanding that they Were of a* docible Wit, *and apt to* Learne) *in that they were curious in attaining the* Eloquence *of the* Latin Tongue.

As for Magick, Pliny *tells us, It flourished in* Britaine, *and that the* People *there were so devoted to it (yea, with all Complements of* Ceremony) *a man would think that even the* Persian *learned his* Magick *thence.*

A Germane Poet, *sayes, that when the World was troubled with* Pannonick Invasions, England *flourished in the knoWledge of all* good Arts; *and Was able to send of her* Learned Men *into other Countries, to propogate* Learning ; *and instances* Winifrid (*alias* Boniface *the* Devonshire *Man) and* Willebroad (*the* Northerne *Man) that were sent into* Germany.

Nay more, England *was twice* Schoole-Mistris *to* France (*for so saith* Peter Ramus) *viz. First by the* Druydæ (*Who taught them their* Discipline) *and afterwards by* Alcunius, *in* Charles the Great's *time, through whose perswasions the* Emperour *founded the* University *of* Paris.

For the Saxons, *it is not to be denied but that many of them , after their conversion to* Christianity, *were exceedingly* Learned, *and before that, much addicted to* Southsaying, Augury, *Divination* by the Neighing *of* Horses, *&c. And tis worth the Enquiry (there being more in it then we ordinarily apprehend) why they in Generall worshiped* Herthus [*i. e. Dame* Earth] *for a* Goddesse, *and honoured* Mercury *above all the* Gods *of the* Germanes, *Whom they called* Wooden, (*hence* Wodensday *now our* Wednesday:) *For, they believed that this Dame* Herthus *Intermediated in* Humane Affaires *and* Relieved *the* Poore; *whose* Image *was made* Armed, *standing among* Flowers, *having in its* right hand *a* Staffe, *and in it a* Banner, *wherein was painted a* Rose; *In the other* Hand *a* Ballance, *and upon the* Head *thereof a* Cock; *on the* Brest *a carved* Beare, *and before the* Midle, *a fixed* Scutchion; *in* Chiefe *whereof was also a* Ballance; *in* Face, *a* Lyon; *and in* Point, *a* Rose. *And for their* God Wooden *they esteemed him as their* God *of* Battaile, *representing him by an* Armed Man. *Insomuch that wee to this very day retaine the Word* Wood *among us, to Signifie Fierce, Furious, Raging,* [*as When one is in a great* Rage, *we usually say he is* Wood:] *So the* Mercury *of the* Philosophers *is shaddowed under the fierce and terrible Names of* Lyon, Dragon, Poyson, *&c. But this is not* All, *although it be* Something.

And now to come yet neerer to our Selves; *we must needs say that of* Later Times *(since the* Conquest) *our Nation hath produced such* Famous *and* eminently learned Men, *as have equall'd (if not surpast) the greatest* Schollers *of other* Nations, *and happy were We if now we could but partake of those* Legacies *they left; and which* Envy *and* Ignorance *has defrauded us of: (Howsoever the small remainder which is left, we have good reason to prize,*

For out of olde Fields as Men saythe,
Cometh alle this new Corne fro yeare to yeere:
And out of olde Bokes in good faythe
Cometh alle this Scyence, that Men leare.)

That England *hath beene successively enrich'd with such* Men, *our Country men* John Leland *(and I never heard he was* Partiall) *abundantly* Testifies: *who avers, That* Generally *Wee have had a great number of excellent* Wits *and* Writers, *learned With the best as* Times *served, who besides their knowledge in the* foure Tongues, *in which*

which part of them excelled, there was no Liberall Science or any Feate concerning Learning, in which they have not shewed certainte Arguments of great Felicity and Wit. And thus much for the Generality of Learning.

Now for a Particular account of the Hermetique Science, vouchsafe (Ingenious Reader) to accept the ensuing Collections, yet not so, as if therein were contained all the Workes of our English Hermetique Philosophers, (for more are design'd in a Second Part to follow and compleate this a full Theatrum; the which GOD allowing me further Time and Tranquility to run through it, as I have already this, I intend shortly to make ready for the Presse.) Whereby yet more to manifest what Men we have had, no lesse famous for this kinde of Philosophy, then for all other Commendable Arts and Sciences.

To adde any thing to the praise thereof, were but to hold a Candle before the Sunne; or should I here deliver a full Account of the Marvellous Operations and Effects thereof, it would be as far beyond the limits of a Preface, as remote from the Beliefe of the generality of the World. Nor doe I expect that all my Readers should come with an Engagement, to believe what I here write, or that there was ever any such thing in rerum natura as what we call A Philosophers Stone, nor will I perswade them to it, (though I must tell them I have not the vanity to publish these Sacred and Serious Mysteries and Arcana, as Romances) tis enough that I know Incredulity is given to the world as a punishment. Yet Ile tell them what one of our Ancient Poeticall Philosophers sayes,

If yow wyl lysten to my Lay,
Something thereby yow maie finde,
That may content your minde:
I will not sweare to make yow give credence,
For a Philosopher will finde, here in Evidence
Of the Truth; and to Men that be Lay,
I skill not greatly what they say.

I must professe I know enough to hold my Tongue, but not enough to Speake; and the no lesse Reall then Miraculous Fruits I have found in my diligent enquiry into these Arcana, lead me on to such degrees of Admiration, they command Silence, and force me to lose

my

my Tongue. *Yet, as one greatly affecting my* Native Countrey, *and the satisfaction of all* Ingenious Artists, *I have published (for their use) these ensuing* Collected Antiquities; *and shall here say something more then they speak of.*

He who shall have the happinesse to meet with S. Dunstans *Worke* De Occulta Philosophia, (*a Booke which* E.G.A.I. *made much use of, and which shall chiefly back what here I am about to say) may therein reade such* Stories *as will make him* amaz'd *to think what* stupendious *and* Immense *things are to bee performed by vertue of the* Philosophers Mercury, *of which a* Taste *onely and no more.*

And first, of the Minerall Stone, *the which is wrought up to the degree onely that hath the power of* Transmuting *any* Imperfect Earthy Matter *into its utmost degree of* Perfection; *that is, to convert the basest of* Metalls *into perfect* Gold *and* Silver; Flints *into all manner of* Precious Stones; [*as* Rubies, Saphirs, Emeralds, *and* Diamonds, *&c.*] *and many more* Experiments *of the like nature. But as this is but a* part, *so it is the least share of that* Blessing *which may be acquired by the* Philosophers Materia, *if the full vertue thereof were knowne.* Gold *I confesse is a delicious* Object, *a goodly* Light, *which we admire and gaze upon* ut Pueri in Junonis avem; *but, as to make* Gold (*saith an incomparable* Authour) is the cheifest intent of the Alchimists, so was it scarce any intent of the ancient Philosophers, *and the lowest use the* Adepti *made of this* Materia.

For they being lovers of Wisdome *more then* Worldly Wealth, *drove at* higher *and more* Excellent Operations: *And certainly* He *to whom the whole* Course *of* Nature *lyes open, rejoyceth not so much that he can make* Gold *and* Silver, *or the* Divells *to become* Subject *to him, as that he sees the* Heavens *open, the* Angells *of* God *Ascending and Descending, and that his own Name is fairely written in the* Book of life.

Next, to come to the Vegitable, Magicall, *and* Angelicall Stones; *the which have in them no part of the* Minerall Stone (Quatenus *a* Stone, Fermented *with* Metalline *and* Earthy Nature) *for they are marvelously* Subtile, *and each of them differing in* Operation *and* Nature, *because* Fitted *and* Fermented *for severall* Effects *and* Purposes. *Doubtlesse* Adam (*with the* Fathers *before the* Flood, *and since)* Abraham, Moses, *and* Solomon, *wrought many* Wonders *by them, yet the utmost of their* Vertues *they never fully understood; nor indeed any* but GOD the Maker of All things in Heaven and Earth, blessed for evermore.

For. by the Vegitable *may be perfectly known the* Nature *of* Man, Beasts, Foules, Fishes, *together with all kinds of* Trees, Plants, Flowers, *&c. and how to* produce *and make them* Grow, Flourish & beare Fruit; *how to encrease them in* Colour *and* Smell, *and when and where we please, and all this not onely at an instant,* Experimenti gratia, *but* Daily, Monethly, Yearly, *at any* Time, *at any* Season; *yea, in the depth of* Winter. *And therefore not unlike, but the* Wallnut-Tree *which anciently grew in* Glastenbury Church-yard, *and never put forth* Leaves *before S.* Barnabies Day, *yet then was fully loaded with them, as also the* Hawthorne *there, so greatly fam'd for shooting forth* Leaves *and* Flowers *at* Christmas, *together with the* Oake *in* New-Forrest *in* Hampshire *that bore greene* Leaves *at the same* Season; *may be some* Experiments *made of the* Vegitable Stone.

Besides the Masculine *part of it which is wrought up to a* Solar Quality, *and through its exceeding* Heat *will* burne *up and* destroy *any* Creature, Plant, *&c. That which is* Lunar & Feminine *(if immediately applyed) will mitigate it with its extreme* Cold: *and in like manner the* Lunar Quality *benums and congeals any* Animall, *&c. unlesse it be presently helped and resolved by that of the* Sun; *For though they both are made out of* one Natural Substance *yet in working they have contrary* Qualities: *neverthelesse there is such a* naturall Assistance *between them, that what the one cannot doe, the other both can, and will perform.*

Nor are their inward Vertues *more then their* outward Beauties; *for the* Solar *part is of so* resplendent, transparent Lustre, *that the* Eye *of* Man *is scarce able to indure it; and if the* Lunar *part be expos'd abroad in a* dark Night, Birds *will repaire to (and circulate about) it, as a* Fly *round a* Candle, *and submit themselves to the* Captivity *of the* Hand: *And this invites mee to believe, that the* Stone *which the ancient Hermet (being then* 140 *Years old) tooke out of the* Wall *in his* Cell, *and shewed* Cornelius Gallus, *Ann.* 1602. *was of the Nature of this* Vegitable Stone: *For, (upon the opening his* Golden Box *wherein it was inclosed) it dilated its* Beames *all over the* Roome, *and that with so great* Splendor, *that it overcame the* Light *that was kindled therein*; *Besides the* Hermet *refused to* project *it upon* Metall (*as being unworthy of it*) *but made his* Experiment *upon* Veronica *and* Rue.

By the Magicall *or* Prospective Stone *it is possible to discover any* Person *in what part of the* World *soever, although never so secretly concealed or hid*; *in* Chambers, Closets, *or* Savernes *of the* Earth: *For there it makes a strict* Inquisition. *In a Word, it fairely presents to your view even the* whole World, *wherein to* behold, heare, *or* see *your* Desire. *Nay more, It enables Man to* understand *the Language of the* Creatures, *as the* Chirping *of* Birds, Lowing *of* Beasts, *&c. To* Convey *a* Spirit *into an* Image, *which by observing the* Influence *of* Heavenly Bodies, *shall become a true* Oracle; *And yet this as* E. A. *assures you, is not any wayes* Necromanticall, *or* Devilish; *but* easy, wonderous easy, Naturall *and* Honest.

Lastly, as touching the Angelicall Stone, *it is so* subtill, *saith the aforesaid* Author, *that it can neither be* seene, felt, *or* weighed; *but* Tasted *only. The* voyce *of* Man (*which bears some proportion to these subtill properties,*) *comes short in comparison*; *Nay the* Air *it selfe is not so penetrable, and yet (Oh mysterious wonder!)* A Stone, *that will lodge in the* Fire *to* Eternity *without being prejudiced. It hath a* Divine Power, Celestiall, *and* Invisible, *above the rest*; *and endowes the possessor with* Divine Gifts. *It affords the* Apparition *of* Angells, *and gives a power of conversing with them, by* Dreames *and* Revelations: *nor dare any* Evill Spirit *approach the* Place *where it* lodgeth. *Because it is a* Quintessence wherein there is no corruptible Thing: and where the Elements are not corrupt, no Devill can stay or abide.

S. Dunston *calls it* the Food of Angels, *and by others it is tearmed* The Heavenly Viaticum; The Tree of Life; *and is undoubtedly (next under GOD) the true* Alchochodon, *or* Giver of Years; *for by it* Mans Body *is preserved from* Corruption, *being thereby inabled to* live *a long time without* Foode: *nay 'tis made a question whether any* Man *can* Dye *that uses it. Which I doe not so much admire, as to think why the* Possessors *of it should desire to* live, *that have those* Manifestations *of* Glory *and* Eternity, *presented unto their* Fleshly Eyes; *but rather desire to be* Dissolved, *and to enjoy the full* Fruition, *then live where they must be content with the bare* Speculation.

After

After Hermes *had once obtained the* Knowledge *of this* Stone, *he gave over the use of all other* Stones, *and therein only delighted:* Moses,*and* Solomon,(*together with* Hermes *were the only three,that*) *excelled in the* Knowledge *thereof, and who therewith wrought* Wonders.

That there is a Gift *of* Prophesie *hid in the* Red-stone, Racis *will tell you; for thereby* (saith he) Philosophers *have* foretold things to come*: And* Petrus Bonus *avers, that they did* Prophesie, *not only* Generally *but* Specially; *having a* Fore-knowledge *of the* Resurrection, Incarnation *of* Christ, day *of* Judgement, *and that the* World *should be consumed with* Fire*: and this not otherwise, then from the* Insight *of their Operations.*

In Briefe, by the true and various use *of the* Philosophers Prima materia (for there are diversities of Gifts, but the same spirit) *the perfection of* Liberall Sciences *are made known, the whole* Wisdome *of* Nature *may be grasped: And* (*Notwithstanding what has been said, I must further adde*) There are yet hid greater things then these,for we have seen but few of his Workes.

Howbeit, there are but a few Stocks *that are fitted to Inoculate the* Grafts *of this* Science *on: They are* Mysteries Incommunicable *to any but the* Adepti, *and those that have beene* Devoted *even from their* Cradles *to* serve *and* waite *at this* Altar: *And how rarely* such *have been heard of, may appear by* Norton:

> For few (saith he) or scarcely One
> In Fifteene Kingdomes had our Red Stone.

And they *perhaps were* (*with S.*Paul) Caught up into Paradice, and *as he*, heard unspeakeable Words, *so they, wrought unoperable Workes*; such as it is not lawfull for to utter.

Of such *as these therefore* will I glory,yet of my selfe I will not glory,but of mine Infirmities. *And truly* whether such were in the Body or out of the Body I cannot tell, GOD knoweth, *doubtlesse* they were not far from the Kingdome of GOD.

But I feare I have waded *too farre; and therefore now to give some* Particular Account, *aswell touching the* Publication *of this* Worke, *as also the* Disposition *thereof,and the* Nature *of the* Obselete Language *wherein tis written: I shall in the First place acquaint the* Reader, *that the kinde* Acceptance *my former* Endeavours *received at the Hands of* Candid Artists,*in publishing some* Chemicall Collections; *very earnestly invited me to finde out a* Second Piece

 where-

wherewith to present those Gratefull Persons. *Whereupon I intended to rally up some of my own* Conceptions *in this* Science, *and expose them also to the* Test: *But (to this end, reviewing the* Philosophers.) *I found that many (assuming that Name) wrote what their* Fancies, *not their* Hands *had wrought, and further then in* Apprehension *had not seene* Projection; *(amongst whom our* Ripley *was sometime One, as appeares by his Ingenious* Retractation, *hereafter mentioned:) and being truly sensible of the great* Injury *such* Workes *have done young* Students *(at the first not able to distinguish, who have written upon their undeceveable* Experience, *who not; and consequently, not which to follow, or which to avoyde) I withdrew my* Thoughts *(having never as yet set my selfe* Effectually *upon the* Manuall Practise *) lest I should adde to the many* Injuries *the* World *has already suffered, by delivering the bare* Medley *of my* Dubious Apprehensions, *without the confident* Attestation *of* Practise: *and be justly esteemed as* indiscreete *as those whom* Ripley *mentions, that prate*

Of Robin Hode and of his Bow,
Which never shot therein I trow.

Yet still casting about what to make choyce *of, at length (by the incouragement of some that are* Industrious *after* publique benefit) *Centred my* Thoughts, *and fix'd them on this* designe *of* Collecting *All (or as many as I could meete with) of our own* English Hermetique Philosophers, *and to make them* publique.

Nor did I change this Resolution *with my* Clothes, *notwithstanding the* Difficulties *I saw, ready to encounter and obstruct the* Undertaking: *For, besides the* Paines *and* Care *that was thereunto requisite, the* Feare *of not meeting with, or obtaining the* Originall Manuscripts, *or* Authentique Copies *of this* Nature, *(which I knew to be in some* Mens hands, *yet wanting them my selfe,) shrewdly beset, though nothing discourag'd me: yet was I therewith freely and plentifully supplyed by some* worthy *and* intimate Friends, *whom I would gladly here* mention, *but that I well know they delight not to see their* Names *in* Print. *These had, My* Care *was next to* dispose *them in such a* Series *as might be answerable to the* Respective Times, *wherein each* Author Flourished; *and withall to the best* Advantage *of the laborious* Student: *the which I have manag'd with so just an* Adequation, *as (I hope) will neither detract from the due* Honour *of the* One, *nor yet disturbe or darken the direct* path *of the* Other.

But

But whilst I was doing this, I made a Question *(in regard some* Philosophers *had writ in* Verse, *others in* Prose *) which of these should take* Precedency; *and after some* Consideration *adjudged it to the* Poetique part: *And that, not only because its* Originall *may probably* Anticipate *the time of* Orpheus, *(although he be noted by* Maierus, Primus Antistes, Sacerdos, Theologus, *VATES*, & Doctor totius Græcorum nationis) *because that* Linus *is said to be the most* Perite *of any* Lyrick Poet, *and so* Ancient *that some suppose him Master to* Orpheus, *who writ that admirable* Allegory *of the* Golden Fleece, *and was the first of all the* Grecians *that brought the* Chemick Learning (*with other* Sciences) *out of* Ægipt, *as the other the first that brought the* Phænician Learning *to the* Grecians: *I say not only for that it is the* Ancientest, *and* Prose *but of* Latter *use with other* Nations: *but because* Poetry *hath bin most* Anciently *used with* us, *and (as if from a* Grant *of* Nature) *held unquestionable.*

Again, the Excellent Melody *thereof is so* Naturall *and* Universall, *as that it seemes to be* borne *with all the Nations of the* World, *as an* Hereditary Eloquence *proper to all* Mankinde: *Nor was this all, for I considered that it Claimes a* Generall succession, *and* Reception, *in All* Nations, *all* Ages, *who were never without a* Homer, *a* Virgil, *or an* Ovid: *No not this small* Segment *of the* World [England] *without a* Rasis Cestrensis *and an* Hortulanus; *For the* First *of these, His* Liber Luminum, *and his* Lumen de Luminum, *are the* Ancientest *now extant in* Latine Verse: *In the latter of which, I cannot omit this* Title *of his,* [Responsio Rasis Cestrensis Filio suo Merlino;] *whereby it appeares he was* Merlin's Contemporary *(at least) if not his* Master, *in this* Abstruse Mystery. *These* Workes *of his are both Published by* Hermannus, *but very* Imperfectly, *as I found by Comparing them with a* Manuscript, *as ancient as* King John's Time. *And for the* Second *He was the first* Christian Philosopher *after* Morienus, *who (travelling abroad, and returning hither in the* Raigne *of* William *the* Conquerour) *because he was the first that* Transplanted *the* Chemicall Muses *from remotest* Parts *into his own* Country; *is called* Garland, ab Coronam Hermeticam & Poeticam. *But, to returne to our* Matter.

If neither its Antiquity, *nor the* Naturall Ratification, Generall Succession, *and* Reception *thereof, were enough to allow it the* Right-hand *of* Fellowship, *yet I suppose the* Effects *thereof, (which so affect and delight the* Eare, *rejoyce the* Heart, *satisfie the* Judgement,

ment, *and indulge the* Hearers) *justly may : In regard* Poesy *has a* Life, *a* Pulse, *and such a secret* Energy, *as leaves in the* Minde, *a far deeper* Impression, *then What runs in the slow and evenlesse* Numbers *of* Prose : *whereby it won so much upon the* World, *That in* Rude Times , *and even amongst* Barbarous Nations, *When other sorts of* Learning *stood excluded, there was nothing more in* Estimation. *And for that we call* Rythme ; *the Custome of divers of our* Saxon *and* Norman Poets, *shewes the* Opinion *they had thereof ; whilst the* Latine *(notwithstanding its* Excellency *) could not sufficiently delight their* Eares, *unlesse their* Verses *(in that* Language, *) were form'd with an* Harmonicall Cadence , *and brought into* Rythme : *Nor did the* Ancients *wrap up their* Chiefest Mysteries, *any Where else, then in the* Parobolical *&* Allusive *part of* Poetry, *as the most* Sacred, *and* Venerable *in their* Esteeme, *and the securest from* Prophane *and* Vulgar Wits. *For such was the goodnesse of our* Fathers, *that they Would not willingly hazard(much lesse throW)their* Childrens Bread *among* Dogs ; *And therefore their* Wisdome *and* Policy *was, First, to finde out a* way *to* Teach , *and then an* Art *(which was this) to* Conceale. *In a* word, *to prefer* Prose *before* Poetry, *is no other, or better, then to let a* Rough-hewen-Clowne, *take the* Wall *of a* Rich-clad-Lady *of* Honour *: or to* Hang *a* Presence Chamber *With* Tarpalin, *instead of* Tapestry.

And for these Reasons, *and out of these* Respects, *the* Poeticall*(as I conceiv'd) deserved the* Precedency.

HoWbeit probably some of these Pieces *(now brought to* publique Light) *had welnigh* perish'd *in a silent* Ruine ; *and* Destruction *got a compleate Victory over them , but that my* Diligence *and* Laborious Inquisition *rescued them from the* Jawes *thereof : being almost quite shrouded in the* Dust *of* Antiquity, *and involv'd in the* obscurity *of* forgotten things, *with their* Leaves *halfe* Worme-eaten. *And a wonder it is, that (like the* Creatures *in* Noahs Arke) *they were hitherto so safely preserved from that* Universall Deluge, *Which (at the* Dissolution of Abbies) *overfloWed our greatest* Libraries.

And in doing thus, I presume it no Arrogance *to challenge the* Reputation *of performing a* Worke, *next that of a* Mans *own : and something* more, *in that (as if having the* Elixir *it selfe) I have made* Old Age *become* Young *and* Lively, *by restoring* each of the Ancient Writers *not only to the* Spring *of their severall* Beauties, *but to the* Summer *of their* Strength *and* Perfection.

As

As for the whole Worke *it selfe, it is* sheav'd *up from a few* gleanings *in part of our* English Fields; *where though I have bestowed my* Industry *to pick up here and there, what I could finde in my* way, *yet I believe there are many other* Pieces *of this* Nature *in private* Hands, *which if any are pleas'd (out of the same* Ingenious score *that I have* published *these,) to* Communicate *to me: I shall set thereon a* value *sutable to the* worth *of their* Favours, *and let the* World *know its* Obligation *to them besides.*

The Style *and* Language *thereof, may, I confesse (to some) seeme* Irksome *and* Uncouth, *and so it is indeed to those that are* strangers *thereunto; but withall very* Significant: *Old* words *have strong* Emphasis; *others may look upon them as* Rubbish *or* Trifles, *but they are grosly* Mistaken: *for what some light* Braines *may esteem as* Foolish Toys; *deeper* Judgements *can and will value as sound and* serious Matter.

We English have often varied our Fashions (such is the levity of our Fancies) *and therefore if you meet with* Spellings *different from those in use; or uncouth* Words *as strangely ridiculous, as a* Maunch, Hood, Cod-piece, *or* Trunke-hose, *know; as they were the fashionable* Attyres, *so these the usuall* Dialects *of those* Times: *And* Posterity *will pay us in our own* Coyne, *should we deride the* behaviour *and* dresse *of our* Ancestors. *For we must consider that* Languages *which are daily used in our* Discourse, *are in as continuall* Mutation: *what* Custome *brings into* habit, *is best lik'd for the* Present, *whether it be to revive what is* lost, *or introduce something* new; *or to piece up the* present, *with the retained shreds of what* preceded; *But* learned Tongues (*which are contain'd in* Books) *injoy a more* immutable Fate, *because not* subject *to be washt away with the daily* tyde *and* current *of* Times. *They are like the* fashion *and* Drapery *wrought on* Marble Statues, *which must ever be retained without* alteration.

And therefore that the Truth *and* Worth *of their* Workes *might receive no* Diminution *by my* Transcription, *I purposely* retain'd *the old* Words *and manner of their* Spelling, *as I found them in the* Originalls (*except only some palpable* Mistakes *and* Blemishes *of former* Transcribers, *which I took upon me to* correct and purge *as litle more then* Litterall Imperfections:) *yet not to leave the* Reader *unsatisfied, have added a* Compendious Table, *for the* Interpretation *of* Old, unusuall, *and* obsolete Words, *and thereby smooth'd (as I suppose) the* Passage *for such as have not hitherto bin* Conversant *in these* Ancient Rough-hew'd Expressions.

Where-

Prolegomena.

Wherefore you that love to converse with the Dead, *or consult with their* Monuments, *draw near : perhaps you may find more benefit in them, then the* Living; *There you may meet with the* Genii *of our* Hermetique Philosophers, *learne the* Language *in which they woo'd and courted* Dame Nature, *and enjoy them more* freely, *and at Greater* Command, *(to satisfie your* Doubts*) then when they were in the* Flesh; *For, they have* Written *more then they would* Speake; *and left their* Lines *so* Rich, *as if they had dissolved* Gold *in their* Inke, *and clad their* Words *with the* Soveraign Moysture.

My Annotations *are limited within the Bounds of what is* Historicall, *or what* occasionally *must needs intrench on the* Confines *of other* Arts, *and all* Glosses *upon the* Philosophicall Worke *purposely omitted, for the same* Reasons *that I chose to send forth other* Mens Children *into the* World, *rather then my own. And what* presumptuous Mistaks, *or* Errors, *the* Candid Reader *shall meet with, will (I hope) be* Censured *with no lesse* Favour *and* Charity, *then that whereby they are wont to* Judge *the* Faults *of those they esteem their* Friends *and* Well-wishers.

And now to Conclude : *May the GOD of NATURE be gratiously pleased (out of the Immense Treasury of his* Goodness*) to vouchsafe all such (whose good* Angells *direct them to, or have already Religiously Engaged them in this* Mysterious *knowledge) the Full and Entire* Accomplishments *of a True and Pious* Philosopher, [*To wit,* Learning, Humility, Judgement, Courage, Hope, Patience, Discretion, Charity & Secrecie:] *That so they may enjoy the* Fruits *of their* Labours, *which otherwise will be but* vain, *and* unpleasant: *and causelesly render the* Divine Science *and* Secret *it selfe,* Contemptible.

Farewell (Industrious Students) *and let your* Goodnesse *still invite me to accomplish the* End *I have proposed : In doing which, (I presume) you may one* Day *esteeme me, better deserving your* Patronage; *At least-wise, your charitable* Censure: *which is all the* Recompence Expected *or* Merited, *by him, who is*

Yours Really Devoted,

26 Jan. 165 1/2.

E. Ashmole.

THE ORDINALL OF ALCHIMY.

VVritten by

THOMAS NORTON

OF

BRISTOLL.

Liber iste Clericis monstrat scientiam,
Liber sed Laicis auget inscitiam:
Liber, honores juvans per copiam:
Et Liber pauperum fugans inopiam:
Liber fiduciæ est & veritatis:
Regibus consilium, doctrina Prælatis:
Et Liber utilis viris beatis
Vivere qui cupiunt absque peccatis.
Liber secretum, Liber doni Dei,
Electis semita, vires bonæ spei,
Valens constantibus firmæ fidei:
Ve non credentibus verbis oris mei.
Quærunt Alchimiam, falsi quoque recti:
Falsi sine numero, sed hi sunt rejecti,
Et cupiditatibus (heu) tot sunt infecti,
Quod inter mille millia, vix sunt tres electi,
Istam ad scientiam multi sunt vocati
Nobiles, & pauperes, inscii, literati;
Qui noelunt labores, neque tempus pati;
Ideo non perficient, quia sunt ingrati.
Liber Artis filios docet iste satis,
Quibus hæc percipere deus dedit gratis,
Versiculis propheticis quatuor bis credatis,
Omnia dat gratis divinæ fons pietatis.
Hæc nobilis scientia est tantum illis data,
Qui diligunt justitiam, mente cum beata;
Dolosis, & raptoribus sed est denegata,
Propter peccata tardantur munera grata.

Sæpe

THis Booke the greatest *Clearkes* may teach,
But *shorteneth* the *Vulgar-Reach*:
A Booke that gets (by Wealth) *Renowne*,
And *Boggles* at a *thred-bare-Gowne*:
A *trusty-Booke* of *faithfull-Things*;
Instructing *Priests*, Advising *Kings*:
A Booke that's fitted for the *sence*
Of Man, who lives without *offence*:
A Booke of *secrets* given by *God*;
To men *Elect, a Beaten-Trod*:
Availing such as *constant* be
In *Faith*, and *Hope*, and *trusting Me.*
Good Men and *Bad*, even Numberlesse,
(The latter, but without successe)
Desire the *Art*: But still (Alas!)
They are so given to *Avarice*,
That of a *Million*, hardly *three*
Were ere Ordaind for *Alchimy*.
Yet many *called* every *Houre*,
Learn'd and *Unlearned*, *Rich*, and *Poore*;
Who'll neither *Tend*, nor take the *Paines*;
And therefore *Trudge* without the *Gaines*.
On whom *God* doth this *Art* bestow,
Her *Sons* may herein fully know:
By these * *foure-lines* you may believe
Heaven doth all things gratis give.
This *Art* in such you only finde
As *Justice* love, with *spotles-Minde*:
But tis deny'd to *guilefull Men*;
For sin protracts the gifts of Heaven.

* These foure Prophetick lines extracted from Sir *John Abbot of Bridlingtons* Prophecies, *Ubi de Tauro, &c.*

These

Sæpe Reges Angliæ decorasset hæc res;
Firma si in domino fuisset eorum spes;
Ille sed qui capiet per hanc rem honores,
Antiquos mores mutabit in meliores.
Iste cumque venerit, regnum reformabit,
Virtutibus & moribus, & exemplum dabit
Sempiternum Regibus; plebs tunc jubilabit,
Et mutuo se diligens laudes Deo dabit:
O Rex, hæc facturus! Deum Regem ora,
Et ejus auxilium pro re hac implora:
Tunc regi justo fulgenti mente decora
Grata supervenient *quâ non sperabitur hora.*

These had adorn'd the *English-Throne*,
If they had trusted *God* alone:
For he that hereby *Honor* winns,
Shall change the old for better things.
And when he comes to *rule* the Land,
Reforme it with a *vertuous hand:*
Leaving *examples* of *good deedes*
To every *King* that him *succeedes:*
Then shall the People *Jubilize*
In *mutuall love*; and *sacrifise*
Praises to *God*. O *King* that shall
These *Workes!* implore the *God* of all
For timely helpe, in this *good thing:*
So to a *Just*, and *Glorious King*,
Most goodly Graces *shall descend,*
When least look'd for: *To Crowne his End.*

The Proheme.

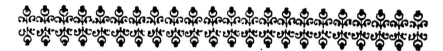

TO the honor of *God*, One in Perſons three,
This Boke is made, that *Lay-men* ſhulde it
And Clerks alſoe, after my deceaſe, (ſee,
Whereby all *Lay-men* which putteth
(them in preaſe,
To ſeech by *Alkimy* great ryches to winn
May finde good Counſell er they ſuch warke begin;
And greate deceipts they may hereby eſchewe,
And by this doctrine know falſ men from trewe.
Nathles Clerks greate ſeacreats heere may leare,
But all *Lay men* ſhall finde heere cauſe to feare,
And to beware of falſ illuſions,
Which *Multiplyers* worke with their Concluſions:
But for that I deſire not worldly fame,
But your good prayers, unknowne ſhall be my name.
That no man ſhulde therafter ſearch, ne looke,
But wiſely Conſider the flowers of this booke:
Of every eſtate that is within Mankind
If yee make ſearch much people ye may finde,
Which to *Alkimy* their Corage doe addreſs
Only for appetite of Lucre and Riches.
As *Popes* with *Cardinalls* of *Dignity*,
Archbyſhopes with *Byſhopes* of *high* degree;
With *Abbots* and *Priors* of Religion,
With *Friars*, *Heremites*, and *Preeſts* manie one,
And *Kings* with *Princes* and *Lords* great of blood,
For every eſtate *deſireth* after good;

And Merchaunts alſo which dwell in the fiere
Of brenning Covetiſe, have thereto deſire;
And *Common-workemen* will not be out-lafte,
For as well as *Lords* they love this noble Crafte;
As *Gouldſmithes* whome we ſhulde leſt repreve
For *ſights* in their Craft meveth them to beleeve:
But wonder it is that *Wevers* deale with ſuch warks,
Free Maſons and *Tanners* with poore *Pariſh Clerks*;
Tailors and *Glaſiers* woll not thereof ceaſe,
And eke ſely *Tinkers* will put them in the preaſe
With greate preſumption; but yet ſome collour there was,
For all ſuch Men as give Tincture to Glaſſe:
But many *Artificers* have byn over-ſwifte
With haſty Credence to fume away their thrifte:
And albeit that loſſes made them to ſmarte,
Yet ever in hope continued their hearte,
Truſting ſome tyme to ſpeede right well,
Of many ſuch truly I can tell,
Which in ſuch hope continued all their lyfe,
Whereby they were pore and made to unthriſe:
It had byne good for them to have left off
In ſeaſon, for noughte they founde but a ſcoffe,
For trewly he that is not a greate *Clerke*
Is nice and lewde to medle with this warke;
Ye may truſt me well it is no ſmall inginn
To know all ſecreats pertaining to the Myne;
For it is moſt profound *Philoſophie*,
The ſubtill ſcience of holy *Alkimy*,
Of which Science here I intend to write,
Howbeit I may not curiouſly indite.
For he that ſhulde all a common people teache,
He muſt for them uſe plaine and common ſpeache;
Though that I write in plaine, and hoemely wiſe
No good Man then ſhulde ſuch writenge diſpise.

All

All *Masters* that write of this Soleme werke
They made their Bokes to many Men full derke,
In Poyses, Parables, and in Metaphors alsoe,
Which to Shollers causeth peine and woe:
For in their practise whan they would it assay,
They leese their Costs, as men see aldaye.
Hermes, *Rasis*, *Geber*, and *Avicen*,
Merlin, *Hortolan*, *Democrit*, and *Morien*,
Bacon, and *Raimond*, with others many moe
Wrote under covert, and *Aristotle* alsoe.
For what hereof they wrote with their penn,
Their Cloudy Clauses dulled many Men:
Fro *Lay-men*, Fro *Clearks*, and so fro every Man
They hid this *Art* that no Man finde it cann.
By their bokes do they shew Reasons faire,
Whereby much people are brought into dispaire.
Yet *Anaxagoras* wrote plainest of them all
In his boke of *Conversions naturall*;
Of the old *Fathers* that ever I founde
He most disclosed of this *Science* the grownde;
Whereof *Aristotle* had greate envy,
And him rebuked unrightfully
In many places, as I can well report,
Intending that men to him shulde not resort:
For he was large of his cunning and love,
God havē his soule in blisse with him above:
And suche as sowed envious seede,
God forgive them their misdeede.
As the *Mounke* which a Boke did write
Of a *thousand receipts* in mallice for despight;
Which be coppied in many a place
Whereby hath beene made pale many a Face;
And many *Gownds* have byne made bare of hewe,
And men made fals which before tyme were trewe.

Wherefore

Wherefore my Pitty doth me constreyne
To shew the trewth in fewe words and plaine,
Soe that you may fro false doctrine flee,
If ye give Credence to this boke and mee;
Avoide your Bokes written of Receipts,
For all such Receipts are full of Deceipts;
Trust not such Receipts, and lerne well this Clause,
Nothing is wrought but by his proper Cause:
Wherefore that Practise falleth farr behinde
Wher Knowledge of the cause is not in minde:
Therefore remember ever more wisely, (whic.
That you woorke nothing but you knowe howe and
Alsoe he that would in this *Arte* procee d e
To eschewe falshood he hath greate need:
For trewth is good which this *Arte* must guide,
Wherefore to falshood ye may never slide;
But stedfastly your minde must be set,
Fals Colloured Metall never to Counterfett;
As thei that seeke Blanchers or Citrinacions,
Which woll not abide all Examinacions,
Wherewith fals Plate they make as they cann
Or Money to beguile some good trew Mann:
But *God* hath made that of this blessed *Arte*,
All that be fals shall have thereof noe parte;
He must have Grace that would for this *Arte* sue,
Therefore of right him needeth to be trew:
Also he may not be trobled in his Minde
With outward charges, which this *Arte* would finde:
And he that would have his intent,
He must have Riches sufficient.
In many wayes he maie not looke
But only pursue the order of this Boke;
Named of *Alkimy the Ordinall*,
The Crede mihi, *the Standard perpetuall:*

D For

For like as the *Ordinall* to *Preests* setteth out
The service of the dayes as they goe aboute:
Soe of all the Bokes unordered in *Alkimy*
The effect is here set out Orderly:
Therefore this Boke to an *Alchimister* wise,
Is a Boke of incomparable price;
Whose trewth shall never be defiled,
Though it appeare in homely wise compiled:
And as I had this *Arte* by Grace from Heaven,
I give you the same here in *Chapters seaven*:
As largely as by my fealty I may,
By licence of the dreadfull Judge at domes daye.
The *first Chapter* shall all Men teache
What manner People may this *Science* teache,
And whie the trew *Science* of *Alkimy*,
Is of old Fathers called *Blessed and Holy*.
In the *second Chapter* maie be sayne,
The nice Joyes thereof, with the greate paine.
The *third Chapter* for the love of One,
Shall trewly disclose the Matters of our Stone;
Which the *Arabies* doon *Elixir* call,
Whereof it is, there understonde you shall.
The *fowerth Chapter* teacheth the grosse Werke,
A foule laboure not kindly for a *Clerke*.
In which is found full greate travaile,
With many perills, and many a faile.
The *fift Chapter* is of the subtill Werk,
Which *God* ordeyned only for a *Clerke*;
Full few *Clerks* can it comprehend,
Therefore to few Men is the *Science* send.
The *sixt Chapter* is of Concord and love,
Between low *natures*, and heavenly spheares above:
Whereof trew knowledge advanceth greatly *Clerks*,
And causeth furtherance in our wonderfull werks.

The

The *seaventh Chapter* trewly teach you shall,
The doubtfull Regiments of your Fires all.

NOw Soveraigne *Lord God* me guide and speede,
For to my Matters as now I will proceede,
Praying all men which this Boke shall finde,
With devoute Prayers to have my soule in minde;
And that noe Man for better ne for worse,
Chaunge my writing for drede of *Gods curse*:
For where quick sentence shall seame not to be
Ther may wise men finde selcouthe previtye;
And chaunging of some one sillable
May make this Boke unprofitable.
Therefore trust not to one Reading or twaine,
But twenty tymes it would be over sayne;
For it conteyneth full ponderous sentence,
Albeit that it faute forme of Eloquence;
But the best thing that ye doe shall,
Is to reade many Bokes, and than this withall.

liter age, et confortet cor tuum
Alkymiæ secretè servas
Secreta
ccipe donum Dei sub
Sacrato
Ro: Vaughan sculp:

Nortons *Ordinall.*

CHAP. I.

M*AIS*tryefull merveylous and Archimaſtrye
Is the tincture of holi *Alkimy*:
A wonderfull *Science*, ſecrete Philoſophie,
A ſingular grace & gifte of th'almightie:
Which never was founde by labour of
But it by Teaching, or Revelacion begann. (Mann,
It was never for Mony ſold ne bought,
By any Man which for it hath ſought:
But given to an able Man by grace, (ſpace.
Wrought with greate Coſt, with long layſir and
It helpeth a Man when he hath neede,
It voydeth vaine Glory, Hope, and alſo dreade:
It voydeth Ambitiouſneſſe, Extorcion, and Exceſſe,.
It fenceth Adverſity that ſhee doe not oppreſſe.
He that thereof hath his full intent,
Forſaketh Extremities, with Meaſure is content.
Some people would not have it cauled *Holy*,
And in this wiſe thei doe replye,
Thei ſay how *Painims* maie th's *Arte* have,
Such as our *Lord God* woll never ſave:
For their wilfull fals infidelitie,
The cauſe of goodnes, poſſeſſours cannot be.
Alſoe it maketh none other thing
But Gold or Silver, for Mony, Cupp, or Ring.
Whiche of wiſe men is proved and well founde
Leaſt verteous thing that is upon the Ground.
Wherefore concluding all men of that ſect,
Say, how this Science n'is holy in effect.
To this we ſay and wittnes as we cann
How that this *Science* was never tought to Man;

Chap. 1. But he were proved perfectly with space,
Whether he were able to receyve this Grace:
For his Trewth, Vertue, and for his stable Witt,
Which if he faulte he shall never have it;
Also no man coulde yet this *Science* reach,
But if *God* send a *Master* him to teach:
For it is soe *wonderfull* and soe selcouth,
That it must needes be tought from mouth to mouth:
Also he must (be he never soe loath)
Receive it with a most sacred dreadfull Oath,
That as we refuse greate dignitie and fame,
Soe he must needly refuse the same.
And also that he shall not be so wilde
To teach this seacret to his owne childe;
For nighnes of Blood ne Consanguinity
May not accepted be to this dignity:
Soe blood as blood, may have hereof noe part,
But only vertue winneth this holy *Arte*:
Therefore straightly you shall search and see,
All manners and vertues with th'abilitie
Of the person which shall this *Scyence* leere,
And in likewise make him straightlie swere:
Soe that noe man shall leave this *Arte* behinde,
But he an able and approved Man can finde;
When Age shall greeve him to ride or goe,
One he may teach, but then never no moe:
For this *Science* must ever secret be,
The Cause whereof is this as ye may see;
If one evill man had hereof all his will
All Christian Pease he might hastilie spill,
And with his Pride he might pull downe
Rightfull *Kings* and *Princes* of renowne:
Wherefore the sentence of perill and jeopardy,
Upon the *Teacher* resteth dreadfully.

Soe

So than for doubt of ſuch pride and wreach,
He muſt be ware that will this *Science* teach:
No Man therefore maie reach this greate preſent,
But he that hath vertues excellent.
Soe though Men weene Poſſeſſours not to aide,
To hallow this *Science* as before is ſaid;
Neither ſeeme not bleſſed effectually,
Yet in her Order this *Science* is *holy*.
And foraſmuch as noe Man maie her finde
But only by grace, ſhe is holy of her kinde.
Alſo it is a worke and Cure divine,
Foule Copper to make Gold or Silver fine:
No man maie finde ſuch chaunge by his thought,
Of divers kinds which *Gods* hands have wrought.
For *Gods* Conjunctions Man maie not undoe,
But if his Grace fully conſent thereto,
By helpe of this *Science*, which our *Lord* above
Hath given to ſuch Men as he doth love;
Wherefore old *Fathers* conveniently
Called this *Science Holy Alkimy*.
Therefore noe Man ſhulde be too ſwifte,
To caſt away our *Lords* bleſſed guift:
Conſideringe how that Almighty *God*
From great Doctours hath this *Science* forbod,
And graunted it to few Men of his mercy,
Such as be faithfull trew and lowly.
And as there be but *Planets* ſeaven
Amonge the multitude of ſtarrs in Heaven:
Soe among millions of millions of Mankinde,
Scarſlie ſeaven men maie this *Science* finde.
Wherefore *Lay-men* ye may lere and ſee
How many *Doctors* of great authoritie,
With many ſearchers hath this Science ſought,
Yet all their labours have turned into nought;

If

Chap. 1. If thei did coſt, yet found thei none availe,
For of their purpoſe every tyme thei faile;
And in deſpaire thei reaſon and departe,
And then thei ſaid how there is noe ſuch arte;
But fained Fables thei name it where thei goe,
A fals fond thing thei ſay it is alſoe:
Such Men preſume too much upon their minde,
They weene their witts ſufficient this *Arte* to finde.
But of their ſlaunder and words of outrage,
We take thereof trewlie little Charge:
For ſuch be not invited to our feaſt,
Which weeneth themſelves wiſe and can doe leaſte.
Albeit ſuch Men liſt not lenger to perſue,
Yet is this *Science* of *Alkimy* full trew;
And albeit ſome proude *Clerks* ſay nay
Yet every wiſe *Clerke* well conſider may,
How he whiche hereof might no trewth ſee
Maie not hereof lawfull wittnes be,
For it were a wonderous thing and queinte,
A man that never had ſight to peinte.
How ſhoulde a borne blinde Man be ſure
To write or make good Portrature.
To build Poules ſteeple might be greate doubt,
For ſuch proude *Clerks* to bring aboute;
Such might well happ to breake their crowne,
Ere they coude wiſely take it downe.
Wherefore all ſuch are full farr behinde,
To fetch out the ſecreateſt pointe of kinde;
Therefore all Men take theire fortune and chaunce,
Remit ſuch *Clerks* to their Ignorance.

Now ye that will this *Science* purſue,
Learne ye to know fals Men from trew.
All trew ſearchers of this *Science* of *Alkimy*,
Muſt be full learned in their firſt Philoſophie:

Elſe

Elſe all their laboure ſhall them let and greive,
As he that fetcheth Water in a Sive ;
The trew men ſearch and ſeeke all alone
In hope to finde our delectable ſtone,
And for that thei would that no Man ſhulde have loſſe,
They prove and ſeeke all at their owne Coſte ;
Soe their owne Purſes they will not ſpare,
They make their Coffers thereby full bare,
With greate Patience thei doe proceede,
Truſting only in *God* to be their ſpeede.

THe fals man walketh from Towne to Towne,
For the moſt parte in a threed-bare-Gowne;
Ever ſearching with diligent awaite
To winn his praye with ſome fals deceit
Of ſwearing and leaſing ; ſuch will not ceaſe,
To ſay how they can Silver plate increaſe.
And ever they rayle with perjury;
Saying how they can Multiplie
Gold and Silver,and in ſuch wiſe
With promiſe thei pleaſe the Covetiſe,
And Cauſeth his minde to be on him ſett,
Then Falſehood and Covetiſe be well mett.
But afterwards within a little while
The Multiplier doth him beguile
With his faire promiſe, and with his fals othes,
The Covetiſe is brought to threed-bare clothes:
But if he can haſtily be well aware,
Of the Multiplier and of his Chaffare ,
Of whoſe deceipts much I can reporte,
But I dare not leaſt I give comforte
To ſuch as be diſpoſed to Treachery ;
For ſo much hurte mought come thereby ;
Wherefore adviſe you and be wiſe,
Of them which proffer ſuch ſerviſe.

Chap. 1. If they had Cunning have ye no doubt,
They woll be loath to shew it out:
When such men promise to Multiplie,
They compasse to doe some Villony,
Some trew mans goods to beare awaye;
Of such fellowes what shulde I saye?
All such false men where ever thei goe,
They shulde be punished, thei be not so.
Upon *Nature* thei falsely lye
For Mettalls doe not Multiplie;
Of this Sentence all men be sure,
Evermore Arte must serve *Nature*.
Nothing multiplieth as Auctors sayes,
But by one of theis two wayes,
One by rotting, called Putrefaction,
That other as Beasts, by Propagation;
Propagation in Mettalls maie not be,
But in our Stone much like thing ye may see.
Putrefaction must destroy and deface,
But it be don in its proper place.
Mettalls of kinde grow lowe under ground,
For above erth rust in them is found;
Soe above erth appeareth corruption,
Of mettalls, and in long tyme destruction,
Whereof noe Cause is found in this Case,
But that above Erth thei be not in their place.
Contrarie places to nature causeth strife,
As Fishes out of water losen their Lyfe:
And Man, with Beasts, and Birds live in ayer,
But Stone and Mineralls under Erth repaier.
Physicians and Appoticaries faut appetite and will,
To seech water flowers on a dry hill:
For *God* hath ordeyned of his wisdome and grace,
All things to grow in their naturall place.

Against

Against this doctrine some Men replie,
And say that Mettalls doe Multiplie:
For of Silver, Lead, Tinn, and al so Brasse,
Some veyne is more, and some is lasse,
Or which diversitie Nature shulde cease,
If Mettalls did not multiplie and increase;
Wherefore they say that reason sheweth nowe,
How that under Erth they multiplie and growe;
Why not then above Erth in vessells close and faire,
Such as shulde preserve them from Fire Water and Aier?
Hereto we say this reason is but rude,
For this is noe perfect similitude;
For cause efficient of Mettalls finde ye shall
Only to be the vertue Minerall,
Which in everie Erth is not found,
But in certaine places of eligible ground;
Into which places the Heavenly Spheare,
Sendeth his beames directly everie yeare.
And as the matters there disposed be
Such Mettalls thereof formed shall you see.
Few grownds be apt to such generation:
How shoulde then above ground be Multiplication?
Also all men perceyven that be wise,
How Water conjealed with Cold is yse;
And before tyme it harded was
Some lay in more places and some in lasse,
As water in fosses of the Carte-wheele,
Were veynes smale whan they began to keele,
But water in ditches made veynes more,
For plenty of water that was therein froare.
Hereupon to say it were noe good advice,
That therefore of yse should multiply more yse.
Soe though there be of Mettalls veynes more and lasse,
It proveth not that they increase more then it was,

Chap. 1. Alsoe ye may trust without any doubt,
If Multiplying should be brought about:
All th'engredience must draw to simplcity,
And breake Composition as yearly ye may see:
For Multiplying of Hearbes how *Nature* hath provided,
That all things joyned in the seede be divided:
Else stalke and leaves which vertually therein be,
May not come forth actually that eye mought them see.
But Mettall holdeth his holle Composicion,
When corrasive waters have made dissolucion:
Therefore syth yse is nerrer to simplicity,
Then is Mettall, and maie not increased be,
Trewly ye maie trust as I said before,.
How of one ounce of Silver, maie Silver be noe more.
Also nothing multiplyed shall ye finde,
But it be of Vegetative or of Sensitive kinde:
Where Mettalls be only Elamentative,
Having noe seede, nether feeling of life;
Wherefore concluding all Multipliers must cease,
For Mettalls once Mettalls shall noe more increase;
Nathlesse one Mettall transmuted we finde,
Unto a Mettall of another kinde,
For propinquity of matter that in them was,
As it is knowne betwixt *Iron* and *Brasse*.
But to make trew *Silver* or *Gold* is noe ingin,
Except only the Philosophers medicine.
Wherefore such leasings as Multipliers use,
Clerks reprove and utterly refuse;
Such art of Multiplying is to be reproved,
But holy *Alkimy* of right is to be loved,
Which treateth of a precious Medicine,
Such as trewly maketh *Gold* and *Silver* fine.:.
Whereof example for Testimonie,
Is in a Citty of *Catilony*.

Which

Which *Raymond Lully, Knight*, men ſuppoſe;
Made in ſeaven Images the trewth to diſcloſe;
Three were good *Silver*, in ſhape like Ladies bright,
Everie each of Foure were *Gold* and did a Knight:
In borders of their Clothing Letters like appeare,
Signifying in Sentence as it ſheweth here.
1. Of old Horſhoes (ſaid one) I was yre,
Now I am good *Silver* as good as ye deſire.
2. I was (ſaid another) *Iron* fet from the Mine,
But now I am *Gould* pure perfect and fine.
3. Whilome was I *Copper* of an old red pann,
Now am I good *Silver*, ſaid the third woman.
4. The fourth ſaide, I was *Copper* growne in the filthy
Now am I perfect *Gould* made by *Gods* grace. (place,
5. The fift ſaid, I was *Silver* perfect through fine,
Now am I perfect *Goulde*, excellent, better then the prime.
6. I was a Pipe of *Leade* well nigh two hundred yeare,
And now to all men good *Silver* I appeare.
7. The ſeventh ſaid, I *Leade* am *Gould* made for a Maiſtrie,
But trewlie my fellowes are nerer thereto then I.
This *Science* beareth her name of a King,
Called *Alchimus*, without leaſing:
A glorious Prince of moſt noble minde,
His noble vertues holpe him this arte to finde;
He ſearched *Nature*, he was nobil *Clerke*,
He left Extorcion, than ſought and found this werke.
King *Hermes* alſoe he did the ſame,
Being a *Clerke* of Excellent fame;
In his *Quadripartite* made of *Aſtrologie*;
Of *Phyſique* and of this *Arte* of *Alkimy*,
And alſo of *Magique naturall*,
As of four *Sciences* in nature paſſing all.
And there he ſaid that bleſſed is hee
That knoweth things truly as thei bee.

Chap. 1. And blessed is he that maketh due proofe,
For that is roote of cunning and roofe;
For by opinion is many a Man
Deceived, which hereof litle cann.
An old Proverbe, *In a Bushell of weeninge,*
Is not found one handfull of Cunninge:
With due proofe and with discreet assaye,
Wise men may leare new things every day.
By Cunninge, Men know themselves and every thinge;
Man is but a Beast and worse without Cunninge:
But litle favour hath every Man
To Science whereof he litle can;
And litle Cunning maketh men proud and wilde,
Sufficient Cunning maketh men full milde.
Nobil men now in manner have despighte
Of them that have to Cunning appetite:
But noble Kings in auncient dayes,
Ordained (as olde Auctors saies,)
That the seven *Sciences* to learne and can,
Shulde none but only a *Noble man*;
And at the least he shulde be so free,
That he mought Studie with libertie;
Wherefore old Sages did them call
The seaven Sciences liberall:
For he that would leare them perfectly and well,
In cleere liberty he must dwell.
From worldly warkes he must withdrawe,
That would lerne but Mans Lawe:
Much more the Worlde he must forsake,
Which many Sciences woulde overtake.
And for that cause Men may well see,
Why Cunninge men dispised be.
Yet nobil Memory shall never cease,
Of him which Cunninge doth increase.

Hee

Hee which loveth Cunning, Justice, and Grace
Is set aside in many a place;
But whoe to Courte bringeth in with guile,
Profit, or present, he is the Man that while.
Wherefore this *Science* and many Graces moe,
Be lost and be departed all ye fro.
And furthermore remember what I say,
Sinn caleth fast for his ending day:
Covetise and Cunninge have discorde by kinde;
Who lucre coveteth this *Science* shall not finde;
But he that loveth Science for her owne kinde,
He may purchase both for his blessed minde.
Of this *Chapter* more I need not teach,
For here appeareth what men may it reach:
That is to remember only the trewe,
And he that is constant in minde to pursue,
And is not Ambitious, to borrow hath no neede,
And can be Patient, not hasty for to speede;
And that in *God* he set fully his trust,
And that in Cunning be fixed all his lust;
And with all this he leade a rightfull lyfe,
Falshoode subduinge, support no sinfull strife:
Such Men be apt this *Science* to attaine.
The Chapter following, is of Joy and paine.

CHAP. II.

NORmandy nurished a *Monke* of late,
Which deceived Men of every state.
But before that done he in his fantazie,
Weened he had caught this *Art* fully.
Such rejoycing thereof he had,
That he began to dote and to be madde.

Of

Chap. 2. Of whose *Joyes* (albeit they were ſmalle)
For an enſample I write this Tale.
This *Monke* had walked about in *Fraunce*,
Raunging Apoſtata in his pleſaunce.
And after he came into this lond,
Willing Men ſhould underſtonde;
How that of *Alkimy* he had the grounde,
By a Boke of *Receipts* which he had founde.
In ſurety thereof he ſet all his minde,
Some nobil Acte to leave behinde;
Whereby his name ſhould be immortall,
And his greate Fame in laude perpetuall.
And ofte he muſed where to beginne,
To ſpend the riches that he ſhulde winn.
And ever he thought loe this I cann,
Where mought I finde ſome truſty Man,
Which would accorde now with my will,
And help my purpoſe to fulfill.
Then would I make upon the plaine
Of *Salisbury* glorious to be ſaine,
Fifteen *Abbies* in a little while,
One *Abbie* in the end of every mile.
Hereupon this *Monke* to me reſorted,
Of truſt (he ſaid) which men of me reported,
His foreſaid mind he did to me tell,
And prayd me to keep his great Councell.
I ſaid before an Image of Saint *Jame*,
That I would never diſcloſe his name;
Yet I may write without all vice,
Of his deſires that were ſo nice.
When he had diſcovered his great Cunning,
He ſaid that he ſaughted nothing,
But a good meane for his ſolace,
To labour to the *Kings* good grace,

To

To get lycence of his eſtate,
And of his *Lords* mediate,
To purchaſe lond for the *Abbies* aforeſaid,
For which all coſte ſhould be well paied;
But yet he had great doubt and feare,
How to purchaſe, of whom, and where.
When I had heard of this greate werke,
I ſearched (to wit) what manner of *Clerke*
He was, and what he knew of Schoole,
And therein he was but a Foole.
Yet I ſuffered, and held me ſtill,
More to lerne of his lewd Will.
Then ſaid I, it were a lewd thinge,
Such matter to ſhew unto the *Kinge*;
But if the proofe were reaſonable,
He would thinke it a fooliſh Fable.
The *Monke* ſaide how that he had in fire,
A thing which ſhulde fulfill his deſire,
Whereof the trewth within forty dayes,
I ſhulde well know by trew aſſaies.
Then I ſaid, I would no more that tyde,
But forty dayes I ſaid I would abide.
When forty dayes were gone and paſt,
The *Monkes* Crafte was cleane overcaſt.
Then all his *Abbies* and all his thought,
Was turned to a thing of nought;
And as he came, he went full lewde,
Departing in a minde full ſhrewd:
For ſoone after within a little while,
Many trewe men he did beguile;
And afterwards went into *Fraunce*.
Loe! this was a pittifull chance,
That fifteene *Abbies* of Religion,
Shulde in this wiſe fall to confuſion.

Chap. 2. Great wonder was what thing he meant,
And why he set all his intent
Abbies to build; then was it wonder,
Why nould he live Obedient under,
But be Apostata, and range about,
This blessed *Science* to finde out:
But as I wrote above in this Boke,
Let no Deceiver after this *Science* looke.

AN other Ensample is good to tell,
Of one that trusted to doe as well
As *Raymond Lully*, or *Bacon* the Frier,
Wherefore he named himselfe *saunce peere*;
He was *Parson* of a little Town,
Not farr from the Citty of *London*,
Which was taken for halfe a Leach,
But little cunning had he to Preach;
He weened him sure this *Arte* to finde;
His Name he would have ever in minde
By meanes of a *Bridge*, imagined in dotage,
To be made over *Thames* for light passage:
Whereof shulde grow a Common ease,
All the Countrey thereabout to please.
Yet though he might that warke fulfill,
It might in no wise suffice his will;
Wherefore he would set up in hight,
That *Bridge* for a wonderfull sight,
With Pinacles guilt shining as goulde,
A glorious thing for men to beholde.
Then he remembred of the newe,
How greater fame shulde him pursue,
If he mought make that *Bridge* so bright,
That it mought shine also by Nighte.
And so continue and not breake,
Than all the Londe of him would speake.

But

But in his minde ran many a doubt,
How he might bring that warke about;
He trowed that Lampes with lights of fire,
Shulde well performe his nice desire;
Wherefore Lampes for that intent,
He would ordaine sufficient:
But then he fell in full great dreade,
How after the time that he were deade;
That light to find Men would refuse,
And chaunge the Rent to some other use.
Then thoughte he well is him that wiste,
In whom he mought set all his trust;
At the laste he thought to make the light,
For that Bridge to shine by nighte,
With *Carbuncle Stones*, to Make men wonder,
With duble reflexion above and under:
Then new thoughts troubled his Minde,
Carbuncle Stones how he mought find;
And where to find wise men and trewe,
Which would for his intent pursue,
In seeking all the Worlde about,
Plenty of *Carbuncles* to find out;
For this he tooke soe micle thought,
That his fatt flesh wasted nigh to nought:
And where he trusted without despaire,
Of this *Science* to have been heire,
When the yeare was fully come and goe,
His *Crafte* was lost, and thrift also;
For when that he tooke up his Glasse,
There was no matter for *Gold* ne *Brasse*:
Then he was angry and well neere wood,
For he had wasted away his good:
In this wise ended all his disporte,
What should I more of him report.

Chap. 2.

But that *Lay-men* and *Clerks* in Schooles,
Maie know the dotage of theis two fooles,
Remember this example where ye goe,
For in such Mindes be trewlie many moe:
Theie lewdly beleeve every Conclusion,
Be it never so false an elusion:
If it in boke written they may finde;
Thei weene it trewe, thei be so lewde of minde.
Such lewde and hasty confidence,
Causeth poverty and lewde expence.
Of trust of this *Arte* riseth Joyes nice,
For *lewde hope is fooles Paradice.*
The trewe tought Children made this confession,
Lord without thee all is digression;
For as thou arte of our *Science* begininge,
Soe without thee may be noe good endinge.

Confiteor; Altissime, nullus ista rapit; Licet vrius didicit, absque te nil sapit:
Nam tanta stat gratia te Deum semper apud: Perficere sicut capere, nam finis es, et caput

As of the *Joyes* of this *Arte* ye have seene;
Soe shall ye now heare some deale of the *Paine*:
Albeit contrary to the appetite
Of them that hath to this *Science* delight.

The

The first *Paine* is to remember in minde,
How many seeken, and how few doe finde,
And yet noe Man may this *Science* wynn,
But it be tought him before that he beginn;
He is well lerned, and of full cleere witt,
Which by teaching can surely learne it:
Of many diversities he must be sure,
Which secreats woulde know of working Nature:
Yet teaching maie not surely availe,
But that sometime shall happ a man to faile;
As all that be now dead and gone
Failed before theie found our *Stone*:
One tyme or other, first tyme or laste,
All Men failed till trew Practise were paste;
No Man sooner faileth in heate and colde,
Then doth the *Master* which hasty is and boulde:
For noe Man sooner maie our Worke spill,
Then he that is presuminge his purpose to fulfill:
But he that shall trewlie doe the deede:
He must use providence and ever worke with dreade;
For of all paines the most grevious paine,
Is for one faile to beginn all againe.
Every man shall greate *Paine* have
When he shall first this *Arte* covet and crave;
He shall oft tymes Chaunge his desire,
With new tydings which he shall heare;
His Councell shall oftentimes him beguile,
For that season he dreadeth noe subtile wile:
And oftentymes his minde to and fro,
With new Oppinions he shall chaunge in woe:
And soe long tyme continue in Phantasie,
A greate adventure for him to come thereby:
Soe of this *Arte* be ye never so faine,
Yet he must taste of manie a bitter paine.

Chap. 2. OF *Paines* yet I must shewe more,
Against your appetite though it be full sore:
It is greate *Paine,* as all wise-men gesse,
To witt where a trewe *Master* is;
And if ye finde him, it will be *Paine,*
Of his trewe love to be certeyne.
Forasmuch as noe Man maie teach but one,
Of the making of our delicious stone;
And albeit yee finde him that will ye teach,
Yet much trouble and paines may ye reach;
For if your minde be verteously set,
Then the *Devil* will labour you to lett;
In three wises to let he woll awaite,
With *Haste,* with *Despaire,* and with *Deceipte*:
For dreade of Vertue which ye maie doe,
When ye shulde attaine this grace unto.
The first perill aforesaide is of Haste,
Which causeth most destruction and waste;
All Auctors writing of this *Arte,*
Saye haste is of the *Devils* parte:
The little Boke writ of the Philosophers feast,
Saith, *omnis festinatio ex parts diaboli est*:
Wherefore that Man shall soonest speede,
Which with greate Leasure wisely woll proceede;
Upon assay ye shall trewly knowe
That who most hasteth he trewly shalbe slowe;
For he with haste shall bringe his warke arreare,
Sometymes a Moneth, and sometymes a whole Yeare
And in this *Arte* it shall ever be soe,
That a hasty Man shall never faile of woe:
Alsoe of haste ye may trewly be sure
That she leaveth nothing cleane and pure;
The *Devil* hath none so subtill wile
As with hastinesse you to beguile;

Therefore

Therefore oft tymes he will assault,
Your minde with haste to make defanlt;
He shall finde grace in Towne and Land,
Which can hastines all tymes withstand:
I say all tymes, for in one pointe of tyme,
Haste may destroy all your engine;
Therefore all haste eschewe and feare,
As if that she a *Devil* were.
My witt trewly cannot suffice,
Haste sufficiently for to despise;
Many Men have byne cast in greate care,
Because thei would not of haste beware:
But ever call upon to see an end,
Which is temptation of the Fende:
Noe more of haste at this present,
But blessed be ever the Patient.

WHen with *Haste* the Feind hath noe availe,
Then with *Despaire* your mind he will assaile;
And oft present this Sentence to your minde,
How many seeken, and how few maie finde,
Of wiser Men then ever were yee:
What suretie than to you maie be?
He woll move ye to doubt also
Whether your Teacher had it or noe;
And also how it mought so fall,
That part he tought you but not all;
Such uncertainety he woll cast out,
To set your minde with greevous doubt;
And soe your *Paines* he woll repaire
With wann hope and with much Despaire;
Against this assault is no defence,
But only the vertue of Confidence:
To whome reason shulde you leade,
That you shall have noe cause to dreade;

If

Chap. 2. If you wisely call to your minde
The vertuous manners, such as you finde
In your *Master* and your *Teacher*,
Soe shall you have noe neede to feare;
If you consider all Circumstances about,
Whether he tought you for Love or for Doubt;
Or whether Motion of him began,
For it is hard to trust such a Man:
For he that profereth hath more neede
Of you, then you of him to speede.
This wise certainely ye maie well win,
Before that you your warkes do begin;
When such certainety ye truly have,
Fro Dispaire ye maie be sure and save.
But who can finde such a *Master* out,
As was my *Master*, him needeth not to doubt:
Which right nobil was and fully worthy laude,
He loved Justice, and he abhorred fraude;
He was full secrete when other men were lowde,
Loath to be knowne that hereof ought he Could;
When men disputed of Colours of the Rose,
He would not speake but keepe himselfe full close;
To whome I laboured long and many a day,
But he was solleyn to prove with straight assaye,
To search and know of my Disposition,
With manifold proofes to know my Condition:
And when he found unfeigned fidelity,
In my greate hope which yet nothing did see,
At last I conquered by grace divine
His love, which did to me incline.
Wherefore he thought soone after on a tyde,
That longer delayes I ne shulde abide;
My manifold letters, my heavie heart and cheere,
Moved his Compassion, thei perced him full neere;
Wherefore

Wherefore his Penn he would noe more refraine,
But as heere followeth soe wrote he againe.

MY very trusty, my deere beloved *Brother*,
I must you answer, it may be none other;
The tyme is come you shall receive this Grace,
To your greate comfort and to your solace:
Your honest desire with your greate Confidence,
Your Vertue proved with your Sapience;
Your Love, your Trewth, your long Perseverance,
Your stedfast Minde shall your Desire advance:
Wherefore it is neede that within short space,
Wee speake together, and see face to face:
If I shulde write, I shulde my fealty breake,
Therefore Mouth to Mouth I must needes speake;
And when you come, mine *Heier* unto this *Arte*
I will you make, and fro this londe departe.
Ye shall be both my *Brother* and myne *Heier*,
Of this greate secrete whereof *Clerkes* despaire:
Therefore thanke *God* which giveth this renowne,
For it is better then to were a Crowne:
Next after his Saints, our *Lord* doth him call
Which hath this *Arte* to honour him withall:
Noe more to you at this present tyde,
But hastily to see me, dispose you to ride.

THis *Letter* receiving, I hasted full sore,
To ride to my *Master* an hundred miles and more;
And there Forty dayes continually,
I learned all the secreats of *Alkimy*:
Albeit *Philosophy* by me was understonde,
As much as of many other in this Londe;
Nethles fooles which for their *Science* sought,
Ween that in forty dayes it wilbe wrought.
Betweene Forty dayes warke now ye may see,
And Forty dayes lerninge is greate diversitie;

Chap. 2. Then darke doubts to me appeared pure,
There fownd I disclosed the ***Bonds of Nature:***
The cause of Wonders were to me soe faire,
And so reasonable, that I could not dispaier.
If your *Master* and ye resemble all aboute
My good *Master* and me, than have ye no doubte.

THe third impediment deceipt we call,
Amongst other to me the worst all;
And that is of *Servaunts* that should awaite
Upon your warke, for some can much deceipte;
Some be negligent, some sleeping by the fire,
Some be ill-willd, such shall let your desire;
Some be foolish, and some be over bold,
Some keepe no Counsell of Doctrine to them tould;
Some be filthie of hands and of sleeves,
Some meddle straunge Matter, that greately greeves;
Some be drunken, and some use much to jape,
Beware of thes if you will hurt escape,
The Trew be foolish, the Witty be false,
That one hurts me Sore, that other als:
For when I had my warke well wrought,
Such stale it away and left me nought.
Then I remembring the cost, the tyme, and the paine,
Which I shulde have to begin againe,
With heavie hearte farewell adieu said I,
I will noe more of *Alkimy*.
But howe that chaunce befell that Season,
Few men would it beleeve by reason:
Yet Tenn persons be witnes trew all
How that mishapp did me befalle,
Which might not be only by Man,
Without the Devil as they tell can.
I made also the *Elixer* of life,
Which me bereft a Merchaunt's wife:

The

The *Quinteſsens* I made alſo,
With other ſecrets manie moe,
Which ſinfull people tooke me fro,
To my greate paine and much more woe:
Soe in this worke there is no more to ſaine,
But that every *Ioy* is medled with his *paine*.

OF *Paine* there is a litle yet behinde,
Which is convenient to be had in minde;
That fell upon a bleſſed Man;
Whereof the trewth report I cann.
Thomas Daulton this good man height,
He ſerved *God* both day and night,
Of the Red Medicine he had greate Store,
I trowe never Engliſh man had more.
A *Squier* for the body of *King Ehward*,
Whoſe name was *Thomas Harbert*,
Tooke this *Daulton* againſt his deſier,
Out of an *Abbie* in *Glouceſter-ſhier*,
And brought him in preſence of the *King*,
Whereof *Deluis* had ſome tiding,
For *Daulton* was whilome *Deluis*'s Clerke;
Deluis diſcloſed of *Daultons* werke.
Deluis was *Squier* in confidence
With *King Edward* oft in his preſence.
Deluis reported that in a little ſtounde,
How *Daulton* had made to him a thouſand pound
Of as good Goulde as the Royall was,
Within halfe a daye and ſome dele laſſe;
For which *Deluis* ſware on a Booke.
Then *Daulton* on *Deluis* caſt his looke,
And ſaid to *Deluis*, Sir you be forſwore,
Wherefore your hert hath cauſe to be ſore.
Of nothing ſaid he, that I now have told,
Witnes our *Lord* whom *Judas* ſould.

Chap. 2. But once said *Deluis* I sware to thee,
That thou shouldst not be uttered by me;
Which I may breake well I understand,
For the *Kings* weale and for all his Lande.
Then said *Daulton* full soberlie,
This answer voydeth no perjury.
How should the *King* in you have Confidence,
Your untrewth confessed in his presence.
But Sir said *Daulton* to the *Kings* Grace,
I have bin troubled oft in many a place
For this Medicine greviously and sore,
And now I thought it should hurt me no more:
Wherefore in the *Abbie* where I was take,
I cast it in a foule and Common lake
Going to the River which doth ebb and flowe,
There is destroyed as much riches nowe,
As would have served to the Holy land,
For twenty thousand men upon a band.
I kept it longe for our *Lords* blessed sake,
To helpe a *Kinge* which that journey would make.
Alas *Daulton* then saide the *Kinge*,
It was fowly don to spill such a thinge.
He would have *Daulton* to make it againe,
Daulton said it might not be certeine:
Why (said the *Kinge*) how came ye thereby?
He said by a *Channon* of *Lichfielde* trewly,
Whose workes *Daulton* kept dilligently,
Many yeares till that *Channon* must dye.
And for his service he said in that space,
The Cannon gave him all that thereof was;
The *Kinge* gave to *Daulton* Marks foure,
With liberty to goe where he would that houre.
Then was the *Kinge* in his herte sore,
That he had not knowne *Daulton* before.

And

And ever it happneth without leasinge,
That Tyrants be full nigh to a Kinge.
For *Herberte* lay for *Daulton* in waight,
And brought him to *Stepney* with deceipte.
The servaunts of *Herbert* the mony tooke away
Which the King gave to *Daulton* that day.
And after *Herbert* carried *Daulton* farr,
From thence to the Casle of *Gloucester*,
There was *Daulton* prisner full longe,
Herbert to *Daulton* did mickle wronge:
Fro thence he had him to prison fast
To *Troy*, till foure yeares were nigh past,
And after he brought him out to dye;
Daulton to death obeyed lowly,
And said *Lord Jesue* blessed thou be,
Me thinks I have byne too longe from thee.
A *Science* thou gavest me with full greate charge,
Which I have kept without outrage.
I founde noe man yet apt thereto,
To be myne Heyer when I am goe:
Wherefore (sweete *Lord*) now I am faine
To resigne this thy guift to thee againe.
Then *Daulton* made devout prayers, and still
Withsmiling cheere he said now doe your wil.
When *Herbert* sawe him so glad to dye,
Then ran water from *Herberts* Eye:
For Prison ne Death could him not availe
To winn this *Arte*, his Crafte did him faile.
Now let him goe said *Herbert* than,
For he shall never hurt ne profett man.
But when *Daulton* from the block should rise;
He looked forth in full heavie wise,
And so departed with full heavie cheere,
It was not his will to live one yeare.

Chap. 2.

This was his *Paine* as I you tell,
By men that had no dread of Hell.
Herbert dyed ſoone after in his bed,
And *Deluis* at *Teuxbury* loſt his head;
This wiſe greate *Paine*, as you may ſee,
Followeth this *Arte* in every degree.
Heere loſt the *King* all his intent,
For *Herbert* was proude and violent,
Soe nobil a man to oppreſſe with pride,
And like a Fellone him leade and guide;
Where that by goodneſſe patience and grace,
There might have growen full great ſolace,
As well to the *King*, ye may underſtonde,
As for th'eaſe of Commons of this londe;
But wonder not that grace doe not fall,
For ſinn reygneth in this londe over all.
Loe here was grace full ready at honde,
To have ceaſed Taxes and Tallages of this londe;
Whereby much Love and Grace would have be,
Betweene Knight-hood Prieſt-hoode and Comminaltie.
Here ye maie ſee how vicious violence
Maie not purchaſe the vertue of ſapience:
For vice and vertue be things contrary,
Therefore the vicious maie not come thereby;
If Vicious men mought lerne this *Science*,
They would therewith doe wondrous violence:
And with Ambitiouſneſſe grow evermore
Worſe of Conditions then they were before.
Now is this *Chapter* of *Joy* and *Paine* gone,
The *Chapter* following ſheweth *Matters of our Stone.*

CHAP.

CHAP. III.

TONSile was a labourer in the fire
Threescore years and more to win his desire:
Brian was another, with *Holton* in the Weste,
Thes were ever busie, & could practice with (the best:
But yet this *Science* thei never founde,
For thei knew not the Matters, ne the Grounde,
But rumbled foorth, and evermore they sought,
They spent their lyfe and their goods to nought;
Much losse, much cost, much anguish they bought,
Amonge their Receipts which they had wrought:
Then made *Tonsile* to me his greate complainte,
With weeping Teares he said his heart was fainte,
For he had spended all his lusty dayes
In fals Receipts, and in such lewde assayes;
Of Herbes, Gommes, of Rootes and of Grasse,
Many kindes by him assayed was,
As Crowefoote, Celondine and Mizerion,
Vervaine, Lunara, and Martagon:
In Antimony, Arsenick, Honey, Wax and Wine,
In Haire, in Eggs, in Merds, and Urine,
In Calx vive, Sandifer, and Vitriall,
In Markasits, Tutits, and every Minerall,
In Malgams, in Blanchers, and Citrinacions,
All fell to nought in his opperacions:
For he considered not how he did rage,
When to *Gods* proportions he layde surcharge:
After all this, he thought nothing so good,
To worke upon as shulde be mans Blode;
Till that I said how blode would waste and fume
In mighty fire, and utterly consume.

For

Chap. 3. For *Christ* his love then saide he teach me,
Whereof the substance of our *Stone* should be:
Tonsile (said I) what shulde it you avayle
Such thing to know? your lims doth you faile
For very Age, therefore cease your lay,
And love your Beades, it is high time to Praye;
For if you knew the Materialls of our *Stone*,
Ere you could make it your dayes would be gone.
Thereof no charge good *Master* said he,
It were sufficient Comfort now to me
To know the trewe Materialls without wronge
Of that *Stone* which I have sought soe longe:
Tonsile (said I) It is noe litle thinge,
Whereof you would have trewe tydinge;
For many Auctors write of this doubte,
But none of them sheweth it Cleerly oute:
For Auctors which of this *Arte* doe write,
Besought *God* (as witnesseth *Democrite*,)
That he unpained would fro this Worlde take
Their Soules whom he tought Bokes thereof to make;
For greatly doubted evermore all suche,
That of this *Scyence* they may write too muche:
Every each of them tought but one pointe or twayne,
Whereby his fellowes were made certayne;
How that he was to them a *Brother*,
For every of them understoode each other;
Alsoe they wrote not every man to Teache,
But to shew themselves by a secret Speache:
Trust not therefore to reading of one Boke,
But in many Auctors works ye may looke;
Liber librum apperit saith *Arnold* the greate *Clerke*,
Anaxagoras said the same for his werke:
Who that slothfull is in many bokes to see,
Such one in Practice prompt shall never be;

But

But *Tonsile* for almes I will make no store
Plainly to disclose it that never was done before,
By way of answer for your recreation,
If ye cann wisely make *Interrogation.*
Good *Master* (saide he) then teach me trewly,
Whether the matters be *Sol* or *Mercury?*
Or whether of *Sol* or *Lune* it maie be,
Or whether I shall take them all three,
Or *Sol* by it selfe, or *Mercury* alone,
Or *Sulpher* with them, for matters of our Stone?
Or whether I shall *sal Almoniack* take,
Or *Minerall meanes*, our *Stone* thereof to make?
Here be many questions *Tonsile*, said I,
Wisely remembred and full craftily;
You name it not yet but onely in generall;
For you must take some deale of theis things all;
Of these and of other you must take a parte,
One time or other to minister this *Arte*:
Many things helpeth to apt our *Stone*,
But *two be Materialls*, yet our *Stone* is one;
Betweene which two is such diversity,
As betweene the *Mother* and the *Childe* may be:
An other diversity betweene them find ye shall,
Such as is found betweene *Male* and *Female*:
Theis two kindes shall doe all your service,
As for the *White worke* (if you can be wise;)
One of thes kindes a Stone ye shall finde,
For it abideth fire as stones doe by kinde:
But it is no Stone in touching ne in sight,
But a subtill Earth, browne, roddy, and not bright:
And when it is separate and brought to his appearage,
Then we name it our grounde *Litharge.*
First it is browne, roddy, and after some deale white,
And then it is called our chosen *Markasite*:

Chap. 3. One ounce thereof is better then fifty pounde;
It is not to be sould in all Christian grounde;
But he that would have it he shalbe faine
To doe it make, or take himselfe the paine:
But one greate grace in that labour is saine,
Make it once well and never more againe.
Olde fathers called it thinge of vile price,
For it is nought worth by way of Marchandise:
Noe man that findeth it woll beare it awaie,
Noe more then thei would an Ounce of Claye;
Men will not beleeve that it is of high price,
No man knoweth it therefore but he be wise.
Here have I disclosed a greate secret wonder,
Which never was writ by *them* which been erth under.

ANother *Stone Tonsile* you must have withall,
Or else you fawte your cheefe Materiall;
Which is a Stone gloriouse faier and bright,
In handling a Stone, and a Stone in sight;
A Stone glittering with perspecuitie,
Being of wonderfull Diaphanitie;
The price of an Ounce Conveniently,
Is twenty shillings or well neere thereby:
Her name is *Magnetia*, few people her knowe,
She is fownde in high places as well as in lowe;
Plato knew her property and called her by her name,
And *Chaucer* reherseth how *Titanos* is the same,
In the *Channons Yeomans Taile*, saying what is thus,
But *quid ignotum per magis ignotius*:
That is to say, what may this be,
But unknowne by more unknowne named is she;
Nethles *Tonsile* now I will trewlie teach
What is *Magnetia* to say in our speache:
Magos is Greeke, *Mirabile* in Latine it ys,
Æs is *Money*, *ycos Science*, *A* is God ywisse.

Tha

That is to ſay it is ſuch a thinge,
Wherein of Money is wonderous divine Cunninge;
Now here you may know what is *Magnetia*,
Res æris in qua latet ſcientia divinaque mira.
Thes two *Stones Tonſile* ye muſt take
For your materialls, *Elixir* if ye make.
Albeit the firſt tyme materialls be no more,
Yet many things helpeth as I ſaide before.
This ſecrete was never before this daye
So trewly diſcovered, take it for your praye;
I pray *God* that this turne not me to Charge,
For I dread ſore my penn goeth too large:
For though much people perceive not this Sentence,
Yet ſubtill *Clerks* have too much Evidence;
For many *Clerks* be ſo cleere of witt,
If thei had this ground, thei were ſure of it;
Wher our Lord hath ordained that no man it finde,
But only he that is of verteous minde:
Wherefore olde Fathers Covered for great reaſon,
The Matters of our *Stone* diſcloſed at this ſeaſon.
Other Materials ye ſhall none take,
But only theis two oure *white ſtone* to make;
Except *Sal Armoniack* with *Sulphur* of kinde,
Such as out of *Mettals* ye can finde;
Theis two woll abide to fulfill your deſire,
The remnant will void when thei come to fire;
Sulpher woll brenn and chaunge Collours faſt,
But our *Litharge* abideth firſt and laſt:
Ye may not with mettals or Quickſilver beginn,
To make *Elixir* if you intend to winn:
Yet if you deſtroy the whole Compoſition,
Some of their Compounds will help in Concluſion;
And that is nothing Els of that one or that other,
But only *Magnetia* and *Litharge* her Brother.

Geberus
Hermes
corpus
Ro: Vaughan sculp:

CHAP. IV.

Chap. 4.

OF the grosse Warke now I wil not spare,
Though it be secrete, largely to declare:
To teach you the trewth is myne intente,
As far forth as I dare for *Gods* Com-
(maundement.
I will informe and guide you in the way,
In such wise as you may finde your praye:
If you consider how the partes of Werkes,
Be out of Order set by the old *Clerks*.
As I saide before, the *Masters* of this *Arte*,
Every each of them disclosed but a parte:
Wherefore though ye perceived them as ye woulde,
Yet ye cannot order and joyne them as ye shulde.
Arnold sheweth in his writinge,
How our finall secret is to know the thinge
Whereupon our worke shulde take her grounde,
And how pure Natures & simple may be found:
In this Boke begining *multipharie*,
He saith in our grounded Matter two kindes be;
But how to find them he kept that in store,
Ye have their Names the last *Chapter* before.
Freer Bacon disclosed more of that pointe,
When he said, Departe ye every joynte
In Elementa propinqua: take good heede thereto;
But unwise Doctours never worken soe,
But headly they proceed as men well nigh madd,
To the Matters divisible moe Matters they adde:
Soe when thei weene to bringe forth a Flower,
They doe nothinge but multiply Errour.
There cesed *Bacon*, and so doe other such,
For very dread least they shulde shew too much

Chap.4. *Avicen in Porta* wrote, if ye remember,
How ye shulde proceede perfection to ingender,
Trewly teaching as the pure trewth was,
Comedas ut bibas, et bibas ut Comedas,
Eate as it drinketh, and drinke as it doth eate,
And in the meane season take *it* a perfect sweate.
Rasis set the Dietary and spake some deale farr,
Non tamen comedat res festinanter,
Let not your Matters eate over hastilie,
But wisely consume their foode leasurelie.
Hereof the *Prophet* made wondrous mention,
Yf ye applie it to this intention.
Visitasti terram, & inebriasti eam,
Multiplicasti locupletare eam
Terram fructiferam in salsuginem,
Et terram sine aqua in exitus aquarum.
If it I have plenty of Meate and of Drinke,
Men must wake when they desier to winke:
For it is laboure of watch and paines greate.
Also the Foode is full costly meate;
Therefore all Poore men beware said *Arnold,*
For this *Arte* longeth to greate men of the worlde.
Trust to his words ye Poore men all,
For I am witnes that soe ye finde shall.
Esto longanimis & suavis said he,
For hasty men th'end shall never see.
The lengthe of clensing of Matters infected,
Deceyveth much People, for that is unsuspected.
Wherefore Poore men put ye not in prease,
Such wonders to seech, but in season cease.
Excesse for one halfe quarter of an howre,
May destroy all: therefore cheefe succoure
Is *Primum pro quo, & vultimum pro quo non,*
To know of the simperinge of our *Stone.*

Till

Till it may noe more ſimper doe not ceaſe,
And yet longe Continuance may not cauſe increaſe.
Remember that Water will buble and boyle,
But Butter muſt ſimper and alſo Oyle.
And ſoe with long leaſure it will waſte,
And not with bubling made in haſte:
For doubt of perrills many moe then one,
And for ſupergreſſion of our ſtone.
Amongſt groſſe Workes the fowleſt of all
Is to clarifie our meanes Minerall.
Extremities may not be well wrought,
Without many Meanes wiſely ſought.
And everie Meane muſt be made pure,
If this worke ſhulde be made ſure.
For foule and cleane by naturall lawe
Hath greate diſcord, and ſoe hath ripe and rawe.
Stedfaſt to ſtedfaſt will it ſelfe combinde,
And fleeting to fleeting will drawe by kinde:
And ever where as the Concordance is more,
Natures will drawe that were elſwhere before;
This groſſe Worke is fowle in her kinde,
And full of perrills as ye ſhall it finde.
No mans witt can him ſoe much availe,
But that ſometyme he ſhall make a fayle.
As well as the *Lay-man* ſoe ſhall the *Clerke*,
And all that labour the groſſe werke:
Whereof *Anaxagoras* ſaid trewlie thus,
Nemo primo fronte reperitur diſcretus.
And once I heard a wiſe man ſay,
How in *Catilonia* at this day,
Magnetia with Minerall meanes all,
Be made to ſale if ye for them call,
Whereby the honds of a cleanly *Clerke*,
Shall not be ſiled about ſo foule a werke.

And

Chap. 4. And longe tyme sooner your Worke I understonde,
Shulde be farr onward before honde.
For if you shulde make all things as I cann,
Ye might be weary before your worke begann.
The Philosophers warke doe not begin,
Till all things be pure without and within.
We that must seeke Tincture most specious,
Must needely avoyd all things vild and vicious.
Of manifold meanes each hath his propertie,
To doe his Office after his degree:
With them hid things be out sett,
Some that will helpe and some that would lett.
Our *Appoticaries* to dresse them can no skill,
And we to teach them have no manner of will:
Whereof the cause trewly is none other,
But that they will counterfaict to beguile their Brother,
Rather then they will take the paine
Thereto belonging, ere they should it attaine:
It is there use whereof my hert is sore,
Much to desire and litle to doe therefore.
Who would have trewe warke he may no laboure spare,
Neither yet his Purse, though he make it bare:
And in the Grosse Warke he is furthest behinde,
That daily desireth the end thereof to finde.
If the grosse warke with all his Circumstance,
Were don in three yeares, it were a blessed chance:
For he that shall end it once for certeyne,
Shall never have neede to begin againe,
If he his Medicine wisely can Augment;
For that is the Mastrie of all our intent.
It needeth not to name the meanes Minerall,
For *Albert* writeth openly of them all.
Much I might write of nature of Mynes,
Which in this Grosse Warke be but engines;

For

For in this Warke finde ye nothing ſhall,
But handie-crafte called Arte Mechanicall:
Wherein an hundreth wayes and moe,
Ye maie committ a faulte as ye therein goe.
Wherefore beleeve what old Auctors tell,
Without Experience ye maie not doe well.
Conſider all Circumſtances, and ſet your delight
To keepe Uniformity of all things requiſite.
Uſe one manner of Veſſell in Matter and in Shape,
Beware of Commixtion that nothing miſcape.
And hundreth faultes in ſpeciall,
Ye maie make under this warning generall.
Nethles this Doctrine woll ſuffice,
To him that can in Practiſe be wiſe.
If your Miniſters be witty and trew,
Such ſhall not neede your warkes to renew.
Therefore if ye woll avoyde all dreade,
In the Groſſe Warke doe by my read:
Take never thereto no Houſhold-man,
Thei be ſoone weary as I tell cann;
Therefore take noe man thereto,
But he be Waged, however you doe;
Not by the Moneth, as nigh as ye maie,
Ne by the Weeke, but by the Daye:
And that your Wages be to their minde,
Better then thei elſewhere can finde;
And that thei neede not for Wages ſue,
But that their Payment be quick and trewe;
For that ſhall cauſe them to love and dreade,
And to their Warks to take good heede,
For doubt leaſt thei be put awaye,
For Negligence of them in one daye:
Houſhold-men woll not doe ſoe,
From this Warke therefore let them goe.

Chap. 4. If I had knowne this, and had done soe,
I had avoyded mickle woe.
Alsoe in this Warke must be Liberty,
Without impediment, in everie degree,
With divers Comforts peynes to release
Of labours continuall which maie not Cease;
Els anguish of Labour and Melancholly,
Mought be Cause your Warkes to destroy.
Of the grosse Warke it needes to shew noe more,
For old men have tought the remnant before;
And what is necessary that thei last out,
This Boke sheweth it without doubt.
Wherefore this litle Boke the *Ordinall*,
Is in *Alkimy* the Complement of all;
The *Chapter* following convenient for a *Clerke*,
Sheweth the *Councells* of the subtill Werke.

CHAP.

Ro: Vaughan sculp.

Chap. V.

BRISE by Surname when the chaunge of
(Coyne was had,
Made some Men sorry, and some Men glad:
And as to much people that chaunge,
Seemed a newe thinge and a straunge;
Soe that season befell a wonderous thinge,
Tuching this *Science* without leasinge.
That three *Masters* of this *Science* all
Lay in one Bed nigh to *Leaden-Hall*,
Which had *Elixirs* parfite White and Red,
A wonder such Three to rest in one Bed,
And that within the space of dayes Tenn,
While hard it is to finde One in Millions of Men.
Of the *Dukedome* of *Loraine* one I understand
Was borne, that other nigh the *Midle* of *England*;
Under a Crosse, in the end of *Shires* three,
The third was borne; the youngest of them is he.
Which by his *Nativity* is by *Clerks* found,
That he shulde honour all English ground;
A Man mought walke all the World aboute,
And faile such Three *Masters* to finde oute;
Twayne be fleeting, the Youngest shall abide,
And doe much good in this *Londe* at a Tyde.
But sinne of *Princes* shall let or delaye
The Grace that he shulde doe on a daye.
The eldest *Master* chaunted of him a Songe,
And said that he shulde suffer much wronge.
Of them which were to him greately behould,
And manie things moe this *Master* tould,
Which sith that tyme hath trewly befall,
And some of them hereafter shall,

Whereof

Whereof one is trewlie (said he)
After Troubles great Joy shalbe
In every quarter of this *Londe*,
Which all good Men shall understonde:
The Younger asked when that shulde be,
The old Man said when Men shall see
The *holy Crosse* honored both day and night,
In the Lond of *God* in the Lond of Light;
Which maie be done in right good season,
But long delayed it is without reason:
When that beginneth note well this thinge,
This *Science* shall drawe towards the *Kinge*;
And many moe Graces ye maie be boulde,
Moe then of us shall now be tould;
Grace on that *King* shall descend,
When he ould Manners shall amende:
He shall make full secreate search,
For this *Scyence* with doulced speech;
And amonge the Solitary,
He shall have tidings certainly.
So sought *King Kalid* of manie Men,
Till he met with *Morien*,
Which helped *Kalid* at his neede,
His Vertues caused him to speede.

NOwe of such Matters let us cease,
And of the suttill Warke reherse;
Greate need hath he to be a *Clerke*,
That would perceive this suttill Werke.
He must know his first Philosophie,
If he trust to come by *Alkimye*:
And first ye shall well understonde,
All that take this Werke in honde;
When your materialls by preparation,

Chap.5. Be made well apt for Generation,
Then thei must be departed a twinn,
Into foure Elements if ye would to winn:
Which thing to doe if ye ne can,
Goe and lerne it of *Hortolan*.
Which made his Boke of that Doctrine,
How ye shulde part the Elements of Wine.
Moreover ye must for your succour,
Know th'effects of the quallities fower;
Called Heate, Colde, Moisture, and Drines,
Of which fower all things Compounded is;
And sith in this *Arte* your cheefe desire
Is to have Colour which shulde abide fier,
Ye must know before you can that see,
How everie Colour ingendred shall be,
For every Colour whiche maie be thought,
Shall heere appeare before that White be wrought.
Yet more ye would have to this summe,
Swiftly to melt as Wex or Gumme:
Els mought it not enter and perce
The Center of Mettalls as Auctors reherse;
Soe ye would have it both fix and flowe,
With Colour plenty if ye wist howe;
Such three Contraries joyntly to meete
In one accord is a greate Secret.
Nethles he that is cleere of Minde,
In this Chapter maie it well finde;.
And first to give you a short Doctrine,
Of the aforesaid qualities prime:
Heate, and Cold, be qualities Active
Moisture, and Drines, be qualityes Passive;
For they suffren the Actives evermore,
As Stones to be Lyme, and Water to be Froare.
Hereupon to Judge, ye maie be bold,

Chap. 5.

Nothing is full wrought but by Heate and Cold;
Nethles the Passives have some Activity,
As in Handicrafts men ye maie daily see;
In Bakinge, and Brewinge, and other Crafts all,
Moisture is opperative and soe Drines be shall.
Aristotle in his *Phisicks* and other manie moe,
Said *ab actionibus procedit speculatio*;
They said that Practise is roote and beginning,
Of Speculation and of all Cunning:
For the properties of every thinge,
Be perceaved by their working;
As by Colours of *Urins* we may be bold
To give sentence of Heate and Colde;
By thes aforesaid foure qualities prime,
We seeche Colours with length of tyme;
Of White Colour we be not full sure,
To seeche it but in a substance pure:
Greate Doctrine thereof lerne now ye maie,
When ye know how Colours growe all day.

Colour is the utmost thinge of a Body cleere,
Cleere substance well termined is his matter heere;
If Heate hath maistery in matter that is drye,
White Colour is ever thereof certainely;
As it appeareth in sight of brent Bones,
And in making of all Lyme Stones.
Where Cold worketh in matter moist & cleere,
Yet of such working Whitnes woll appeare:
As it sheweth in Ice and Frosts hore;
The cause is set out in Philosophie before:
I write not here of common Philosophie,
But by example to teach *Alkimy*;
That one maie be perceived by that other,
As is the Child perceived by the Mother.

If

Chap. 5. If Heate in moyst matter and grosse withall,
Warke, thereof *Black* Colour ingender shall;
Example hereof if ye of me desire,
Behold when you see greene Wood set on a fire;
When Cold worketh in matter thick and drye,
Black Colour shall be, this is the cause whie;
Such matter is compacted and more thick,
With Cold constreyning, enimy to all quick,
Thicknes made Darknes with privation of Light,
Soe Collour is private, then Black it is to Sight,
Therefore evermore remember this,
How cleere matter is matter of Whitenes;
The cause efficient maie be manyfold,
For somewhile it is Heate, and sometime Cold:
But White and Black, as all men maie see,
Be Colours contrary in most extremitie:
Wherefore your warke with Black must beginn,
If the end shulde be with Whitenes to winn.
The midle Colour as *Philosophers* write,
Is *Red* Colour betweene Black and White:
Nethlesse trust me certainly,
Red is last in work of *Alkimy*.
Alsoe they say in their Doctrine,
How theis two Colours Rufe and Citrine,
Be meane Colours betweene White and Red,
And how that Greene, and Colour wan as Lead,
Betweene Red and Black be Colours meane,
And freshest Colour is of matter most Cleane.
Physitians in *Urines* have Colours Nynteene,
Betweene White and Black as thei weene;
Whereof Colour underwhite *Subalbidus* is one,
Like in Colour to *Onychyne* stone:
Of such like Colour *Magnetia* found is,
But *Magnetia* glittereth with Cleerenes:

In

In our suttill warke of *Alkimy* *Chap. 5.*
Shall be all Colours that hath beene seen with Eye:
An hundreth Colours more in certeyne,
Then ever hath been seene in *Urine.*
Wherein so many Colours mought not be,
But if our *Stone* conteyned every degree,
Of all Compositions found in warke of kinde,
And of all Compositions imaginable by minde.
Of as manie Colours as shall therein be saine,
So manie graduations your wisdome must attaine:
And if you knowe not such graduations all,
Lerne them of *Raymond* in his *Atre Generall.*
Gilbert Kymer wrote after his devise,
Of 17. Proportions, but thei maie not suffice
In this *Science*, which he coude never finde;
And yet in *Phisick* he had a nobil minde.
Wher the royalty of the nature of Man,
Advaunceth ofte Medicines of the Phisitian:
And so honoreth oft times his Crafte,
When that the Medicines peradventure mought be lafte;
But it is not so in Phisick of *Mines*,
For that Arte exceedeth all other engines:
And resteth only in the wisdome of Man,
As by experience wise men witnes can.

AND soe of *Alkimy* the trew foundation,
Is in *Composition* by wise graduation
Of Heate and Cold, of Moist and of Drye,
Knowing other Qualities ingendered thereby;
As hard and soft, heavy and light,
Rough and smoothe, by ponders right,
With Number and Measure wisely sought,
In which three resteth all that *God* wrought:
For *God* made all things, and set it sure,

Chap. 5. In Number Ponder and in Measure,
Which numbers if you doe chaunge and breake,
Upon *Nature* you must doe wreake.
Wherefore *Anaxagoras* said Take good heede,
That to *Conjunction* ye not proceede,
Till ye know the Ponders full compleate
Of all Componects which shulde therein meete;
Bacon said that old Men did nothing hide,
But only *Proportion* wherein was noe guide:
For none old Auctor, King, Prince, ne Lord,
Writing of this *Science* with others did accorde
In the Proportions; which if ye would reach,
Raymond, with *Bacon*, and *Albert*, done it teach,
With old *Anaxagoras*, of them fowre ye shall
Have perfect knowledge, but not of one have all:
And if you would joyne fowre Qualities to intent,
Then must ye Conjoyne every Element:
As Water and Erthe after your desire,
Well compounded with Ayer, and Fier:
Knowing the worthiest in his activitie,
The second, the third, every-each in his degree;
The fourth, and the vilest maie not be refused,
For it is profitable and best to be used;
And best maie extend his Multiplication,
In whome is the virtue of our Generation;
And that is the Erthly *Lytharge* of our *Stone*,
Without him Generation shall be none;
Neyther of our Tincture fixation,
For nothing is fixt but Erthe alone;
All other Elements moveable be,
Fier, Ayer, and Water, as ye daily see:
But Fier is cause of extendibility,
And causeth matters permiscible to be,
And cleere brightnes in Colours faire

Is

Is caused of kinde evermore of Ayer,
And Ayer also with his Coaction,
Maketh things to be of light liquefaction:
As Wax is and Butter, and Gummes all,
A little heate maketh them to melt and fall:
Water clenseth with ablution blive,
And things mortifyed causeth to revive.
Of multiplying of Fier is no greater wonder,
Than is of multiplying of Erth set under:
For Erth beareth Herbes daily new and newe,
Without number, therefore it is trewe
That Erth is wonderfull as well as Fier,
Though one sparke maie soone fill a Sheere:
If all a Sheere were filled with Flaxe,
One sparke than would wonderfully waxe:
Fier and Erth be multipliers alone,
And thei be causers of multiplying our *Stone*.
Of this Erth showeth *Albert* our great Brother,
In his *Mineralls*, which *Lytharge* is better than other.
For the white *Elixir* he doth it there rehearse,
And the booke of *Meeter* showeth it in a verse.

Now to *Conjunction* let us resorte,
And some wise Councell thereof reporte:
Conjoyne your Elements *Grammatically*,
With all their Concords conveniently:
Whiche Concords to healpe a Clerke,
Be cheefe Instruments of all this werke:
For nothinge maie be more contrary nowe,
Than to be fixt and unperfectly flowe:
All the *Grammarians* of *England* and of *Fraunce*,
Cannot teach you this Concordance:
This *Ordinall* telleth where ye maie it see,
In *Phisick* in the Boke *de Arbore*.

Chap. 5. Joyne them also in *Rhetoricall* guise,
With Natures Ornate in purified wise.
Sithens our Tincture must be most pure and faire,
Be sure of pure Erth, Water, Fier and Ayre.
In *Logicall* wise be it early or late,
Joyne trewe kindes not sophisticate;
Ignorance hereof hath made many Clerks,
Lewdly to leese their labour and their werkes.
Joyne them together also *Arithmetically*,
By suttill Numbers proportionally.
Whereof a litle mention made there was,
When *Boetius* said *tu numeris elementa ligas*.
Joyne your Elements *Musically*,
For two causes, one is for Melody:
Which there accords will make to your mind,
The trewe effect when that ye shall finde.
And also for like as *Diapason*,
With *Diapente* and with *Diatesseron*,
With *ypate ypaton*, and *Lecanos muse*,
With other accords which in Musick be,
With their proporcions causen Harmony,
Much like proportions be in *Alkimy*,
As for the great Numbers Actuall:
But for the secreate Numbers Intellectuall;
Ye must seeche them as I said before,
Out of *Raymond* and out of *Bacons* lore.
Bacon sheweth it darkly in his three letters all,
And *Raymonde* better in his *Arte Generall*.
Many men weene which doth them reade,
That theie doe understonde them when theie doe not (indeede.
With *Astrologie* joyne Elements also,
To fortune their Workings as theie goe:
Such simple kindes unformed and unwrought,
Must craftily be guided till the end be sought.

All

All which seafon theie have more obedience,
Above formed Natures to Sterrs influence.
And Science *Perfpective* giveth great evidence,
To all the Minifters of this *Science*.
And fo done other Sciences manie moe
And fpecially the Science *de Pleno & Vacuo*;
But the chiefe Miftris among Sciences all,
For helpe of this *Arte*, is *Magick Naturall*.

WHen the foure Elements wifely joyned be,
And every-each of them fet in his degree,
Then of divers degrees and of divers digeftion,
Colours will arife towards perfection.
For then worketh inward heate naturall,
Which in our fubftance is but Intellectuall:
To fight unknowne, hand maie it not feele,
His working is knowne to few Men and feild;
And when this heate naturall moved be fhall
By our outward heate artificiall,
Then Nature excited to labour will not ceafe,
Many diverfities of degrees to increafe.
Which is one caufe by reafon you maie fee,
Whie in our warke fo manie Colours be:
Therfore it caufeth in this *Arte* great doubt,
Ignorance of heate within and without,
To know how theis two heates fhulde accord,
And which of them in working fhulde be Lord.

D*igeftion* in this warke hath great likeneffe
To digeftion in things of Quicknes:
And before other (as I witneffe can)
It is moft like to digeftion of Man.
Therefore faid *Morien*, our *Stone* in generation
Is moft like thing to Mans Creation,

Chap. 5. In whom saith *Raymond* the fowre degrees all
Of the fowre Complexions together finde ye shall,
And that actually, which ye cannot finde
Amongst Creatures in none other kinde.
Wherefore amonge Creatures theis two alone
Be called *Microcosmus*, *Man* and our *Stone*.
Now of Digestion the aliment and foode
Perfectly to know is needfull and full good.
It is humor sollid constant with siccitie,
Mightily medled after some degree,
In opposite passives mixed duly,
Ingendered by inward and outward heat trewly.
Soe nothing else is our Digestion,
But of humour substantiall a create perfection.
I pray ye *Laymen* have me excused,
Though such Tearmes with you be not used,
I must use them, for all Auctors affirmes,
How *every Science hath his proper Tearmes*.
Digestion sometimes advanced maie be
By outward cold, as yearly ye maie see
How in Winter men eaten more meate
Than in Summer, when expansed is their heate;
For colde maketh heate inward then to flye,
And ligge nigh together, then stronger is he;
Which by his strength his power is more
To make Digestion than he mought before.
But our cheefe Digesture for our intent,
Is virtuall heate of the matter digerent;
Nethles heate of the digestible thinge,
Helpeth digestion and her working:
Feaverly heate maketh no digestion,
Baines maie helpe and cause also destruction.
Wine digested hath more heate naturall,
Than hath new Muste, whose heate is accidentall:

Coagula-

Coagulation is noe forme ſubſtantiall,
But onlie paſſion of things materiall.

MOre ye muſt know, when Colours appeare,
Who is principall Agent in that matter Cleere.
For ſometimes it is Heate, and ſometimes Cold it is,
And ſometime Moyſture, and ſomewhile Drines.
The principall Agent to know at every ſeaſon,
Requireth great ſearch made by ſuttill reaſon:
Which is not perceived but of *Maſters* fewe,
For thei mark not how Colours ariſe by rewe:
The principall Agent of the qualities fowre,
Hath power royall as Lord of moſt honour
The remnant of qualities to Converte to his kinde,
Of which converſion *Anaxagoras* maketh minde
In his Boke of *Converſions Naturall*,
Whereof *Raymond* ſheweth cauſes ſpeciall:
It is no Jape neither light to lerne
Your principall Agent all ſeaſons to diſcerne:
Which I teach you to knowne by ſignes fowre,
By *Colour*, *Odour*, *Sapor* and *Liquore*.

ANd firſt by *Colour* to ſerve your intente,
To know thereby your principall Agent.
Looke in your Veſſell which Colour ſheweth moſt,
He that cauſeth him is principall of the hoſt
As for that ſeaſon, whoſe pride ye maie ſwage,
By this our Doctrine, if ye ſee him rage:
Which ye maie doe when ye well underſtonde,
The cauſe of all Colours which ye have in honde.
Which I woll teach you now ſhortly withall,
Bycauſe here and there ſeeke them ye ne ſhall:
Whitnes is cauſed of manie matters cleere,
In another thing termined, and ſoe it is heere;

Blacknes

Chap. 5. *Blacknes* is when parts of a body darke,
With thicknes oppresseth the cleernes of the Warke;
Or els it is of a Combust terrestrietie;
But of such Combustion greate hardnes shall be;
And by Commixion of Darke Cleere and Cleane,
Shall be ingendered all the Colours meane:
Every cleere thinge perspicuate and fayre,
Standeth by the matters of Water and Aire,
Whome a pure Erth doth apprehend,
Such as shall not their cleerenes offend;
And if in such cleerenes and perspicuitie,
Ye can noe speciall Colour see,
Thereupon to Judge you maie be bold,
The cause of such things was exceeding Colde:
As *Christall*, *Berill*, and other things moe,
Diversitie betweene them lerne ere ye goe;
Christall hath Water declyning toward Ayer,
Wherefore it is cleere, perspicuous and faire;
But where it declineth towards Water more,
It is darke as Berill or Ice hard frore;
But when matters draweth toward siccitie,
Darknes with hardnes ingendred shall be;
As it appeareth in the *Adamant Stone*,
And in other things manie one.
Twinckling and glittering as in *Magnetia* is,
Light is cause thereof within matter of Cleerenes;
Which is superduced upon waterly vapour,
Beforetyme incenced with Heate be ye sure;
Now after cleerenes and Colours in extremitie,
Of meane Colours a litle shew will I.
Ruby colour is of a thinn fume succended
In a cleere Body, which alsoe is amended
When in that Body reyneth plenty of light,
For more or les thereof maketh more or les bright:

As

As the *Amatist* followeth the Ruby in dignity,
In leſs Cleerenes and more Obſcuritie:
And a *Calcedonie* in Slymy ſubſtance,
Followeth the *Berill* in degrees of variance.
Greene as a *Smaragde* is of Water cleere,
With Erthy ſubſtance Combuſt mixt full neere:
And the cleerer ſubſtance that the Erth be,
The cleerer greeneſs thereof ye ſhall ſee.
Tawney is of Cleerenes terminate,
Infuſed with thick Fumoſity congregate
Of Water, and alſoe of Erth ſuccended,
Whereby the cleerenes of Aier is ſuſpended.
Wann or leady Colour ingendred is
Of Waterie and Erthy parts without amiſſe;
And where ſuch parts be cold and thick,
Ever Wann Colour theron ſhall ſtick;
As it appeareth in old layen Lead,
And in Men that be wellneere dead:
This Wann Colour called Lividitie,
In Envious Men uſeth much to be;
Naturall heate and blood done reſorte,
To the Hert, them to comfort,
And leaveth Cold and Dry the Face,
For heate and blood is parted fro that place.
Likewiſe when Fevers be in extremitie,
The Nailes of Hands of this Colour wilbe.
The *Saphire* Colour, that Orient Blewe,
Like in Colour to the heavenlie hue,
Is much fairer than Wann Colour to ſight,
For therein is more of Aier Water and Light
Than is in Wann Colour, and that by manifold,
Wherefore ſuch Colour is more deerer ſolde;
All other *Blewes* the ſadder that they be,
Thei have leſſe of Aier and more of Terreſtriety.

L *Silver*

Chap. 5. Silver to Azure ſoone broght will be;
The cauſe thereof is perſpicuitie,
Which is in Silver cauſed of Ayer,
Wherefore it turneth to hevenly Colour faire;
And Quickſilver plenty within him is,
Cauſeth in Silver all this brightnes:
Subtiler Erth, pure Water, with cleerenes of Air,
Cauſeth ſuch brightnes to Quickſilver to repaire.
Citrine Colour Yellowe as ye ſee in Gould,
Is Colour moſt liking for ſome men to behould:
Cauſed of mighty and ſtrong digeſtion,
For humor in him have ſtrong decoction;
Such Colour with Heate ingendred be ſhall,
As it in Honey, Urine, Lye, and Gall:
The ſhining of *Gould* is cauſed as I tell,
Of pure and ſubtile Water termined full well,
Perſpicuouſly condenſed; for Water pure and fine,
The more it is Condenſed, the better it woll ſhine;
For of a Mirrour the cauſe none other is,
But moiſture termined, as all Clerks geſſe,
Soe that it be polible withall;
For Aier Figures receive never ſhall;
For Aier maie not be terminate in his kinde;
So cauſe of ſhining in Water ye ſhall finde.
With White and Red well medled pure and fine
Woll be ingendred faire Colour Citrine.
Soe divers Comixtions of *Elements*,
Maketh divers Colours, for divers intents:
With divers Digeſtions, and divers degrees,
All Colours be made which your Eyen ſees.
Of Elements ye muſt the proper Colour lerne,
Whereby of Colours ye maie better diſcerne;
Phiſitians ſaie of good Herbs and ſoote,
Some be colde outward and hot within the roote;

Example

Chap. 5.

Example hereof if ye list to gett,
Behold the working of the gentle Violet:
Common Philosophie the cause doth disclose,
Whie colde is within and red without the Rose:
Anaxagoras said in his *Coversions naturall*,
Inward and Outward be contrary in things all,
Which is trewe except such things as be
Of little composition, and nigh simplicitie;
As is Scammonye, and Lawrell the Laxative,
Which be not nourishing to vegetative.
Remember how in every mixt thinge,
Evermore one Element desireth to be Kinge:
Which proude appetite of Elements and vicious,
Moveth men to be Ambitious:
Wherefore our *Lord* that best dispose cann,
Hath made Ordeynance for sinfull Man,
All proude appetites to equalitie to bringe;
When *Requiem æternam* the Church shall singe,
Than shall everie ambitious thought,
Plainely appeare how that it was nought:
Lords, and Beggars, and all shall be
In the Charnell brought to equalitie.
Your Principall Agent so rebate shall ye,
When he usurpeth above equality;
Therefore *Aristotle* said Compound ye our Stone
Equall, that in him repugnance be none;
Neither division as ye proceede;
Take heede thereto, for it is greate neede;
And when it falleth that ye shall see
All Colours at once that named maie be;
Than suffer Nature with her operation,
At her owne leasure to make Generation:
Soe that amonge so manie Colours all,
Nature maie shew one principall:

Chap. 5. Such as ſhall draw towards your intent,
According to your deſired Element.
This wiſe by Colours yee maie provide
How in your workes yee ſhall yee guide.
Manie moe things of Colours I maie write,
But this is ſufficient my promiſe to acquite,
As farr forth as Colours maie ſerve your intent,
By them to know your principall agent.
But manie Clerks wonder why you may ſee
Soe manie Colours as in our Stone woll be,
Before that perfect White and Cleere,
And unchaungeable woll appeare,
Conſidering the fewnes of the ingredients;
I woll that anſwer to pleaſe their intents,
And teach them the trewth of that greate doubte.
By kinde of *Magneſia* ſuch Colours paſſe out,
Whoſe nature is of ſuch Convertibilitie,
To everie proportion, and to everie degree,
As Chriſtall to his Subject is founde;
For of everie thing that is upon the grounde,
Which that ye woll Chriſtall ſet under,
Such Colour hath Chriſtall, therefore ceaſe to wonder:
Wherefore *Hermes* ſaid not untruly ne Envious,
Ad perpetranda miracula rei unius:
God hath ſo ordeyned ſaith *Hermes* the Kinge,
To fulfill the miracles of one thinge:
Common *Philoſophers* thereof cannot finde
The vertues of our *Stone* exceeding far their minde.

S*Melling* maie helpe forth your intente,
To know your reigning Elemente;
And be with Colour a Teſtimony,
To know your principall Agent thereby;
And ye which would by ſmelling lerne

Of

Of your principall Agent trewly to discerne. Chap. 5.
As White, and Black, be Colours in extremitie,
Soe of Odors, soote and stinking be:
But like as Fishes know not by sight
Noe meane Colours, because their Eyne bright
Have none Eyelidds for their sight closinge,
Soe meane Odors shall not by smellinge
Be knowne of you, this is the cause whie,
For Nostrills be open as the fishes Eye:
Therefore meane Odors be not in certaine
Smelled by the Nose, as meane Colours be seene.
Heavie Smell is not as Clerks thinke
The midle Odor, but only the lesse Stinke.
Old Fathers wrote by their Doctrine,
Of their Experience which is maturine,
That if ye medle sweete Savour and redolente
Equally with stinking to prove your intent;
The soote shall be smelled, the stinking not soe,
The cause ye may lerne now ere ye goe;
All sweete smelling things have more puritie,
And are more spirituall than stinking maie be:
Wherefore it is in Aier more penetrative,
And is more extendible, and is alsoe to life
More acceptable, as friend to Nature,
And therefore rather received be ye sure.

ODor is a smokish vapour resolved with heate,
Out of substance, by an invisible sweate;
Which in the Aier hath free entringe,
And chaungeth the Aier and your Smellinge;
As Sapor of Meates chaungeth your Tastinge,
And as Sounds chaungeth your Hearinge,
And as Colour chaungeth your Sight,
Soe Odor chaungeth Smelling by might.

Chap.5. The cause of Odours to know if you delight,
Foure things thereto be requisite;
First that suttill matter be Obedient
To the working of Heate, for to present
By a fume the liknes of the same thinge,
From whome that fume had his beginninge;
Also to beare forth that pure fume and faire,
There is required a cleere thinn Aier:
For thick Aier woll not beare it farr,
But it woll reteyne it much faster;
And soe thick matter Obedience hath none,
To the working of Heate, as it sheweth in Stone:
Heate maketh Odours, Cold shrinketh, by reason
Dunghills in Summer stink more than in Winter season;
Pleasant Odours ingendered be shall
Of cleane and Pure substance and fumigale,
As it appeareth in Amber, Narde, and Mirrhe,
Good for a Woman, such things pleaseth her;
But of Pure substance with a Meane heate,
Be temperate Odours, as in the Violet;
Of a Meane heate with substance Impure,
Is Odours missliking, as Aloes and Sulphure:
But when Naturall heate beginneth to spill,
Then thereof ariseth heavie smell;
As Fish smelleth that is kept too longe,
Naturall heate rotteth, soe the smell is stronge;

STinch is a Vapour, a resolved fumositie
Of things which of Evill Complexions be.
And when Humor onlie is in Corruption,
Soe that the Substance be not in Destruction,
Thereof shall onlie heavie smell arise,
But not verie Stinch come in that wise.
Of everie Stinch the cause of that Chaunce

Is

Is only corruption of the selfe substance;
And when Evill substance shall putrifie,
Horrible Odour is gendred thereby:
As of Dragons and Men that long dead be,
Their stench maie cause greate Mortalitie.
It is not wholsome to smell to sume Cole,
For quenching of some Snuffe a Mare woll cast her Foale.
When the Qualities of a thing according is
To your Nature, good Odour will not misse:
But when the substance is contrary to your kinde,
The Odours thereof odious you shall finde.
Fishes love Soote smell, also it is trewe,
Thei love not old Kydles as thei doe the new.
All things that are of good Odour,
Have naturall Heate for their succour;
Though Camphire, Roses, and things colde,
Have soote Odours, yet Auctors tould,
How Heate virtually inclosed is the skell,
With Purenes of substance, whic they so smell:
This olde opinion you maie teach your Brother,
How noe good Odour is contrary to another;
But it is not soe of stinking smells,
For stinch of Garlick voydeth stinch of Dunghills.
Of Odours this Doctrine is sufficiente,
As in *Alkimy* to serve your intente,
Your Warks to understonde thereby,
When things begin to putrifie;
Alsoe by Odours this you maie lerne,
Suttilnes and grosnes of Matters to discerne:
Alsoe of Meane substance knowledge ye may get,
With knowledge of Corruption of Naturall heate;
And knowledge of Diversitie by good attendance,
When Humour corrupteth and when the Substance.
But our Substance was made so pure and cleane,
And

Chap. 5. And is conserved by vertue of the meane,
That ye no stinke thereof shall finde,
Albeit that it putrifie fro his owne kinde.

THe third signe and the third Testimony
To understand your principall Agent by,
Is *Sapor* called, of Mouth the Taste,
Which evermore is cause of waste
Of the substance of the same thinge
Whereof ye make proofe by Tastinge
Sapor shulde be much better Judge
Then Colour or Odour, and more refuge,
Were not Taste a perillous thinge,
While our *Stone* is in workinge;
For it is hurting to health and life,
It is so greatly penetrative;
Above all subtill things it hath Victory,
And peirceth solid things hastily,
Wherefore it is perill and not good,
Much or oft to Tast of that foode:
It Comforteth Mettalls as we well finde,
But it is Perillous for all Mankinde,
Till perfect Red thereof be made,
Such as in Fier woll never fade.
A lewde Man late that served this Arte,
Tasted of our *white Stone* a parte,
Trusting thereby to find releefe
Of all sicknes and of all greefe,
Whereby the Wretch was sodenly,
Smitt with a strong Paralisie;
Whom my *Master* with great Engine,
Cured with *Bezoars* of the Mine.
Therefore though Tast by Common reason,
Shulde be best judge at every season,

You

Yet for that Tast is abominable
Sapor is heere not profitable.
Yet of some parts seperable,
A Tast maie well be Convenable
Before Conjunctions to make assay,
Whether they be well wrought or nay;
Howbeit a Wiseman hath helpe sufficient,
By Colour and Odour to have his intent:
For manie Men can chuse good Wine,
By Colour and Odour when it is fine;
But for new Wine not fined in generall,
The trew Tast is most suertie of all;
For Smelling hath Organalls but one,
Nothing discerning but fumous things alone;
But Tast hath six Organalls without doubt,
To feele qualitie of things within and without,
Which Nature ordain'd against perill and strife,
For more suertie of things haveing life:
An Ape chuseth her Meate by Smelling,
Men and Popinjayes trusten to Tasting:
For manie things be of good Smell,
Which to Tast be found full ill:
For they maie be abhominable sower,
Over-sharpe, too bitter, or of greate horrour,
Or Venamous, stinking, or over-stronge,
The Tast is judge and voideth such wronge.
Old men wrote in antient time,
How that of *Sapors* there be fully Nyne;
Which ye maie lerne in halfe an hower,
As Sharpe tast, Unctuous, and Sower,
Which three doe suttill matter signifie;
And other three doe meane matter testifie,
As Bitinge tast, Saltish and Weerish also,
Other three come thicke substances fro,

Chap. 5. As Bitter tast, under Sower, and Douce;
Thes Nyne be found in manie a Noble House;
Five of these Nyne be ingendred by Heat,
Unctuons, Sharpe, Salt, Bitter, and Doulcet;
But of the Nyne the remnant all fower,
Be made with cold, as is the Sapor Sower,
And so is Sowerish tast called Sapor Pontick,
And lesse Sower allso called Sapor Stiptick,
Also is Weerish tast called Unsavoury,
With Cold ingendered effectually.
Sapor of two things hath his Conception,
Of divers Substance and of divers Complection.

OF Hot and Moyst in the Second degree,
With a Thick substance, Doulcet Tast will be;
The same degrees of the same Complexion,
To a Meane substance knit by connexion,
Unctuous Sapor ingender ever shall;
But where it is Hott and Dry withall,
With a Meane substance in the Second degree,
The Tast thereof must needs Saltish be;
When a thing in the Third degree Hot and Dry is,
With a substance Thick, there is Bitternes;
But in the Fowerth degree matter Hot and Dry,
With a Suttill substance, Sharpe Tast is thereby;
So five Tasts, as I said before,
Be ingendered with Heat, and not one more.
Of Cold and Dry in the Second degree by kinde,
With a Suttill substance, full Sower ye shall it finde;
As by Faces of People ye maie Deeme,
When thei tast Crabs while thei be greene:
The same Complexion in the same degree,
In a thing which of Meane substance shall be,
Of that is ingendred ye maie well suppose,

A

A Bitinge Tast as is of the Roase, *Chap.* 5.
But Sower, and Sowrish, and least Sower, all three
Be of Cold and Dry in High and Low degree:
And Cold and Moyst in the First degree of all,
A Weerish Tast ingender ever shall,
As of an Egg it showeth in the glaere,
And in pale Women over White and Fayer:
For such be Cold, and of Humiditye
Thei have trewly greate superfluity,
Therefore to Men thei have lesse delight;
Cold rebateth luxurious appetite.
Isaac said there be but Tastes seaven,
For Sower and lesse Sower was one but uneven,
But in Complexion thei were of one foundation,
For Unsavoury was but of Tast privation;
Compound Tasts be found also,
As Doulce Eger and others manie mo;
So by Tast men maie Craftily know
Divers complexions and degrees high and low;
And when ye doubt by Tast to make report,
Than to your other testimonies resort.
As in *Phisicke* trust not to Urine
Onely, but also take witnes and Doctrine
Of your Pulses, and wisely considering
Six things not naturall the Body concerning,
Having respect also therewithall,
Unto these Seaven things naturall;
And take heed if ye woll be sure,
Of Three things contrary to nature:
Compleat theis Sixteene wisely to your ground,
A lewd *Phisition* least that ye be found:
For so of (*had I wist*) ye maie beware,
And helpe the Sick man from his care:
So of this *Science* if ye woll advaunce

Chap. 5. Your works, take heed of everie Circumstance,
Wisely Considering your testimonyes fower,
Three be now passed, the fowerth is Liquor.

Liquor is the Comfort of this Werke;
Liquor giveth evidence to a Clerke
Thereby to fasten his Elements,
And also to loose them for some intents;
Liquor conjoyneth Male with Female Wife,
And causeth dead things to resort to Life;
Liquors clenseth with theire ablution,
Liquors to our *Stone* be Cheefe nutrition;
Without Liquor no Meate is good;
Liquors conveieth all Aliment and Food
To every part of Mans Body,
And so thei doe with us in *Alkimy*.
Ye must consider the puritie
Of all your Liquors and quantitie;
And how thick thei be or thinn,
Or else thereof shall ye litle winn;
But not as *Phisitions* maketh mention;
For *Elixir* is a thing of a second intention;
Wherefore ye shall more Wondrous natures find
In his working, than in all other kind;
Phisitions say the thicker Urine be,
The more it signifieth Humidity,
Where thick Liquor with us hath siccity,
And suttill Liquor betokneth Humidity.

Manie Liquors be requisit
To our *Stone* for his appetite:
In the Booke of *Turba*-*Aristeus* deposed,
How Ayre in Water was secreatly inclosed,
Which bare up Erth with his Aierly might.

Pithagoras

Pithagoras said that was spoke with right.
Aristotle Craftilye his words set he,
Saying, *cum habueris aquam ab Aere.*
Plato wrote full sapiently,
And named it *stilla roris madidi:*
Which was kindly spoken for *Alkimy.*
But common Students in first Philosophie,
Say Ayre condensed is turned into Raine,
And Water rarified becomes Ayre againe.
Some said how *May* was first season and faire
To take such Water as is made of Ayre.
Some said such Waters come heaven fro,
When the *Sunn* entereth into *Scorpio.*
Some said all Liquors shulde be refused,
Which Frost infected shulde not be used:
The cause whie as telleth Autors old,
Is that theire accuity is duld with cold.
Some *Philosophers* said that ye shulde take
Milke for the Liquor *Elixir* to make:
And other sort said after their intent,
No Liquor so good for the Complement,
As Water of *Litharge* which would not misse,
With Water of *Azot* to make *lac virginis:*
But *Democrit* said best Liquor to present
Elixir withall was Water permanent:
Whose naturall vertue and propertie,
Was fier to abide and never to flye:
Rupiscissa said that cheefe Liquor
Was *Aqua-vitæ Elixir* to succour;
For she was spirituall, and would revive
Dead things fro death to live,
Shee was *Quintessence*, the fift thing,
Whereof *Aristotle* by his writing
In his Boke of *Secrets* saith soe,

Chap. 5. How that all perfection was *in quinario.*
Rupiscissa called it best Liquor of all,
For it maketh grosse matter spirituall:
But of *Pithagoras* ye maie finde,
Our *Aqua-vitæ* of another kinde;
He saith it was *Vivificans* in his sentence,
Fac fugiens fixum & fixum fugiens,
For in such wise with strong Coaction,
Fixt matters were made of light liquefaction.
Another sort said no Liquor was above
The Liquor which Congers most desier and love:
Therefore such Liquors are best found,
Nigh to Islands, and to such ground
Which the Ocean Sea hath compassed about,
For there such Liquors be soonest fet out.
Of another Liquor wise men tell,
Which is fresher than Water of the Well;
Fresher Liquor there is none in tast,
Yet it woll never consume ne waste;
Though it be occupied evermore,
It will never be lesse in store;
Which *Democrit* named for his intent,
Lux umbra carens, Water most Orient;
Hermes said no Liquor so necessarie,
As was Water of crude Mercury:
For he shall stand said that Noble Clerke,
For the Water within our werke.
Now lerne ye which for this *Science* have sought,
By all these Liquors our *Stone* must be wrought.

L*iquor* is a thing moveable,
Of fleeting substance and unstable.
All such things follow the *Moone*,
More then standing kindes doone;

And

And that appeareth to a Clerke,
In working of the white Werke;
Liquors washen and maken cleane
Both Extremities and the Meane;
God made Liquors for Mans use,
To clense foule things in everie howse;
Liquor bringeth without doubt,
Hidden things in Bodyes out,
As Landres witnes evidently,
When of Ashes thei make their Lye;
Liquor comforteth the roots of Grasse,
And of Trees such as drye was;
For Liquors of Nature woll restore
Humors that were lost before.
Liquors departeth Qualities asunder,
Substance resolving in Attomes with wonder;
Liquors also bringeth into one
Many things to be one Stone.
Liquors helpeth to flux and to flowe
Manie things, and lerne ye maie now
How Liquor is in manie manners found
Out of things that be on the ground,
Some by cutting, as Turpentine;
Some with Pressing, as Sider and Wine;
Some with grinding, as Oyle is had;
Some with stilling, as Waters be made;
Some with Brenning, as Colophonie;
And some with Water, as Women make Lye;
Some be otherwise brought about,
And by naturall working set out,
As Urin, Sweat, Milk, and also Blood,
And Renniet which for Cheese is good:
By as manie manners and moe by one,
We seek Liquors for our *Stone*.

Every

Chap.5. Every of the forenamed woll cleave
To that thei touch, and some deale leave:
But Quicksilver albeit it is fleeting,
Yet he woll never cleave to any thinge,
But to a Mettall of one kinde or other,
For there he findeth Sister or Brother.
Medling with suttill Erth doth him let,
To cleave to things such as he meet:
All the said Liquors which rehearsed be,
Conteyne fower Elements as well as he;
As Milke conteyneth Whey, Butter, and Cheese,
So done trewly every-each of all these:
Which fower maie be departed a twinn,
And after conjoynd to make ye winn.
But much more craftily they be heere sought,
Then Cheese, and Butter, and Whey be wrought;
And drawe neerer to simplicitie,
Then Cheese, Butter, or Whey maie be.
Of all Liquors which be in our *Stone*,
None is called simple but Water alone.
Of every Liquor which to our *Stone* shall goe,
Ye must know complexion and degree allso,
And than with Liquor ye maie abate
The principall Agent from his Estate,
If he permanent and abiding be,
In any point of superfluitye:
As if the reigning qualitie be Drines,
Ye maie amend it with humour of Moistnes.
Now more, now lesse, as ye see need,
And so in all qualities proceede:
And in such wise order at your will,
The principall Agent, your purpose to fulfill:
With knowledge of diversity, contrarietie, and accord,
Ye maie chuse which quality shall be Lord.

Your

Your Liquors be ordained to add and ſubtray, *Chap.* 5.
To make equalitie by wiſdome of aſſay;
But truſt not that any thing maie be
Hot and Moiſt both in one Degree:
For all that truſt two qualities to be ſoe,
Shall be deceived where ever thei goe.
Common Schooles (ſo teaching) be not true,
Leave that Opinion, and lerne this of new
All Old men in that were overſeene,
To ſet in one degree anie qualities twaine:
Elſe thei ſaid ſo that Schollers ſhulde not finde
The ſecret mixtures of Elementall kind.
Therefore who cannot his graduations,
Maie not be perfect in our operations:
For in true Number *God* made every thing;
Without true Number no Man trulie maie ſing;
Who faileth of his Number faileth of his Song,
Who faileth with us muſt doe Nature wrong.

COnſider alſo the nature of the meane,
When it is in the Third degree made cleane;
The purer that your meanes be,
The more perfection thereof ye ſhall ſee.
The meanes reteyne a great part
Of the vertues of this *Arte*:
For the Principle maie not give influence
To the Finall end, neither the refluence
Unto his Principall without ſuccour and aid
Of meanes conteyning the extremities aforeſaid:
For like as by meanes of a treble Spirit,
The Soule of Man is to his Body knit,
Of which three Spirits one is called Vitall,
The ſecond is called the Spirit Naturall.
The third Spirit is Spirit Animall,

Chap. 5. And where they dwell now lerne ye ſhall:
The Spirit Vitall in the Hert doth dwell,
The Spirit Naturall as old Auctors tell
To dwell in the Liver is thereof faine,
But Spirit Animall dwelleth in the Braine:
And as long as theſe Spirits three
Continue in Man in there proſperitie:
So long the Soule without all ſtriſe
Woll dwell with the Body in proſperous life,
But when theis Spirits in Man maie not abide,
The Soule forthwith departeth at that tide:
For the ſuttill Soule pure and immortall,
With the groſſe Body maie never dwell withall,
He is ſo heavie, and She ſo light and cleane,
Were not the ſuttilneſſe of this Spirit meane.
Therefore in our worke as Auctors teach us,
There muſt be *Corpus Anima & Spiritus*:
Alſo in our worke ye ſhall ſo finde,
That our meanes muſt accord in every kinde
Of both extremities with wiſdome ſought,
Els all our worke ſhall turne cleere to nought:
For prudent Nature maie not by workinge,
Make Complement of appetite of a thing,
And ſo paſſe betweene extremities,
But if ſhe firſt paſſe by all degrees
Of everie meane, this is truth unfained,
Wherefore Nature manie meanes ordained.

NOw after all this to lerne ye had need,
Of ſeven Circulations of Elements for your ſpeede,
According to number of the Planets ſeaven;
Which no man knoweth but he have grace from heaven.
Old *Philoſophers*, men of great engine,
Said how of Circulations there ſhulde be Nine;

It

It is the surer to doe by their advice,
Nethles Seaven maie your worke suffice,
By inventions late found of new,
Of later *Philosophers* whos workes be trewe.
But for Circulations of Elements,
Some Clerks ween to have their intents.
When they fro Fier ordaine to descend,
To Aire (thei ween not to offend)
If thei to Water doe then proceed,
And thens to Erth when thei see need,
And in such wise by order fall,
From the highest to the lowest of all:
Upon these words they tooke their ground,
That *Aer est cibus ignis* found.
But trust me that such Circulation,
Is but only a rectification,
Better serving for separation,
And for correction than for transmutation.
But the truth is that appetite of the Fier,
Hath to worke in Erth his cheese desire,
As upon his cheese foode materiall,
For Fier with Erth hath most concord of all;
Because that siccitie is the lyme of heate,
But Ayre of her kind is most wet;
Yet Fire without Ayre worketh not,
For Faces of Elements be knit with a knot
Of *Gods* hand that they maie not depart,
By noe engine ne craft of Mans art;
As in Plomps ye have example faire,
Where heavie Water ariseth after Ayre;
Whereof noe cause reasonable ye shall finde,
But Connexion of faces of Elementall kinde.
But our Circulation is from Fier on high,
Which endeth with Water his most contrary.

Chap. 5. Another Circulation beginneth with Ayre,
Ending with his Contrary cleane Erth and faier.
Fro Fier to Erth, fro thence to Water cleane,
Fro thence to Ayre, then fro thence by a meane,
Passing to Erth, then eftsoones to Fier,
To such Circulations the Red worke hath desire.
Other Circulations be better for the White,
That be rehearsed for her appetite.
Every Circulation hath her proper season,
As her lightnesse accordeth with reason.
For as one Planet is more ponderous
Then is another and slower, in his course:
So some Circulations which Clerks seeks,
Must for her time have full thirtie Weeks;
Other Circulations shall oft time have lesse,
As one Planet is lighter then another was:
But the time of one with another will amount
To twenty six Weekes proved by accompt.
After all grosse workes made before hand,
And after all Circumstances had I understande;
Ignorance hereof deceiveth manie a Man,
Causing them to cease where Wisemen began.
Common People which for this *Science* have sought,
Ween how in forty dayes it mought be wrought.
They know not how Nature and things of Arte,
Have a proper time assigned for their part,
As it appeareth by this Similitude,
The Elephant for that she is great and rude,
Goeth with Foale years full twayne,
And fifty yeares ere that Foale gender againe.
Anaxagoras said in his Consideration,
That Mettals had for their generation
A thousand Yeares, wherefore him list to say,
In respect thereof our Worke is but one Day.

Alsoe

Alſo ye muſt worke by good advice,
When ye ſee Erth above Water riſe;
For as Water beareth Erth which we goe on,
So woll it doe in working of our *Stone*:
Wherefore Well-ſprings with ſtrokes ſoft,
Soberly make ye muſt in tymes oft;
Whereby Water maie ſoberly flowe,
For violent Fluxes be perilous as nowe.

MOreover it healpeth in *Alkimy*
To know ſeaven Waters effectually:
Which be Coppied with manie a Man,
While thei be common ſeeke them as ye can,
Deſire not this Boke to ſhow things all,
For this Boke is but an *Ordinall*.
By thoſe Waters men Weene in mind
All faults to amend of Metaline kinde;
Alſo thei weene of the Elements fower,
The effects to weene by their ſuccour:
For thei ſuppoſe with confidence unfeined,
That all Vertues requiſit in them be conteyned;
Some to molifie Mettalls hard wroght,
And ſome to harden Mettalls that be ſoft,
Some to purifie, ſome to make malleable;
Everie-each according that he was able,
Such Liquors to know it is profitt and good,
Howbeit thei maie not to our *Stone* be food:
Noble Auctors men of glorious fame,
Called our *Stone Microcoſmus* by name:
For his compoſition is withouten doubt,
Like to this World in which we walke about:
Of Heate, of Cold, of Moyſt and of Drye,
Of Hard, of Soft, of Light and of Heavy,
Of Rough, of Smooth, and of things Stable,

Chap. 5. Medled with things fleetinge and moveable;
Of all kinds Contrary broght to one accord,
Knit by the doctrine of *God* our blessed *Lord*:
Whereby of Mettalls is made transmutation,
Not only in Colour, but transubstantiation,
In which ye have need to know this thing,
How all the vertues of the Elements transmuting,
Upon the transmuted must have full domination,
Before that the substance be in transmutation;
And all partes transmuted must figured be
In the Elements transmuting impressed by degree.
So that the third thinge elemented of them all,
Of such condition evermore be shall.
That it trewly have it maie be none other,
But her Substance of that one, and her Vertue of that (other.
A Child at his Nativitie can eate his meate and cry,
Our *Stone* at his Nativity woll Colour largly.
In three years after a Child can speake and goe,
Then is our *Stone* more Colouring also.
One upon a Thousand his tincture trewly is,
Of clean washen Mettall I am trew witnes,
Fastiely (beleeve it) and fully in your thought,
It maketh good Silver as of the Myne is wrought;
And also our *Stone* woll augment and increase,
In quantitie, and qualitie, and thereof never cease;
And therefore his growing and augmentation,
Is likned to Man in waxing and creation.
Nathles one pointe of trewth I woll reporte,
Which to some Men maie be discomforte;
At the first making of our *Stone*,
That time for winninge looke for none;
If ye then cease, I understande
Ye shall departe with loosinge hand,
The Costs be so great before,

Expended

Expended and ſet upon the ſcore;
But at the firſt augment of all
Which tyme our *Stone* depart ye ſhall
In parts twaine full equally,
With ſubtill ballance and not with Eye:
One for the Red, that other for the White,
To mainteyne both for your delight;
Then winning firſt beginneth to ariſe:
But afterwards if ye be wiſe,
At every augment continually,
Profit ſhall grow comodiouſly;
In this our White Warke alone,
As well as in the Ruby Stone;
Whereof ſaid *Maria* Siſter of *Aron*,
Lyfe is ſhort, and Science is full long.
Nathles it greately retardeth Age,
When it is ended by ſtrong Courage;
But ſome that have byne tought trewlie,
Have forſooke their worke lewdly;
When their greate labour have byne paſte,
For thei know not how at the laſte
Groweth the profit and the winninge,
Which thei would have at the beginninge,
Therefore I finde that it is neede,
The trewth to tell when ye ſhulde ſpeede,
For when I am paſt and out of minde,
This my Witnes ſhall reſt behinde,
For which cauſe I doe not ſpare,
Of this *Arte* the trewth to declare;
As much as I dare, that I be not ſhent
For breaking of *Gods* Commandement.
This wiſe endeth all our *White Werke*
Shewed ſufficiently for an able Clerke.

After

Chap. 5.

After all this upon a day
I heard my noble *Master* say,
How that manie men patient and wise,
Found our *White Stone* with Exercise;
After that thei were trewlie tought,
With great labour that *Stone* they Caught;
But few (said he) or scarcely one,
In fifteene Kingdomes had our *Red Stone*:
And with that word he cast his Eye,
Looking on me full steadilye,
Of his words he saw me woe,
I said alas what shall I doe?
For above all Erthly thinge,
I most desire and love Cunninge.
And for the *Red Stone* is preservative,
Most precious thinge to length my Life;
The *Red Stone* said I is lever to me,
Then all were Gould that I would soe to be.
He said I was to younge of Age,
Of Body lusty and likely to outrage,
Scantly of the age of twenty eight yeares,
He said *Philosophers* had noe such Compeers;
This woefull answer then he made to me,
Till ye be elder he said it maie not be.
Alas good *Master* remember said I,
Howbeit my Body be light and lustie,
Prove and assay and you shall finde
Age sufficient within my Minde,
He held his words full still that tyde,
And so long tyme he did abide;
After this sudainely in wonderous wise,
He tempted me after the *Philosophers* guise.
Which to reherse it were too longe,
And to shew how I should doe wronge;

For

For that must be kept secreate,
For them which shall with this *Science* meete;
Yet at the last with leasure and with space
I wan his love, by help of *Gods* Grace;
So that I had with Grace the trewe doctrine
Of Confection of the *Red medicine*;
Whom to seeke it availeth right nought,
Till the *White medicine* be fully wrought.
Alsoe both Medicines in their beginninge
Have one manner of Vessell and Workinge,
As well for the White as also for the Red,
Till all quick things be made dead;
Then Vessells and forme of operation
Shall chaunge, in Matter, Figure, and Graduation.
But my herte quaketh, my hand is tremblinge,
When I write of this most selcouth thinge.
Hermes brought forth a true sentence and blounte,
When he said *Ignis & Azot tibi sufficiant*.
The Expositor of *Hermes* and *Aristotle* joynte,
In that joynte worke shewd a straunge pointe,
He said *Albertus Magnus* the Black Freere,
Nether Freer *Bacon* his compeere;
Had not of our *Red stone* consideration,
Him to increase in multiplication.
The Expositor knew it sufficiently,
And my *Master* tought me trewly,
Albeit that I never made assaye
Of the *Red worke* before this Daye:
The cause appeareth in this Boke before,
When I was robbed then I would no more.
Nethlesse I have put me so farr in preass,
That secreate Trewth to shew I cannot cease;
Rehersing such as were greately too bold,
So great secreats to shew as thei tolde:

Chap. 5. Thei ſaid that within the Center of incompleate White
Was hid our *Red Stone* of moſt delight:
Which maie with ſtrength and kinde of Fier,
Be made to appeare right as we deſier.
Pandulphus in *Turba* ſaide, *mente ſecura,*
Et ejus umbra in vera tinctura.
Maria confirmed it *in fide oculata,*
Quod in ipſa albedine eſt rubedo occultata.
The Boke *Laudabile Sanctum* made by *Hermes,*
Of the *Red Worke* ſpeaketh in this wiſe:
Candida tunc rubeo jacet uxor nupta marito,
That is to ſaie, if ye take heede thereto,
Then is the faire White Woman
Married to the Ruddy Man.
Underſtandinge thereof if ye would gett,
When our *White Stone* ſhall ſuffer heate,
And reſt in Fier as red as Blood,
Then is the Marriage perfect and good;
And ye maie trewly know that tyme,
How the ſeminall ſeed Maſculine,
Hath wrought and won the Victory,
Upon the menſtrualls worthily;
And well converted them to his kinde,
As by experience ye ſhall finde:
Paſſing the Subſtance of *Embrion,*
For then compleate is made our *Stone*;
Whom wiſe Men ſaid that ye ſhulde feede
With his owne Venome when it is need.
Then ride or goe where ye delight,
For all your Coſts he woll you quite.
Thus endeth the *ſubtill Warke* with all her ſtore,
I need not, I maie not, I woll ſhew no more.

CHAP.

Libra. 24.
Leo. 15.
Virgo: 28.
Scorp: 12
Can: 0.
Sagit: 2
Gem: 2.
Capri: 0
Tau: 12
Pisses 28
Aquar: 15.
Aries 24
Libra. 24
Leo. 15.
Virgo 28
Scorp: 12
Can: 0.
Sagit: 2
Gem: 2
Capric: 0
Tau: 12
Pisses. 28
Aquar: 15
Aries 24
Libra. 24.
Leo 15
Virgo 28
Scorp: 12
Canc: 0
Figura superior dividit, Seperat, et Corrigit.
Hæc operatione Naturæ Secreta comfortat.
Sagit: 2
Gem: 2
Capri: 0
Tau: 12
Pisses. 28
Aquar: 15
Aries: 24
Libra. 24
Leo. 15
Virgo. 28.
Scorp. 12
Canc: 0
Superior figura est Elementorũ conjunctionis atque Elementatorum. Inferior hæc perficit et terminat omnia.
Sagit: 2
Gem: 2
Capri: 0
Tau: 12
Pisses 28
Aquar: 15
Aries: 24
Vaughan sculp:

Chap. VI.

TOwards the Matters of Concordance,
Consider there be no variance
Betweene such things as shulde accorde;
For of variance maie grow discord,
VVhereby your VVarkes maie be lost,
VVith all your labour and all your cost:
He that wol take our VVarke in hande,
Five Concords he must understande.
The *first Concord* is neede to marke
VVhether his *Minde* accorde with the *Warke*,
VVhich shalbe Lord to paie for all,
Els all your labour destroy ye shall.
The *second Concord* is needfull to kenn,
Between this *Crafte* and her *Workemen*.
The *Third* shall serve well your intents,
VVhen *Warke* accordeth with *Instruments*.
The *fourth Concord* must welbe sought,
VVith the *Place* where it shall be wrought:
For trewlie it is no little grace
To find a perfect working Place.
The *Fift* is of *Concord* and of *Love*,
Betweene your VVarkes and the Spheare above.
Of theis *five Concords* reherse we shall,
Beginning with the first of all.

FOr the *first* ye shall well finde
That full few Lords be stable of *Minde*;
Thei be hasty, the VVarke is longe,
Thei woulde have you doe Nature wronge.
Some now be onward as hasty as fier,

Halfe

Halfe a yeare after have noe desire;
And some in a Weeke, it is noe Nay,
Woll chaunge their mindes, and some in a day,
And for one Moneth have full beleife,
And the next Moneth thei woll the *Arte* repreeve.
It were much better for such to cease,
Than for this *Arte* to put them in preasse;
Let such like Butterflies wander and passe,
And lerne this lesson both more and lasse,
Following the Sentence of this holie letter,
Attingens à fine usq; ad finem fortiter,
Disponens omnia suaviter:
That is, proceede mightily to the End
From the Beginning, maugre the feinde,
All things disposing in the meane space,
With great suavity that commeth of grace.
All short-witted Men and mutable,
Such must needs be variable;
And some doe every Man beleive,
Such credence doth their Cofers greive;
To everie new Tale to them tolde,
They give Credence and leave the olde.
But some Lords be stable of wit,
Such be apt to finish it.
Everie such *Lord* or *Master* of this Werke,
Be he *Layman* or be he *Clerke*,
Be he rich man, *Knight*, *Abbot* or *Lorde*,
He hath with this *Arte* greate Concorde.

THe *seconde Concorde* with this *Arte* is,
When ye can finde apt *Ministers*.
Noe Minister is apt to this intent,
But he be sober, wise, and diligent;
Trewe, and watchfull, and also timerous,

Chap.6. Close of Tongue, of Body not vitious,
Clenly of hands, in Tuching curious,
Not disobedient, neither presumptuous;
Such Servants maie your workes of Charge
Minister, and save from all outrage;
But trust not that two such Servants or three,
Maie sufficient for your worke be;
If your Matter be of quantity reasonable,
Then Eight such Servants be convenable;
But upon litle quantity, finde ye shall
Foure men able to performe all;
That one halfe of them must werke
While the other Sleepeth or goeth to Kerke;
For of this *Arte* ye shall not have your praye,
But it be ministred as well by Night as Daye
Continually, except the holy Sonday alone;
From Evensong begin till Evensong be done.
And while thei worke thei must needes eschewe
All Ribaudry, els thei shall finde this trewe,
That such mishap shall them befall,
Thei shall destroy part of their Works or all;
Therefore all the Ministers must be Men,
Or else thei must be all Weomen;
Set them not occupied one with another,
Though some to you be Sister or Brother:
Yet thei must have some good disporte
Their greate labours to recomforte:
Then nothinge shall better avaunce
Your worke than shall this Concordance.

THe *Third Concord* is to manie full derke,
To ordeyne *Instruments* according to the Werke:
As everie *Chapter* hath divers intents,
Soe hath it divers Instruments;

Both

Both in Matter and alſo in Shape,
In Concord that nothing may mis-happ:
As workes of Diviſion and Seperation
Have ſmall Veſſells for their Operation;
But Veſſells broade for Humectation,
And ſome deale broad for Circulation;
But longe Veſſells for Precipitation;
Both ſhort and long ſerve Sublimation:
Narrowe Veſſells and foure inches high
Serve Correction moſt properly.
Of Veſſells, ſome be made of Leade,
And ſome of Clay both quick and deade;
Dead Clay is called ſuch a thinge
As hath ſuffered greate roaſtinge;
Such medled in powder with good raw Claye,
Will Fier abide and not goe away;
But manie Claies woll leape in Fier,
Such for Veſſells doe not deſire.
Other Veſſells be made of Stone,
For Fier ſufficient but few or none;
Amonge Workemen as yet is founde
In any Country of Engliſh grounde,
Which of Water nothing drinke ſhall,
And yet abide drie Fier withall,
Such Stones large for our intente,
Were a precious Inſtrument;
All other Veſſells be made of Glaſſe,
That ſpirituall matters ſhould not out-paſſe;
Of Aſhes of Ferne in this Lond everi-each one
Be made, but els-where be of Stone:
Of our Glaſſes the better kinde,
The morning ſtuffe ye ſhall it finde,
Which was Aſhes the night before,
Standing in Heate all night and more,

The

Chap. 6. The harder stuffe is called Freton,
Of clipping of other Glasses it come:
Tincture with anealing of Glasiers
Will not perse him as thei reherse.
By this Doctrine chuse or refuse,
Take which you woll unto your use,
But for figures of Vessells kinde,
Everie Man followeth his owne minde,
The best fashion is ye maie be sure,
She that best concordeth with Vessell of Nature;
And figure that best Concordeth with quantity,
And with all Circumstances, to matter best is she,
And this sheweth well *Albertus Magnus*,
In his Boke *De Mineralibus*.
Hereof a Secreate disclosed was,
By my good *Master*, to more and lesse,
Saying, *Si Deus non dedisset nobis vas*
Nihil dedisset, and that is Glasse.

I*Nstruments* needefull there be more,
As be *Furnaces* ordeyned therefore.
Olde Men imagined for this *Arte*
A speciall Furnace for everie parte,
Everie each divising after his owne thought;
But manie Furnaces of them be naught;
Some were too broade and some too longe,
Manie of them did Nature wronge:
Therefore some Furnaces maie be well used,
But manie of them must be refused,
For theie were made but by advice
Of them which seemed, and were not wise:
The most Commendable Fashion of them all,
In this Boke portraied finde ye shall.
One Furnace by me is found of newe,

Such

Such as Olde Men never knewe, Chap.6.
Whose secreate Power with study sought,
And with greate Cost was dearely bought;
In him wilbe at one tyme wrought,
Threescore Warkes, and cost right nought,
More than it shulde for one Warke or twaine,
Therefore profitable it is certaine;
Threescore degrees divers ye maie gett,
For threescore warkes, and everie-ech of divers Heate,
Within that Furnace, to serve your desire,
And all thei served with one litle Fier,
Which of a Foote square onlie shalbe,
Yet everie-ech of the threescore as greate space as he:
Manie purposes ye maie thereby fulfill,
For here you shall have Heate after your will.
Of this Instrument all Men maie not be sure,
Therefore it is not formed in Picture.
Another Furnace woll serve threescore
Glasses trewly, and yet farr more,
Everie-ech of them standing in like Heate,
As by the Picture, Doctrine ye maie gett:
Another Furnace for this operation,
By me was found by Imagination,
Notably serving for Seperation
Of dividents, and for Altification,
And for Dis-junction called Division,
And for Correction called Ablution,
Yt woll for some things serve Desiccation,
Yt serveth full well for Preparation;
Soe for six things it serveth well,
And yet for all at once as I can tell:
This is a new thinge which shall not be
Set out in Picture for all men to see;
Another Furnace in Picture be shall,

P More

Chap. 6. More full of perills than other Furnaces all,
Made for *Magnetia*, whereof bould Men had doubte,
To tuch with hands a poore lynine Cloute,
Which in the midle thereof unbrenned ſtoode,
For feare of flames brenning fierce and woode;
Which ſuttill Furnace I deviſed alſoe,
In which I found manie wonders moe
Than is convenient at this ſeaſon to tell,
Whoſe graduation is doubtfull and caſuell:
Wherein *Magnetia*, matter of greate coſte,
Muſt quickly be ſerved or ſuddainly be loſte:
Of whoſe graduation if you woll not miſſe
Conſider your Stoples, and lerne well this,
The more is the Stople the leſſe is the Heate,
By manifould Stoples Degrees ye maie gett;
Whoe knoweth the power, the working and kinde,
Of everie Furnace, he maie well trewth finde,
And he which thereof dwelleth in Ignorance,
All his Warke faleth upon Chaunce:
Noe man is ſure to have his intent,
Without full concord of *Arte* with Inſtrument.
Manie more Inſtruments occupied ye ſhall ſe,
Than in this *Chapter* now rehearſed be,
Which ye muſt ordeyne by good or ſad advice
And prove them before hand oft if ye be wiſe.

THe *fourth Concord* is full notable
Betweene this *Arte* and *Places Convenable*.
Some Places muſt needes be evermore dry,
Cloſe from Aier, no waies Windy;
Some muſt be darke and dimme of ſight,
In which Sun-beames none maie light;
But for ſome Places the trewth ſo is,
Thei cannot have too much brightnes:

Some

Some Places must needes be Moist and Cold Chap.6.
For some workes as Auctors toulde;
But in our Warkes in everie place,
Winde will hurt in everie Case:
Therefore for everie Warke in season,
Ye must ordaine Places by reason.
Philosophers said by their engine,
How it shulde be wrought within locks Nyne:
Astrologers said it was a grace,
To finde a Chosen Working Place;
For manie things woll wonderous doe
In some Places and elsewhere not soe,
But contrarie wonders be of one thinge
In contrarie Countries wrought without leasing;
Whereof none other cause maie appeare,
But only contrarie places of the *Sphere*:
Whereto Places contrarie of the grounde,
To them Concordaunt and Obedient be found;
Hereof great Evidence and wittnes full cleere,
In the *Magnets Stone* openly doth appeare,
Whose North pointe draweth toward his Countrie,
Which under the Southe starr driveth Needles awaye;
Wherefore wise Men which for this *Arte* sought,
Found some Places concordant, some Places nought;
Trewly such Places where Lechery is used
Must for this *Arte* be utterly refused.

THe *fift Concord* is knowne well of *Clerks*, (*Werks*.
Betweene the *Sphere of Heaven* and our *Suttill*
Nothing in Erth hath more Simplicitie,
Than th'elements of our *Stone* woll be,
Wherefore thei being in warke of Generation,
Have most Obedience to Constellation:
Whereof Concord most kindly and convenient

Chap.6. Is a direct and firie *Ascendent*,
Being signe common for this Operation,
For the multitude of their Iteration:
Fortune your *Ascendent* with his *Lord* also,
Keeping th' aspect of *Shrewes* them fro;
And if thei must let, or needely infect,
Cause them to looke with a *Trine* aspect.
For the *White warke* make fortunate the *Moone*,
For the Lord of the *Fourth house* likewise be it done;
For that is *Thesaurum absconditum* of olde Clerks;
Soe of the *Sixt house* for *Servants* of the Werks;
Save all them well from greate impediments,
As it is in Picture, or like the same intents.
Unlesse then your *Nativity* pretend infection,
In contrariety to this Election,
The vertue of the Mover of the Orbe is formall,
The vertue of the Eight Sphere is here Instrumentall,
With her Signes and Figures and parts aspectuall,
The Planets vertue is proper and speciall,
The vertue of the Elements is here materiall,
The vertue infused resulteth of them all:
The first is like to a workmans Minde,
The second like his Hand ye shall finde.
The third is like a good Instrument,
The remnant like a Thing wrought to your intent.
Make all the Premises with other well accord,
Then shall your merrits make you a greate Lord.
In this wise the *Elixir* of whom ye make mention,
Is ingendered, a thing of a second intention.
Trust not in *Geomantie* that superstitious Arte,
For *God* made Reason which there is set aparte.
Trust not to all *Astrologers*, I saie whie,
For that Arte is as secreat as *Alkimy*.
That other is disproved and plainely forbod,

By

By holy *Saincts* of the Church of *God.*
Trust not, ne love not *Negromancy*,
For it is a property of the Devill to lye.
Trust to this *Doctrine*, set here n your desires,
And now lerne the Regiment of your Fiers.

CHAP. VII.

A parfect *Master* ye maie him call trowe,
Which knoweth his Heates high and lowe.
Nothing maie let more your desires,
Than ignorance of Heates of your Fiers.
Of manie Auctors written ye maie see,
Totum consistit in ignis regimine:
Wherefore in all Chapters you must so proceed,
That Heate worke not more ne lesse than it need;
Wherein manie of *Gebars Cookes*
Deceived were, though thei be wise in Bokes.
Such Heate wherewith Pigg or Goose is Scalded,
In this *Arte* Decoction it is called;
For Minerall meanes serveth such heate,
And to make our *Letharge* to give sweate.
Such Heate as dryeth lawne Karcheeses fayre,
In thirty operations serveth for our Ayre;
But for Divisions you must use such heate,
As Cookes make when they roast grosse Meate;
The same Heate with a circular Fier,
For Separation of Dividents we desire;
But for Circulation of Elements,
Ignis candens observeth our intents;
Which Fier must ever be Coequall
In every minute, and yet perpetuall:
For it maie never abate ne increase,
And yet the Fier maie never cease.
Study wisely, and looke about
Such a Fier trewlie to finde out.
And in that Fier no moisture maie be,
Which Hand maie feele or Eye maie see.

Ignis

Chap. 7. *Ignis humidus* an other Fier alsoe
Is, and yet it seemeth *oppositum in adjecto*:
Such Heate disevereth at certaine tydes
Matters cleving to Vessells sides.
Manie moe things that Heate maie wynn,
It maketh oft thick Matters to be thynn.
A *Philosopher* mistely spake of this Heate,
And saide, the highest degree thereof to get.
Shall cause and gender such Siccitie,
As of drie heate shall be in the First degree.
Another Fier is Fire of Disiccation,
For matters which be imbibed with Humectation.
An other Fier is Fier of Conservation,
For all drie things of his operation:
For *Magnetia* is Fier of effusion,
Full of perills and full of illusion,
Not onely perill which to the Warke maie fall,
But such alsoe which the *Master* hurte shall;
Against which once received is noe boote,
Ordaine therefore to fetch breath from your foote;
Provide for Mouth, Eyes, Eares, and Nose,
For it is worse than ten times the Pose.
Men hereby hath found paines sore,
Because they had not this warning before.
Ignis corrodens serveth in this *Arte*,
Elementa propinqua wisely to departe.
By one point of excesse all your Warke is shent,
And one point too little is insufficient;
Who can be sure to finde his trewe degree,
Magister magnus in igne shall he be.
It is the harder to know trewly his might,
There is no triall for it but our Eye sight:
Therefore all men faile in his presence,
Where Heate is lerned with cost of Experience.

Of

Of this Heate in speciall *Anaxagoras* said thus,
Nemo primo fronte reperitur discretus.
Another is Heate of mighty Coaction,
For Mineralls that be of hard Liquefaction:
This Heate cannot be too stronge,
Be he continued never so longe.
Another is Heate of Calcination
For fowle Mettalls for their Preparation;
Which maie not brenn, ne doe them melte,
For so all thei maie soone be spilte.
The twelfte is Heate for to Sublime
All rhe Spirits of the Mine.
The last Heate of theis goeth for all,
When to Projection our *Stone* shall fall.
Use maketh Masterie, there is noe more to sayne,
But he that faileth must needs begin againe.
Now have I tought you everie thing by name,
As Men teach other the way to *Walsingham*,
Of every Village, Water, Bridge, and Hill,
Whereby wise Men their Journey maie fulfill:
Soe maie a Clerke by this Doctrine finde
This *Science* well if he be cleere of minde;
All other maie finde himselfe hereby a foole
To deale therewith, which litle can of Schoole;
For this is the end of all worldly Cunninge,
Where to attaine can neither Pope ne King
By their Honours, ne by their great Councell,
But only by Vertue and Grace as Auctors tell.
This precious *Stone* will not be found ne wrought
But he be right devotely sought.
The Auctors forenamed with this Boke of mine,
Sheweth of *Alkimy* all the Doctrine,
If ye compleate their Sentences all,
Not by Opinion, but after this *Ordinall*;

Chap.7. For in this *Ordinall* I set you from all doubt,
Is nothing set wronge, nor one point left out.
The dayes were when that this Doctrine and ground
Had pleased me more than a Thousand pound;
Three Hundred pounds was not for my desire,
As would have byne this *Chapter* of the Fier.
And mervaile not Lords, ne ye freinds all,
Why soe noble a *Scyence*, as all Men this *Arte* call,
Is here set out in *English* blunt and rude,
For this is soe made to teach a Multitude
Of rude people which delen with this Werkes,
Ten Thousand *Laymen* against ten able *Clerks*:
Whereby yearely greate Riches in this *Londe*
Is lewdly lost, as Wisemen understonde;
And manie men of Everie degree
Yearely be brought to great Povertee.
Cease *Laymen*, cease, be not in follie ever;
Lewdnes to leave is better late than never.
All that hath pleasure in this Boke to reade,
Pray for my Soule, and for all both Quick and deade.
In this yeare of *Christ* One thousand foure Hundred
(seaventy and seaven,
This Warke was begun, *Honour to God in Heaven*.

The

THE *COMPOUND* OF ALCHYMIE.

A most excellent, learned, and worthy worke, written by Sir *George Ripley*, Chanon of *Bridlington* in *Yorke-shire*, Conteining twelve Gates.

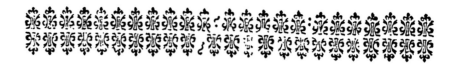

Titulus Operis.

HEre begynneth *The Compound of Alchymie,*
Made by a Chanon of *Bridlington,*
After his learning in *Italy*
At *Yxning* for tyme he there did wonne:
In which be declared openly
The secrets both of *Sunne* and *Moone,*
How they their kinde to multiplye,
In one body togeder must wonne.

Which Chanon Sir *George Ripley* hight,
Exempt from Claustrall observance,
For whom pray ye both day and night,
Sith he did labour you to advance.
He turned darknes into light,
Intending to helpe you to happy chaunce,
Gyving Counsell that ye live right,
Doeing to God no displeasaunce.

George

GEORGE RIPLEY
UNTO
King Edward the fourth.

O Honorable Lord, and most victoryous Knyght,
With Grace and Fortune abundantly endewed,
The savegard of England, *& maynteyner of right;*
That God you loveth indeede he hath well shewed:
Wherefore I trust thys Lond shalbe renewed
With Joy and Riches, with Charyty and Peace,
So that old ranckors understrewed,
Tempestuous troubles and wretchednes shall cease.

And now syth I see by tokens right evident,
That God you guydeth, and that ye be vertuous,
Hating synne, and such as be insolent,
How that also Manslaughter to you is odious,
Upon the Indygent also that ye be piteous,
Greate ruth it were if ye should not lyve longe:
For of your great fortune ye be not presumptuous,
Nor vengeable of mynde to wreke every wrong.

Theis considered, with others, in your most noble Estate,
Like as God knoweth, and people doe witnesse beare,
So entyrely me meveth, that I must algate
Recorde the same, and therein be no flatterer:
And that not onely, but also to write here,
And to your Highnes humbly for to present
Great Secretts which I in farre Countryes did lere,
And which by grace to me most unworthy are lent.

Once to your Lordship such thyngs I did promise,
What tyme ye did command to send unto me;
And since that I wrote in full secret wise,
Unto your Grace from the Universitie
Of Lovayne, *when God fortuned me by Grace to see*
Greater secretts and moch more profyte,
Which onely to you I wyll disclosed to be:
That is to say the great Elixirs *both Red and White.*

For like it you to trust that trewlie I have found
The perfect waye of most secrete Alchimy,
Which I wyll never trewly for Merke ne for Pounde
Make common but to you, and that conditionally
That to your selfe ye shall keepe it full secretly,
And onely it use as may be to Gods pleasure,
Els in tyme comming, of God I should abye
For my discovering of his secrete treasure.

Therefore advise you well wyth good delyberation,
For of this Secrete shall know none other Creature
But onely you, as I make faithfull Protestation,
For all the tyme that I here in lyfe endure:
Whereto I wyll your Lordship me to ensure,
To my desyre in thys by othe to agree,
Least I should to me the wrath of God procure;
For my revealing his greate gift and previtie.

And yet moreover I wyll your Hyghnes to pardon me,
For openly wyth pen I wyll it never wryte,
But when that ye list by practice ye shall see;
By Mouth also this pretious secret most of delyght,
How may be made Elixirs *Red and Whyte,*
Playne unto your Hyghnes it shall declared be,
And if it please you with easy expence and respyte
To help, I wyll them make by helpe of the Trinitie.

Yet

But notwythstanding for perill that might befall,
Though I dare not here plainly the knot unbinde,
Yet in my writeing I wyll not be so Mysticall,
But that ye may by studie the knowleige finde:
How that eche thing multiplicable is in hys kinde,
And that likenes of bodies Metalline be transmutable
I wyll declare, that if ye feele me in your minde
Ye shall prove my wryting true and noe fayned fable.

And if God graunt you by me to wynne thys treasure,
Serve him devoutly with more Laud and thanking,
Praying his Godhead in lyfe ye may so endure,
His gifts of grace and fortune to use to his pleasing,
Most specially intending over all thing,
To your power and connyng his precepts tenne
So to keep, that into no daunger your selfe ye bring;
But that ye may in glorie see him hereafter, Amen.

As the Philosopher *in the boke of* Meteors *doth wryte,*
That the lykenesse of bodyes Metalline be not transmutable,
But after he added theis words of more delyte,
Without they be reduced to theyr beginning materiable.
Wherefore such bodies which in nature be liquable,
Minerall and Mettaline may be Mercurizate,
Conceave ye may that this Scyence is not opinable,
But very true by Raymond *and others determynate.*

In the said Boke the Philosopher *speaketh also,*
Therein if it please your Highnes for to reade,
Of divers Sulphurs, *but especially of two;*
And of two Mercuryes *Joyned to them indede:*
Whereby he doth true understanders leade
To the knowledge of the principles which be true;
Both Red most pure, and White, as have I spede,
Which be neverthelesse founden but of right few.

And

And these two things be best he addeth anone
For them that worketh the Alchimy *to take,*
Our Gold and our Silver therewith to make alone;
Wherefore I say, who will our Pearle and Ruby make,
The said principles looke that he not forsake:
For at the beginning if his principles be trewe,
And that he can by crafte them so bake;
Trewly at the end his Worke shall him not rewe.

But one greate secret ryght nedefull it is to knowe,
That though the Philosophers *speake plurally,*
All is but one Thing, ye may me trowe,
In kinde, which is our Base principally,
Whereof doth spring both Whyte and Red naturally;
And yet the Whyte must come fyrst of the Red:
Which thyng is not wrought manually,
But naturally, Craft helping oute of our Leade.

For all the parts of our most precious Stone,
As I can preve, be Coessentiall and concrete;
Moreover there is no true principle but one;
Full longe it was er I therwith could mete:
Who can reduce it, and knoweth his Heate,
And only kinde with kinde can redresse,
Till filth originall be clensed from his Seat,
Likely he is to finde our secrets both more and lesse,

Onlie therefore worke Kynde, with his owne Kynde,
And all your Elements Ioyne that they not strive,
This poynte also for any thing beare in mynde;
That passive natures ye tourne into active;
Of Water, Fire, and Winde, of Erthe make blive;
And of the Quadrangle make ye a Figure round,
Then have ye honie of our bene hive;
One ounce well worth a thousand pound.

The

The principall ſecrete of ſecretes all
Is true Proportion which may not be behinde,
Wherein I councell yow be not ſuperficiall,
The true concluſion if ever ye thinke to fynde,
Turne Erth to Water, and Water into Wynde,
Therof make Fire, and beware of the Floode
Of Noe, *wherein many one be blinde;*
That by this Science *thei get but little good.*

I councell you to eate and drinke temperatly,
And be well ware that Ipoſarcha *come not in place;*
Neſh not your Wombe by drinking ymmoderatly,
Leſt ye quench your naturall Heate in lyttle ſpace;
The colour wyll tell appearing in your Face:
Drinke no more therefore, then ye may eate;
Walke up and downe after an eaſie pace,
Chafe not your Body too ſore for to ſweate.

With eaſy Fire after meving when ye ſweate,
Warme your Body and make it dry againe;
By Rivers and Fountaines walke after meate:
At morrowe tymely viſit the high Mountaine,
That Phiſicke *ſo byddeth I reade certeyne:*
So hygh the Mountaine nevertheles ye not aſcende,
But that ye may downeward the way have plaine,
And with your Mantell from cold ye yow defende.

Such labour is holſome, your ſweat if ye wyll drie
With a napkin, and after it take no cold,
For groſſe humors be purged by Sweat kindly;
Uſe Diacameron, *then confect with perfect Gold*
Hermodactilus *for watrie humors good I hold,*
Uſe Hipericon Perforate *with mylke of* Tithimall;
And Sperma Cete *ana with redd Wyne when ye wax old,*
And Gotes Mylke ſoddẽ with Gold nouriſheth moiſture radical.

R But

But a good Phiſytian who ſo intendeth to be,
Our lower Aſtronomy *him nedeth well to knowe*
And after that to lerne, well, Urine in a glaſſe to ſee,
And if it nede to be chafed, the Fyre to blowe,
Then wyttily, it, by divers wayes to throwe,
And after the cauſe to make a Medicine blive,
Truly telling the ynfirmities all on a rowe:
Who thus can doo by his Phyſicke is like to thrive.

We have an Heauen yncorruptible of the Quinteſſence,
Ornate with Elements, Signes, Planetts, and Starrs bright,
Which moiſteth our Erthe by Suttile influence:
And owt thereof a Secrete Sulphure hid from ſight,
It fetteth by vertue of his attractive might;
Like as the Bee fetcheth Hony out of the Flowre
Which thing can doo none other Erthly wight;
Therefore to God only be glory and honour.

And like as Yſe to Water doth relente,
Whereof congealed it was by violence of greate Cold,
Whence Phebus it ſmiteth with his Heate influent:
Right ſo to Water mynerall, reduced is our Gold,
(As writeth playnly Albert, Raymond, *and* Arnold)
With heate and moiſture by craft occaſionate,
With congelation of the Spyrite, Lo! now have I told
Howe our materialls togeather muſt be proportionate.

Att the Dyers craft ye may lerne this Science,
Beholding with Water how they decoctions make
Uppon theyr Woad and Maddre eaſyly and with patience,
Till the Tinctures appeare which the Cloath doth take
Therein ſo fixed that they wyll never forſake
The Cloth for waſhing after they joyned be;
Right ſo our Tinctures with Water of our Lake
We draw by boyling with Aſhes of Hermes tree.

Which

Which Tinctures when they by craft are made parfite,
So dieth Mettalls with Colours evermore permanent,
After the qualitie of the Medycine Red or White;
That never away by eny Fire, will be brente:
To this Example, if you take good tent
Unto your purpoſe the rather ſhall ye wynne,
And ſee your Fire be eaſy and not fervent;
Where Nature did leave off, what tyme look ye begynn.

First Calcine, and after that Putrefye,
Dyſſolve, Dyſtill, Sublyme, Deſcende, and Fyxe,
With Aquavite oft times, both waſh and drie,
And make a marriage the Body and Spirit betwixt;
Which thus togeather naturally if ye can myxe,
In loſinge the Body the Water ſhall congealed bee,
Then ſhall the Body dy utterly of the Flixe,
Bleeding and chaunging Colours as ye ſhall ſee.

The third daye againe to Life he ſhall upriſe,
And devour Byrds, and Beaſts of the Wildernes,
Crowes, Popingayes, Pyes, Pekocks, and Mavies;
The Phenix, the Egle whyte, the Griffon of fearfulnes,
The Greene Lyon and the Red Dragon he ſhall deſtres;
The white Dragon alſo, the Antlope, Unicorne Panther,
With other Byrds, and Beaſts both more and leſſe;
The Baſiliske alſo which allmoſt eche one doth feare.

In Bus *and* Nubi *he ſhall ariſe and aſcend*
Up to the Moone, *and ſith up to the* Sonne,
Through the Ocean Sea, which round is without end:
Only Shypped within a little glaſen Tonne,
When he commeth thither, then is the Maiſtrie Wonne:
About which Iourney greate good ſhall ye not ſpend,
And yet ye ſhall be glad that ever it was begonne;
Patiently if ye liſte to your worke attend.

For then both Body and Spirit alſo both Oyle and Water,
Sowle and Tincture one thing both White and Red,
After Colours variable it conteyneth what ſo men clatter;
Which alſo called is when he hath once bene Dedd:
And is revived our Marchaſite, *our* Magnete, *and our* Lead,
Our Sulphure, *our* Arſenicke, *and our true* Calcevive:
Our Sonne, *our* Moone, *our* Ferment *of our Bread:*
Our Toade, *our* Baſiliske, *our unknowne* Body, *our* Man,
(*our* Wife.

Our Body thus naturally by crafte when it is renovate
Of the firſt ordre is Medicine called in our Philoſophy,
Which oftentimes muſt againe be Spiritualizate:
The rounde Whele turning of our foreſaid Aſtronomy:
And ſo to the Elixir *of Spirites muſt ye come, for why*
Till the ſame of the fixed by the ſame of the flier be over-
Elixir *of Bodyes named it is only;* (*gone*
And this ſecrete poynt truly deceaveth many one.

This naturall proceſſe by helpe of craft thus conſummate
Diſſolveth the Elixir *ſpirituall in our unctuous Humiditie;*
Then in Balneo *of* Mary *togeather let them be Circulat,*
Like new Hony or Oyle till they perfectly thicked be,
Then will that Medicine heale all manner Infirmitie,
And turne all Mettalls to Sonne *&* Moone *moſt perfectly:*
Thus ſhall ye have both greate Elixir, *and* Aurum Potabile,
By the grace and will of God, to whom be lawd eternally.

Incipit Prologus.

CHyld of thys Dyſſyplyne incline to me (thyne Ere,
And harkyn to my doctryne with all thy (dylygence;
Thes words of wyſdome in mynde doe (thou bare,
Which of old Fathers be trew in ſentence;
Live clene in ſoule, to God doe none offence:
Exalt thee not but rather keepe thee Lowe,
Ells wyll thy God in thee no Wyſdome ſowe.

Fro fayned Doctryne and wycked thought,
The holy ſpryt doth hym wythdraw;
Nylling to dwell where Syn is wrought,
Dred God therefore and obay his Lawe
A ryghteous Man forſooke I never ſawe:
Nether hys ſeed begg bread for need,
In holy *Scrypture* thus doe I rede.

Make Wyſdome therefore thy Siſter to be,
And call on Prudence to be thy Frynd,
By pathes of truth they wyll gyde thee,
Wyth love and honeſty wher ſo thou wend:
Both vertuoſe to be, curteous and hend:
Pray God therefore that thou may fynde
Wyſdome and Prudence with mouth and mynde.

All manner good cum wyth them ſhall,
And honeſtie by ther hands innumerable,
Then into combraunce ſhall thou not fall;
Soe be they in ryches Incomparable:
To worſhyp and profyt they wyll thee able,
To conyng and to all manner of grace,
Both here and after thy lyvys ſpace.

For theſe benefyts which they don bryng,
In parte ynnumeryd by ſapyence,
To them I can compare no thyng;
No rychys, no ſpyces of redolence:
Above all treſure ſuch is ther exellence,
That whatſoever erthly that precyous ys,
To them comparyd ys but as cley ywys.

Infynyte treaſure to Man they be,
Who uſyth them ſhall fryndſhyp have
With God in Heven, and there hym ſe,
After them vyvelyche therefor thou crave,
For Body and Soule both wyll they ſave;
And herein Goods doth multiplye,
And afore Prynces they dygnyfy.

Thynke how *Adam* loſt hys wyſdome,
Sampſon hys myght that was ſoe ſtrong,
Kyng *Saule* alſo loſt hys Kyngdome;
And *Davyd* was punnyſhed ſoare for hys wrong:
In the Oake by the here fayre *Abſolon* hong,
Kyng *Ezeky* by ſyckneſſe had puniſhment,
And many one moe for ſynne was ſhent.

But

But ſee how other that livyd well,
And to their God did none offence,
Such chaſtyſment did never fele,
But God ſhewed ever to them benevolence;
Enok and *Ely* were caryed hence,
To Paradyſe, and other good livers were
Of God rewarded in dyvers manner.

Sum had gret Fortune, ſum gret Cunnynge,
Sum had gret Peace, ſum gret Ryches,
Sum conquered Londs to ther wonyng;
Sum were exalted for ther gret mekenes,
Sum other were ſaved fro the cruelnes
Of Tyrants, Lyons, and hot Fornacys,
As *Danyell* and other in many places.

Thus to good Livers God ſend gret grace,
And unto Synners ſore poniſhment;
Sum to amend in thys lyfe had ſpace,
Sum ſodenly with fyre fro Heavyn were brent,
Synfull *Sodomyts* for ever were ſhent;
With *Dathan* and *Abyron* and other moe,
Which ſank for Syn to endles wo.

Thus ever ſyth the World was wrought,
God hath rewardyd both evyll and good;
Thus yf it maye reſt in thy thought,
Fro ſynfull livyng wyll chaung thy moode.
Yf ſynfull people thys underſtood,
They ought to be aferd God to offend,
And ſoone ther ſynfull lyfes to amend.

Therefore

Therefore with God looke thou begyne,
That he by grace may dwell with thee,
So ſhall thou beſt to Wyſdom wyn,
And knowledge of our grete prevyte;
Noryſh Vertues, and Vices looke thou flee,
And truſtyng thou wylt thee well diſpoſe,
Our ſecrets to thee I wyll dyſcloſe.

Keep thou them ſecret and for me pray,
Looke that you uſe them to Gods pleaſure;
Do good wyth them what ever thou may,
For tyme thou ſhalt thys lyfe endure,
That after thy endyng thou may be ſure
In Hevyn for to rewardyd be,
Whych God graunt both to thee and me.

The Preface.

O Hygh Yncomprehenſyble and gloryous
(Mageſte,
Whoſe Luminos Bemes obtundyth our
(ſpeculation;
One-hode in Subſtance, O Tryne hode
(in Deite,
Of Hierarchycall Jubyleſtes the gratulant gloryfycation;
O pytewouſe puryfyer of Soules and puer perpetuation;
O deviaunt fro danger, O drawer moſt deboner;
Fro thys envyos valey of vanyte, O our Exalter.

O Power, O Wyſdom, O Goodnes inexplycable;
Support me, Tech me, and be my Governour,
That never my lyvyng be to thee dyſplycable,
But that I aquyte me to thee as a trew profeſſor:
Att thys begynnyng good Lord here my prayer;
Be nygh with Grace for to enforce my wyll,
Graunt well that I may my entent fulfyll.

Moſt curyoſe Coffer and copyoſe of all treſure
Thou art, fro whom all goodnes doth deſſend,
(To Man) and alſo to every-ech Creature;
Thyne Handy-warke therefore vouchſafe to defend,
That we no tyme in lyvying here myſpend,
With truth thou graunt us our lyvelode to wyn
That in no daunger of Synfulnes we renne.

And for soe much as we have for thy sake
Renowncyd the World, our Wylls, and the Fleshys Lust,
As thyne owne wylfull professyors us take;
Syth in thee only dependyth all our trust,
We can no ferther, to thee enclyne we must:
Thy secret Tresorars, vouchsafe to make us,
Show us thy Secrets, and to us be bounteous.

Among other which be professyd to thee
I me present, as one wyth humble Submyssyon,
Thy Servant besechyng that I may bee,
And trew in levyng acording to my professyon:
In order Chanon reguler of *Brydlyngton*;
Besechyng the Lord that thou wylt me spare,
To thy trew Servaunts thy secretts to declare.

In the begynnyng when thou madyst all of nought,
A globose Mater and darke under confusyon,
By thee Begynner merveloufly was wrought,
Conteynyng naturally all thyngs withoute dyvysyon,
Of whych thou madyst in six Dayes dere dystynction;
As Genesys apertly doth recorde
Then Heavyn and Erth perfeytyd were wyth thy word.

So thorow thy Wyll and Power owte of one Mase
Confusyd was made all thyngs that being ys;
But yn thy glory afore as maker thou was,
Now ys and shall be wythout end I wys;
And puryfyed Sowls upp to thy blys
Shall come a pryncyple, thys may be one,
For the declaryng of our *Stone*.

For

For as of one Mase was made all thyng,
Ryght soe must hyt in our practyse be,
All our secrets of one Image must spryng:
In *Phylosophers* Bokes therefore who lust to se,
Our *Stone* ys callyd the *lesse World* one and three,
Magnesia also of *Sulphure* and *Mercury*,
Propotionat by Nature most perfytly.

But many one mervelyth whych mervel may,
And muse on such a mervelous thyng,
What ys our *Stone* syth *Phylosophers* doth say,
To such as ever be hyt sechyng:
Yet Fowles and Fyshys to us doth yt bryng,
Every-ech Man yt hath, and ys in every place,
In thee, in me, in every tyme and space.

To thys I answer, that *Mercury* it ys I wys
But not the comyn callyd Quicksylver by name,
But *Mercury* withoute whych nothyng beyng ys;
All true *Phylosophers* record and say the same:
But symple serchers puttyth them in blame,
Saying they hyd hyt, but they be blame worthy,
Which be no *Clerks*, and medlyth with *Phylosophy*.

But though hyt *Mercury* be yett wysely understond,
Wherein it ys, where thou shalt it seech,
Ells I thee Councell take not this warke in hond,
For *Philosophers* flattryth Foolys with fayre Speche:
But lyst to me, for trewly I wyll thee teche,
Whych ys thy *Mercury* most profyttable,
Beyng to thee nothing dysseveable.

It ys more nythe in ſum things than in ſum,
Therefore take tent what I unto the wryt,
For yf thou never to the knowledge cum,
Therof yet ſhalt thou me not twytt:
For I wyll trewly now thee excite,
To underſtand well *Mercurys* three,
The keys which of our *Scyens* be.

Raymond hys Menſtrues doth them call,
Without which trewly no truth ys done,
But two of them are Superfycyall:
The third eſſentyall of Soon and Moone;
Theyr propertyes I wyll declare ryght ſoone,
And *Mercury* of other Mettalls eſſencyall,
Ys the pryncipall of our *Stone* materyall.

In Soon and Moone our Menſtrue ys not ſene
Hyt not appeareth but by effect to ſyght,
That ys the *Stone* of whych we mene;
Who ſo our wrytyng concevyth aryght,
Hyt ys a Soule, a ſubſtance bryght:
Of Soon and Moone, a ſubtyll influence,
By whych the Erth receyveth reſplendence.

For what ys Gold and Sylver ſayth *Avycen*,
But Erth whych ys pure Whyte and Red,
Take fro that the ſayd clernes, and then
That Erth wyll ſtond but lyttyll in ſtede;
The hole compound ys called our Lede,
The qualyte of clernes fro Soon and Moone doth com
These be our Menſtrues both all and ſum.

Bodyes

Bodyes wyth the fyrst we Calcene naturally
Perfyt, but none whych be unclene,
Except one whych usually
Namyd by *Phylosophers* the *Lyon Greene*,
He ys the meane the Soon and Moone betweene:
Of joynyng Tynctures wyth perfytnes,
As *Geber* thereto beryth wytnes.

Wyth the Second whych ys an Humydyte
Vegetable revyvyng that earst was dede,
Both pryncyples materyalls must loosed be;
And formalls, els standyth they lytle in stead:
The Menstrues therefore know I the rede:
Wythout whych neyther trew Calcynatyon,
Don may be, nether yet naturall Dyssolutyon.

Wyth the thyrd humydyty most permanent
Incombustyble and unctuous in hys nature,
Hermes Tre to ashes must be brent:
Hyt is our *Naturall Fyre* most sure,
Our *Mercury*, or *Sulphure*, or *Tyncture* pure:
Our *Soule*, our *Stone*, borne up wyth wynd
In the Erthe ingendered, bere thys in thy mynde.

Thys *Stone* alsoe tell thee I dare,
Is the vapor of Mettalls potentyall,
How thou shall gett hyt thou must beware:
For invysible ys truly thys Menstruall:
Howbehytt with the second Water phylosophycall,
By seperatyon of Elements yt may appeare,
To syght in forme of Water cleere.

Of our Menſtrue by labour exuberate
And wyth hyt may be made *Sulphure* of nature
If itt be well and kyndly acuate;
And cyrculate into a Spryt pure:
Then to dyſſolve thou muſt be ſure
Thy Baſe wyth hyt in dyvers wyſe,
As thou ſhalt know by thy practyſe.

That poynt therefore in hys dew place
I wyll declare wyth other mo,
If God wyll graunt me ſpace and grace:
And mep reſerve in lyfe from wo;
As I thee teche loke thou doe ſo,
And for thy fyrſt ground pryncypall
Underſtond thy Water menſtruall.

And when thou haſt made true Calcination,
Encreſyng and not Waſtyng moyſture radycall,
Tyll thy Baſe by ofter ſubtylyatyon
Wyll lyghtly flow as Wex uppon Mettall;
Then lowſe hyt wyth thy vegetable Menſtruall,
Tyll thou have Oyle thereof in Colour bryght,
Then ys your Menſtrue viſible to ſyght.

And Oyle is drawne owte in colour of Gold,
Or lyke thereto out of our fine Red Lead,
Whych *Raymond* ſayd when he was old,
Much more then Gold wold ſtond hym in ſtede,
For whan he was for age nygh dede,
He made thereof *Aurum Potabile*,
Whych hym revyvyd as Men myght ſee.

For

For ſo together may they be Cyrculate,
That ys to ſay, Oyle and the vegetable Menſtruall,
Ether ſo by labour exuberate,
And made by Crafte a Stone Celeſtyall:
Of Nature ſo fyrye that we yt call
Our *Baſelysk*, otherwyſe our *Cokatryſe*,
Our great *Elixir* moſt of pryſe.

Whych as the ſyght of a *Baſylysk* hys object
Kylyth, ſo ſleyth it crude *Mercury*,
When thereon itt ys project,
In twynke of an Eye moſt ſodenly,
That *Mercury* teynyth permanently;
All bodyes to Son and Moone perfyt,
Thus gyde thy baſe both Red and Whyte.

Aurum potabile thus ys made,
Of Gold, not comyn calcynat;
But of our Tyncture whych wyll not vade,
Out of our Baſe drawen wyth the Menſtrue circulate,
But naturall Calcynatyon muſt Algate
Be made, ere thy Gold dyſſolved be,
That Pryncypall fyrſt I wyll tell thee.

But into Chapters thys Treatis I ſhall devyde,
In number Twelve with dew Recapytulatyon;
Superfluous rehearſalls I ley aſyde,
Intendyng only to geve trew Informatyon,
Both of the Theoryke and Practycall operatyon:
That by my wrytyng who ſo wyll guyded be,
Of hys intente perfytly ſpeed ſhall he.

The

The Fyrst Chapter shalbe of naturall *Calcination*;
The Second of *Dyssolution* secret and Phylosophycall;
The Thyrd of our Elementall *Separation*;
The Fourth of *Conjunction* matrymonyall;
The Fysthe of *Putrefaction* then followe shall;
Of *Congelatyon*, albyfycative shall be the Syxt,
Then of *Cybatyon* the Seaventh shall follow next.

The secret of our *Sublymation* the eyght shall shew;
The nynth shall be of *Fermentation*,
The Tenth of our *Exaltation* I trow;
The Eleventh of our mervelose *Multyplycatyon*;
The Twelfth of *Projectyon*; then *Recapytulatyon*;
And so thys Treatyse shall take an end,
By the help of God as I entend.

Of Calcination.

The first Gate.

1\. C*Alcinacion* is the purgacyon of our *Stone*,
Restauryng also of hys naturall heate;
Of radycall moysture it lesyth none;
Inducyng Solucion into our *Stone* most mete,
After *Philosophy* I you behyte,
Do not after the comyn gyse,
Wyth Sulphure and Salts preparat in dyvers wyse.

2\. Nether with Corrosyves nor with Fire alone,
Nor with Vyneger nor Water ardent,
Nether with the vapour of Lede our *Stone*
Is Calcyned to our intente:
All they to Calcyne whych so be bent
Fro thys hard *Scyence* withdraw theyre hond,
Till they our *Calcyning* better understonde.

3\. For by such Calcynyng theyre bodyes be shent,
Whych mynysheth the moysture of our *Stone*;
Therefore when bodyes to powder be brent,
Dry as askys of Tre or Bone,
Of such Calx then wyll we none,
For moysture we multiply radycall,
In Calcynyng, mynyshyng none at all.

T And

4. And for a sure ground of our trew *Calcynacyon*,
Woorch wyttyly kynde only wyth kynde ;
For kynd to kynde hath appetyble inclynacyon ;
Who knoweth not thys yn knowledge is but blynd :
He may forth wander as Myst doth wyth the Wynd ;
Woting never wyth perfytnes where to lyght,
Because he cannot consceve our words aryght.

5. Joyne kynd to kynd therefore as reason ys,
For every Burgeon answereth to his owne Seed ;
Man begetteth Man, a Beast a Beast lykewyse ;
Ferther of thys to trete it is no need,
But understond thys poynt yf thou wylt spede ;
Every thyng ys fyrst Calcyned in hys owne kynd,
Thys well consevyng, frute thereyn shalt thou fynde.

6. And we make Calxes unctious both Whyte and Red,
Of three degrees or our Base be perfyt ;
Fluxyble as Wex, ells stond they lyttle in sted ;
By ryght long processe as *Phylosophers* wryte,
A yere we take or more for our respyte :
For in lesse space our Calxe wyll not be made,
Able to tayne with colour whych wyll not vade.

7. As for the Proporcyon thou must beware,
For therein many one ys beguylyd,
Therefore thy warke that thow not marre ;
Lat the Body be sotelly fylyd
With *Mercury*, as much then so subtylyd :
One of the *Sonn*, two of the *Moone*,
Tyll altogether lyke pap be done.

Then

8. Then make the *Mercury* foure to the *Sonne*,
Two to the *Mone* as hyt should be,
And thus thy worke must be begon,
In fygure of the Trynyte;
Three of the Body and of the Spryt three:
And for the unytye of the substance spirituall,
One more than of the substance corporall.

9. By *Raymonds Reportory* thys ys trew,
Proporcyon there who lyst to looke,
The same my *Doctour* to me did shew;
But three of the Spryt *Bacon* tooke,
To one of the Body for thys I wooke:
Many a nyght or I hyt wyst,
And both be trew take whych you lyst.

10. If the Water be equall in Proporcyon
To the Erthe whych hete in dew mesure,
Of hym shall spryng a new burgyon;
Both Whyte and Red in pure tyncture,
Whych in the Fyre shall ever endure:
Kyll than the quyck, the ded revyve,
Make Trynyte Unyte wythout any stryve.

11. Thys ys the best and the surest Proporcyon,
For here ys lest of the part spyrytuall,
The better therefore shall be Solucyon;
Then yf thou dyd it wyth Water small,
Thyne Erth over glutyn whych losyth all:
Take heede therefore to potters loome,
And make you never to nesh thy wome.

12. That loome behold how yt tempered ys,
The meane allso how thou hyt Calcenate;
And ever in mynd loke thou bare thys,
That never thyne Erth wyth Water be suffocate,
Dry up thy moysture wyth heate most temperate:
Helpe *Dyssolucyon* wyth moysture of the Mone,
And *Congellacyon* wyth the Son, then hast thou done.

13. Foure Natures shall into the fyfth so turne,
Whych ys a Nature most perfect and temperate;
But hard hyt ys with thy bare foote to spurne,
Agaynst a brodyke of Iyron or Stele new acuate:
Soe many one doth whych bene infatuate,
When they such hygh thyngs don take in hond,
Whych they in noe wyse understonde.

14. In Eggs, in Vitryoll, or in Blod,
What ryches wene they there to fynde;
Yf they *Phylosophy* understode,
They wold not in worchyng be so blynd,
Gold to seke or Sylver out of kynd:
For lyke as Fyre of brennyng the pryncyple ys,
So ys the pryncyple of gildyng, Gold I wys.

15. Yf thou intend therefore to make
Gold and Sylver by craft of our *Philosophy*;
Therto nother Eggs nor Blood thou take,
But Gold and Sylver whych naturally,
Calcyned wysely, and not manually,
And new generacyon wyll forth bryng,
Incresyng theyr kynde as doth ech thyng.

And

16\. And yf yt true were that perfyt myght be,
In thyngs which be not mettallyne:
In which be Colours plesaunt to see,
As in Blood, Eggs, Here, Uryn, and Wyne,
Or in meane Mettalls dyggyd out of the Myne:
Yet must theyr Elements be putrefyed and separate,
And wyth Elements of perfyt Bodys be dysponsate.

17\. But fyrst of these Elements make thou Rotacyon,
And into Water thy Erth turne fyrst of all;
Then of thy Water make Ayre by Levygacyon;
And Ayre make Fyre; then MASTER I wyll thee call
Of all our secretts greate and small:
The Wheele of Elements thou canst turne about,
Trewly consevyng our Wrytyngs wythowt dowte.

18\. Thys done, go backward, turnyng thy Wheele againe,
And into thy Water then turne thy Fyre anon;
And Ayre into Erth, ells laboryst thow but in vayne:
For soe to temperment ys brought our *Stone*,
And Natures contraryose, fower be made one,
After they have three times ben Cyrculat,
And alsoe thy Bace perfytly consummate.

19\. Thus under the moysture of the *Moone*,
And under the temperate hete of the *Sonne*,
Thy Elements shalbe incynerate sone,
And then thow hast the Maistery wone;
Thanke God thy worke was then begon:
For there thow hast one token trew,
Whych fyrst in blacknes to thee wyll shew.

20. The hede of the Crow that tokyn call we,
And ſum men call hyt the Crows byll;
Sum call hyt the Aſhes of *Hermes* Tre,
And thus they name hyt after theyer wyll,
Our Tode of the Erth whych etyth hys fyll:
Sum name hyt by whych it ys mortyfycat
The ſpyryt of the Erth wyth venome intoxycate.

21. But hyt hath Names I ſay to the infynyte,
For after each thyng that Blacke ys to ſyght;
Namyd hyt ys tyll the tyme that hyt wex Whyte,
For after blackneſſe when yt wexeth bryght,
Then hath hyt names of more delyght:
After Whyte thyngs, the Red after the ſame,
Rule of Red thyngs, doth take hys name.

22. At the *fyrſt Gate*, now art thou in,
Of the *Phyloſophers Caſtle* where they dwell;
Proceede wyſely that thou may wyne
In at mo Gates of that Caſtell,
Whych Caſtle ys round as any Bell:
And Gates hath Eleven yet mo,
One ys conquered, now to the *Second* go.

The end of the firſt Gate.

Of Solution.

The second Gate.

1. OF *Solucion* now wyll I speke a word or two,
Whych sheweth owt that err was hyd from syght,
And makyth intenuate thyngs that were thyk also;
By the vertue of our fyrst Menstrue clere and bryght,
In whych our Bodyes eclypsyd ben to syght:
And of ther hard and dry Compactyon subtylyat
Into ther owne fyrst nature kyndly retrogradate.

2. One in Gender they be and in Nomber not so,
Whose Father the Son, the Moone truly ys Mother,
The mean ys Mercury, these two and no mo
Be our *Magnesia*, our *Adrop*, and none other;
Thyngs there be, but only *Syster* and *Brother*:
That ys to wene *Agent* and *Pacyent*,
Sulphure and *Mercury* coessentyall to our entent.

3. Betwyxt these two in qualyte cotraryose,
Ingendred ys a Mene most mervyllosely
Whych ys our *Mercury* and Menstrue unctuose;
Our secrett *Sulphur* worchyng invysybly,
More fersely than Fyre brennyng the body,
Into Water dyssolvyng the Body mynerall,
Which Nyght fro darknes in the North parte we call.
But

4. But yet I trow thou underſtandyſt not utterly
The very ſecrett of Phyloſopers *Dyſſolucion*;
Therefore conceve me I councell thee wyttyly:
For I wyll tell thee trewly wythout deluſyon;
Our *Solucyon* ys cauſe of our *Congelacyon*;
For the *Dyſſolucyon* on the one ſyde corporall
Cauſyth *Congelacyon* on the other ſyde Spyrytuall.

5. And we Dyſſolve into Water whych weytyth no hond,
For when the Erth ys integrally yncynerat;
Then ys the Water congelyd, thys underſtond;
For the Elements be ſo concatenat,
That when the body fro hys fyrſt forme ys alterate:
A new forme ys inducyd immediately,
For nothyng being wythout all forme ys utterly.

6. And here a ſecret to thee I wyll dyſcloſe,
Whych ys the ground of our ſecrets all;
And yf thou hyt not know thou ſhalt but loſe
Thy labour and coſts both great and ſmall,
Take hede therefore in Errour that thou not fall:
The more thyne Erth and the leſſe thy Water be,
The rather and better *Solucyon* ſhall thou ſee.

7. Behold how Yſe to Water doth relent,
And ſo hyt muſt, for Water hyt was before;
Ryght ſoe agayne to Water our Erth is bent,
And Water thereby congelyd for evermore,
For after all *Phyloſophers* whych ever was bore:
Every Mettall was ons Water myneral,
Therefore wyth Water they turne to Water all.

In

8. In whych Water of kynde occasyonate
Of qualytes bene repugnaunce and dyversyte,
Thyngs into thyngs must therfore be rotate,
Untyll dyversyte be brought to parfyt unyte,
For Scrypture recordyth when the Erth shall be
Trowbelyd, and into the depe Sea shall be cast
Mountaynes, our Bodyes lykewyse at the last.

9. Our Bodyes be lekenyd convenyently
To Mountaynes whych after hygh Planets we name;
Into the depenes therfore of *Mercury*.
Turne them and kepe the out of blame,
Then shall ye se a Nobyll game;
How all shall become powder soft as sylke,
So doth our Runnett by kynde curd our Mylke.

10. Then hath our Bodys ther fyrst forme loste,
And other be enducyd ymedyately;
Then hast thow well beset thy cost,
Wheras some other uncunning must goe by,
Not knowyng the secretts of our *Phylosophy*:
Yet one poynt I more must tell thee,
Every Body how hyt hath dymencyons three.

11. *Altytude*, *Latytude*, and *Profundyte*,
By whych algates turne we must our Whele;
Knowyng thy entraunce in the West shall be;
Thy passage forth into the North yf thou do well,
And there thy Lyghts lose theyre Lyght eche-dele:
For there thou must abyde by Ninety Nyght
In darknes of Purgatory wythowten Lyght.

V Then

12. Then take thy course up to the Este anon
By Colours passyng varyable in manyfold wyse,
And then be Wynter and Vere nygh over-gon
To the Est, therfore thyne assendyng devyse,
For there the Son wyth Day-lyght doth uprysе
In Somer, and there dysporte the wyth delyght,
For there thy Warke shall becom parfyt Whyte.

13. Forth fro the Est ynto the South assend,
And sett thou up therein thy Chayre of Fyre,
For there ys Harvest, that ys to say an end
Of all thys Warke after thyne owne desyre:
Ther shynyth the Son up in hys owne sphyre,
And after the Eclyps ys in rednes wyth glory
As Kyng to rayne uppon all Mettalls and Mercury.

14. And in one Glasse must be done all thys thyng,
Lyke to an Egg in shape, and closyd well,
Then must you know the mesure of fyryng;
The whych unknowen thy Warke ys lost ech dele,
Lett never thy Glasse be hotter then thow may feele:
And suffer styll in thy bare hand to holde
For dread of losyng as *Philosophers* have the tolde.

15. Yett to my Doctryne furthermore intend,
Beware thy Glasse thou never opyn ne meve
Fro thy begynnyng, tyll thou have made an end;
If thou do contrary thy Warke may never cheve:
Thus in thys *Chapter* whych ys so breve,
I have the taught thy trew *Solucion*;
Now to the *Thyrd Gate* goe, for thys ys won.

OF

OF SEPARATION.

The third Gate.

1. S*Eparacyon*, doth ech parte from other devyde,
The subtill fro the groce, fro the thyck the thyn;
But *Separacyon* manuall look thou put asyde:
For that pertaynyth to folys whych lyttyll good don
But in our *Separacyon* nature doth not blyn: (wyn,
Makyng dyvysyon of qualytes Elementall
Into the fyfth degree tyll they be turned all.

2. Erth ys turnyd into Water black and bloe,
And Water after into Ayre under very whyte:
Ayre ys turned into Fyre, Elements there be no mo;
Of thys ys made by crafte our *Stone* of grete delyte,
But of thys *Separacyon* much more must we wryte;
And *Separacyon* ys callyd by *Phylosophers* dyffynycyon
Of the sayd Elements tetraptatyve dyspersyon.

3. And of thys *Separacyon* I fynde a lyke fygure
Thus spoken by the *Prophet* yn the Psalmody,
God brought out of a Stone a flud of Water pure,
And out of the hardyst Stone Oyle abundantly:
Ryght so of our precyose *Stone* yf thou be wytty,
Oyle incombusteble and Water thou shalt draw,
And thereabout thou nedyst not at the Coles to blow.

4. Do thys wyth hete esy and mesuryng
Fyrst wyth moyst Fyre, and after wyth the dry;
The flewme by Pacyence owt drawyng;
And after that thy other natures wyttyly,
Dry up thyne Erth tyll hyt be thrysty:
By Calcenyng els thou laboryst all in vayne,
And then make hyt drynke up his moysture agayne.

5. *Separacyon* thus must thou ofte tymes make,
Thy Matter dyvydyng into parts two;
So that the Symple fro the groce thou take
Tyll Erth remayne benethe in color bloe,
That Erth ys fyx for to abyde all wo:
The other parte ys Spyrytuall and fleyng,
But thou must turne hem all into one thyng.

6. Than Oyle and Water wyth Water shall dystyll
And thorow her help receve menyng:
Kepe well thys two that thou not spyll,
Thy Wark for lack of dew closyng,
Make thy Stopell of glas meltyng
The top of thy Vessle together wyth yt,
Than Phylosopher-lyke usyd ys hyt.

7. The Water wherwyth thou must renew thy *Stone*
Looke thou dystyll afore thou warke wyth hyt
Oftentymes by it selfe alone:
And by thy syght thou shalt well wyt,
Fro feculent feces when hyt ys quytt:
For sum men can wyth *Satúrne* it multeply,
And other Substance which we defye.

Dystyll

8. Dystyll hyt therfore tyll hyt be clene,
And thyn lyke Water as hyt shold be,
As Hevyn in Color bryght and shyne,
Kepyng both fygure and ponderosyte,
Therwith dyd *Hermes* moysture hys Tre:
Wythyn hys Glas he made to grow upryght,
Wyth Flowers dyscoloryd bewtyosely to syght.

9. Thys Water ys lyke to the venemous Tyre,
Wherewyth the myghty Tryacle ys wrought;
For yt ys Poyson most stronge of yre;
A stronger Poyson can none be thought:
Att the Potecarys therfore oftyn yt ys bought:
But no man shall be by hyt intoxycate,
After the tyme yt ys into Medycyne Elevate.

10. For then as ys the Tryacall trew,
Hyt ys of poysons most expulsyse;
And in hys working doth mervells shewe,
Preservyng many from deth to lyfe,
Loke thou meng yt wyth no corrosyve:
But chese hyt pure and quick rennyng,
Yf thou thereby wylt have wynnyng.

11. It ys a mervelose thyng in kynde,
And Wythout hyt may nought be done;
Therefore *Hermes* calleth hyt hys *Wynde*,
For it ys up flying fro Sonn and Mone,
And makyth our *Stone* flye wyth hyt Sone:
Revyvyng the ded and gevyng lyfe
To Son and Mone, Husband and Wyfe.

12. Whych yf they were not by craft made quick,
And ther fatnes wyth Water drawn out;
And so the thyn dyssevered from the thyke,
Thou should never bryng thys worke about:
Yf thou wylt speed therefore wythout doubt,
Reyse up thy Byrds out of theyre nest,
And after agayne bryng them downe to rest.

13. Water wyth Water accord wyll and assend,
And Spryt wyth Spryt, for they be of kynde;
Whych after they be exalted make to dyssend,
And soe thou shalt devyde that nature before dyd bynde,
Mercury essencyall turnyng into wynde:
Wythout whych naturall and subtyll *Seperacyon*,
May never be compleat profytable Generacyon.

14. Now to help thee in at thys *Gate*,
The last Secret I wyll tell to thee;
Thy Water must be seven tymes Sublymate,
Ells shall no kyndly Dyssolucyon be,
Nor Putryfyyng shall thou none see,
Like lyquyd pytch nor colours apperyng,
For lack of fyre wythin thy Glasse workyng.

15. Fower Fyers there be whych you must understond,
Naturall, Innaturall, against Nature, alsoe
Elementall whych doth bren the brond;
These foure Fyres use we and no mo:
Fyre against Nature must doe thy bodyes wo;
That ys our *Dragon* as I thee tell,
Fersely brennyng as Fyre of Hell.

Fyre

Fyre of Nature ys the thyrd Menſtruall,
That fyre ys naturally in every thyng;
But fyre occaſionat we call Innaturall,
And hete of Askys and balnys for putrefying:
Wythout theſe fyres thou may not bryng
To Putrefaccyon for to be ſeperat,
Thy matters togeather proportyonat.

Therefore make fyre thy Glaſſe wythin,
Whych brennyth the Bodyes more then fyre
Elementall; yf thou wylt wyn
Our Secret accordyng to thy deſire,
Then ſhall thy ſeeds both roote and ſpyre,
By help of fyre Occaſionate,
That kyndly after they may be ſeperat.

Of *Seperacyon* the Gate muſt thus be wone,
That furthermore yet thou may procede,
Toward the Gate of ſecret *Conjunccion*,
Into the Caſtle whych wyll the Inner leade,
Do after my Councell therefore yf thou wylt ſpede;
Wyth two ſtrong locks thys Gate ys ſhyt,
As conſequently now thou ſhalt wyt.

The end of the third Gate.

Of Conjunction.

The fourth Gate.

1. AFter the Chapter of naturall *Separacion*
By which the Elements of our *Stone* dyſſeveryd be
The Chapter here followyth of ſecret *Conjunccion*;
Whych natures repugnant joyneth to perfyt Unyte,
And ſo them knyttyth that none from other may fle;
Whan they by Fyre ſhall be examynate,
Soe be they together ſurely conjugate.

2. And therſore *Phyloſophers* geveth thys deffynycyon,
Seyng thus *Conjunccion* ys nought ells
But of dyſſeveryd qualytes a Copulacyon;
Or of Pryncypylls a coequacyon as other tells,
But ſome wyth *Mercury* whych the Potecarys ſells,
Medleth Bodyes whych cannot dyvyde
Ther matter, and thereſore they ſtep aſyde.

3. For unto tyme the Sowle be Separate
And clenſyd from hys orygynall Syn
Wyth the Water and purely ſpyrytualyzate:
Thy trew *Conjunccion* may thou never begyn,
Therfore the Soule fyrſt fro the Body twyn:
Then of the corporall parte and of the ſpyrytuall,
The Soule *Conjunccion* ſhall cauſe perpetuall.

Of

4. Of two *Conjunccions Phylosophers* don mentyon make,
Groce when the Body with *Mercury* ys reincendat,
But let hyt passe, and to the second tent thou take,
Which as I sayd ys after *Separacion* celebrat:
In whych the partys be left whych left so collygate;
And so promotyd unto most perfyt temperance,
Then never after may be among them Repugnance.

5. Thus causyth *Separacion* trew *Conjunccion* to be had
Of Water, Ayre, Earth and Fyre,
But that every Element may into other be lad,
And so abyde for ever to thy desyre;
Do as done Laborours with Clay and Myer,
Temper them thyke, and make them not to thyn,
For so to up drying thou shalt the rather wyn.

6. But manners there be of thys *Conjunccion* three,
The fyrst ys callyd by *Phylosophers* Dyptative,
Betwyxt the Agent and the Patyent which must be
Male and Female, *Mercury* and *Sulphure* vive;
Matter and forme, thyn and thyke to thryve.
Thys lesson wyll helpe thee wythout any dowte,
Our *Conjunccion* trewly to bryng about.

7. The second manner ys called Tryptative,
Whych ys *Conjunccion* made of thyngs three,
Of Body, Sowle, and Spyrit tyll they not stryve,
Whych Trynite must be brought to perfyt unyte,
For as the Sowle to the Spyrit the bond must be;
Ryght to the Body the Sowle to hym must knyt,
Out of thy mynde let not thys lesson flyt.

X The

8. The thyrd manner and also the last of all,
Fowre Elements together whych joynyth to abyde,
Tetraptative contently *Phylosophers* doth hyt call,
And specyally *Guydo de Montayno* whose fame goyth.
And therfore the most laudable manner thys tyde,(wyde;
In our *Conjunccion* four Elements must be aggregat,
In dew proportion fyrst whych asonder were separat,

9. Therefore lyke as the Woman hath Vaynes fyfteene,
The Man but five to the act of her fecundyte,
Requyryth in our *Conjunccion* fyrst I mene,
So must the Man our Sun have of hys water three;
And (nine) hys Wyfe, whych three to hym must be:
Then lyke whych lyke wyll joy have for to dwell,
More of *Conjunccion* me nedyth not to tell.

10. Thys Chapter I will conclude right sone therefore,
Groce *Conjunccion* chargyng the to make but one,
For seldome have Strumpetts Chyldren of them I bore,
And so thou shalt never cum by our *Stone*,
Wythout you suffer the Woman to lygg alone;
That after she hath conceyved of the Man,
The Matryce of her be shyt from all other than.

11. For such as addyth evermore crude to crude,
Openyng theyr vessells, and lettyng ther matter kele:
The sperme concevyd they norysh not, but delude
Themselfes, and spyllyth ther work every dele;
If thou therefore lyst for to do well,
Close up the Matryce and norysh the seed, (spede.
Wyth heat contynuall and temperate if thou wilt

And

12. And whan thy Veslle hath stond by Monyths five,
And Clowds and Clypsys be passed ech one;
That lyght apperen increase thy hete then blyve,
Tyll bryght and shyneing in Whytnesse be thy *Stone*,
Then may thou opyn thy Glasse anone,
And fede thy Chyld whych ys then ybore
Wyth mylke and mete ay more and more.

13. For now both moyst and dry be so contemperate,
That of the Water erth hath recevyd impressyon;
Whych never assunder after that may be seperate,
And ryght soe Water to Erth hath given ingressyon,
That both together to dwell hath made professyon:
And Water of Erth hath purchasyd retentive,
They fower be made one never more to strive.

14. And in two thyngs all our entent doth hing,
In dry and moyst whych be contraryous two;
In dry that hyt the moyst to fyxing bryng,
In moyst that hyt geve lyquyfaccion the Erth unto,
That of them thus contemperate may forth go
A temperament not so thyk as the Body ys,
Nother so thyn as Water wythout mys.

15. Losyng and knyttyng therefore be Princypalls two
Of thys hard *Scyence*, and Poles most pryncypall;
How be hyt that other pryncyples be many mo,
As shyneyng fanells whych shew I shall:
Proceed therefore unto another wall
Of thys strong Castle of our wysdome,
That Inner at the *Fyft Gate* thou may come.

Of Putrefaction.

The fift Gate.

1. Now begynnyth the Chapter of *Putrefaccion*,
Wythout whych Pole no sede may multyply,
Whych must be done only by contynuall accyon
Of hete in the body, moyst, not manually,
For Bodies ells may not be alterat naturally: (Whete
Syth Chryst do it wytnes, wythowt the grayne of
Dye in the ground, encrese may thou not gete.

2. And in lykewyse wythout thy Matter do Putrefye,
It may in no wyse trewly be alterate,
Nor thyne Elements may be devyded kyndly;
Nor thy *Conjunccion* of them perfytly celebrat:
That thy labor therfore be not frustrate,
The prevyte of *Putrefying* well understond,
Or ever thou take thys Warke in hond.

3. And *Putrefaccyon* may thus defyned be,
After Phylosophers sayings it ys of Bodyes the sleyng,
And in our Compound a dyvysyon of thyngs thre,
The kyllyng Bodyes into corrupcyon forth ledyng,
And after unto Regeneratyon them ablyng:
For thyngs beyng in Erth wythowt dowte
Be engendryd of rotacyon of the Hevyns aboute.

And

4. And therfore as I have seyd afore
Theyn Elements comyxt and wysely coequat,
Thou keepe intemperat heate, eschuyng evermore,
That they by violent hete be never incynerat;
To powder dry unprofytably Rubyfycate,
But into powder blacke as a Crowes byll
Wyth hete of Balne, or ells of our Dounghyll.

5. To tyme that Nyghts be past nynty,
In moyst hete kepe them fro eny thyng;
Sone after by blacknes thow shalt espy
That they draw fast to putrefying,
Whych thow shalt after many colers bryng
To perfyt Whytenes wyth Pacyence esyly,
And so thy sede in hys nature shall multeply.

6. Make ech on other to hawse and kysse,
And lyke as Chyldren to play them up and downe,
And when ther sherts be fylyd wyth pysse,
Then lat the Woman to wash be bound,
Whych oftyn for fayntnes wyll fall in a sound:
And dye at the last wyth her Chyldren all,
And go to Purgatory to purg ther fylth orygynall.

7. When they be there, by lyttyll and lyttyll encrese
Ther paynys by hete ay more and more,
The Fyre from them lat never cese:
And se thy Fornace be apt therfore,
Whych wyse men do call *Athenor*:
Conservyng hete requyryd most temperately,
By whych the Water doth kyndly putrefy.

8. Of thys Pryncypull ſpekyth Sapyent *Guydo*,
And ſeyth by rottyng dyeth the Compound corporall,
And then after *Moryen* and other mo,
Upryſyth agayne Regenerat, Sympill, and Spyrytuall,
And were not hete and moyſture contynuall,
Sperme in the wombe myght have now abydyng,
And ſo ther ſhold therof no frute upſpryng.

9. Therfore at the begynnyng our Stonys thou take,
And bery ech on wyth other wythin ther Grave;
Then equally a Marryage betwyxt them make
To ly together ſix wekys; then lat them have
Ther ſede conſevyd kyndly to noryſh and ſave;
From the ground of ther grave not ryſyng that while,
Whych ſecret poynt doth many on begyle.

10. Thys tyme of Conceptyon wyth eſye hete abyde,
The Blacknes ſhowing ſhall tell the when they dye;
For they together lyke lyquyd Pyche that tyde,
Shall ſwell and burbyll, ſetyll, and *Putrefye*,
Shyning Colors therin thou ſhalt eſpye:
Lyke to the Raynbow mervelose unto ſyght,
The Water then begynnyth to dry upryght.

11. For in moyſt Bodys hete noryſhyng temperate,
Ingendryth Blacknes fyrſt of all which ys
Of kyndly Commyxyon to the tokyn aſſygnate;
And of trew *Putrefying*, remember thys,
For then to alter perfytly thou may not myſſe;
And thus by the Gate of Blacknes thou muſt cum in
To lyght of Paradyce in Whytenes yf thou wylt wyn.

For

12. For fyrst the Son in hys uprysyng obscurate
Shalbe, and passe the Waters of *Noyes* flud
On Erth, whych were a hundred dayes contynuate
And fyfty, away or all thys Waters yode,
Ryght so our Waters as wyse men understode
Shall passe, that thou wyth *Davyd* may say
Abierunt in sicco flumina: bare thys away.

13. Sone after that *Noe* plantyd hys Vyneyard,
Whych really floryshed and brought forth Graps anon:
After whych space thou shalt not be aferd;
For in lykewyse shall follow the floryshyng of our *Stone*:
And sone uppon that thyrty dayes overgone,
Thou shalt have Graps ryght as the Ruby red,
Whych ys our *Adrop*, our *Ulyser* red and our *Lede*.

14. For lyke as Sowles after paynys transytory
Be brought into paradyce where ever ys yoyfull lyfe;
So shall our *Stone* after hys darknes in Purgatory
Be purged and joynyd in Elements wythoute stryfe,
Rejoyse the whytenes and bewty of hys wyfe:
And passe fro the darknes of Purgatory to lyght
Of paradyce, in Whytnes *Elyxer* of gret myght.

15. And that thou may the rather to *Putrefaccyon* wyn
Thys Exampull thou take to the for a trew conclusyon,
For all the secrett of *Putrefaccyon* restyth therein;
The heart of Oke that hath of Water contynuall infusyon
Wyll not sone putrefy, I tell the wythout delusyon:
For though yt in Water ly a hundred yeres and more,
Yet shold thou fynd it sound as ever it was afore.
But

16. But and thou kepe hyt somtyme wete, & sometyme dry,
As thow many se in Tymber by usuall experyment,
By prosses of tyme that Oke shall utterly Putrefy:
And soe in lykewyse accordyng to our entent,
Sometyme our Tre must wyth the Son be brent:
And then wyth Water sone after we must hyt kele,
That by thys menes thou shalt to rottyng bryng hyt (wele

17. For nowe in wete and nowe agayne in dry,
Now in grete hot and now agayne in cold
To be, shall cause yt sone for to putrefy:
And so shalt thow bryng to rottyng thy Gold,
Entrete thy Bodys therfore as I have thee told:
And in thy Putrefying wyth hete be not so swyft,
Lest in the Askys thou seke after thy thryft.

18. Therfore thy Water out of the Erth thow draw,
And make the soule therwyth for to assend;
Then downe agayne into the Erth hyt throw,
That they oft tymes so assend and dessend,
From vyolent hete and sodayne cold defend
Thy Glasse, and make thy fyre so temperat,
That by the sydys thy Water be never vytryfycate.

19. And be thou wyse in chesing of thy Water,
Medyll with no Salt, Sulphure, nor mene Minerall,
For whatsoever any Water to the do clatter;
Our *Sulphure* and *Mercury* be only in Mettall,
Which Oylys and Waters som men call:
Fowlys, and Byrds wyth other namys many one,
Because that folys shold never know our *Stone*.

For

20. For of thys World our *Stone* ys callyd the sement,
Whych mevyd by craft as Nature doth requyre;
In hys encrese shall be full opulent,
And multeply hys kynd of thyne owne desyre:
Therfore yf God vouchsafe thee to enspyre
To know the trewth, and fancies to eschew,
Lyke unto the shalbe in ryches but few.

21. But many be mevyd to worke after ther fantasy
In many subjects in whych be Tynctors gay,
Both Whyte and Red, devydyd manually
To syght, but in the Fyre they fle away,
Such brekyth Potts and Glassys day by day:
Enpoysonyng themselfs, and losyng of theyr syghts
Wyth Odors and smoks and wakeyng up by nyghts.

22. Their Clothes be bawdy and woryn threde-bare,
Men may them smell for Multyplyers where they go;
To fyle theyr fyngers wyth Corrosyves they do not spare
Theyr Eyes be bleryd, & theyr Chekys both lene & bloe:
And thus for *(had I wyst)* they suffer losse an d wo;
Such when they have lost that was in theyr purse,
Then do they chyd and *Phylosophers* sore accurse.

23. For all the whyle that they have *Phylosophers* ben,
Yet cowde they never know our *Stone*.
Som sought in Soote, Dung, Uryne, som in Wyne:
Som in Sterr slyme, for thyng yt ys but one;
In Blood, Eggs; Som tyll theyr thryst was gone:
Devydyng Elements, and brekyng many a pott,
Multyplying the sherds, but yet they hyt yt not.

24. To se theyr Howsys it ys a noble sport,
What Fornaces, what Glassys there be of divers shape;
What Salts, what Powders, what Oyles, and waters fort,
How eloquently, *de materia prima* they clape,
And yet to fynde the trewth they have no hap:
Of our *Mercury* they medle and of our *Sulphur vyve*,
Wherein they dote, and more and more unthryve.

25. They take of the Red Man and hys whyte Wyfe,
That ys a speciall thyng and of *Elixers* two,
Of the *Quintessence* and of the *Elixers* of lyfe,
Of Hony, Celydony, and of Secundyns also,
These they devyde into Elements wyth other mo;
No Multeplyers but *Phylosophers* callyd wyll they be,
Whych naturall Phylosophye dyd never rede nor see.

26. Thys felyshyp knowyth our *Stone* ryght wele,
They thynke them rycher then ys the *Kyng*;
They wyll hym helpe, he shall not fayle
Fraunce for to wyn, a wonders thyng;
The *holy Cresse* home wyll they bryng:
And yf the *King* were prysoner I take,
Anon hys Raunsome would they make.

27. A mervell yt ys that *Westminster* Church,
To whych these *Phylosophers* do haunte;
Syth they so much ryches can woorche,
As they make boste of and avaunte,
Drynkyng dayly the wyne a due taunte,
Ys not made up perfytly at ons,
For truly hyt lackyth yet many Stonys.

Folys

28. Folys doe folow them at the tayle,
Promotyd to ryches wenyng to be;
But wyll ye here what worshyp and avayle,
They wyn in *London* that nobyll cyte,
Wyth Sylver Macys as ye may se:
Sarjaunts awayting on them every owre,
So be they men of great honour.

29. Sarjaunts sekyth them fro Strete to Strete,
Marchaunts and Goldsmyths leyeth after them watch;
That well ys he that wyth them do mete,
For the great advantage that they doe cache,
They hunt about as doth a Rache:
Wenyng to wyn so grete tresure,
That ever in ryches they shall endure.

30. Som wold cache theyr goods agayne,
And some more good would aventure;
Som for to have wold be full fayne,
Of Ten pound one I you ensuer:
Som whych hath lent wythout mesure
Theyr goods, and be with powerte bestad;
To cache a Nobyll wold be full glad.

31. But when the Sarjaunts do them arest,
Ther Paukeners be stuffed wyth *Parrys* balls;
Or wyth Sygnetts of *Seynt Martynes* at the lest,
But as for Mony yt ys pyssyd on the walls:
Then be they led as well for them befalls
To *Newgate* or *Ludgate* as I you tell,
Because they shall in safegard dwell.

32. Where ys my Mony becom seyth one,
And where ys myne seyth he and he?
But wyll ye here how suttell they be anon,
In answeryng, that they excused may be,
Saying, Of our *Elyxers* robbyd we be:
Ells myght we have payd you all your Gold,
Yf yt had been more by ten folde.

33. And then theyer Creditors they begyn to flatter,
Promysyng to worke for them agayne;
The *Elyxers* two in short space after,
Dotyng the Merchaunts that they be fayne
To let them go, but ever in vayne:
They worke so long, tyll at the last
They be agayne in Pryson cast.

34. Yf any then aske them why they be not ryche,
They sey they make fyne Gold of Tynn;
But he they sey may surely swym in dyche,
Whych ys upholden by the chyn;
We have no stock, therefore may we nought wyn:
Whych yf we had we wold some worche,
I now to fynysh up *Westmynster* Churche.

35. And some of them be so Devowte,
They wyll not dwell out of that place;
For there they may wythowten dowte,
Do what them lyst to their Solace,
The *Archedeacon* ys so full of grace:
Yf that they please hym wyth the Crosse,
He forsyth lyttyll of other menys losse.

And

36. And when they there syt at the wyne,
These Monkys they sey have many a pound,
Wolde God (seyth one) that som were myne;
Hay hoe, careaway, lat the cup go rounde:
Drynk on, seyth another, the mene ys founde:
I am a Master of that Arte,
I warrant us we shall have parte.

37. Such causyth the Monkys then evyll to don,
To wast ther Wagys thorow theyr dotage;
Som bryngeth a Mazer and som a Spone;
There *Phylosophers* gevyth them such corage,
Behotyng them wynnyng wythout damage:
A pound for a peny at the lest agayne,
And so fayre promys makyth folys fayne.

38. A ryall Medycyne one upon twelve
They promys them thereof to have,
Whych they could never for themselfe
Yet bryng abowte, so God me save:
Beware such *Phylosophers*, no man deprave:
Whych helpyth these Monkys to ryches so,
Wyth thread-bare Cowlys that they do go.

39. The *Abbot* well ought to cherysh thys Company,
For they can tech hys Monkys to leve in poverte,
And to go clothyd and monyed relygyously,
As dyd *Seynt Benet*, eschuyng superfluyte,
Esyng them also of the ponderosyte
Of theyr pursys, wyth pounds so aggravate,
Whych by *Phylosophy* be now allevyat.

40 Lo who ſo medlyth wyth thys rych Company,
Gret boſt of ther wynnyng may they make,
For they ſhall have as much by ther *Phyloſophy*,
As they of the tayle of an Ape can take;
Beware therſore for Jeſus ſake:
And medyll wyth nothyng of gret coſt,
For and thou do, yt ys but loſt.

41. Theſe *Phyloſophers* (of whych I ſpake afore)
Medlyth and blondryth wyth many a thyng,
Renuyng in errors more and more,
For lac of trew underſtandyng,
But lyke muſt lyke alway ferth bryng:
So God hath ordeyned in every kynde,
Wold Jeſus they wold thys bere in mynde.

42. Wene they of a Nettyll to have a Roſe
Or of an Elder an Apple ſwete,
Alas that wyſe men ther goods ſhold loſe:
Truſtyng ſuch Loſells when they them mete,
Whych ſeyth our *Stone* ys trodyn under fete:
And makyth them therfore vyle thyngs for to ſtyll
Tyll at theyr howſys wyth ſtench they fyll.

43. Som of them never lernyd a word in Scolys,
Such thynk by reaſon to underſtond *Phyloſophy*:
Be they *Phyloſophers*? nay, they be folys:
Therfore ther Warkes provyth unwytty;
Medyll not wyth them yf thou be happy:
Leſt wyth theyr flatteryng they ſo the tyll
That thou agre unto ther wyll.

Spend

44. Spend not thy Mony away in waste,
Geve not to every speche credence;
But fyrst examyn, grope and taste;
And as thou provyst, so put thy confydence,
And ever beware of grete expence:
But yf thy *Phylosopher* lyve vertuosely,
Trust the better to hys *Phylosophy*.

54. Prove hym fyrst and hym oppose
Of all the Secretts of our *Stone*,
Whych yf he know not thou nedyth not to lose;
Medyll thou not ferther, but let hym gone,
Make he never so pytyose a mone:
For than the Fox can fagg and fayne
When he wold faynyst hys prey attayne.

46. Yf he can answer as ought a Clarke,
How be hyt he hath not provyd indede;
And yf thou wylt helpe hym to hys Warke,
Yf he be vertuose I hold hyt mede,
For he wyll the quyte yf ever he spede:
And thou shalt weete by a lytyll anon
Yf he have knowledge of our *Stone*.

47. One thyng, one Glasse, one Furnace and no mo,
Behold thys pryncypyll yf he take,
And yf he do not, then lat hym go;
For he shall never thee rych man make:
Trewly yt ys better thou hym forsake,
Then after wyth losse and varyaunce,
And other manner of dysplesaunce.

But

48. But and God fortune the for to have
Thys *Scyence* by doctrine whych I have told;
Dyscover yt not whoever thee crave,
For Favor, Fere, Sylver, nor Gold:
Be none Oppressor, Lecher, nor boster bold;
Serve thy God, and helpe the powre among,
Yf thou thys lyfe lyst to continew long.

49. Unto thy selfe thy secretts kepe
From synners whych hath not God in dred;
But wyll the cast in Pryson depe,
Tyll thou them tech to do hyt in dede,
Then slander on the sholde spryng and sprede,
That thou dyd coyne then wold they sey,
And so undo the for ever and aye.

50. And yf thou teche them thys conyng,
Their synfull levyng for to mayntayne;
In Hell therfore myght be thy wonnyng,
For God of the then would disdayne,
As thow nought cowd for thy selfe sayne:
That Body and Soule you may bothe save,
And here in pece thy levyng have.

51. Now in thys Chapter I have the tought,
How thou the bodys must *Putrefy*:
And so to guide the thou be not cawght,
And put in duraunce, losse, and vylanye:
My doctryne therefore remember wyttyly,
And passe forth toward the *Syxth Gate*,
For thys the *Fysthe* ys tryumphate.

Of

OF CONGELATION.

The sixt Gate.

1. OF *Congelacyon* I nede not much to wryte,
But what yt ys now I wyll fyrst declare:
It ys of soft thyngs Induracyon of Colour Whyte,
And confyxacyon of Spyrits whych fleyng are:
How to congele thee nedyth not much to care;
For Elements wyll knyt together sone,
So that *Putrefaccyon* be kyndly done.

2. But *Congelacyons* be made in dyvers wyse,
And Spyryts and Bodys dyssolvyd to water clere,
Of Salts also dyssolvyd ons or twyse,
And then to congele in a fluxyble Mater;
Of such *Congelyng* folys do clatter:
And some dyssolvyth devydyng manually
Elements, them after congelyng to powder dry.

3. But such Congelyng ys not to our desyre:
For unto owers yt ys contraryose.
Our *Congelacion* dredyth not the fire:
For yt must ever stond in yt unctuos,
And also in hys Tincture be full bounteous,
Whych in the Ayre congelyd wyll not relent
To Water, for then our Worke were shent.

4. Moreover Congele not into so hard a *Stone*
As Glasse or Crystall whych meltyth by fusyon;
But so that hyt lyke wax wyll melt anon
Wythouten blast: and beware of Delusyon;
For such Congelyng longyth not to our Conclusyon
As wyll not flow and ren to water agen,
Lyke Salts congelyd, then laboryst thou in vayne.

5. Whych *Congelacyon* avaylyth us never a dell,
Hyt longyth to Multyplyers whych Congele vulgarly;
Yf thow therefore lyst to do well,
(Syth thy Medcyne shall never flow kyndly,
Nether Congele, wythout thow fyrst yt Putrefye)
Fyrst Purge and Fyx the Elements of our *Stone*,
Tyll they together Congele and flow anone.

6. For when the Matter ys made parfyt Whyte,
Then wyll thy Spryte wyth the Body Congelyd be;
But of that tyme thou must have long respyte,
Yer yt appere Congelyd lyke Pearles unto the,
Such *Congelacyon* be glad for to see;
And after lyke graynys red as blod,
Rychyr then any worldly good.

7. The erthly Grosnes therefore fyrst mortyfyed
In Moystnes, Blacknes ingendryd ys;
Thys pryncypell may not be denyed,
For naturall *Phylosophers* so seyth I wys,
Whych had, of Whytenes thou may not mys:
And into Whytenes yf thou Congele hyt ons,
Thou hast a *Stone* most presyose of all Stonys.

And

8. And by the Dry lyke as the Moyst dyd putrefy,
Whych causyd in colors Blacknes to appere;
Ryght so the Moyst Congelyd by the Dry,
Ingendryth Whytenes shyneyng with myght full clere,
And Drynes procedyth as Whytyth the matter:
Lyke as in Blackyng Moysture doth hym show,
By colors varyante aye new and new.

9. The cause of all thys ys Hett most temperate,
Workyng and mevyng the Mater contynually;
And thereby also the Mater ys alterate,
Both inward and outward substancyally,
And not to as doth folys to syght sophystycally:
But every parte all fyre for to endure,
Fluxybly fyxe and stabull in tyncture.

10. And *Physycke* determyneth of eche Dygestyon,
Fyrst don in the Stomack in whych ys Drynes,
Causyng Whytnes wythout questyon,
Lyke as the second Dygestyon causyth Rednes,
Complet in the Lyver by Hete and temperatnes;
And so our *Stone* by Drynes and by Hete,
Dygestyd ys to Whyte and Red complete.

11. But here thou must another secret knowe,
How the *Phylosophers* Chyld in the Ayre ys borne:
Besy thee not to fast at the Cole to blowe,
And take that nether for mock nor skorne,
But trust me truly else thy work ys all forlorne:
Wythout thyne Erth wyth Water revyvyd be,
Our trew *Congelyng* shalt thou never see.

12 A sowle betwyxt Hevyn and Erth beyng,
Arysyng fro the Erth as Ayre wyth Water pure,
And causyng lyse in every lyvely thyng,
Incessably runnyng uppon our foresayd Nature,
Enforsyng to better them wyth all hys cure;
Whych Ayre ys the Fyre of our *Phylosophy*,
Namyd now Oyle, now Water mystyly.

13. And thus mene Ayre, whych Oyle, or Water we call,
Our Fyre, our Oyntment, our Spryte, and our *Stone*,
In whych one thyng we grownd our wysdomes all,
Goyth nether out nor yn alone,
Nether the Fyer but the Water anone;
Fyrst yt outeledyth, and after bryngyth yt yn,
As Water with Water whych wyll not lyghtly twyn.

14. And so may Water only our Water meve,
Whych mevyng causyth both Deth and Lyfe,
And Water doth kyndly to Water cleve
Wythout repugnance, or any stryse,
Whych Water to Folys ys nothyng ryfe;
Beyng of the kynd wythowten dowte
Of the Spryte, callyd Water and leder owte.

15. And Water ys the secret and lyfe of every thyng
That ys of substance in thys world y found;
For of the Water eche thyng hath begynnyng,
As showyth in Woman when she shallbe unbound
By water whych passyth afore, if all be sound,
Callyd *Albyen*, fyrst from them rennyng,
Wyth grevose throwys afore ther chyldyng.

And

16. And truly that ys the cause pryncypall,
Why *Phylosophers* chargyd us to be pacyent
Tyll tyme the Water were dryed to powder all,
Wyth nurryshyng hete contynuall but not vyolent,
For qualytes be contrarious of every element,
Tyll after Black in Whyte be made a unyon,
And then forever congelyd wythout dyvysyon.

17. And furthermore the preparacion of thys conversyon
Fro thyng to thyng, fro one state to another,
Ys done only by kyndly and descrete operacion
Of Nature, as ys of Sperme wythin the Mother:
For Sperme and Hete as Syster be and Brother,
Whych be converted wythin themself as Nature can
By accion, and passyon, and at the last to parfyt Man.

18. For as the bodely part by Nature whych ys consumate
Into Man, ys such as the begynner was,
Whych though yt thus fro thyng to thyng was alterat,
Not owt of kynd to menge with other kynds dyd yt pas;
And so our Mater spermatycall wythin one Glas,
Wythin hyt selfe must turne fro thyng to thyng,
By hete most temperate only hyt noryshyng.

19. Another example naturall I may thee tell,
How the substance of an Egg by nature ys wrought
Into a Chyk, not pasyng out of the shell,
A playner example cowd I not have thought,
And there conversions be made tyll forth be brought
Fro state to state the lyke by lyke yn kynd,
Wyth nurryshyng hete: only bere thys yn mynd.

20. Another example here may you also rede,
Of Vegetable thyngs takyng consyderacyon;
How every Plant growyth of hys owne sede,
Thorow Hete and Moysture by naturall operacyon,
And therefore Mineralls be nurryshyd by mynystracyon;
Of Moysture radycall, whych theyr begynnyng was,
Not passiyng theyer kynd wythin one Glas.

21. There we them turne fro thyng to thyng agayne,
Into ther Moder the Water when they go;
Whych pryncyple unknowen thou labourest in vayne:
Then ys all Sperme, and thyngs ther be no mo,
But kynd wyth kynd in number two;
Male and Female, Agent and Pacyent,
Wythin the matryce of the Erth most oryent.

22. And these be turnyd by Hete fro thyng to thyng
Wythin one Glas, and so fro state to state,
Tyll tyme that Nature do them bryng
Into one substance of the Water regenerate,
And so the Sperme wythin hys kynde ys alterate,
Abyll in lykenes hys kynde for to Multeplye,
As doth in kynde all other thyngs naturally.

23. In the tyme of thys seyde processe naturall,
Whyle that the Sperme consevyd ys growyng,
The substance ys nurryshed wyth hys owne Menstruall,
Whych Water only out of the Erth dyd bryng,
Whose colour ys Greene in the fyrst showing,
And for that tyme the Son hydyth hys lyght,
Taking hys course thorow owte the North by nyght.

The

24. The ſeyd Menſtrue ys, (I ſay to the in councell)
The blod of our *Grene Lyon*, and not of Vytrioll,
Dame *Venus* can the trewth of thys the tell,
At thy begynnyng to councell and yf thou her call:
Thys ſecret ys hyd by *Phyloſophers* grete and ſmall;
Whych blode drawen owte of the ſeyd *Lyon*,
For lac of Hete had not perfyt Dygeſtyon.

25. But thys blode our ſecret Menſtruall,
Wherewyth our Sperme ys nurryſhed temperatly,
When it ys turnyd into the ſecys Corporall,
And becom Whyte perfytly and very Dry,
Congelyd and Fyxyd into hys owne body;
Then bruſtyn blod to ſyght yt may well ſeme,
Of thys warke namyd the *mylke whyte Dyademe*.

26. Underſtonde now that our ſyery Water thus acuate,
Is called our Menſtruall water, wherein
Our Erth ys loſyd and naturally Calcenat
By *Congelacyon* that they may never twyne:
Yet to Congele more water thou may not blyn
Into thre parts of the acuate water ſeyd afore,
Wyth the 4th. part of the Erth congelyd & no more.

27. Unto that ſubſtance therefore ſo congelat,
The fowerth part put of water Cryſtallyn
And make them then together to be Dyſponſat
By *Congelacyon* into a myner metallyne,
Whych lyke a ſworde new ſlypyd then wyll ſhyne,
After the Blacknes whych ſyrſt wyll ſhowe,
The fowerth parte geve yt them of water new.

Mo

28. Mo *Inbybycyons* many must we have yett;
Geve yt the second, and after the thyrd also,
The seyd proporcyon kepe well in thy wyt;
Then to another the fowerth tyme loke thou go,
The fyfth tyme and the syxth, passe not there fro:
But put two parts at eche tyme of them three,
And at the seventh tyme fyve parts let there bee.

29. When thou hast made thus seven tymes *Inbybycion*,
Ageyne then must thow turne thy Whele,
And Putrefy all that Matter wythowte addycyon:
Fyrst Blacknesse abydyng yf thow wylt do well,
Then into Whytenes congele yt up eche dele,
And by Rednes into the Sowth assend,
Then hast thou brought thy Base unto an end.

30. Thus ys thy Water then devydyd in partyes two,
Wyth the fyrst party the Bodys be Putryfycat,
And to thyne *Inbybycions* the second part must go,
Wyth whych the Matter ys afterwards Denygrat,
And sone uppon by esy *Decoccyon* Albyfycate:
Then yt ys namyd by *Phylosophers* our *Sterry Stone*,
Bryng that to Rednes, then ys the *syxth Gate* woon.

Of

Of Cibation.

The seventh Gate.

1. NOw of *Cibacion* I turne my pen to wryte,
Syth yt must here the seventh place occupye;
But in few words yt wylbe expedyte,
Take tent therto, and understond me wyttyly;
Cibacion ys callyd a fedyng of our Matter dry
Wyth Mylke, and Mete, whych moderatly they do,
Tyll yt be brought the thyrd order unto.

2. But geve yt not so much that thou hyt glut,
Beware of the Dropsy, and also of *Noyes* Flood;
By lyttyll and lyttyll therfore thou to hyt put
Of Mete and Drynke as semyth to do hyt good,
That watry humors not overgrow the blood:
The Drynke therfore let hyt be mesuryd so,
That kyndly appetyte thou never quench therfro.

3. For yf yt drynke to much, then must yt have
A Vomyte, ells wyll yt be syk to long;
Fro the Dropsy therfore thy Wombe thou save,
And fro the Flux, ells wyll hyt be wrong,
Whych rather lat yt thyrst for drynke amonge:
Then thou shold geve yt overmuch at ons
Whych must in youth be dyattyd for the nons.

4. And yf thou dyatt hyt (as Nature doth requyre)
Moderatly tyll hyt be growen to age,
Fro Cold hyt kepyng and nurryshyng wyth moyst Fyre;
Than shall yt grow and wax full of corrage,
And do to thee both plesure and advauntage:
For he shall make darke Bodys hole and bryght,
Clensyng theyer Leprosenes thorow hys myght.

5. Thre tymes thus must thou turne about thy Whele
Abowte kepyng the rewle of the seyd *Cibacyon*,
And then as sone as yt the Fyre doth fele,
Lyke Wax yt wylbe redy unto Lyquacyon;
Thys Chapter nedyth not longer protestacion:
For I have told thee the dyatory most convenyent
After thyne Elements be made equypolent.

6. And also how thou to Whytnes shalt bryng thy Gold,
Most lyke in fygure to the lenys of an hawthorn tre,
Callyd *Magnesya* afore as I have told;
And our *Whyte Sulfur* wythowte conbustebyllyte,
Whych fro the fyer away wyll never fle:
And thus the *seventh Gate* as thow desyred
In the upspryng of the Son ys conqueryd.

Of

Of Sublimation.

The eight Gate.

1\. HEre of our *Sublimacion* a word or two,
I have to ſpeke, whych the eyghth *Gate* ys
Folys do Sublyme, but Sublyme thou not ſo,
For we Sublyme not lyke as they do I wys;
To Sublyme trewly therfore thou ſhall not mys:
If thou can make thy Bodys firſt ſpirituall,
And then thy Spyryts as I have tought the corporall.

2\. Som do *Mercury* from *Vitriall* and *Salt* ſublyme,
And other ſpryts fro Scales of Yern or Steele,
Fro Eggſhells calcynyd and quyk lyme,
And on theyer manner hyt they Sublyme ryght well,
But ſuch Sublymyng accordyth never adele
To our entent, for we Sublyme not ſo,
To trewe *Sublymyng* therfore now wyll I go.

3\. In *Sublymacyon* fyrſt beware of one thyng,
That thou Sublyme not to the top of thy Veſſell,
For without vyolence thou ſhalt yt not downe bryng
Ageyne, but there yt wyll abyde and dwell;
So hyt rejoyſyth wyth refrygeracion I the tell:
Kepe hyt therfore wyth temperat hete adowne
Full forty dayes, tyll hyt wex black abowen.

4. For then the Sowle begynnyth for to com owte,
Fro hys owne vaynys ; for all that ſubtyll ys,
Wyll wyth the Sprytsaiſend withouten dowte:
Bere in thy mynde therfore and thynkeon thys,
How here eclypſyd byn thy Bodys:
As they do Putrify Sublymyng more and more,
Into the Water tyll they be all up bore.

5. And thus ther venom when they have ſpowtyd out
Into the water, than Black yt doth appeare,
And become ſpirituall every dele withoute dowte,
Sublymyng eſyly on our manner
Into the water which doth hym bere:
For in the Ayre one Chyld thus muſt be bore
Of the Water ageyne as I have ſeyd before.

6. But when theſe to *Sublymacyon* continuall
Be laboryd ſo, wyth hete both moyſt and temperate,
That all ys Whyte and purely made ſpirituall ;
Than Hevyn uppon Erth muſt be reitterate,
Unto the Sowle wyth the Body be reincorporate:
That Erth becom all that afore was Hevyn,
Whych wyll be done in *Sublymacyons* ſevyn.

7. And *Sublymacyon* we make for cauſys thre,
The fyrſt cauſe ys to make the Body Spirituall;
The ſecond that the Spryt may Corporall be,
And becom ſyx wyth hyt and ſubſtancyall:
The Thyrd cauſe ys that fro hys fylth orygynall
He may be clenſyd, and hys fatnys ſulphuryoſe
Be mynyſhyd in hym whych ys infectuoſe.

Then

8. Then when they thus togeder depuryd be,
They wyll Sublyme up whyter then Snow;
That syght wyll gretly comfort the;
For than anon parfytly shalt thou know
Thy Sprytts shall so be a downe I throw:
That thys *Gate* to the shalbe unlockyd,
Out of thys *Gate* many one be shyt and mockyd.

Of Fermentation.

The ninth Gate.

1. TRew *Fermentacyon* few Workers do understond,
That secrett therfore I wyll expounde to the,
I travelyd trewly thorow many a Lond:
Or ever I myght fynde any that cold tell hyt me;
Yet as God wolde, (evermore blessed he be,)
At the last I cum to knowledge therof parfyt,
Take heede therfore, therof what I do wryte.

2. *Fermentyng* in dyvers maners ys don,
By whych our Medcyns must be perpetuate,
Into a clere Water, som lesyth *Son* and *Mone*;
And wyth ther Medcyns makyth them to be Congelate;
Whych in the Fyer what tyme they be examynate;
May not abyde nor alter wyth Complement,
For such *Ferments* ys not to our intent.

3. But yet more kyndly som other men don
Fermentyng theyer Medcynes in thys wyse,
In *Mercury* dyssolvyng both *Son* and *Mone*,
Up wyth the Spryts tyll tyme wyll aryse,
Sublymyng them together twyse or thryse:
Then *Fermentacyon* therof they make,
That ys a way, but yet we hyt forsake.

4. Som other ther be whych hath more hap
To touch the trothe in parte of Fermentyng;
They *Amalgam* ther Bodys wyth *Mercury* lyke papp;
Then theruppon ther Medcyns relentyng,
These of our Secretts have som hentyng:
But not the trewth wyth parfyt Complement,
Because they nether Putrefy nor alter ther Ferment.

5. That poynt therfore I wyll dysclose to thee,
Looke how thou dydyst wyth thy unparfyt Body,
And do so wyth thy parfyt Bodys in every degre;
That ys to sey fyrst thou them Putrefye
Her prymary qualytes destroying utterly:
For thys ys wholey to our entent,
That fyrst thou alter before thou Ferment.

6. To thy Compound make Ferment the fowerth parte,
Whych Ferments be only of *Son* and *Mone*;
If thou therfore be Master of thys *Arte*,
Thy *Fermentacion* lat thys be done,
Fyx Water and Erth together sone:
And when the Medcyn as wax doth flowe,
Than uppon *Malgams* loke thou hyt throw.

And

7. And when all that together ys myxyd
Above thy Glasse well closyd make thy fyre,
And so contenew hyt tyll all be fyxid,
And well Fermented to desyre;
Than make *Projeccyon* after thy pleasure:
For that ys Medcyn than ech dele parfyt,
Thus must you Ferment both Red and Whyte.

8. For lyke as flower of Whete made into Past,
Requyreth Ferment whych Leven we call
Of Bred that yt may have the kyndly tast,
And becom Fode to Man and Woman most cordyall;
Ryght so thy Medcyn Ferment thou shall,
That yt may tast wyth the Ferment pure,
And all assays evermore endure.

9. And understond that ther be Ferments three,
Two be of Bodys in nature clene,
Whych must be altryd as I have told thee;
The thyrd most secret of whych I mene,
Ys the fyrst Erth to hys owne Water grene:
And therfore when the *Lyon* doth thurst,
Make hym drynke tyll hys Belly burst.

10. Of thys a Questyon yf I shold meve,
And aske of Workers what ys thys thyng,
Anon therby I sholde them preve;
Yf they had knowledge of our *Fermentyng*,
For many man spekyth wyth wondreng:
Of Robyn Hode, and of his Bow,
Whych never shot therin I trow.

But

11. But *Fermentacion* trew as I the tell
Ys of the Sowle wyth the Bodys incorporacyon,
Restoryng to hyt the kyndly smell;
Wyth tast and color by naturall conspyssacyon
Of thyngs dysseveryd, a dew redyntegracyon:
Wherby the Body of the Spryte takyth impression,
That eyther other may helpe to have ingression.

12. For lyke as the Bodys in ther compaccyon corporall
May not show out ther qualytes effectually
Untyll the tyme that they becom spyrituall:
No more may Spryts abyde wyth the Bodys stedfastly,
But they wyth them be fyrst confyxat proportionably:
For then the Body techyth the Spryt to suffer Fyer,
And the Spryt the Body to endure to thy desyre.

13. Therfore thy Gold wyth Gold thou must Ferment,
Wyth hys owne Water thyne Erth clenyd I mene
Not ells to say but Element wyth Element;
The Spryts of Lyfe only goyng betweene,
For lyke as an Adamand as thow hast sene:
Yern to hym draw, so doth our Erth by kynde
Draw downe to hym hys Sowle borne up wyth Wynd.

14. Wyth mynd therfore thy Sowle lede out and in,
Meng Gold wyth Gold, that is to say
Make Elements wyth Elements together ryn;
To tyme all Fyre they suffer may,
For Erth ys Ferment wythouten nay
To Water, and Water the Erth unto;
Our *Fermentacion* in thys wyse must be do.

Erth

15. Erth ys Gold, so ys the Sowle also,
Not Comyn but Owers thus Elementate,
And yet the Son therto must go,
That by our Whele yt may be alterate,
For so to Ferment yt must be preparat:
That hyt profoundly may joynyd be
Wyth other natur es as I seydto thee.

16. And whatsoever I have here seyd of Gold,
The same of Sylver I wyll thou understond,
That thou them Putresye and alter as I have told;
Ere thou thy Medcyn to Ferment take in hond,
Forsowth I cowde never fynde hym wythin *Englond*:
whych on thys wyse to Ferment cowde me teche
Wythout errour, by practyse or by speche.

17. Now of thys Chapter me nedyth to trete no more,
Syth I intend prolixite to eschew;
Remember well my words therfore,
Whych thou shalt preve by practys trew,
And *Son* and *Mone* loke thou renew:
That they may hold of the fyfth nature,
Then shall theyr Tynctures ever endure.

18. And yet a way there ys most excellent,
Belongyng unto another workyng,
A Water we make most redolent:
All Bodys to Oyle wherwyth we bryng,
Wyth whych our Medcyn we make floyng:
A Quyntessens thys Water we call
In man, whych helyth Dysesys all.

Bb But

19. But wyth thy Bace after my Doctryne preperat,
Whych ys our Calx, thys must be don;
For when our Bodys be so Calcenat,
That Water wyll to Oyle dyssolve them sone;
Make therfore Oyle of *Son* and *Mone*
Which ys *Ferment* most fragrant for to smell,
And so the 9th *Gate* ys Conquered of thys Castell.

Of Exaltation.

The tenth Gate.

1. PRocede we now to the Chapter of *Exaltacion*,
Of whych truly thou must have knowledge pure,
Full lyttyll yt ys dyfferent from *Sublymacyon*,
Yf thou conceve hym ryght I thee ensure:
Herto accordyth the holy Scrypture:
Chryste seyng thus, *Yf I exalted be,*
Then shall I draw all thyngs unto me.

2. Ower Medycyn yf we Exalt ryght so,
Hyt shall therby be Nobylyzate,
That must be done in manners two;
Fro tyme the parts be dysponsate,
Whych must be Crusyfyed and examynat:
And then contumulate both Man and Wyfe,
And after revyvyd by the Spyryts of Lyfe.

Than

3. Than up to Hevyn they must Exaltyd be,
Ther to be in Body and Sowle gloryfycate;
For thou must bryng them to such subtylyte,
That they assend together to be intronyzate,
In Clowds of clerenesse, to Angells consociate:
Then shall they draw as thou shalt se
All other Bodys to ther owne dygnyte.

4. Yf thou therfore thy Bodys wyll Exaltat,
Fyrst wyth the Spryts of Lyfe thou them augment,
Tyll tyme thy Erth be well subtylyate,
By naturall rectyfyyng of eche Element;
Hym up exaltyng into the Fyrmament:
Than much more presyose shall they be than Gold,
Because they of the Quyntessence do hold.

5. For when the Cold hath overcum the Hete,
Then into Water the Ayre shall turnyd be;
And so two contrarys together shall mete,
Tyll ether wyth other ryght well agre,
So into Ayre thy Water as I tell the;
When Hete of Cold hath gott domynacyon,
Shalbe convertyd by craft of *Cyrculacyon.*

6. And of the Fyer then Ayer have thou shall,
By losyng Putrefyyng and Sublymyng;
And Fyer thou hast of the Erth materyall:
Thyne Elements by craft thus dysseveryng,
Most specyally the Erth well Calcenyng:
And when they be eche on made pure,
Then do they hold all of the fyfth nature.

7. On thys wyse therfore make them to be Cyrculat,
Ech unto other exaltyng by and by,
And in one Glas do all thys surely sygylate,
Not wyth thy honds, but as I teche the naturally,
Fyer into Water then turne fyrst hardely;
For Fyer ys in Ayer wych ys in Water exystent,
And thys Conversyon accordyth to our entent.

8. Than ferthermore turne on thy Whele,
That into Erth thy Ayre convertyd be,
Whych wylbe don also ryght well:
For Ayre ys in Water beyng in the Erth trust me,
Then Water into Fyre contraryose in ther qualyte:
Sone turne thou may, for Water in Erth ys,
Whych ys in Fyer conversyon, true ys thys.

9. Thy Whele ys now nygh turnyd abowte,
Into Ayre turne Erth, whych ys the proper nest
Of other Elements ther ys no dowte,
For Erth in Fyre ys, whych in Ayre takyth rest,
Thys *Cyrculacyon* thou begyn must in the West:
Then forth into the Sowth tyll they exaltyd be,
Procede dewly as in the Fygure I have towght the.

10. In whych proces thou may clerly se,
From an extreame how to another thou may not go.
But by a mene, syth they in qualyte contraryose be;
And reson wyll forsoth that hyt be so,
As hete into cold wyth other contraryose mo:
Wythout theyr menys as moyst to hete and cold,
Examples suffycyent afore thys have I told.

Thus

11. Thus have I tawght the how for to make,
Of all thy Elements a parfyt *Cyrculacyon*,
And at thy Fygure example for to take,
How thou ſhalt make thys foreſayd *Exaltacyon*,
And of thy Medcyn in the Elements trew graduacyon:
Tyll hyt be brought to a quynaryte temperat,
And then thou haſt conqueryd the *Tenth Gate*.

OF MULTIPLICATION.

The eleventh Gate.

1. MUltyplycacyon now to declare I procede,
Whych ys by *Phyloſophers* in thys wyſe dyfynyd,
Augmentacyon yt ys of that *Elixer* indede,
In goodnes, in quantyte, both for Whyt and Rede,
Multyplycacyon ys therfore as they have ſeyd:
That thyng that doth Augment the Medcyns in ech degre,
In Color, in Odor, in Vertue, and alſo in Quantyte.

2. And why thou may thy Medcyn multeply,
Infynytly the cauſe forſoth ys thys.
For yt ys Fyer whych tyned wyll never dye:
Dwellyng wyth the as Fyer doth in houſys,
Of whych one ſparke may make more Fyers I wys;
As musk in Pygments, and other ſpycys mo,
In vertue multyplyeth and our Medcyn ryght ſo.

3. So he ys ryche the whych Fyer hath les or more,
Because he may so gretly Multeply;
And ryght so ryche ys he whych any parte hath in store
Of our *Elixers* whych be augmentable infynytly:
One way yf thou dyssolve our Powders dry,
And oft tymes of them make Congelacyon,
Of hyt in goodnes thou makyst then Augmentacyon.

4. The second way both in goodnes and in quantyte,
Hyt Multyplyeth by Iterat *Fermentacion*,
As in that Chapter I showyd playnly unto the,
By dyvers manners of naturall Operacyon,
And also in the Chapter of our *Cybacyon*:
Where thou may know how thou shalt Multeply
Thy Medycyn wyth *Mercury* Infynytly.

5. But and thou bothe wyll Loose and also Ferment,
Both more in quantyte and better wyll hyt be;
And in such wyse thou may that so augment,
That in thy Glas yt wyll grow lyke a Tre,
The *Tre of Hermes* namyd, seemly to se:
Of whych one Pepyn a thowsand wyll *Multyply*,
Yf thou can make thy *Projeccyon* wyttyly.

6. And lyke as Saffron when yt ys pulveryzate,
By lyttyll and lyttyll yf hyt in Lycour be
Temperyd, and then wyth mykyll more Lycour dylate;
Tyngyth much more of Lycour in quantyte, (se
Than beyng hole in hys owne grose nature: so shall thou
That our *Elixers* the more they be made thyn,
The farther in Tyncture sothfastly wyll renne.

Kepe

7. Kepe in thy Fyer therfore both evyn and morow,
Fro house to house that thou nede not to renne
Amonge thy Neyghbors, thy Fyer to sech or borow,
The more thou kepyst the more good shall thou wyn,
Multyplyyng ey more and morethy Glas wythin:
By fedyng wyth *Mercury* to thy lyvys end,
So shall thou have more than thou nedyst to spend.

8. Thys mater ys playne, I wyll no more
Wryte now therof, lat Reson the guyde;
Be never the bolder to Syn therfore,
But serve thy God the better at ech tyde;
And whylls that thou shall in thys lyfe abyde,
Bere thys in mynde, forget not I the pray,
As thou shalt apere before thy God at domys day.

9. Hys owne gret Gyfts thefore and hys Tresure,
Dyspose thou vertuosely, helpyng the poore at nede,
That in thys World to the thou may procure
Mercy and Grace with Hevenly blys to mede,
And pray devoutly to God that he the lede
In at thys eleventh *Gate* as he can best,
Sone after then thou shalt end thy conquest.

Of

Of Projection.
The twelfth Gate.

1. IN *Projeccyon* hyt ſhalbe provyd yf our practiſe be profy-
Of wch yt behovyth me the ſecrets here to meve; (table
Therfore yf thy Tyncture be ſure and not varyable,
By a lyttyll of thy Medcyn thus ſhall thou preve
Wyth Mettall or wyth Mercury as Pyche yt wyll cleve:
And Tynct in *Projeccyon* all Fyers to abyde,
And ſone yt wyll enter and ſpred hym full wyde.

2. But many for Ignorans doth mar that they made,
When on Mettalls unclenſyd *Projeccyon* they make,
For be cauſe of corrupcyon theyr Tynctures muſt vade;
Whych they wold not awey fyrſt fro the Bodys take,
Whych after *Projeccyon* be bryttyl, bloe, and blacke:
That thy Tyncture therfore may evermore laſt,
Uppon *Ferment* thy Medcyn loke fyrſt that thou caſt.

3. Then brottyl wyll thy *Ferment* as any glas be,
Uppon Bodys clenſyd and made very pure,
Caſt thy brottyll ſubſtance and ſone ſhall thou ſe,
That they ſhalbe curyoſely coleryd wyth Tyncture,
Whych at all aſſays for ever ſhall endure:
But at the Pſalmys of the Sawter example thou take
Profytable *Projeccyon* parfytly to make.

On

4. On *Fundamenta* cast fyrst thys *Psalme Nunc Dimittis*,
Uppon *Verba mea* then cast *Fundamenta* blyve;
Than *Verba mea* uppon *Diligam*, conseve me wyth thy wytts;
And *Diligam* on *Attende* yf thou lyst to thryve:
Thus make thou *Projeccyons* thre fowre or fyve,
Tyll the Tyncture of thy Medcyn begyn to decrese,
And then yt ys tyme of *Projeccyon* to cese.

5. By thys mysty talkyng I mene nothyng ells,
But that thou must cast fyrst the lesse on the more,
Incresyng ever the Number as wyse men the tells,
And kepe thou thys Secrett to thy selfe in store,
Be covetuose of connyng yt ys no burden sore:
For who that joyneth not the *Elixers* wyth Bodys made clene,
He wot not what sykerly *Projeccyon* doth mene.

6. Ten yf thou Multyply fyrst into ten,
One hundreth, that number wyll make sykerly;
Yf one hundreth into an hundreth be Multyplyed then,
Ten thousand ys that number counte hyt wyttyly,
Then into as much more ten thousand multyply:
That ys a thousand thousand, whych multyplyeth I wys,
Into as much more as a hundred myllyons ys.

7. That hundred myllyons beyng multyplyed lykewys,
Into ten thousand myllyons, that ys for to sey,
Makyth so grete a number I wote not what yt ys,
Thy number in *Projeccyon* thus Multyply alwey:
Now Chyld of thy curtesy for me thou pray;
Syth that I have told the our secretts all and some,
To whych I beseche God by Grace thou may com.

8. Now thow hast conqueryd the *twelve Gates*,
And all the Castell thou holdyst at wyll,
Kepe thy Secretts in store unto thy selve;
And the comaundements of God looke thou fulfull:
In fyer conteinue thy glas styll,
And Multeply thy Medcyns ay more and more,
For wyse men done sey *Store ys no sore*.

The end of the Twelve Gates.

THE RECAPITULATION.

1. FOr to bryng thys *Tretys* to a fynall end,
And brevely here for to conclude these Secretts all,
Dylygently loke thou, and to thy Fygure attend:
Whych doth in hyt conteyne these secrets grete & small,
And yf thou conceve both Theorycall and Practycall:
By Fygures, and by Colors, and by Scrypture playne,
Whych wyttely consevyd thou mayst not work in vayn.

2. Consyder fyrst the Latytude of thy Precyous *Stone*,
Begynnyng in the fyrst syde notyd in the West,
Where the *Red Man* and the *Whyte Woman* be made one,
Spowsyd wyth the Spryts of lyfe to lyve in love and rest,
Erth and Water equaly proportyond that ys best;
And one of the Erth ys good and of the Spryts thre,
Whych twelve to fowre also of the Erth may be.

Three

3. Thre of the Wyfe and one of the Man then must thou take,
And the lesse of the Spryts there be in thys dysponsation,
The rather thy *Calcynatyon* for certeyne shall thou make,
Then forth into the North procede by obscuratyon;
Of the *Red Man* and hys *Whyte Wyfe* callyd *Eclypsation*:
Losyng them and alteryng betyxt Wynter and Vere,
Into Water turnyng Erth darke and nothyng clere.

4. Fro thens by colors many one into the Est assends,
There shall the Mone be full apperyng by day lyght;
Then ys she passyd her Purgatory and course at an end;
There ys the uprysyng of the Son apperyng whyt and bryght,
There ys Somer after Vere, and day after nyght: (Ayre;
Than Erth and Water whych were so black be turnyd into
Than clouds of darknes be overblowyn & all aperyth faire.

5. And lyke as the West begynnyng was of the Practyse,
And the North the parfyt mene of profound Alteratyon,
So the Est after them the begynnyng of Speculacyon ys; (tion
But of thys course up in the Sowth the Son makyth Consumma-
Ther be thy Elements into Fyre turnyd by Cyrculacyon:
Then to wyn to thy desyre thou needst not be in dowte,
For the Whele of our *Phylosophy* thou hast turnyd abowte.

6. But yet ageyne turne abowte two tymys thy Whele,
In whych be comprehendyd all the Secretts of our *Phylosophy*,
In Chapters 12 made playne to the if thou conseve them well;
And all the Secretts by and by of our lower *Astonomye*,
How thou Calcin thy Bodys, parfit, dissolve, devide & putrefie:
Wyth parfyt knowledge of all the polys whych in our Hevyn
Shynyng with colors inexplycable never were gayer sene. (ben

7. And thys one Secrett conclusyonal know thou wythouten fayle,
Our *Red Man* teyneth not tyll he teynyd be;
Therfore yf thou lyst thy selfe by thy craft to avayle,
The Altytude of thy Bodys hyde & show out theyr profundyte,
In every of thy Materyalls dystroyyng the fyrst qualyte:
And secundary qualytes more gloryose repare in them anon
And in one Glas wyth one governaunce 4 Naturs turne into one.

8. Pale, and Black, wyth falce Citryne, unparfyt Whyte & Red,
Pekoks fethers in color gay, the Raynbow whych shall overgoe
The Spottyd Panther wyth the Lyon greene, the Crowys byll (bloe as lede;
These shall appere before the parfyt Whyte, & many other moe
Colors, and after the parfyt Whyt, Grey, and falce Citrine also:
And after all thys shall appere the blod Red invaryable,
Then hast thou a Medcyn of the thyrd order of hys owne (kynde Multyplycable.

6. Thow must devyde thy *Elixer* whyte into partyes two,
After thou rubify and into Glassys let hym be don,
If thou wylt have the *Elixers* both for *Son* and *Mone* do so;
Wyth *Mercury* then hem Multeply unto gret quantyte sone:
Yf thow at the begynnyng had not as much as wold into a spone:
Yet moght thou them so Multeply both the Whyte & Red,
That yf thou levyd a thousand yere they shold the stond in (stede.

10. Have thou recourse to thy Whele I councell the unto,
And stody tyll thou understond eche Chapter by and by,
Medyll with no falce Fantesys, Multeplyers, let them go,
Which wyll the flatter & falcely sey they are connyng in *Phyloso-* (*phye*,
Do as I byd the and then dyssolve these foreseyd Baces wyttely;
And turne hym into parfyt Oylys with our trew water ardent,
By Cyrculacion that must be don accordyng to our entent.

These

11. Thefe Oylys wyll fyx crude *Mercury* and convert Bodys all,
Into parfyt *Sol* and *Lune* when thou fhalt make *Projeccyon*,
That Oylyfh fubftance pure and fyx *Raymond Lully* dyd call
Hys *Bafylyske*, of whych he made never fo playne deteccyon,
Pray for me to God that I may be of hys eleccyon:
And that he wyll for one of hys on Domys Day me kene,
And graunt me in hys blys to reygne for ever wyth hym, *Amen.*

Gloria tibi Domine.

An Admonition, wherein the Author declareth his Erronious experiments.

1. AFter all thys I wyll thou underftonde,
For thy favegarde what I have done,
Many Experyments I have had in hond;
As I found wryten for Son and Mone,
Whych I wyll tell the reherfyng fone:
Begynnyng wyth Vermylion whych provyd nought,
And Mercury fublymyd whych I dere bought.

2. I made *Solucyons* full many a one,
Of Spyrytts, Ferments, Salts, Yerne and Steele;
Wenyng fo to make the *Phylofophers Stone*:
But fynally I loft eche dele,
After my Boks yet wrought I well;
Whych evermore untrew I provyd,
That made me oft full fore agrevyd.

3. Waters corrosyve and waters Ardent,
With which I wrought in divers wyse,
Many one I made but all was shent;
Eggs shells I calcenyd twise or thryse,
Oylys fro Calcys I made up-ryse;
And every Element fro other I did twyne,
But profyt found I ryght none therein.

4. Also I wrought in Sulphur and in Vitriall,
Whych folys doe call the *Grene Lyon*,
In Arsenike, in Orpement, fowle mot them fall;
In debili principio was myne Incepcyon:
Therefore was frawde in fyne the Conclusyon;
And I blew my thryft at the Cole,
My Clothys were bawdy, my Stomache was never hole.

5. Sal Armonyake and Sandever,
Sal Alkaly, sal Alembroke, sal Attinckarr,
Sal Tarter, sal Comyn, sal Geme most clere;
Sal Peter, sal Sode, of these beware;
Fro the odor of Quycksylver kepe the fare:
Medyll not wyth Mercury precipitate,
Nether wyth imparfyt Bodys rubyfycate.

6. I provyd Uryns, Eggs, Here, and Blod,
The Scalys of Yern whych Smethys do of smyte,
Æs Ust, and Crokefer whych dyd me never good:
The sowle of Saturne and also Marchasyte,
Lythage and Antemony not worth a myte:
Of whych gey Tyntures I made to shew,
Both Red and Whyte whych were untrew.

Oyle

7. Oyle of Lune and water wyth labour grett,
I made Calcynyng yt with salt precipytate,
And by hyt selfe with vyolent hett
Gryndyng with Vynegar tyll I was fatygate:
And also with a quantyte of Spyces acuate;
Uppon a Marble whych stode me oft in cost,
And Oyles with Corrosyves I made; but all was lost.

8. Many Amalgame dyd I make,
Wenyng to fix these to grett avayle,
And thereto Sulphur dyd I take;
Tarter Egges whyts, and the Oyle of the Snayle,
But ever of my purpose dyd I fayle:
For what for the more and what for the lesse,
Evermore somethyng wantyng there was.

9. Wyne, Mylke, Oyles, and Runnett,
The Slyme of Sterrs that falleth to the grownde,
Celydony and Secundynes wyth many moe yett,
In these I practysyd as in my books I found,
I wan ryght nought, but lost many a pownde;
Of Mercury and Mettalls I made Chrystall stones,
Wenyng that hyt had ben a worke for the nonys.

10. Thus I rostyd and boylyd as one of *Gebers* Cooks,
And oft tymes my wynnyng in the Asks I sought;
For I was dyscevyd wyth many falce Books
Wherby untrue thus truly I wrought:
But all such Experyments avaylyd me nought;
But brought me in danger and in combraunce,
By losse of my goods and other grevaunce.

For

11. For the love of our Lady such lewdnes eschue,
Medyll wyth no falshood whych never prevyd well;
Assay when thow wylt and thow shalt fynde me treue;
Wynn shalt thou nought but lose every dele,
Pence in thy Pauwkner fewe shalt thou feele:
In smokes and smells thow shalt have myckle wo,
That unnethe for syknes on Erth shalt thow go.

12. I never saw true worke treuly but one,
Of whych in thys tretys the trewth I have told.
Stody only therfore to make our *Stone*:
For therby may thow wyn both Sylver and Gold,
Uppon my wrytynge therfore to ground the be bold:
So shalt thow lose nought yf God be thy gyde,
Trust to my Doctryne and therby abyde.

13 Remember how Man ys most noble Creature,
In erths. Composycyon that ever God wrought,
In whom are the fowre Elements proportyonyd by nature:
A naturall Mercuryalyte whych cost ryght nought,
Out of hys myner by Arte yt must be brought;
For our Mettalls be nought ells but myners too,
Of our Soon and our Moone, wyse *Reymond* seyd so.

14. The clerenes of the *Moone* and of the *Soone*, bryght,
Into these two Myners desendyth secretly,
Howbeyt the cleernes be hyd fro thy syght:
By craft thou shalt make ytt to appere openly,
Thys hyd *Stone*, thys one thyng therfore putrefye:
Wash hym wyth hys owne broth tyll whyte he becoom,
Then Ferment hym wyttely, nowe here ys all and soom.

Now

Now to God Almyghty I thee Recommend,
Whych graunte the by Grace to knowe thys one thing,
For now ys thys *Treatys* brought to an end:
And God of hys Mercy to hys blysse us bryng,
Sanctus, Sanctus, Sanctus, where Angells do syng:
Praysyng without ceasynge hys gloriose Magestye,
Whych he in hys Kyngdome graunte us for to see.

An. Dom. 1471.

Explicit Alchimiæ Tractatus Philosophiæ,
Cujus Rypla George, *Canonicus*, *Auctor erat*;
Mille, quadringentis septuaginta unoq;
Annis qui scriptus compositusq; fuit.
Auctori lector præbe præce, quæso Iuvamen,
Illi purgamen leve post vitam ut sit Amen.

Englished.

Thus heere the *Tract of Alchimy* doth end,
Whych *(Tract)* was by *George Ripley* Chanon pen'd;
It was Composed, Writ, and Sign'd his owne,
In *Anno* twice Seav'n hundred seav'nty one:
Reader! Assist him, make it thy desire,
That after Lyfe he may have gentle Fire.

Amen.

LIBER PATRIS SAPIENTIAE.

THow that in thys Boke beginneth to rede, (spede:
Keepe well thys Councell the better schalt thow
Be thow in a place secret by thy selfe alone, (done.
That noe man see or here what thow schalt say or

2. Yet ere thow begyn to rede much, take thow good hede,
Wyth whom thow kepest company I councell thee indede;
Trust not thy freind too much, wheresoere thow goe,
For he that thow trustest best sometyme may be thye Foe.

3. And take hede to the words of the Fader of Wysdom,
How he techeth hys Sonne how he schould done;
To kepe hys presepts of bodely governance
And wyth hys Conyng he wyll the gretly advance.

4. And yf thow wylt not to hys wordys take hede,
Thow schalt stand here oft in gret feare and dred.
For he that hath a fore wytt he nedes not do amysse,
And he that doth Folly the Folly schalbe hys.

5. Now my dere *Sonne* be thow not a know
To Lerned nor to Leud, to Hygh nor to Low:
Neyther to Young nor Old, Rych nor Poore,
Unto them thow tech nothyng my Lore.

6 Also

6. Alſo to ſcuche men that hold themſelves wyſe;
And ſo forth to the foolys that glyde on the Ice:
They weene in grete Bokes ſchould be the *Art*
Of the Science of *Alchemy*, but they be not worth a fart.

7. Therefor my *Sonn* to thee thys *Science* I may well teach,
And yf thow wylt upon thy enemy be wreach;
Or to purchaſe or build any good thyng,
It ſchalbe to thy gret furtheryng.

8. Thys worthy *Scyence* of *Alchemy* if thow wylt it leare,
A lyttle mony out of thy purſe thow muſt forbeare;
To buy therewyth *Flos Florum* it is moſt worthieſt,
And to build well her Cabyn and her Neſt.

9. And if thow put out mony for any other thing,
It is to thy loſſe; and to thy great hindring:
Except yt be for thy workes naturall Foode,
Which is had out of Stone, Ayre and Wood.

10. And if thow have all thyngs wythin the growing,
Then thow needeſt not to buy any manner of thing,
That ſchould be to thys *Science* belonging,
But beware of thy ſelfe for feare of hanging.

11. For then thow and thys *Scyence* were for ever loſt,
If thow make thereof any manner of boaſt,
To any Man or Woman, Old or Young,
Beware of thy ſelfe for feare of diſcovering.

12. For if thow make any man privie
Of thy Councell, Rich or Needy,
Thow muſt ſo beware Sleeping or Waking,
For once ymagining of Money making.

13. For yf God ſends thee grace and underſtanding,
Wyth thys *Scyence* thow mayſt have good lyving:
But beware of ſpeach of Women liberall,
And of the voice and ſight of Children generall.

14. *Sonn* in thyne owne howse thow maist well gett
A good Morsell of meat thy mouth to sweet,
Both Pheasant, Partridge, Plover and Leveret,
Though thow cry yt not owte in the common Market.

15. Therefore kepe close of thy Tongue and of thy Hand,
From the Officers and Governours of the Land;
And from other men that they of thy Craft nothing know,
For in wytnes thereof they wyll thee hang and draw.

16. And thereof the People will the at Sessions indight,
And great Treason against the they wyll write;
Wythowt that the Kings grace be to thee more,
Thow schalt for ever in thys world be forlore.

17. Alsoe wythowt thow be sure of another thyng,
To purchase the Lycence of thy King:
For all manner of doubts thee schall betide,
The better thow maiste Worke, and both goe and ride.

18. Also another thing I schall thee lere,
The poore People take thow nothing deare,
But ever serve thy God alway at the b gynnyng,
And among the poore People the better schalbe thy livyng.

19. Now my *Chylde* to my precepts looke thow take hede,
Whatsoever fall after the better schall thow spede.
Better it ys to have a thyng, then for it to wish,
For when thow feelst a Sore tis hard for thee to get a Leech.

20. Now my deare *Son* to the I wyll declare,
More of thys Warke which schalbe thy welfaire;
If thow canst consider all my sayings,
For therewyth thow mayest finde a full precious thing.

21. And *Son* though thys Writing be made in Ryme,
Yet take thow thereat noe greate disdaine.
Till thow hast proved my words in deede and in thought,
I watt it well it schalbe set at nought.

22. There-

22. Therefor of all Bodyes and Spyrits more or lesse,
Mercury is called *Flos Florum* and worthiest Pryncesse:
For her Birth and marvelous dealing,
Sche ys most worthiest to have byne King.

23. For sche ys Erth and Water most heviest,
And sche will conjoyne wyth Fire and Aire most lyghtest;
And so forth wyth her love sche will run and flee,
For sche delighteth noe other game or glee.

24. Some say that of *Sulphur* and *Mercury* all Bodyes minerall
Ingendered in the Erth with divers Colours cladd: (are made,
By the vertue of Decoccion before Preperacion,
To the lykenes of every body Mynerall in ther fashion.

25. I will first begin wyth *Saturne* after other mens sayings,
How he ys ingendered in the Erth wyth unclene *Mercury* flying:
And of *Mercury* he ys most heviest wyth black Sulphury Erth
Save he ys soft of fusion, and hys Sulphur nothing fixed. (mixed,

26. *Iupiter* is a whyte Body made of pure *Mercury* outward,
And of clere *Sulphur* som what Erthly and white inward;
He ys in kynde softest and well in his fixation,
For he is almost fixt, but he lacketh Decoction.

27. *Mar's* ys a white Body most of unclene ☿ in the Erth y'made,
And he ys hardest of fusion with *Sulphur* Erthly cladd;
To blacknes and rednes he will soonest consume,
By heate or by corrosive when the Spirit beginneth to fume.

28. *Sol* is the purest, somwhat red, & is made of clene ☿ & *Sulphur*
Ingendered with clere red *Sulphur*, in the Erth well mixed, (fixed,
And therefor he ys without defalt and lacketh no degree;
For he ys almost hardest of Fusion and heviest in ponderossity.

29. *Venus* ys a Body more red of pure ☿ made in hys substance,
Most of red *Sulphur* and greene and therein is greate variance:
In the Erth ingendered with Corrosive and bitter substance,
Well fixed and hard of fusion, rude in governance.

30. *Mercury* ys a Body if he be with a Subſtance moved,
Mixing one kinde with his kinde, ſo ſchall he be loved;
One Spirit received wyth another, the which of them be maine,
Is cauſe of ingeneration of every body Mettalyne.

31. *Luna* ys a pure white Body of clene *Mercury* & *Sulphur* white
And ſche is a litle hard of fuſion & almoſt well fixed, (ingendered
And ſche is next cleaneſt in Tincture of whitenes,
Of Ponderoſity light, of *Iupiter* bearing his whitenes.

32. And ſoe after the Colour of that Erth ys Sulphuri and re-
Some men do ſay ys engendered every Mettall; (ceptuall,
But my *Son* the perfect worke of thys alteration,
I ſchall informe the true way of another faſhion.

33. Now have I declared the working of the Bodies Mynerall,
Whereof they be ingendered after other mens ſayings over all;
And as in place of the Erth one Body was fully wrought,
Soe muſt the artificiall Medicine, be or elſe it ys nought.

34. Now will I declare the worthines of *Mercury* in ſpeciall,
How ſche ys the notableſt Spirit that ys mynerall,
Moſt marvelous in working and in degree,
Sche ys called the Matter principalleſt of the three.

35. Alſo ſche ys very ſubtile in many things artificiall,
Sche will both give and take Tincture moſt ſpeciall,
To hym or of hym that ſche loveth moſt beſt,
In ſpeciall when ſche ys warmed in her Neſt.

36. My Son *Mercury* ys called the mightieſt *Flos florum*,
And moſt royall, and richeſt of all *Singulorum*;
Sche ys very Patron and Princes moſt royall,
And ſche ys very Mother of every Mettall.

37. Sche ys Vegitable, Animalle and Minerall,
Sche ys Foure in kinde, and One in generall:
Sche ys Erth, Aire, Water and Fyre,
Among all other ſche hath no Peere.

38. Sche

38. Sche kylleth and slayeth, and also doth calcine
Sche dyeth, and also doth sche live againe;
Sche giveth lyfe and also ingression,
For joyntly sche ys three in one.

39. Sche ys a very frendly mixar,
The progeneration of a greate *Elixar*:
Sche ys both Body Soule and Spirite,
In Colour very red, black and white.

40. Many be the wooers that hang on her tayle,
But sche will not with them I'deale;
They would her wedd against her will,
With foemen that liken her full ill.

41. Sche will deale with no manner of wight,
But with her Husband as it ys greate right:
With him sche will beare much fruite,
For he ys by nature of her selfe same sute.

42. My *Son* of hem Fooles have much dispight,
And therin such Fooles loose their light:
For sometymes he ys darke, and sometymes bright,
For he ys lyke no other wight.

43. For if they have their kynde ingendering,
Their naturall foode and good keeping,
They schall increase frute by dene,
Very red and white, King and Queene.

44. My *Son* in thys *Scyence* I doe deny,
All things that be discording truly,
All manner of Salts I doe defie,
And all manner of Sulphurs in waters of Corrosie.

45. Also Alloome, Vitriall, Auripigmentum and Haire,
Gold, Silver, Alkaly and Sandiver;
Honey, Wax, and Oyles or Calx else,
Gumms, Galls, and also Egg shells.

46. Also

46. Alſo I defie Antimony, Berrall, and Chriſtall,
Roſin, Pitch, alſo Amber, Jett and Corrall ;
Hearbs, Dated Stones, Marble, or Tinglas,
If there come any of all theſe it ys the worſe.

47. Alſo Berrills, Gotts Hornes, and Alome plome,
Good with them will none be done ;
All things that diſcordeth from Mettall,
It ys contrary to thys worke in generall.

48. My *Son* many fooles to me have ſought,
But they and I accord right nought ;
I leave them there as I them finde,
And as Fooles I make them blinde.

49. For whych *Mercury* they have errd full ſore
And then when they had they could doe no more,
Therefor in *Phyloſophers* ſche bear'th the floower,
For ſche ys King, Prince, and Emperour.

50. Yet my deare *Son* be thow not a knowne
To Learned, nor to Lewde, to High, nor to Low ;
That thys worke ſtandeth by *Mercury* and in her fire,
Her owne ſpeciall Love both life and deare.

51. For he ys her Son, ſche ys hys Fright,
In whome ſche worketh all her myght :
He ys her Son, ſche ys hys Mother,
Sche loveth him peramore and no other.

52. In *Sol*, and *Lune*, in her meeting ys all love,
For of *Mercury* only ys all her behove,
And with them ſche worketh all her might,
Bnt they may never increaſe on fright.

53. Therefor it ys poſſible to caſt a Projection pure,
Upon a Million to make a perfect Body of tincture :
Wyth Medicine of Spirits well joyned and fixed,
It ſchall not be perceived where it ys well mixed.

54. And

54. And therefor if there com Silver or Gold in at thy Gate,
The which men use in Aoyne or in common Plate;
I sweare by God that all thys world hath wrought,
All thy labour and warke schall turne to nought.

55. For with what Mettall soever that *Mercury* be joyned,
Because of her Coldnes and Moistnes sche ys acloyd:
Put them never so close togeder sche will fume anon,
And when they come into the fire sche wil sone be gone.

56. Therefore *Mercury* hath a Lover that passeth them
A thousandfold, who so will him ken
And he ys her Lover and her Leman sweete,
And so hys Councell sche will keepe.

57. Both in hys Chamber and also in hys Bedd,
Also alive and when they byne dead;
Seeke yee forth fooles as ʃe have sought,
For in all other things finde yee right nought.

58. Now my deare *Son* to thee I will indight,
The truth in word and deede I will write:
How that a precious *Stone* shalbe made,
Thee to rejoyce and make thee full glad.

59. As I said in the 32. Chapter unto my Conclusion,
How I schould informe the truth after another fashion,
And to performe thys *Scyence* both in word and deede,
In making of our Medicine God must us speede.

60. The which ys called the greate *Elixer*,
And ys verily made with a stronge mixar;
The which is a Stone very Minerall,
And thow maist him well gett ever all.

61. My *Son* thow schalt take to *Mercury* no other thing,
But Erth that's heavy and hard and stiff standing:
The which in himselfe ys derke bright dry and cold,
To joyne them togeder thow maist be full bold.

62. One of them to 10 parts of that Water running most heaviest
And they schalbe both one, and to thy warke most mightiest:
Then hast thow Man and Woman togeder brought,
The which ys done by greate love in a thought.

63. The which two be both Spirits, & one Body most heaviest,
When they be in your Chamber and bed joyned in the Element
The which ys more bigger, and bigger hott and dry, (lightest,
And therein they will both kiss togeder & neither weepe nor cry.

64. For when Erth and Water ys well mixed,
By the vertue of the lightest Element well hardned and fixed:
For before that time they be Water running both,
And then schall turne to fix body be they never so loath.

65. For in theyr bed they schall make a perpetuall Conjunction,
After the feeding of the light Element and of their proportion;
Soe schould they be decoct, having the parfeit fixascion,
In the likenes of a body in fusion having hys fashion.

66. But at the first in their Bed they may indure no greate heate,
Soe as they may well labour in their Bed for sweate:
Att the first if there be in their Chamber overmuch red Colour,
Hastily going thereto will cause greate Dolour.

67. For in their first Nest they schould be both water running,
And because of heate they schould be ever drying.
And so therein become a subtill dry Substance,
The which warke schall thee greately avaunce.

68. Therefor their Nest must be made of a strong kinde,
Of the most hardest and cleerest Body, that they not out winde;
For if it so be that their Chamber or Nest begin to breake,
Anon out thereof they will begin to Creake.

69. And then ys all thy warke and thy greate labour lost,
Then thou maist begin againe upon a new cost,
And so thow mayst not be negligent and hasty, but of the bed be
Without it be hard stuff and cleere it will not indure. (sure,

70. And

70. And if thow wil at the firſt hand give ſuddaine heate,
It will unto thy Warke be nothing meete;
And if thow let him have any ſuddaine greate Cold,
All thys ſchall breke thy warke, then art thow to bold.

71. Let their Neſt be ſomewhat large with a broade rouſe,
And therein they ſchall abide if it be ſtrong and cloſe above;
And in proportion put thereto nothing more nor leſſe,
But as ys ſayd before if thow doe yt ys the worſe.

72. Alſo from the beds head there muſt riſe a highe Spoute,
And another almoſt downe to the bottome that the Spirit go not (out;
For thou muſt ſave the flyers that ſwim into the upper place,
For they may hereafter ingender a body as well as the other in (ſpace.

73. Alſo be ſure that thow put in their Bed no other thing,
Then thereof thow ſchalt have no greate winnyng,
If thow do thys it ſchall be to thee for the beſt
To keepe them cloſe from flying and warme in their Neſt.

74. Firſt with ſoft fyre her Neſt muſt be warmed,
With a litle bigger Fyre with overmuch they ſchalbe harmed,
Under thy Chamber flowre meaſure thy Fyre with tyme,
Then commeth the reward, Gold and Silver fine.

75. After the quantity ſpace and tyme muſt be had,
For to deale togeder they be in their dealing glad.
And how long ſpace and tyme I cannot well ſay,
That they in their Chamber and Neſt wilbe in ſport and play.

76. Behold the uppermoſt of their Neſt what there commeth (out,
The ſweting of their Bodys labouring round aboute,
And when they have played and ſweate and laboured ſo ſore,
They wilbe ſtill, and neither labour nor ſweate any more.

77. Then let them coole eaſily, and draw their breath,
And then there ſchalbe ſome above and ſome beneath:
There thou ſchalt ſee a Stone as it were grey pouther,
Which ſchalbe to the a ryght greate wonder.

78. Then take them out of their Chamber and Bed anon,
And lay them upon a Marble ſtone and breake them thereon:
And looke what thow haſt in of Colour and Ponderoſity,
Put to him as much of *Flos florum* greateſt in dignity.

79. That ys the ſame Spirit that thow hadſt before,
And ſo medle them togeder and leare them the ſame lore;
Altogeder in another Bed and in their Chamber they muſt be,
For a marvelous warke thereof thow ſchalt underſtand and ſee.

80. And thus ſo oft thow muſt Multiplie thy Warke,
To aſcend and deſcend into the Aire as doth the Larke;
For when the Larke ys weary above in hys ſtound,
Anon he falleth right downe to the ground.

81. Behold well their Body, and to their head lay thine Eare,
And harken thow well what warke they make there:
If they begin to ſing any manner of voyce,
Give them more heate till thow heare no noyce.

82. And thus give them more heate in their Chamber and Bed.
Till thou heareſt no manner of noyſe rumbling to nor fro: (alſo,
And thus continue in their Bed in their ſporting playes,
After the quantity thereof continue ſo many dayes.

83. When their play and wreſtling ys all well done,
In their voyce ſinging and crying and ſweating up and downe;
Give their Chamber bigger heate till their Neſt be red,
And ſo bring them downe low and have no feare nor dread.

84. For thus w . n heate they ſchalbe brought full low,
That they ſchall in their Bed ne cry nor crow,
But as a Body lye ſtill downe in their Bed,
In their owne liknes as they were bodyes dead.

85. Of Grey and White ys all hys cheife Colour,
For then he ys paſt all hys greate Dolour:
I ſweare by Almighty God that all hath wrought,
Thow haſt found out that many other Men hath ſought.

86. Then

86. Then take thow hym out of hys Cchamber and Bed,
And thow ſchalt then finde a fixt Body as he were dead;
Keepe thow hym cloſe and ſecretly within thy place,
And thanke Almighty God of hys grace.

(ſought
87. Now my *Son* before thys, after thys *Science* I have right well
And thus to thee I have the White *Elixer* parfetly wrought;
And if thow wilt of the Red *Elixer* parfetly underſtand,
Thow muſt take ſuch another warke in hand.

88. My *Son* whan thow haſt wrought more upon more,
Dubling each time as I ſaid before;
Make thow what thow wilt of Red ſubſtance,
As I did the White warke in manner of Governance.

89. Then thow muſt take the Red Stone that ys all ponder,
And lay on a Mable Stone and breake him aſunder;
And to medle him with the white Spirit and Water cleere,
And ſo put him in hys Bed and Chamber in the Fire.

90. And ſo in hys Chamb. & in hys Bed, he muſt all thys while be
Till thow haſt turn'd and broght him to another manner of glee:
Thys Red *Elixer* if thow wilt open worke heare,
Thys manner of Schoole thow muſt right well leare.

91. Thow muſt hang him in his Chamber with red Colour,
Till he be fixed and brought from hys great Dolour:
Then of thys worthy warke be not thow agaſt,
For in the warke all the worſt ys paſt.

92. And ſo in hys fiery Neſt and Chamber let him be ſure,
For the longer he be in, the better ſchalbe hys tincture;
Soe that he runn not like blood overcoming hys fuſion,
Then haſt thow parfectly thys worke in concluſion.

93. Thus he muſt continue in thys greate heate of Firing,
Till he be full fixed that he be not running nor flying:
Then he will give tincture without Number running like wax,
Unto hys like of fuſion he will both joyne and mix.

94. And yf thy Warke be thus well guided and so forth led.
Then hast thow in thy Warke right well and wittily sped:
For if thow do otherwise then I have thee tould,
In the adventure of thy warke thow maist be to bold.

95. For if thow warke by good measure and parfect tyme,
Thow schalt have very good Gold and Silver fine;
Than schalt thow be richer in thy self than any King,
Wythowt he labour the *Science* and have the same thing.

96. Now my deare *Son* I schall teach thee how to cast a Projecti-
Therein lyeth all the greate prafetnes with the Conclusion: (on,
To leade an imparfect Body to hys greate parfectnesse,
In joyning that like to hys like thow standest in no distres.

97. For when thow hast joyned the milke to the Bodyes dry,
Than hast thow the White and Red *Elixer* truly:
The which ys a Marvilous and very precious Stone,
For therein lieth in thys *Science* all the worke upon.

98. In thys *Science* these Stones be in themselves so precious,
That in their working and nature they be marvelous:
To schew thee the greate vertue furthermore I will declare,
That if thow canst with thys manner of working well fare.

99. First thow must take of that Body which ys next *Sol* in per-
And of his colour toward in ponderosity & proportion: (fection,
Being soluble as it were cleere blood running,
In the hot Element yt ys alwayes lightest and fleeting.

100. Then take parte of the Red *Elixer* that ys the precious
And cast him upon that body that ys blood ronning anon: (Stone
And whan thow hast thus parfectly thys warke wrought,
It schalbe turned into parfect *Sol* with litle labour or nought.

101. On the same wise do for *Luna* that is in the Colour so white,
In joyning with that body that is schining and somewhat light;
In the same proportion cast him the very white Stone,
And then ys all thy greatest warke both made and done.

102. Than

102. Than hast thow both the Red warke and the White,
Therefor blessed be that tyme both day and night:
For thys warke that standeth by greate vertue and love,
Thow must thanke Almighty God in heaven above.

103. *Sonn* in the 21. Chapter there write I a full true Rime,
That ys to say unto thys warke thow have no greate disdaine;
Till thow have proved my words in deede and thought,
I know it well thys *Science* schalbe set at nought.

104. My *Son* to these last precepts looke thow take good hede
For better 'tys to have then to wish for in time of neede:
For who so ys bold in time to a Freind to breake,
He that ys thy Freind may be thy Fo and hys emnity wreake.

105. And therefor my *Son* I schall give thee a greate charge,
In uttering of speech be thow not to large;
To tell every man what thow hast in Silver or Gold,
For to have it from thee many men wilbe right bold.

106. Also use not to revill or ryott that schould exceede
To thy bodily health, the better schalt thow speede;
Use temperate dyet and temperate travell,
For when Physitian thee fayleth thys schall thee availe.

107. And leave all blind warkes that thow hast seene or heard of
Or proved by Sublimations, Preperations, Distillations, or Disso-
Of such manner of things greate Bokes do greatly specifie (lutions;
And all those contrary sayings in this Craft I do plainly deny.
(Conclusions

108. Also my *Son* remember how thow art mortall,
Abiding but a while in thys World which ys terrestriall:
Thow wottest not how long nor hence how soone,
That death schall thee visitt and unto thee Come.

109. And remember thee well at thy departing,
Whome thow lovedst and trustedst best old and young:
Make him thine Heire and most of thy Councell,
And give him thy Cunning or thy Boke every deale.

110. But

110 But beware of flattering and glosing People,
Of Boasters and Crackers for they will thee beguile:
Of thy precious Cunning behinde or beforne,
And when they have their intent they will give thee a scorne.

111. Therefor make no Man of thy Councell rude nor rustie,
But him that thow knowest both true and trustie;
In ryding and going sleeping and waking,
Both in word and deede and in hys disposing.

112. Also in thy owne Chamber looke thow be secret,
That thy dores and windowes be close shet;
For some wyll come and looke in every Corner,
And anon they will aske what thow makest there.

113. And therefore a good excuse must soone be had,
Or else thow schalt verily wine for to run madd;
Say thow labourest sore both sleeping and waking,
To the perfect way of strange Colours making.

114. As yt be sure Bice, Vermillion, Aurum Musicum, & others (moe
Or else with some people thow schalt never have a doe;
Also thereof thow must have many samples to schew,
Or else they that harmes thinke will say so.

115. Also furthermore I give thee right good warning,
Beware of thy warking and also of thy uttering,
For the examination of the People better or worse,
Ere thow have for thy warke thy mony in thy purse.

116. Therefor take heede my *Son* unto these Chapters sixscore
And all manner of things said what schould be don before:
For in *Astronomy* thow must have right good feeling,
Or else in thys Boke thow schalt have simple believing.

117. For thow must know well of seaven principle Characters,
To what Bodyes in heaven moving that they be likned in those (figures
And to understand their properties and their Conditions,
In Colours, qualities, softnes, hardnes, & in their proper fashions.

118. Now

118. Now *Son* to thee that underſtandeſt parfection & Sciences
Whether it be Speculative or Pracktick to my ſentences:
In thys *Science* and labour I thinke it greate ruthe,
Therefore I write to thee very truth.

119. And to thee that underſtandeſt no parfection nor practike
In no concluſion proved that ſchould be to hys warke like,
By Almighty God that all thys world hath wrought,
I have ſaid and performed to thee right nought.

120. Therefore my *Son* before that thow thys Boke begin,
Underſtand wiſely in thys what ys written therein:
For if thow canſt not finde by thys Boke neither *Sol* nor *Moyne*,
Then go forth and ſeeke thow further as other fooles have done.

Explicit Liber dictus Pater Sapientiæ.

Vaughan
sculp.

IN the name of the holy Triniti,
Now send us grase, so hit be:
Fyrst God made both Angel and Heaven,
Na alleso the World wyth Planets seaven;
Man and Woman wyth gret sensewalite,
Sum of estate, and other in hyr degree;
Both Best and Worme for in the grown crepe,
Everyech in hys kynd to receve hys mete.
Egles and Fowles in the Eyre don fle,
And swemynge of Fycheys also in the See:
Wyth vygital moyster and of the red Grap,
And alleso of the whyte hos can hym take:
Alle meneral thyng that growyth in grownd,
Sum to encrese and sum to make an end:
Alle thes bryngeth now to awre howse,
The mighiti Ston that ys so precius,
Thys ryche Reby, that ston of pryce,
The whych wosse send owt of Paradyce:
Thus made the gret God of heven,
Whych alle ben rewled under Planets seaven:
God send us parte of thys secrete,
And of that heven that ys sweet.

AMEN.

Yfe thow wilt thys warke begyn,
Than schrevy the clene of alle thy Seyne:
Contryte in hert wyth alle thy thowght,
And ever thenke on hym that the der bowght.
Satisfaction thow make wyth alle thy myght,
Than thre fayre flowers thow hast in syght;
Yet nedeth the mor to thy conclesyon,
Take thow good hede nowe to thys lessen;
Thow must have Grase, Nature, *and* Resen,
Spekelatif, *and* Coning, *wyth good Condition:*
Yet thow must have more now herto,
Experience, *wyth* Pracktik, Prudent *also;*
Patient *that thow be, and* Holi in Lysyngs,
Thenke thow on thys in thy beginings;
Thes fowrtyn Hestys as I the saye,
Ever kepe thow man both nyght and day,
Of thy desyres thow mayst not mysse,
And alleso of heven that swezt bless.

HERMES BIRD.

PRoblemis of olde likenes and ſuguris,
Wych proved byn fructuos of ſentens;
And have auctorite grounded in Scripture,
By reſemblaunce of notabil apperence;
Wych moralites concludyng on prudence:
Lyke as the Bibel reherſeth be wryting,
How Trees ſum tyme cheſe hemſelfe a Kyng.

2. Firſt in theyre choiſe they namyd the Olyve
To regne among hem, *Iudicium* doth expres;
But he hymſelfe can excuſe hym blyve,
He myght not forſake hys fatnes:
Nor the Fig-tree hys amorus ſwetnes:
Nor the Vyne hys holſum freſche terrage:
Wych gyveth comfort to all manner of age.

3. And semblealbil *Poyetes laureat*,
By derke parables full convenient;
Feyncin that Birdis and Bests of estate
As rial Egeles and Lyons by assent,
Sent owte writtes to holde a Parlement;
And made degrees brevely for to sey,
Sum to have Lordschip and sum to Obey.

4. Egeles in the Eyre hyghest take theyre flyght,
Power of Lyons on the grownde ys sene;
Cedre amonge Trees highest ys of sight,
And the Laurer of nature ys ever grene,
Of flowris all Florra Goddes and Quene:
Thus of all thyng ther byn diversites,
Sum of estate and sum of lower degres.

5. *Poyetys* write wonderfull lyknes,
And Covert kepe hemselfe full clos;
They take Bestes and Fowles to witnes:
Of whos feynyng Fabelis furst a ros,
And here I cast unto my purpos,
Owte of the *Frensche* a tale to transcelate,
Whych in a Pamphlet I red and saw as I sate.

6. Thys Tale wych y make of mencion,
In gros reherseth playnely to declare,
Thre Proverbys payed for raunsome
Of a fayre *Byrde* that was take in a snare,
Wonder desirus to scape owte of hir care:
Of myne Auctor followyng the prosses,
So as it fel in Order y schall expres.

7. Whilom ther was in a small vilage,
As my Auctor maketh rehersal;
A *Chorle* the wich had lust and gret corage,
Within hymselfe by hys deligent travel,
To aray hys Garden with notabil reparel:
Of lenght and brede y lyche square and long,
Heggyd and dychyd to make yt sure and strong.

8. All

8. All the Aleys made playne with Sande,
Benches coverid with new Turves grene,
Set Erbes with Condites at the ende;
That wellid up agen the Sun ſchene,
Lyke Silver ſtremys as any criſtal clene:
The burbeſy Waves up ther on boylyng,
Rownde as Beral theyr bemys owte chedyng.

9. Mides the Garden ſtode a freſh Lawrer,
Ther on a *Byrde* ſyngyng both day and nyght;
With ſhinyng federis brighter then Gold weer,
Wych wyth hir ſong made hevy hertis lyght;
For to behold hit was an hevenly ſyght:
How towerd evyn and in the dawnyng,
Sche dyd her payne moſt ameus to ſyng.

10. Eſperus enforced hyr corage,
Towerd evyn when Phebus went to neſt;
Amonges the braunches to hir avauntage:
To ſyng hir complyn as yt was beſt,
And at the ryſyng to the Quene Alceſt
To ſyng ageyne as hit was to hir dew,
Erly on the morow the day-ſter to ſalew.

11. Hit was a very hevenly melody,
Evyn and Morne to her the *Byrd* ſong;
And the ſote ſugeryd Armony:
Of uncoud Warbelis and twenes drew along,
That al the Garden of the noyſe rong:
Tyll on a morow that Tytan ſchone ful cler,
The *Byrd* was trapped and cawt in a Panter.

12. The *Chorle* was glad that he thys *Byrd* hath take
Mere of cher loke and of viſage:
And in all haſt he caſt for to make
Within hys howſe a lytil prati Cage,
And with hir ſong to rejoyce hys corage:
And at the laſt the ſely *Byrd* abrayde,
And ſobirly to the *Chorle* ſche ſayde:

13. I

13. I am now take and stond under daunger,
Hold streyte that y may not fle;
Adew my song and al my notes cler,
Now that y have lost my liberte,
Now y am thrall and sumtyme was fre:
And trust wel y stand in distres,
Y can nat syng ne make no gladnes.

14. And thogh my Cage forged were of Gold
And the penacles of Beral and Cristal:
Y remember a *Proverbe* sayde of olde;
Who lisit hys fredom in sooth he ys in thral,
For me had laver upon a branche smale,
Merle to syng amonge the wodis grene,
Than in a Cage of Golde bryght and chene.

15. Songe and Presun have non acordaunce,
Trowys thow y wyl syng in Presun,
Song procedet of joy and plesaunce;
And Presun causeth deth and destruction,
Ryngyng of Feteris maketh no mere sown;
Or how schoulde he be glad and jocownde,
Ageyn hys wil that lyth in cheynys bownde.

16. What avayleth a Lyon to be a Kyng of Bestes
Fast schut in a Tower of ston alone;
Or an Egell under stryte cheynys,
Called also the Kyng of Fowlys everichon,
Fy on Lordschyp whan Liberte ys gon:
Answer herto and hit nat a start,
Who syngeth mere that syngeth not with hert.

17. If thow wilt rejoyce the of my syngyng,
Let me go fleen fre fro dawnger:
And every day in the mornyng
Y wyll repayre to thy Lawrer,
And fresshely to syng with notis cler;
Under thi Chaumber or afore thy Hal,
Every season when thow lyst me cal.

18 To

18. To be schut and pyned under drede,
No thyng acordyng to my nature:
Though I were fed with Mylke and Wastelbrede;
And swete Crudis brought to my pasture,
Yet had y lever do m y bese cure:
Erly in the morow to shrape in the Vale,
To fynde my dener amongs the Wormys smale.

19. The Laborer ys gladder at hys Plough,
Erly on the morow to fede hym on bakon:
Then sum ben that have tresour y nowgh;
And of al deyntes plente and foyson;
And no fredom with hys pocession;
To go at large but as Bere at the stake,
To pas hys bondes but yf he leve take.

20. Take thys answer ful for conclusion,
To synge in prison thow schalt not me constreyne:
Tyll y have fredom in woddis up and downe:
To fle at large on bowys both rough and plaine,
And of reson thow schuldest not disdeyn:
Of my desyre but laugh and have good game,
But who ys a Chorle wold every man wer the same.

21. Well quod the *Chorle* sith hit woll not be,
That y desyre by my talkyng;
Magre thy wyll thow schalt chese on of thre:
Within a Cage merele to syng,
Or to the Kychyn y schall thy bode brynge:
Pul thy federis that byn so bryght and clere,
And after rost or bake the to my dynere.

22. Then quod the *Byrde* to resson y sey not ney,
Towchyng my song a ful answer thow hast:
And when my federis pulled byn awey,
If y be rosted or bake in a past,
Thow schalt of me have a smal repaste:
But yf thow wylt werke by my councel,
Thow mayst by me have a gret avayle.

Gg 23. If

23. If thow wolt to my rede assent,
And suffer me go frele fro Preson:
Witowte raunsom or any oder rent;
Y schall the gyf a notabil grete gwerdon,
The thre grete Wysdomys acordyng to reson;
Mor of valew, take hede what y profer,
Than al the Gold that ys shet in thy Cofer.

24. Trust me wel y schal the not deceyve.
Well quod the *Chorle* tel and let se:
Nay quod the *Byrde* a forne conseyve;
Who schal teche of Reson he most go fre,
Hit fitteth a Master to have hys Liberte:
And at large to teche hys lesson,
Hafe me not suspecte y mene no treson.

25. Wel quod the *Chorle* y holde me content,
Y trust the promys which thow hast made to me;
The *Byrde* fle forth the *Chorle* was of sent:
And toke hys flight up to the Lawrer tre,
Then thought sche thus now that y stand fre:
With snaris panters y cast not al my lyve,
Nor wyth no lyme twygges no mor to strive.

26. He ys a Fole that schaped ys daungere,
That broke hys feteris and fled ys fro Preson,
For to resort agene: for brente childe dreds fyre:
Eche man bewar of Wisdom and reson,
Of suger strawed that hideth false poyson;
Ther ys no venom so perilus in scherpnes,
As whan yt hath triakcle of lyknes.

27. Who dredeth no perell in perell he schal falle,
Smothe Watres byn of sithes depe:
The Quayle pipe can most falsely calle;
Tyl the Quayle under the net doth crepe;
A bleryed Fowler trust not thogh he wepe:
Exchew hys thumbe, of weping take no hede,
That smale Byrdys can nyp by the hede.

28 And

28. And now that y ſuch daunger am ſcaped,
Y wyl bewar and afore provide:
That of no Fowlar y wil no more be Japed,
From theyre lyme twygges to fly far aſyde,
There perel ys perel to abyde:
Com ner thow *Chorle*, take hede to my ſpeche;
Of thre Wyſdomys that y ſchal the teche.

29. Yef not of Wyſdom to haſty credens,
To every Tale nor eche tydyng:
But conſyder of Reſon and Prudens;
Among Talys ys many a grete leſyng,
Haſty credens hath cawſed grete hynderyng:
Report of talis and tydyngys broght up new,
Maketh many a man ful on trew.

30. For on party take thys for my Raunſom,
Lerne the ſecond grownded of ſcripture:
Deſyre thow not by no condicion
Thyng that ys ympoſſybyl to recure,
Worldly deſyres ſtante alle in a venture:
And who deſyreth to ſoare hygh a lofte,
Oft tyme by ſoden turne he falleth on ſofte.

31. The thyrd is thys, bewar both even and morrow,
Forget yt nought but lerne thys of me:
For Treſor loſt, make never to grete Sorrow;
Wych in no wyſe may not recovered be,
For who that taketh ſorrow for loſſ in that degree:
Reken fyrſt hys loſſe, and after reken hys peyne,
Of one ſorrow he maketh Sorrowys tweyne.

32. Aftur thys Leſſon the *Byrde* began a ſonge,
Of hyr aſcape gretely rejoycyng:
And ſche remembred hyr alleſo of the wronge
Don by the *Chorle*, fyrſt at hyr takyng,
And of the affray, and of hyr impreſonyng:
Glad that ſche was at large and owte of drede,
Seyde unto hym hoveryng above hys hede,

 33. Thow

33. Thow were quod ſche a very natural Fole
To ſuffer me departe of thy lewdnes:
Thow owthtys of right to complaine and make dole,
And in thy hert have grete hevenes,
That thow haſt loſt ſo paſſyng grete riches:
Wych myght ſufficc by valew in rekeyng
To pay the raunſom of a myghty Kyng.

34. Ther ys a *Stone* wych ys called *Jagownce*,
Of olde engendered within myne entrayle:
Wych of fyne Golde poyſeth a grete unce;
Setryne of Colors lyke Garnetis of entayle,
Wych makyth men victorius in batayle;
And who that bereth on hym thys *Stone*,
Ys ful aſured ageyne hys mortal Fone.

35. Who that hath thys in poſceſſion,
Schal ſuffer no Povert ne non Indygens:
But of Treſour have plente and foyſon,
And every Man ſchal don hym reverence,
And non Enemy ſchal don hym non offence;
But fro thi hondes now that I am gone,
Pleyne gyf thow wilt for thy parte ys none.

36. As y the abrayde her before,
Of a ſtone now that I had:
The wych now thow haſt forlore;
Be alle reſon thow ſchuldys ben ſad,
And in thi hert nothyng glad:
Now *Chorle* y the tel in my device,
I was eyred and bred in ſwite Paradyce.

37. Now mo namys y ſchal the tel,
Of my ſtone that y cal *Jagownce*:
And of hys vertuis with hys ſmel;
That ben ſo ſwete and ſo oleferus,
Wyth *Ennock* and *Ely* hath be my ſervis:
My ſwete ſonge that ſowndeth ſo ſcherpe,
Wyth Angelles voyſe that paſſeth eny harpe.

38. The

38. The nigrum deamond that ys in Morienis sees.
And the white Charbonkkel that rolleth in wave;
The setryne Reby of ryche degrees:
That passeth the stonys of comen sawe,
In the Lapidery ys grown by olde lawe;
He passeth all stonys that ys under hevyn,
After the cowrse of kynde by the Planets sevyn.

39. Hyt ys for none *Chorle* to have schuch tresour,
That exsedeth alle *Stonys* in the lapidery:
And of alle vertuis he bereth the flowr,
Wyth all joy and grace yt maketh man mery,
That in thys worlde schal never byn sory;
Now very *Chorle* thow passeth thy gras,
Y am at my leberte even as I was.

40. As Clerkys fyndeth in the Bybell,
At Paradys yatis whan he was cast;
By an Angel both fayr and styll,
A downe Kyng *Elysawnder* ther I threst,
And of all stonys yt was y lest;
Soche stonys in place few ben y brought,
Soroful ys the *Chorle* and hevy in hys thowte.

41. Now more *Chorle* yt tel y can,
And thow wolt to me take hede:
The Byrde of Ermes ys my name,
In all the worlde that ys so wyde,
Wyth gletering of grace by every syde,
Hose me myght have in hys covertowr,
He wer rychcher than eny Emperowr.

42. *Elysawnder* the conquerowr my *Ston* smot dow
Upon hys helme whan hyt pyght:
No mor then a pese that ys so rownde,
Hyt was ther to no manys syght,
That leyde so pleyne the manly Knyght;
Now y tel the wyth melde Stevyn,
hys myghty grace cam owte fro H.vyn.

43. Hit cawseth Love aud maketh men Gracius,
And favorabel in ever mannes syght:
Hit maketh acorde of two Folks envyus;
Comforteth Sorowful and maketh hevy herts lyght,
Lyke passyng of colur Sunny bryght:
Y am a fole to tel the at onys,
Or to teche a *Chorle* the pryce of precious Stonys.

44. Men schalle not put a precius Margareyt,
As Rubeys, Saferys, and odther Stonys ynde;
Emeraudys, nor rownde Perlys whyte,
Byfore rude Swyne that love dreffe of kynde:
For a Sowe delyteth hyr as y fynde
Mor in fowle draffe hyr Pygges for to glad,
Than al the Perry that comes owte of Granad.

45. Heche thyng drawes to hys semblable,
Fysshes in the See, Bestys on the Stronde;
The Eyr for Fowlys ys commendabyl,
To the Plowghman for to tyll hys Londe,
And to a *Chorle* a Muk-forke in hys honde.
Y lese my tyme eny more to tare
To tell the bewar of the Lapidare.

46. That thow haddest thow getyst no more,
Thi Lyme twygges and Panters y defie;
To let me gon thow were fowle over seen,
To lese the richches only of folye:
Y am now fre to syng and to fle
VVher that my lyst: and he is a Fole at all
That goth at large, and maketh hymselfe thrall.

47. To here of VVisdome thi neres be halfe defe,
Like a Nasse that lysteth upon an Harpe;
Thow must go pype in a Ive leffe:
Better ys to me to syng on Thornes scharpe,
Than in a Cage wyth a *Chorle* to carpe:
For hyt was seyd of Folkes many yere agone,
A Chorles Chorle ys oft woe be gone.

48. Now

48. Now *Chorle* y have the her tolde,
My vertuys her wyth grete experience;
Hyt were to sume man better than Golde;
To the yt ys no fructius a sentence,
A Chepys Croke to the ys better than a Launce:
Adew now *Globbe* wyth herte sore,
In *Chorles* clowchys com y never more.

49. The *Chorle* felt hys herte part in tweyne,
For very sorow and in sunder ryve:
Alas quod he y may wel wepe and pleyne;
As a wreche never lyke to thryve,
But for to indure in povert all my lyve:
For of foly and of wylfulnes,
Y have now lost all holy my ryches.

50. I was a Lorde y crye owte on Fortune,
And had grete Tresor late in my keepyng;
Wych myght have made me long to contune;
Wyth that ilke *Stone* to have levyd a Kyng,
Yf y had set hyt in a Ryng:
Borne it upon me y had gode y nowe,
Than schuld y no mor have gon to the plowe.

51. Whan the *Byrde* saw the *Chorle* thus morne,
That he was hevy of hys chere,
Sche take her flyght and agayne returne:
Toward hym and sayd as ye schal here,
O dull *Chorle* wisdom for to lere;
That y the taute all ys lefe byhynde,
Reysed awey and clene owte of thy meynde.

52. Taw tey the not thys Wysdome in sentens,
To every tale brought up of new,
Not to hastyle gyf not ther to credens;
Unto tyme thow know hit be trew,
All ys not Gold that scheweth Goldys hew:
Nor stonys all by nature as y fynde,
Byn not Saferus that schewyth colour ynde.

35. In

53. In thys Doctryne y lost my labour,
To teche the such Proverbys of substaunce;
Now mayst thow see thy lewd blynde error;
For all my body poysed in Balans,
Weyth not a nounce lewde ys thi remembraunce;
Yet have y mor poyse closyd in myne entrayle,
Than all my Body set for Countervayle.

54. All my Body weyth not an unce,
How myght y have then in me a ston:
That poyseth mor than doth a grete *Jagounce*:
Thy brayne ys dull thi witte almost gon,
Of thre Wysdomys thow hast lost on;
Thow schulds not after my sentence,
To every tale gefe to hastyly credence.

55. I badde also bewar both even and morowe,
For thynge lost by suden adventur;
Thow schulds not make to moche sorow;
Whan thow seyst thow mayst not hit recover,
Her thow faylest wych doth thy besy cure;
In the snare to catch me agayne,
Thow art a Fole thy labor ys in vayne.

56. In the thyrde also thow dost rave,
Y bad thow schulds in no maner wyse
Covet thyng the wych thow mayst not have,
In wych thow hast fogetyn myne empryse,
Thaty may say playnly to devyse,
Thow hast in madnes forgetyn all thre,
Notabyl Wysdomys that y taute the.

57. Hit wer but foly mor wyth the to carpe,
Or to teche of Wysdomys mor or lesse;
Y holde hym madde that bryngs forth hys Harpe,
Theron to teche a rode for dollyd Asse,
And mad ys he that syngyth a Fole a Masse:
And he ys most madd that doth hys besynesse,
To teche a *Chorle* the termys of Gentlenesse.

58. And

Hermes Bird.

58. And semeblabilly in Apryll and in May,
When gentyl Byrds most make melody;
But the Cockow can syng butoo lay;
In odthir tewnys sche hath no fantesy:
Thus every thyng as Clerks do specify;
As Frute c n the Trees, and Folke of every age,
Fro whense they come they have a tallage.

59. The Wynter tretyth of hys Welsom wyndys,
Of the gentyll Frute bostys the Gardener;
The Fysher castyth hys hokys and hys lynys,
To catche Fysshe in the fresh Revyr,
Of tyllyth of Londe tretyth the powre;
The Gentylman tretyth of Gentry,
The *Chorle* delytith to speke rebawdry.

60. All on to a Faucon and a Kyte,,
As good an Owle as a Popyngay;
A dunghyll Douke as deyntieth as a Snyte,
Who servys a *Chorle* hase many a wofull day,
Y cast me never her after mot with the play;
To fore a *Chorle* any more to syng,
Of Wysdome to carpe in my lysyng.

61. The Folke that schall thys Fabyl se and rede,
New Forged Talys y councel them to fle
For losse of Good take not to grete hede,
Be not to Sorowfull for noon adversyte;
Covet not thyng that may not be,
And remember wher ye goan,
A Chorlys Chorle ys ofte wo begon.

62. Unto purpose thys *Proverbe* ys ful ryve,
Redde and reported by olde remembraunce:
A Chyldys Byrde, and a Chorlys Wyfe,
Hath ofte sythys sorow and mischaunce.
VVho hath fredom hath sufficiaunce:
Better ys Fredom wyth lytle in gladnes,
Than to be a *Chorle* wyth all worldly rychches.}

63. Go lytyl Quiar and rcommaunde me
To my *Mayster* wyth humbyl affeccyon,
Be ſekyng hym lowly of merſy and pete
Of thys rude makyng to ha compaſſion:
And as towchyng thys Tranſlacyon
Owte of the *Frenſhe*, how ſo ever the *Englyſh* be,
All thyng ys ſayd under correccyon,
VVyth ſupportation of yowr benygnite.

FINIS.

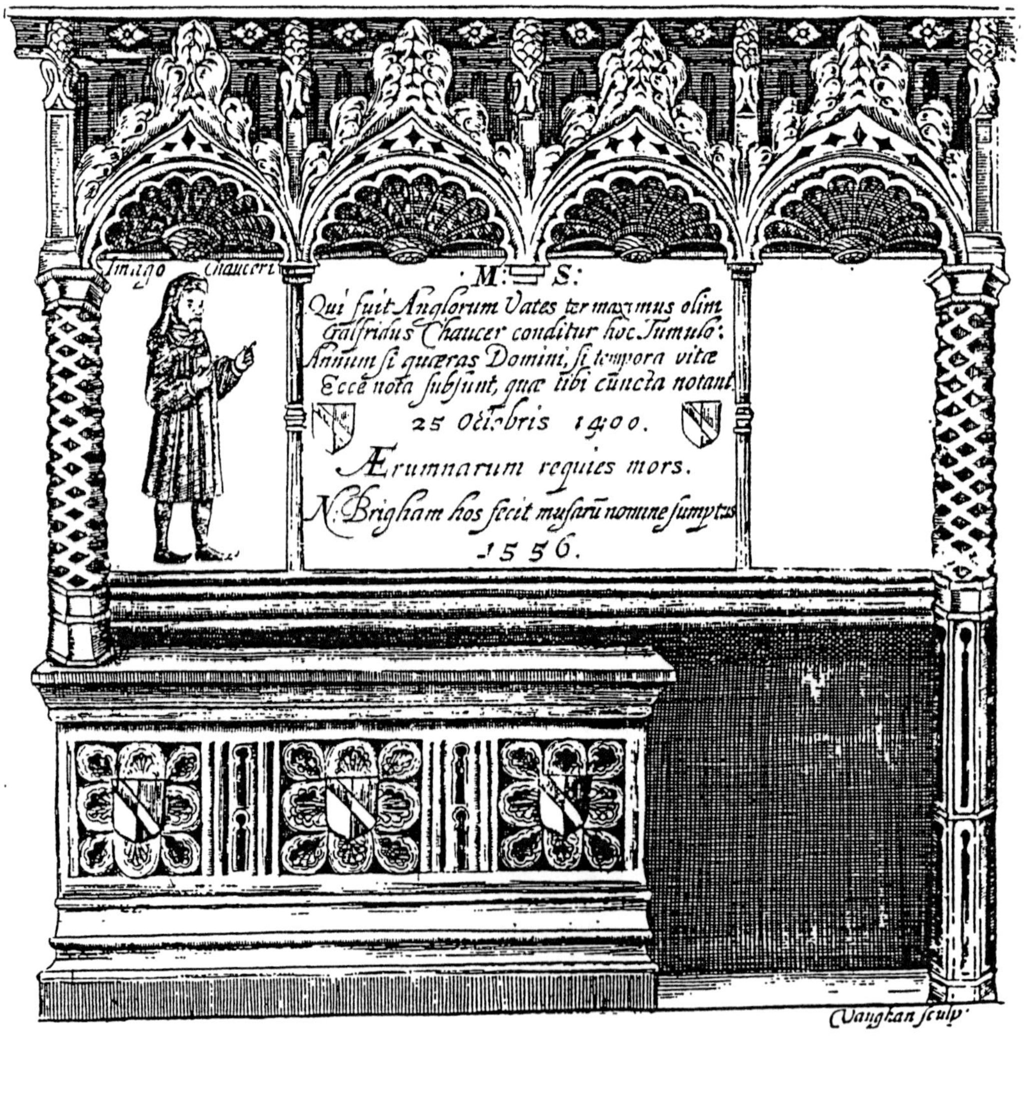

THE TALE OF THE *CHANONS YEOMAN.*

VVritten by our Ancient and famous English Poet, *Geoffry Chaucer.*

THE PROLOGUE OF The Chanons Yeoman.

WHan ended was the Lyfe of Saint Cecyle,
Er we fully had rydden fyve myle :
Att Boughton under the blee *us gan a take*
A Man that clothed was in clothes blake ;
And under that he had a whyte Surplyse,
His hakeny that was all pomely gryse ;
So swete that itt wonder was to see ;
It seemed that he had precked myles three.
The horse eke that his Yoman rode uppon,
So Swete, that vimeth migh he gon:
About the paytrell stode the fome full hye,
He was of fome as flecked as a pye :
A Male twyfolde on his croper lay ;
Itt semed that he carryed letel Aray ;
All light for somer rode this worthy Man,
And in my heart wondren I began,

What

What that he was, till I understode,
How that his cloke was sewed to his hode:
For which whan I had long avysed me;
I demyd him some Chanon *for to be:*
His hatt hynge att his backe by a Lace,
For he had rydden more then trot or pace.
He rode aye pryckyng as he were wode,
A Clote leafe he had layd under his hode,
For Swett and for to keepe his heede from hete,
But itt was joy for to se him swete:
His foreheed dropped as a Stillatorie,
But full of Playntaine or of Peritorie:
And when he was come he gan crye,
God save (quod he) this Iolly company:
Fast have I pricked (quod he) for your sake,
Bycause that I wold you ouertake,
To ryden in this mery company.
His Yoman was eke full of curtesy,
And sayd, Syrs, now in the morowe tyde,
Out of your hostrye I saw you ride,
And warned here my Lord and Soverayne,
Which that to ryden with you is full fayne:
For his disporte, he loveth dalyance.
Frede for thy warning God yeve thee good chance.
Then sayd our Host, certayne itt wold seme
Thy Lord were wyse, and so I may well deme:
He is full Iocunde, alsoe dare I lay,
Can he ought tell a mery Tale or tway,
With which he glad may this company?
Who Sir my Lord? ye without lye,
He can of myrthe and eke of Iolyte,
Not but ynough also Sir trusteth me;
And ye him knew also well as doe I,

Ye

Ye wold wonder how well and thriftely
He con the werke and that in sondry wyse;
He hath taken on him many a great Empryse:
Which were full hard for any that is here,
To bring about, but they of him itt lere.
As homely as he rideth among you,
If ye him knew itt wold ben for your prowe:
Ye nolde not forgon his aquayntaunce,
For Mochel good I dare lay in balaunce
All that I have in my possession;
He is a man of hye discression:
I warne you well he is a passing wyse man.
Wel quod our Hoste) I pray thee tell me than,
Is he a Clerke *or non? tell what he is.*
A Clerke! *nay greater then a* Clerke *I wys,*
Sayd the Yoman, and in words fewe,
Hoste of his Crafte somwhat wol I shew;
I say my Lord can such a subtelte,
But of his Crafte ye may not wete of me:
And somewhat helpe I yett to his worchyng,
That all the ground that we be on rydyng,
Till we come to Canterbury *Towne,*
He could all cleane turne up and downe:
And pave it all of Silver *and of* Gold.
And when this Yoman had thus I told
Unto our Hoste, he sayd benedicite,
This thing is wonder and marvellous to me:
Sens that thy Lord is of so high prudence,
(Because of which men shold him reverence,)
That of his worship recketh he so lyte,
His overest slopp is not worth a myte;
As in effect to him so mote I go,
It is all bawdy and to tore alsoe.

Why is thy Lord soe slotlyche I thee pray,
And is of power better clothes to bey?
If that his dede accord with thy speech,
Tell me that and that I thee beseech.
Why (quod this Yoman) whereto aske ye me?
God helpe mee so, for he shall never ythe:
But I wol not avow that I saye,
And therefore keepe itt secrett I you praye;
He is to wyse in fay as I beleeve,
That is overdone wil not preve;
And right as Clerkes *sayne itt is a vyce,*
Wherefore I holde him in that leude and nyce;
For whan a man hath over greate a witte,
Full ofte it happeth him to misusen itt:
So doth my Lord, and that me greveth sore;
God amend itt, I can say you no more.
Thereof no force good Yoman (quod our Host)
Sens of the connyng of thy Lord thou wost:
Tell how he doth I pray the hertely,
Sens that he is so crafty and so sly,
Where dwellen ye if itt to tell be?
In the Subbarbes of a Towne (quod he)
Lurkeyng in hernes and in lanes blynde,
Where these Robbers, and Theeves by kynde
Holden her privy fearefull residence,
As they that dare not shewen her presence;
Soe fare we if that I shall say the sothe,
Yett (quod our Hoste) lett me talke tothe.
Why art thou soe discolored in thy face?
Peter *(quod he) God yeve itt hard grace;*
I am so used in the hott fyre to blowe,
That itt hath changed my colour as I trow:
I am not wonte in no mirrour to prye,

But

But swynke sore and lerne to Multiplye.
We blondren ever and pooren in the fyre,
And for all that we faylen of our desyre:
For ever we lacken our conclusion,
To moche folke we do illusion:
And borrowe Golde be itt a pound or two,
Or ten or twelve or many somes mo,
And make hem wene at the leste way,
That of a pound we coulde make tway;
Yett is itt false, and ay hav we good hope
Itt for to done, and after it we grope.
But that Science is so ferre us byforne,
We mowe not all though we had itt sworne
Itt overtake, itt flytte away soe faste,
Itt wol us make Beggers at the laste.
Whiles this Yeman was thus in his talking
This Chanon *drew him nere and herde all thing*
Which this Yeman spake, for suspection
Of mennes speche ever had this Chanon:
For Cato *saythe, he that giltye is,*
Deemeth all thing be speke of him Iwys:
Bycause of that he gan so nyghe to draw,
To his Yeman to herken all his saw;
And thus he sayd unto his Yeman tho,
Holde nowe thy peace and speke no words mo,
For if thou doe, thou shalt it sore abye,
Thou slanderest me here in this Companye:
And eke discoverest that thou sholdest hyde.
Ye (quod our Hoste) tell on what soever betyde,
Of all his thretynge recke the not a myte.
In fayth (quod he) no more doe I but lyte.
And whan this Chanon *saw itt wolde not be,*
But his Yeman wolde tel his privyte,

Hec

He fledde away for very sorrow and shame.
A (quod the Yeman) here shall ryse a game,
All that I can anon woll I you tell,
Sens he is gone the foule Fend him quell;
For never hereafter wol I with him mete,
For penny ne for pounde I you behete;
He that me brought first unto that game,
Er that he dye sorrowe have he and shame;
For it is ernest to me by my faith,
That fele I well whatsoe any man saith:
And yett for all my smerte and all my greife,
For all my sorrowe, labour and mischeife,
I couthe never leave it in noe wyse:
Now wolde God my witt might suffyse,
To tellen all that longeth to that Arte.
But nathelesse, yet wol I tell you a parte:
Sens that my Lord is gon I wol not spare;
Such thyng as I know I wol declare.

Here endeth the Prologue of the Chanons
Yeoman, and here followeth his Tale.

The

THE TALE OF
The Chanons Yeoman.

WIth this *Chanon* I dwelt seaven yere,
And of this Science am I never the nere:
All that I had I have lost thereby,
And God wotte soe hath many moe then I,
There I was wonte to be right, fresh and gay,
Of clothing and eke of other good aray;
Now may I weare an hose uppon myne heed:
And where my colour was both fresh and reed,
Now itt is wanne and of a leaden hewe,
Whoe soe itt useth, sore shall him rewe.
And of my swynke yett blered in myne Eye,
Lo which avauntage itt is to Multiply:
That slyding Science hath me made so bare,
That I have noe good where that ever I fare:
And yett I am indetted so thereby,
Of Gold, that I have borrowed truly,
That while I live I shall itt quitt never,
Let every man beware by me ever;
What manner man that casteth him thereto,
If he contynue I hold his thrifte I do:
So helpe me God thereby shall he never wyn,
But empte his purse and make his witts thyn;
And whan he thorow his madnesse and folye,
Hath lost his owne good through Jeopardye:
Than he exiteth other men thereto,

To lese her good as himselfe hath do;
For unto shrewes joy it is and ese,
To have her fellowes in paine and disese;
For thus was I ones served of a *Clerke*;
Of that noe charge, I wol speke of our werke.
  When we be there as we shall exercise
Our elvish Craft, we semen wonder wise.
Our termes ben so Clergiall and so quaynte,
I blow the fyre tyll myn hearte faynte.
  What shold I tell each proportion
Of things which we werchen uppon?
As on fyve or syxe unces, may well be
Of Silver or of some other quantite;
And besye me to tellen you the names,
Of Orpiment, brent Bones, Yron squames;
That into powder grounden ben full small,
And in an Erthen pott how putt is all:
And salt y put in and also pepere,
Before these powdres that I speke of here:
And well y covered with a lompe of Glasse,
And of moch other thing that there was.
And of the potts and glass englutyng,
That of the ayre might passe out nothing;
And of the easy fyre and smerte alsoe;
Which that was made, and of the care and wo
That we had in our matters Sublymeing,
And in Amalgamyng and Calsenyng:
Of Quicksilver icleped Mercurye rude,
For all our sleight we conne not conclude.
Our Orpyment and Sublymed Mercury;
Our grounde Litarge eke on the porphirye:
Of eche of these unces a certayne
Not helpeth us, our labour is in vayne;

Ne eke our Spyrites assnecioun,
Ne yet our matters, that lyen al fyxe adoun:
Mowe in our werkyng nothing avayle,
For lost is our laboure and our travayle.
And all the Coste, a twenty dyvel away,
Is lost alsoe which we uppon itt lay.
There is alsoe full many another thing,
That is to our Craft apertaynyng:
Though I by ordre hem ne reherce can,
Bycause that I am a leud man.
Yet wol I tellen hem as they come to mynde,
Though I ne can sette hem in her kynde,
As bole Armonyake, Verdegreece, Boras,
And sondry Vessles made of Erth and Glas.
Our Urynalls and our Discensories,
Vyols, Crosseletts and Sublimatories:
Concurbytes and Alembykes eke,
And other such dere ynough a leke:
It needeth not to reherce them all,
Waters rubyfyeng and Boles, Gall;
Arsneke, Sal Armonyake and Brymstone,
And herbes could I tell eke many one:
As Egrimonye, Valeryan, and Lunarye,
And other such if that me liste to tarye;
Our Lampes brennyng both night and day,
To bringen about our Crafte if that we may;
Our Fournyce eke of Calcination,
And of our Waters Albifycation.
Unsleked Lyme, Chalke, and glere of an Eye,
Poudres divers, Ashes, Dong, Pisse, and Cley:
Sered pokettes, salt Peter, and Vitriole,
And divers fyres made of wood and cole;
Sal Tartre, Alkaly, and Sal preparate,

And combust matters, and coagulate,
Cley made with horse donge, mans heere and Oyle,
Of Tartre, Alym, Glas, Berme, Worte and Argoyle:
Resalgor and other maters enbybyng,
And eke of our Maters encorporing;
And of our Silver Citrynacion,
Our Cementyng, and eke Fermentacyon;
Our Ingottes, Testes and many mo.
I wol you tel as was me taught also,
The fowre Spyrites and the bodies seven,
By order as oft I herd my lord nemene.
The first Spyrite Quicksilver cleped is,
The second Orpyment, the third I wis
Armonyake, the fourth Brimstone.
The Bodyes seven eke lo here hem anone,
Sol Gold is, and *Luna* Sylver we threpe,
Mars, Iron, *Mercury*, Quicksilver we clepe:
Saturnus Lede, and *Iupiter* is Tynne,
And *Venus* Copper, by my father kynne.
This cursed Crafte whoe soe wol exercyse,
He shall noe good have that may him suffyse;
For all the good he spendeth thereaboute,
He lese shall thereof have I no doute;
Whoso that lysten to utter his folye,
Let him com forth and lerne to *Multiplye*:
And every man that hath ought in his cofer,
Let him apere and wexe a *Philosopher*:
Askaunce that Crafte is so light for to lere;
Nay God wot all be he *Monke* or *Frere*,
Preist, or *Chanon*, or any other wight,
Though he sytte at hys boke both day and night;
In lernyng of this Elvysh nyce lore,
All is in vayne, and parde moche more;

Is

Is to lere a leude man this ſubtelte,
Fye ſpeke not thereof, itt wol not be;
Al coulde he lettrure or coulde he none,
As in effect he ſhall fynd itt all one;
For bothe two by my Salvacyon
Concluden in Multyplycacyon:
Ilyche well whan they have al ydo,
This is to ſayen, they faylen both two.
Yet forgate I moche reherſayle,
Of waters Coroſyfe and lymayle:
And of Bodyes moliſycacion,
And alſo of her Induration:
Oyles, Ablucyons, Mettall fuſyble
To tellen you all, wolde paſſe any Byble:
That O where is, whereſore as for the beſt
Of all theſe names nowe woll I reſt.
For as I trowe I have you told ynowe
To reyſe a Fende, al loke he never ſo rowe.
A nay let be the *Philoſphers Stone*;
Alixer cleped, we ſeken faſte echeone,
For had we him, than were we ſyker ynowe:
But unto God of Heaven I make a vowe,
For al our crafte whan that we han al ydo,
And all our ſleyght, he wol not come us to;
He hath made us ſpend moche goode,
For ſorrow of which almoſt we wexen wode;
But that good hope crepeth in our herte,
Suppoſyng ever though we ſore ſmerte,
To ben releved by him afterwarde,
Suppoſyng, and hope is ſharpe and harde;
I warne you wel it is to ſyken ever,
That future temps hath made men diſcever,
In truſt therof, all that ever they had,

Yet of that Arte, they could not waxe sad;
For unto him itt is a bytter swete,
So semeth itt, for ne had they but a shete:
Which that they might wrappen hem in a night,
And a bratte to walken in a day light;
They wolden hem sel and spend it on this Crafte,
They conne not stynte, tyl nothing be lafte;
And evermore where that ever they gone,
Men may hem ken by smell of Brimstone:
For al the world they stynken as a Gote,
Her Savour is so rammish and so hote:
That though a man a myle from him be,
The savour wol infecte him trusteth me.
Lo thus by smelling and by threde-bare aray,
If that men list this folke know they may:
And if a man wol aske him prively,
Why they be clothed so unthriftely:
Right anon they wil rowne in his ere,
And sayne if that they aspyed were,
Men wold hem flee bycause of her Science,
Lo thus these folke betrayen innocence.
  Passe over this I goe my tale unto,
Ere that the pott be on the fyre ydo:
Of Metalls with a certayne quantyte,
My Lord hem tempreth and no man but he:
Now he is gon I dare say boldly,
For as men sayne, he can done craftely;
Algate I wotte wel he hath such a name,
And yet full oft he renneth in the blame,
And wotte ye how full oft itt happeth so,
The potte to breaketh and farewel all is go.
These Mettalls ben of soe greate violence,
Our walls may not make hem resystence;

But

But if they were wrought of lyme and ſtone,
They percen ſoe and through the wall they gone;
And ſome of them ſynken into the ground,
Thus have we loſt by tymes many a pound:
And ſome are ſcattered all the floore aboute,
Some lepen into the rofe withouten doute:
Tho that the fende not in our ſyght him ſhewe,
I trow that he with us be, that ilke ſhrewe:
In hell where that he is Lord and ſyre,
Ne is there no more wo, ne angre, ne yre:
When that our potte is broke as I have ſaid,
Every man chyte and holte him yvell apayde.
Some ſayd itt was long of the Fyre makeing,
Some ſayd nay, it was on the blowing:
Than was I ferd, for that was myn offyce,
Straw (quod the third) ye ben lewde and nyce;
It was not tempered as it ought to bee,
Nay (quod the fourthe) ſtynte and herken me:
Bycauſe our fyre was not made of beche
That is the cauſe, and none other ſo teche;
I can not tell whereon itt is alonge,
But well I wotte greate ſtrife is us among.
What (quod my lord) ther nys no more to done,
Of theſe perill I will beware ofte ſoone;
I am right Syker that the potte was craſed,
Be as be may, be ye not amaſed;
As uſage is, let ſwepe the floore as ſwythe,
Plucke up your heart and be glad and blythe.
The Mullocke on an heape yſwepte was,
And on the floore caſt a Canvas;
And all this Mullocke in a ſyve y throwe,
And yſyfted and yplucked many a throwe.
Parde (quod one) ſomewhat of our Mettall;

Yet

Yet is there here though we have not all;
And though this thyng miſhapped hath as now,
Another tyme it may ben wel ynowe;
We mote put our good in aventure,
A Marchant parde may not aye endure;
Truſteth me wel in his proſperyte,
Sometyme his good is drowned in the ſee:
And ſometyme it cometh ſafe unto the londe.
Peace (quod my lord) the next tyme I wol fonde,
To bring our Crafte all in another plyte,
And but I doe Syrs lett me have the wyte:
There was default in ſomewhat wel I wote.
Another ſayd the Fyre was over hote.
But be it hotte or colde I dare ſay this,
That we concluden evermore amys:
We faylen of that which we wolde have,
And in our madneſſe evermore we crave;
And whan we be togyther everychon,
Every man ſemeth as wyſe as *Solomon*,
But all thing which that ſhyneth as the Golde,
Is not Golde as I have here tolde:
Ne every Apple that is faire at Eye,
Nys not good what ſo men clappe or cry.
Right ſoe itt fareth among us;
He that ſemeth the wyſeſt by *Ieſus*
Is moſt foole when it cometh to the preſe,
And he that ſemeth trueſt is a Theefe:
That ſhall ye know er that I from you wende,
By that I of my Tale have made an end.
There was a *Chanon* of Religyoun
Amonge us, wolde enfect all a Towne,
Rome, *Alyſaundere*, *Troy*, and other thre,

His

His sleyght and his infynyte falsenesse,
There couthe no man written as I gesse;
Though that he might lyve a thousand yere
In all this worlde of falsenesse nye his pere:
For in his termes he wol him so wynde,
And kepe his words in so slye a kynde,
Whan he comen shall with any wight,
That he wol make him dote anon right.
But it a feude be as himselfe is,
Full many a man hath he begysed er this;
And mo wol, if that he may lyve a whyle,
And yet men ryden and gone full many a myle
Him for to seeke and have acquayntaunce,
Not knowing of his false governaunce:
And if ye luste to give me audience,
I wol it tellen here in your presence.
  But worshipfull *Chanons* relygyouse,
Ne demeth not that I sclaunder your house;
Although my tale of a *Chanon* be,
Of every ordre some shrewe is parde:
And God forbid that al a Companye
Shoulde rue a syngle mannes folye.
To slaunder you is not myn entente,
But to correct that mysse is mente;
This tale was not only told for you,
But eke for other moe ye wotte wel howe;
That among *Christs* Apostles twelve,
There was no traytour but *Iudas* himselve:
Then why shoulde the remenant have blame
That gyltlesse were? by you I say the same:
Save only this, if you wol herken me;
If any *Judas* in your Covent be,
Remeveth him betyme I you rede,

If ſhame or loſſe may cauſen any drede,
And be nothing diſpleſed I you pray,
But in this caſe herkenneth what I ſay.
  In *LONDON* was a *Preeſt* annuellere,
That therin had dwelt many a yere,
Which was ſoe pleſaunt and ſo ſervyſable
Unto the Wyfe, where he was att table;
That ſhe wolde ſuffer him nothing to pay
For borde, ne clothing, went he never ſo gay;
And ſpending Sylver had he right ynowe,
There of no force I wol proceed as nowe:
And tell forth my tale of the *Chanon*,
That brought this *Preeſt* to confuſyon.
  This falſe *Chanon* came uppon a daye
Unto this *Preeſts* chamber where he laye,
Beſeechyng him to leve him a certayne
Of Gold, and he wolde quyte him agen:
Leveth me a Marke (quod he) but dayes thre,
And att my day I wol quyte itt the;
And if it ſo be, that thou fynde me falſe,
Another day hang me by the halſe.
  This *Preeſt* toke him a Marke and that ſwyth,
And this *Chanon* him thanked oft ſyth;
And toke his leve, and went forth his wey,
And att his third day brought his money.
And to this *Preeſt* he toke this Gold ayen,
Whereof this *Preeſt* was gladde and fayn.
  Certes (quod he) nothing anoyeth me
To lend a man a Noble, two or thre;
Or what thing were in my poſſeſſion,
Whan he ſoe true is of Condition:
That in no wyſe he breke wol his day,
To ſuch a man I can never ſay nay.

What

What (quod this *Chanon*) sholde I be untrewe,
Nay ! that were a thyng falsen of newe,
Trouthe is a thyng that wol ever I kepe
Unto the day, in which I shall crepe
Into my Grave, or els God forbede:
Beleveth this as syker as your Crede:
God thanke I and in good tyme be it sayd,
That there was never man yett yvel apayd;
For Gold ne Sylver that he to me lent,
Ne never falsehede in myn herte I ment.
And Sir (quod he) now of my privyte,
Sens ye so goodlych have ben to me;
And kythe to me so great gentlenesse,
Somwhat to quyte with your kyndnesse;
I wol you shewe if ye wol it lere,
(I shall it shewe to you anon right here)
How I can werche in *Phylosophye*:
Taketh good hede ye shall it se with your Eye,
That I woll done a Maistrye or I goe.
Ye Sir (quod the *Preest*) and wol ye so?
Marye thereof I pray you hertely.
Att your Commandement Sir truly,
(Quod the *Chanon*) and els God forbede,
Lo how this thefe con the his servyce bede.
Ful sothe itt is that such profered servyse
Stynketh, as wittnesseth the olde wyse:
And that ful sone I wol it verefye,
In this *Chanon* rote of all trechery,
That evermore delyte hath and gladnesse:
Such fendly thoughts in his herte empresse,
How Christs people he may to mischiefe bring,
God kepe us from his false dissymuling.
What wyst this *Preest* with whom that he delte,

Ne of his harme comyng nothing he felte.
O fely *Preest*, O fely Innocente.
With Covetyse anon thou shalt be blente;
O gracelesse ful blynde is thy conceyte,
Nothyng arte thou ware of his deceyte.
Which that this foxe hath shapen to the,
His wylye wrenches thou mayst not fle.
Wherefore to goe to thy Conclusyon,
That referreth to thy confusyon:
Unhappy man anon I wol me hye,
To tell thyn unwitte ne thy folye:
And eke the falseneffe of that other wretche,
As fer forthe as my connyng wol stretche.
This *Chanon* was my Lord ye wold wene,
Syr hoste in fayth and by the heven Quene:
It was another *Chanon* and not he,
That can an hundredfold more subtelte:
He hath betrayed folke many a tyme,
Of his falseneffe it doleth me to ryme;
Ever whan I speke of his falseheed,
For shame of him my chekes waxen reed:
Algates they begennen for to glowe,
For rednesse have I non right well I knowe
In my visage, for fumes dyverce
Of Metalls which ye have herde me reherce,
Consumed and wasted hath my rednesse,
Now take heed of this *Chanons* Cursednesse.
Syr (quod he) to the *Preest*, set your Man gon,
For Quicksilver that we it had anon;
And lett him bring unces two or thre,
And whan he cometh as faste shul ye se
A wonder thyng which ye saw never er this;
Syr (quod the *Preest*) itt shalbe done iwys:

He

He badd his ſervaunte fetch him this thyng,
And he already was att his bydding;
And went him forth and came anon agayne
With this Quickſylver ſhortly for to ſayne:
And toke theſe unces there to the *Chanoun*,
And he hem ſayd well and fayre adoun:
And bade the ſervaunt Coles for to bryng,
That he anon might go to his werkyng.
The Coles right anon were yfet,
And this *Chanon* toke out a Croſſelett
Of his boſome, and ſhewed it to the *Preeſt*:
This Inſtrument (quod he) which that thou ſeeſt
Take in thy hond, and put thy ſelfe therein
Of this Quickſylver an unce and begyn
In the name of Chiſt to wexe a *Philoſopher*,
There be ful fewe which I wolde it profer;
To ſhewe him this moche of my Science,
For here ſhul ye ſe by experience,
That this Quickſylver I wol mortifye
Right in your ſyght anon withouten lye,
And make it as good Sylver and as fyne,
As there is any in your purſe or myne,
Or elſewhere, and make it malliable,
Or els hold me falſe and unſtable;
Amonges folke ever to appere.
I have a poudre that coſt me deere,
Shall make all good, for it is cauſe of all
My connyng, which I you ſhewe ſhall;
Voydeth your Man, and let him be therout,
And ſhette the dore, whyles we ben about
Our privetie, that no man us eſpy,
Whyles that we *Werken* in our Philoſophye.
Al as he bade fulfylled was indede:

This ylke servant anon out yede,
And his Maister shette the dore anon,
And to her labour spedily they gone.
This *Preest* at this cursed *Chanons* byddyng,
Uppon the fyre anon set this thyng;
And blewe the fyre and besyed him ful faste,
And this *Chanon* into this croslet caste
A pouder, I not wherof it was,
Ymade either of Chalke, Erthe, or Glasse
Or somwhat els, was not worthe a fly,
To blynde with this *Preest*, and bade him hye
These Coles for to couchen al above
The Crosslet for in token that I the love;
(Quod this *Chanon*) thyn hondes two,
Shal werke al thing that here shalbe do;
Graunt mercy (quod the *Preest*) and was ful glad,
And couched coles as the *Chanon* bad.
And whyle he besy was, this fendely wretch,
This false *Chanon*, the foule fende him fetche;
Out of his bosome toke a bechen cole,
In which ful subtelly was made an hole,
And therein was put of Sylver lymayle,
An unce, and stopped was without fayle,
The hole with waxe to kepe the Limayle in.
And understandeth that this false gyn
Was not made there, but it was made byfore;
And other thynges that I shall you tell more
Herafter, that whiche he with him brought,
Er he came there to begyle him he thought:
And so he did er they went a twynne
Till he had turned him, coulde he not blynne,
It dulleth me whan that I of him speke,
On his false hede fayne wolde I me wreke,

If

If I wyste how, but he is here and there,
He is so varyaunt he bydeth no where.
  But taketh heed Syrs nowe for Godds love,
He toke his Cole of which I spake above,
And in his honde he bare it prively,
And whyles the *Preest* couched besily
The Coles, as I told you er this,
This *Chanon* sayd, Frende ye done amys:
This is not couched as it ought to be;
But sone I shall amend it (quod he)
Nowe let me medle therwith but a whyle,
For of you have I pyte by *Saint Gyle*:
Ye ben right hotte, I se wel how ye swete,
Have here a clothe and wype away the wete:
And while the *Preest* him wyped hace,
This *Chanon* toke the Cole, I shrewe his face:
And layd it aboven uppon the mydwarde
Of the Croslet, and blewe wel afterwarde,
Till that the Coles gonne faste brenne.
  Nowe yeve us drinke (quod this *Chanon*) then,
As swythe al shall be wel I undertake,
Sytte we downe and let us mery make;
And whan this *Chanons* bechen Cole
Was brent, al the Limayle out of the hole
Into the Croslet anon fell adoun,
And soe it must needes by resoun,
Sens it so even above couched was,
But thereof wyste the *Preest* nothing alas:
He demed all the coles lyche goode,
For of the sleyght nothing he understoode.
  And whan this *Alkamistre* sawe his tyme,
Ryseth up Syr *Preest* (quod he) and stondeth byme;
And for I wott well yngot have I none:

Gothe

Gothe walketh forth and brynge a chalke ſtone,
For I wol make it of the ſame ſhappe,
That an yngott is if I may have happe;
And bring eke with you a bolle or a panne
Full of water, and you ſhall ſe thanne,
How that our beſyneſſe ſhall happe and preve,
And yet for ye ſhall have no misbyleve,
Ne wronge conceyte of me in your abſence,
I wol not ben out of your preſence:
But goe with you and come with yon agayne.
The Chamber dore ſhortly to ſayne,
They opened and ſhette and went forth her wey,
And forthe with him they carryed the key;
And comen agen withouten any delay,
What ſhulde I tarry all the long day?
He toke the Chalke and ſhope it in the wyſe
Of an yngot as I ſhall you devyſe.
I ſay he toke out of his owne ſleve
A teyne of Sylver, yvel mote he cheve;
Which that was but an unce of weight,
And taketh heed now of his curſed ſleight,
He ſhope his yngot in lenght and in brede
Of the teyne withouten any drede,
So ſlily that the *Preeſt* it not aſpyde,
And in his ſleve agayne he gan it hyde;
And from the fyre toke up his Mattere,
And into the yngot it put with mery chere:
And into the water-veſſele he it caſte
Whan that him liſt, and bade the *Preeſt* as faſte
Looke what there is put in thyn honde, and grope,
Thou ſhalt finde there Sylver as I hope;
What dyvel of hell ſhulde it els be?
Shaving of Sylver, Sylver is parde.

He

He put in his honde and toke up a Teyne
Of Silver fyne, and glad in every veyne
Was this *Preest*, whan he saw itt was so,
Gods blessynge and his Mothers also:
And al hallowes have ye Sir *Chanon*
Sayd this *Preest*, and I her Malyson.
But and ye vouchsafe to teche me
This noble Crafte, and this subtelte;
I wol be yours in al that ever I may.
Quod the *Chanon* yet woll I make assay
The seconde tyme, that ye mowe take heede,
And ben expert of this and in your neede
Another day assay in myn absence,
This Disciplyne and this crafty Science.
Lette take onother ounce (quod he) tho
Of Quicksylver withouten words mo,
And don therwith as I have don er this,
With that other which that nowe silver is.
This *Preest* him besyeth in all that he can,
To don as this *Chanon* this cursed man
Commanded him, and fast blew the fyre
For to come to the effect of his desyre;
And this *Chanon* right in the meane while,
All redy was, this *Preest* efte to begyle;
And for a Countenance in his honde bare
An holow sticke, take keepe and beware;
In thend of which an unce and no more
Of Sylver Lymayle putte was, as before,
Was in his cole, and stopped with wexe wele,
For to kepen in his Lymaile every dele.
And whiles this *Preest* was in his besynesse
This *Chanon* with his sticke gan him dresse
To him anon, and his poudre cast in,

As he did erst, the Dyvell out of his skyn
Him torne, I pray to God for his falshede,
For he was ever false in thought and dede:
And with his sticke above the Crosslette,
That was ordeyned with that false iette,
He styreth the coles tyl all relent gan
The waxe agayne the fyre, as every man,
But he a foole be, wote wel it mote nede,
And al that in the hole was out yede:
And into the crosslette hastely it fell.
The *Preest* supposed nothing but well,
But besyed him fast and was wonder fayne,
Supposing nought but trouthe, soth to sayne:
He was so gladd that I cannot expresse,
In no manere his mirth and his gladnesse;
And to the *Chanon* he profered eft soone
Body and good: ye (quod the *Chanon*) anone,
Though I be poore, crafty thou shalt me fynde,
I warne the yet is there more behynde,
Is there any Copper here within sayd he?
Ye Sir (quod the *Preest*) I trowe there be.
Els go bye some and that aswythe.
Nowe good Sir go forth thy way and hythe.
He went his way and with the Coper he came,
And this *Chanon* in his honde it name;
And of that Coper wayed out but an unce,
All to symple is my tonge to pronounce:
As to ministre by my wytte the doublenesse
Of this *Chanon*, roote of all cursydnesse:
He semed freindly to hem that knew him nought.
But he was fendly both in werke and thought,
It weryeth me to tell of his falsenesse
And nathlesse, yet wol I it expresse,

To

To the entent that men may beware thereby,
And for none other cauſe truly.
He put this unce of Coper into the Crosſlett,
And on the fyre as ſwythe he hath it ſett;
And caſt in pouder, and made the *Preeſt* to blowe,
And in his workeing for to ſtoupe lowe:
As he did erſte, and all nas but a jape,
Right as him lyſte, the *Preeſt* he made his Ape;
And afterward in the yngot he it caſte,
And in the panne put it at the laſte
Of water, and in he put his owne honde,
And in his ſleve, as ye by forehonde
Herd me tell, he had a Sylver Teyne,
He ſlily toke it out, this curſed heyne,
Unwetyng this *Preeſt* of his falſe crafte,
And in the pannes botome he hath it lafte,
And in the water rombleth to and fro:
And wonder prively toke up allo
The coper Teyne, not knowing this *Preeſt*,
And hydde itt, and hent him by the breſt;
And to him ſpake, and thus ſayd in his game,
Stoupeth adowne, by God ye be to blame,
Helpeth me nowe, as I did you whylere:
Put in your honde, and loketh what is there.
This *Preeſt* toke up this Sylver Teyne ano ie,
And then ſaid the *Chanon*, lette us gon
With theſe thre Teynes which we han wrought
To ſome Goldſmythe, and wete if it be ought:
For by my faith, I nolde for my hoode,
But if it were Sylver fyne and goode,
And that as ſwythe wellproved ſhalbe.
Unto the Goldſmythe with theſe Teynes three,
They wént and put them in aſſaye,

To fyre and hammer, might no man ſay nay,
But they were as them ought for to be.
This ſotted *Preeſt* who was gladder then he,
Was never Byrd gladder agenſt the day,
Ne Nightyngale agenſt the ceaſon of May,
Was never none, that lyſt better to ſynge,
Ne Lady luſtier in Carolyng:
And for to ſpeke of love and woman hede,
Ne Knight in armes to done a herdy dede,
To ſtonden in grace of his Lady dere,
Then had this *Preeſt* this crafte to lere,
And to the *Chanon*, thus he ſpake and ſayd
For the love of God, that for us all deyd,
And as I may deſerve it unto yow,
What ſhall this receite coſt, telleth me nowe?
By our Lady (quod this *Chanon*) it is dere,
I warne you well, ſave *I* and *a Frere*:
In *ENGLAND* there can no man it make.
No force (quod he) nowe Sir for Gods ſake,
What ſhall I pay? tell me I you pray.
I wys (quod he) it is ful dere I ſay.
Syr at one word if that ye lyſt it have,
Ye ſhall pay fortye pound, ſo God me ſave:
And nere the freindſhyp that ye did er this
To me, ye ſhulden pay more y wys.
This *Preeſt* the ſome of forty pounde anon
Of Nobles fette, and told hem everychon
To this *Chanon* for this ilke receyte,
All his worchyng was fraude and deceyte.
Syr *Preeſt* he ſaid; I kepe for to have no loos
Of my craft, for I wold itt were kept cloos:
And as ye love me kepeth it ſecre,
For and men knowe all my Subtelte,

By

By God men wolde have soe greate envye
To me by cause of my Phylosophye:
I shulde be deed, ther were none other way.
God it forbid (quod the *Preest*) what ye say:
Yet had I lever spend all the good,
Which that I have, or els waxe I wood
Than that ye shoulde fallen in such mischeife:
For your good wyll have ye right good prefe,
(Quod the *Chanon*) and farewell graunt mercy:
He went his way, and never the *Preest* him sey
After that day: And whan that this *Preest* sholde
Maken assay at such tyme as he wolde,
Of this receyte, farwell it nold not be:
Lo thus bejaped and begyled was he.
Thus maketh he his Introduction,
To bringe folke to her distruction.
Consydereth Sirs, howe in eche estate:
Betwixt Men and Gold is debate,
Soe fer forthe, that unneths there is none,
This Multiplyeng blyndeth so many one;
That in good fayth, I trowe that it be
The greatest cause of such scarsyte:
These *Phylosophers* speken so mistily,
In this Crafte, that men cannot come thereby,
For any witte that men have nowe adayes,
They may well chattre and jangle as doth the Jayes:
And in her termes sett her luste and payne,
But to her purpose shall they never attaine;
A man may lightly lerne if he have ought,
To Multiply and bring his good to nought:
Lo such a Lucre is in this lusty game,
A mans myrthe it wol turne all to grame:
And emptien also greate and hevy purses,

And maken folke to purchase curses:
Of hem that han alsoe her good ylent.
O fye for shame, they that han be brente:
Alas cannot they fly the fyres hete,
Ye that it usen, I rede that ye it lete:
Lest ye lesen al, for bet then never is late,
Never to thryve were to long a date,
Though that ye prolle aye ye shall it never fynde,
Ye ben as bold as is *Bayarde* the blynde;
That blondereth forth, and perill casteth none;
He is as bolde to renne agenst a stone,
As for to go besyde in the way;
So faren ye that multiplyen I say;
If that your Eyen can not sene aright,
Loketh that your Mynde lacke not his sight;
For though ye loke never soe brode and stare,
Ye shall not wynne a myte in that chaffare:
But waste all that ye may repe and renne,
Withdrawe the fyre least it to fast brenne:
Medleth with that Arte noe more I mene;
For yf ye done your thrifte is gone full cleane.
And right as swythe I woll you tellen here,
What that the *Phylosophers* sayne in this mattere.
  Lo thus saith *Arnolde* of the newe toune,
As his *Rosarye* maketh mencioune:
He sayth right thus withouten any lye,
There may noe man *Mercury* mortifye;
But if it be with his brothers knowlegyng;
Lo how that he which firste sayd this thyng
Of Phylosophers father was, *Hermes*.
  He saythe how that the *Dragon* doutlesse
Ne dyeth not, but if he be slayne
With his brother: and this is for to sayne,

By

By the Dragon *Mercurye* and none other,
He underſtood that Brimſtone was his brother.
That out of *Sol* and *Luna* were ydrawe,
And therefore ſayd he, take heed to my ſawe.
Let no man beſye him this *Arte* for to ſeche,
But he that the Entention and ſpeche
Of *Phyloſophers* underſtonde can,
And if he do he is a leud man:
For this *Science*, and this connyng (quod he)
Is of the Secre, of the Secres parde.
Alſoe there was a Diſciple of *Plato*,
That on a tyme ſayd his Maiſter to:
As his booke *Senior* wol bere wytneſſe,
And this was his demaunde in ſothfaſtneſſe.
Tell me the name of the privy Stone?
And *Plato* anſwered unto him anone,
Take the Stone that *Tytanos* men name.
Which is that (quod he?) *Magnatia* is the ſame,
Said *Plato*: ye Sir, and is it thus?
This is *ignotum per ignotius*:
What is *Magnatia* good Sir I you pray?
It is a Water that is made I ſay
Of Elements foure (quod *Plato*)
Tell me the Rocke good Sir (quod he tho)
Of that Water, if it be your wyll.
Nay nay (quod *Plato*) certayne that I nyll,
The *Philoſophers* were y ſworne echone,
That they ſhulde diſcover it unto none;
Ne in no Boke it write in no manere,
For unto *Chriſt* it is ſo lefe and dere,
That he wol not that it diſcovered be,
But where it liketh to his deite;
Man to enſpyre and eke for to defende,

Whan

Whan that him lyketh, lo this is his ende.
  Then conclude I thus, ſens the God of heaven,
Ne wyl not that the *Phyloſophers* nemen:
Howe that a Man ſhall come unto this *Stone*,
I rede as for the beſt, lett itt gone;
For who ſo maketh God his adverſary,
As for to werche any thing in contrary:
Unto his will, certes never ſhall he thrive;
Though that he Multiplye terme of his live,
And there a poynte: for ended is my Tale,
God ſend every true man *Bote of his bale.*

THE

THE WORKE OF JOHN DASTIN.

NOt yet full sleping, nor yet full waking,
But betweene twayne lying in a traunce;
Halfe closed mine Eyne in my slumbering,
Like a Mā rapt of all cheer & countenance;
By a manner of weninge & Remembrance
Towards *Aurora*, ere *Phœbus* uprose,
I dreamed one came to me to doe me pleasaunce
That brought me a *Boke* with seaven seales close.

2. Following upon I had a wonderfull dreame,
As semed unto my inward thought,
The face of him shone as the Sun-beame:
Which unto me thys hevenly Boke brought,
Of so greate Riches that yt may not be bought,
In order set by *Dame Philosophie*,
The Capitall and the flowrishing wrought
By a wise Prince called *Theologie*.

3. Thys Boke was written with letters aureat,
Perpetually to be put in memory,
And to *Apollo* the Chapters consecrate,
And to the seaven *Gods* in the hevenly Consistory:
And in *Mercuries* litle Oratory,
Groweth all the fruite in breese of thys *Science*,
Who can expresse hem and have of hem Victory,
May clayme the tryumph of his Minerall prudence.

4. Of this matter above betweene Starrs seaven,
By *Gods* and *Goddesses* all of one assent,
Was sent *Caducifer* to Erth downe form Heaven:
Saturnus as Bedell by great advisement;
For to summon a generall Parliament,
By concord of all both old and younge of age,
To say in Breife their Councell most prudent:
For Common proffit to knitt up a Marriage.

5. Betweene twaine Borne of the Imperiall blood,
And descended from *Iupiters* line,
Of their Natures most pure and most good;
Wythowte infeccion their seede is most divine:
That noe Eclips may let them for to shine,
So that *Mercury* doth stint all debate,
And restraine their Courage by meaknes them incline;
That of frowardnes they be not indurate.

6. For the *Sunne* that sitteth so heigh a lost,
His golden dew droppes shall cleerely raigne downe,
By the meane of *Mercury* that moven first made soft:
Then there schalbe a glad Conjunccion,
Whan there is made a Seperacion:
And their two Spermes by Marriage are made one;
And the said *Mercury* by devision,
Hath taken his flight and from both is gone.

7. These be the two *Mercuries* cheife of Philosophers,
Revived againe with the Spirit of lyfe,
Richer then Rubies or Pearles shut in Cofeurs;
Washed and Baptized in waters vegitative,
The body dissevered with heate nutrative:
By moderate moysture of Putrefaccion;
So that there is no excesse nor no strife
Of the foure Elements in their Conjunccion.

8. The

8. The graine of Wheate which on the ground doth
But it be dead it may not fructifie, (fall,
If it be hole the vertue doth appayse;
And in no wise it may not Multiplye,
The increase doth begin whan it doth Putrefie;
Of good Grafts commeth Fruites of good lastage;
Of Crabs Verjuyce, of Ash is made Lye,
Of good Grapes followeth a good Vintage.

9. Who soweth good Seede repeth good againe,
Of Cockles sowne there can grow no good Wheate,
For as such a *Ploughman* traveleth in vaine,
To fruitefull Land Cockle is not meete;
Gall is ever bitter, Honey is ever sweete,
Of all things contrary is fals Conneccions,
Let Male and Female together ever meete;
But both be clensed of their Complexions.

10. A Man of Nature ingendereth but a Man,
And every Beast ingendereth his semblable;
And as *Philosophers* rehearse well can,
Diana and *Venus* in marriage be notable,
A Horse with a Swine joyneth not in a stable,
For where is made unkindly geniture,
What followeth but things abominable:
Which is to say *Monstrum* in Nature.

11. All this I finde in the said Boke,
Brought to me when I lay a sleepe;
And of one thing good heede I toke;
The Wolf in kinde is Enemy to the Sheepe.
The Rose full divers to the wild Neepe:
For things joyned that be contrary;
Dame *Nature* complayning doth sit and weepe:
For falce receipts found in her Library.

12. And there it was so pitiously complained,
That men so err by false Opinions
That be so farr from truth away restrained,
Like as they had lost wholly their Reasons,
Not considering in their discretions;
What mischeife followeth as is oft seene,
By these false froward Conneccions:
As doth leapers with folkes that byne cleane.

13. Notwithstanding he that is sate so high in heaven,
Crown'd with a Crowne of bright stones cleere,
Borne there to raine as cheife chosen of seaven:
Equall with *Phœbus* shone in the same sphere,
Without difference as *Clerkes* to us leare,
Sate there most royallin his diadem:
Very Celestiall and Angelike of cheare;
And in all vertue like as he did seeme.

14. And in that Boke I found well by writing,
Like as the processe made mention:
How that there was once a mighty rich King,
Cleane of nature and of Complexion:
Voyde of deformity from head soe forthe downe,
Which for his beauty as it is specified,
And for his cleanes most soverayne of renowne:
Was among *Planets* in heaven stellesyed.

15. Certaine Brethren I found he had in Number,
And of one Mother they were borne every each one:
But a Sicknes did them sore cumber,
That none was whole on his feete to gone,
Hoarse of language, cleere voice had they none:
For with a scabb that was contagious,
They were infected, hole was their none;
For ever exiled because they were Leaprous.

16. The

16. The said King rose up in his Royall see,
Seeing this mischeife cast his Eye downe,
And of his mercy, and fraternall pittye,
Surprized in heart, full of Compassion:
And began to complaine of their Infeccion,
Alas quoth he how came this adventure,
Under what froward or false Constelacion;
Or in what howre had yee your ingendure.

17. But sithence this mischeife ys to you befall,
There is nothing which were more expedient,
Then to chuse one out amongst us all,
Without spott all cleere of his intent,
For you to dye by his owne assent,
To save the people from their Damnation:
And with his blood ere you be fully shent,
To make of his mercy your remission.

18. The which Liquor most wholesome is and good,
Against leprous humors and false infeccions,
When from a veyne taken is the blood;
Cleansing each parte from all corrupcions,
The Originall taken from generacions:
Which is descended downe from stock royall,
Nourished with Milke of pure complexion;
With menstrous which are not superficiall.

19. But when the Brethren of this worthy King
Heard the Language, they fell in full great dread,
Full sore weeping and said in Complayning
That none of them was able to bleede,
Because their blood was infeccious indeede,
And of corrupt blood made is noe Sacrifice,
Wherefore alas there is noe way to speede,
That we can finde, to helpe us in any wise.

20. Of our Birth and of our Originall,
Cleerely and truly to make mencion;
Excuse is there none in parte nor in all;
In sin was first our concepcion:
Our bringing forth and generation,
Fulfilled was in sorrowe and wickednesse,
And our Mother in a short conclusion
With Corrupt milke us fostred in distresse.

21. For who may make that seede to be cleane,
That first was conceived in uncleanes,
For cancred rust may never I meane,
By noe crafte shew forth parfect brightnes:
Now let us all at once our Course addres;
And goe unto our Mother to aske by and by,
The finall cause of our Corrupt sicknes;
That she declare unto us the Cause and why.

22. The said Children uprose in a fury
Of wofull rage, and went by one assent
Unto their Mother that called was *Mercury*:
Requiring her by greate advisement,
Before her *Goddesses* being every one present.
To tell them truly and in noe parte to faine,
Why their nature was corrupt and shent;
That caused them evermore to weepe and complaine.

23. To whome the Mother full bright of face and hew,
Gave this answer remembred in Scripture,
First when I was wedded a new,
I conceived by prosses of true Nature:
A Child of seede that was most cleane and pure,
Undefiled, most orient, faire and bright,
Of all the *PLANETS* cheife of ingendure:
Which now in Heaven giveth so cleere a light.

24. Whose

24. Whose Complexion is most temperate,
In heate and cold and in humidity,
In Erth also that there is noe debate,
Nor noe repugnaunce by noe quallity:
Nor none occasion of none infirmity,
That among them there may be none discord,
So well proportioned every-each in his degree,
Each hower and space they be of so true accord.

25. Whose Nature is so imperiall,
That fire so burning doth him noe distresse:
His royall kinde is so celestiall,
Of Corrupcion he taketh no sicknesse;
Fire, Water, Air, nor Erth with his drines,
Neither of them may alter his Complexion,
He fixeth Spirits through his high noblenes;
Saveth infected bodyes from their Corrupcion.

26. His Heavenly helth death may not assayle,
He dreadeth noe venome, nor needeth no treacle,
Winde Tempest ne Wether against him may prevaile,
Soe high in Heaven is his Tabernacle,
In Erth he worketh many a miracle:
He cureth Lepers and fetcheth home Fugitive,
And to gouty Eyne giveth a cleere Spectacle:
Them to goe that lame were all their lief.

27. He is my Son and I his Mother deare,
By me conceived truly in Marriage;
As touching your Birth the sicknes doth appeare,
Of Menstruous blood brought forth in tender age,
Your Leprie is shewed in Body and in Visage,
To make your hole Medicine is no other
Drinke, nor potion to your advantage,
But the pure blood of him that is your deare Brother.

28. A good Shephard must dye for his Sheepe,
Without grudging to speake in words plaine,
And semblable take hereof good keepe,
Your Brother must dye and newe be borne againe,
Though he be old, be hereof well certaine;
To youth againe he must be renewd,
And suffer passion or else all were vaine,
Then rising againe right fresh and well hewd.

29. Old *Æson* was made young by *Medea*,
With her drinks and with her potions,
Soe must your Brother of pure *Volunta*
Dyeand be young through his operation,
And that through subtile natures Confections,
By whose death plainely to expresse;
Yee shalbe purged from all infeccions:
And your foule leaprie changed to cleanes.

30. With the said words the King began to abrayd
The tale adverting that she had tould,
How might a Man by nature thus he said
Be borne againe, namely when he ys old?
Then said hys Mother by reason manifold:
But if the Gospell thus doth meane,
In Water and Spirit be renovate hott and cold,
That he shall never plainely come into Heaven.

31. The King was tristy and heavy of cheere,
Upon his Knees meekely kneeled downe,
Prayed his Father in full low manner,
To translate the Challice of hys passion,
But for he thought the redempcion
Of his brethren, might not be fulfilled,
Without his death nor their Salvation;
For them to suffer he was right willed.

And

32. And for to accomplish hys purpose in sentence,
By cleere example who so looketh right,
Heavy things from their Circumferance,
Must up assend and after be made light,
And things light ready to the flight
Must descend to the Center downe,
By interchaunging of natures might,
As they be moved by meane of Revolucion.

33. Soe as *Iupiter* in a Cloud of Gold,
Chaunged himselfe by transformacion,
And descended from hys hevenly hold
Like a Golden dewe unto *Danae* downe,
And she conceived as made is mencion,
By influence of hys power divine;
Right so shall *Phœbus* right soveraigne of renowne
To be conceived of his Golden raine decline.

34. And to comfort hys Brethren that were full dull,
The *Sun* hath chosen without warr or strife,
The bright *Moone* when she was at the full,
To be his Mother first, and after hys wedded wife;
In tyme of *Ver* the season vegetative,
In *Aries* when *Titan* doth appeare,
Inspired by grace with the Spirit of lyfe,
This marriage hallowed at midday Spheare.

35. And at this feast were the Godes all,
Saturne from blacknes was turned to white;
And *Iupiter* let his mantle fall,
Full pale and meager of greate delight,
Clothed in lylies that every maner wight,
Of Heaven and Erth, and Gods of the Sea,
Rejoyced in Heart, and were full glad and light,
To be present at this great Solemnity.

36. *Mars* forgot there hys sturdy black hardines,
Cast off his Habergeon fret with old rust;
Venus forsooke her minerall rednes,
Tooke Gold for greene and she againe also for lust,
Because she had in *Phœbus* such a trust,
That he should this feast hold of most noblenes:
Of brotherly pitty needs as he must,
Give her a mantle of Orientall brightnes.

37. After this Wedding here afore devised,
Of faire *Phœbus* and fresh *Lucine*;
Philosophers have prudently practised,
A Closset round by their wise Doctrine,
Cleere as Christall of Glasse a litle shrine;
With heavenly deawe stuffed that dungeon,
Kept night and day with glorious maidens nyne;
To keepe the Queene in her Concepcion.

38. Religiously they kept their Sylence,
Till that from heaven their a royall light,
And there with all in open audience;
Was heard a voyce almost at mid night,
Among the Virgins most amiable of sight,
That said unto them, to save that was forlorne;
I must againe through my imperiall myght,
Be of my Mother new conceived and borne.

39. I must passe by water and by Fire,
The brunt abide and there from not decline,
To save my brethren I have so greate desire,
With new light their darknes to yllumine,
But sore I dread that venomous Serpentine,
Which ever advanceth with his violence,
My tender youth to hurt and to invenome,
But in your keeping doe you your diligence.

The

40. The King thus entred in his bed royall,
The Queene conceived under a Sun bright;
Under her feete a mount like Christall,
Which had devoured her husband anon right,
Dead of desire and in the Maidens sight;
Lost all the Collour of his fresh face,
Thus was he dead, the Maidens feeble of mighr
Dispaired, slept in the same place.

41. The Serpent bold shed out his poyson,
The Queene and Maidens for feare tooke them to flight;
Seaven tymes assending up and downe
With in a vault, now darke, now cleere of light,
Their generation was so strong of might,
Tfter death now passeth Purgatory;
Ao Resurreccion as any Sun bright,
Things that were lost to bring to his glory.

42. The Queene tooke her full possession,
The Soule reviving of the dead King;
But of old hatred the toxicate poyson,
Was by the Serpent cast in to their hindring;
The *Prince* was buried, but of his rising,
The Brethren were glad the truth was seene,
When they were washed by his naturall clensing;
And their old Leprie by Miracle was made cleane.

43. The full *Moone* halfe shaddowed the *Sun*,
To putt away the burning of his light;
Black shaddowed first the skyes were so dunn,
The Ravens bill began who looketh right,
Blacker then Jett or Bugle to sight;
But litle and litle by ordinary apparance,
The temperate fire with his cherishing might
Turned all to white, but with noe violence.

44. Tyme to the Queene approched of Childing,
The Child of Nature was ready to fly,
Passage was there none to hys out going:
He spread hys wings and found no liberty;
Of nyne Virgins he devoured three,
The other six most excellent and faire,
Fearefull for dread in their greatest beauty,
Spread their feathers and flew forth in the Aire,

45. The Child coloured first Black and after White,
Having noe heate in very existence,
But by cherishing of the Sun bright,
Of forraine fire there was noe violence:
Save that men say which have experience,
He dranke such plenty of the Water of the well,
That his six sisters made noe resistance;
But would have devowred; *Dasten* can you tell.

46. Sometymes black, sometymes was he redd,
Now like ashes, now Citrine of Colour:
Now of Safforne hew, now sanguine was his head,
Now white as a lylie he shewed him in his bower,
The Moone gave nourishment to him in his labour;
And with all their force did their buisnes,
To cloath hym fresher then any flowre,
With a mantle of everlasting whitnes.

Pearce

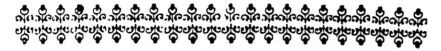

PEARCE
THE BLACK MONKE
upon the Elixir.

TAke Erth of Erth, Erths Moder,
And Watur of Erth yt ys no oder,
And Fier of Erth that beryth the pryse,
But of that Erth louke thow be wyse,
The trew *Elixer* yf thow wylt make,
Erth owte of Erth looke that thow take,
Pewer sutel faire and good,
And than take the Water of the Wood:
Cleere as Chrystall schynyng bryght:
And do hem togeder anon ryght,
Thre dayes than let hem lye,
And than depart hem pryvyly and slye,
Than schale be browght Watur schynyng,
And in that Watur ys a soule reynynge,
Invisible and hyd and unseene,
A marvelous matter yt ys to weene.
Than departe hem by dystillynge,
And you schalle see an Erth apperinge,
Hevie as metale schalle yt be;
In the wych is hyd grete prevety,
Destil that Erth in grene hewe,
Three dayes during well and trew;
And do hem in a body of glass,
In the wych never no warke was.

In a Furnas he must be sett,
And on hys hede a good lymbeck;
And draw fro hym a Watur clere
The wych Watur hath no peere,
And aftur macke your Fyer stronger,
And there on thy Glasse continew longer,
So schal yow se come a Fyer;
Red as blode and of grete yre,
And aftur that an Erth leue there schale,
The wych is cleped the Moder of alle;
Then into Purgatory sche must be doe,
And have the paynes that longs thereto,
Tyl sche be bryghter than the Sune,
For than thow hast the Maystrey wone;
And that schalbe wythin howres three,
The wych forsooth ys grete ferly:
Than do her in a clene Glass,
Wyth some of the Watur that hers was.
And in a Furnas do her againe,
Tyl sche have drunke her Watur certaine,
And aftur that Watur give her Blood,
That was her owne pewre and good,
And whan sche hath dranke alle her Fyer,
Sche wyll wex strong and of grete yre.
Than take yow mete and mylcke thereto,
And fede the Chylde as you schowlde do,
Tyl he be growne to hys full age,
Than schal he be of strong courage;
And tourne alle Bodies that leyfull be,
To hys owne powre and dignitye,
And this ys the makyng of owre *Stone*,
The trewth here ys towlde yow evereech one.
For all that taketh any other wey,
Mouch they looseth and mouch they may,

For

For trewly there ys no other way of righte,
But Body of Body and Lyghte of Lyghte,
Man of Man begottyn ys,
And Beste of Beste to hys lykenes,
Alle the fooles in the worlde seeken;
A thynge that they may never meeten,
They wolde have Metalle owte of hem,
That never was fownde by worldly men:
Ne never was fownde by Goddis myghte,
That they schould beare any such fryghte.
All Saltes and Sulphures far and nere,
I interdite hem alle in fere,
Alle Corosive waters, Blood and Hayre,
Pyss, Hornes, Wormes and Saudiver,
Alume, Atriment, alle I suspende,
Rasalger and Arsnick I defende,
Calx vive, and Calx mort hys Brother,
I suspende them both, one and other,
For of alle things I wyll no moe,
But fowre Elements in Generall I say soe,
Sun and Moone, Erth and Water;
And here ys alle that men of clatter,
Our Gold and Sylver ben no common plate,
But a sperme owte of a Bodi I take,
In the wych ys alle *Sol*, *Lune*, Lyfe and Lyghte
Water and Erth, Fyre and Fryght:
And alle commyth of one Image,
But the Water of the Wood makyth the marryage;
Therefore there ys none other waye,
But to take thee to thy Beades and praye:
For Covetous Men yt fyndyth never,
Though they seek yt once and ever,
Set not your Hearts in thys thyng,
But only to God and good lyvynge.

And.

And he that wyll come thereby,
Must be meeke, and full of mercy:
Both in spyrit and in Countenannce,
Full of Chereti and good Governaunce;
And evermore full of almes deede,
Symple and pewerly hys lyf to leade:
Wyth Prayers, Pennaunces, and Piety,
And ever to God a lover be,
And alle the ryches that he ys sped,
To do God worschyppe wyth Almes deede.
 In Arsenyck sublymed there ys a way streight,
Wyth Mercury calcyned nyne tymes hys weight
And grownde together with the Water of myght
That bereth ingression lyfe and lyght,
And anon as they togyther byne,
Alle runnyth to Water bryght and shene,
Upon thys Fyre they grow togethyr,
Tyll they be fast and flee no whythyr;
But than feede hem fowrth wyth thy hond,
Wyth mylke and meate tyle they be stronge,
And thow schalt have there a good Stone,
Whereof an Ounc on sowrty wyll gone:
Upon *Venus* or on *Mercury*,
Thys Medicyn wyll make thee merry.
 All yow that have sowght mani a day,
Leave worke, take yowre Beades and pray,
For the longer that yow seeken,
The longer yt ys or yow meeten;
And he that now fayne would be sped,
Lysten to my Daughter *Megg*:
For schhe scall tell yow trewth and ryghte,
Hearken now wyth all your myght.
 I am *Mercury* the myghty Flower,
I am most worthy of Honour;

I am sours of *Sol, Luna*, and *Mars*,
I am genderer of *Iovis*, many be my snares:
I am setler of *Saturne*, and sours of *Venus*,
I am Empresse, Pryncesse and Regall of Queenes,
I am Mother of Myrrour, and maker of lyght,
I am head and hyghest and fayrest in syght:
I am both *Sun*, and *Moone*,
I am sche that alle thynges must doone.
I have a Daughter hight *Saturne* that ys my darlyng,
The wych ys Mother of all werkyng,
For in my Daughter there byne hydd,
Fowre thyngs Commonly I kydd:
A Golden seede, and a spearme rych,
And a Silver seede none hym lich;
And a *Mercury* seede full bryght,
And a *Sulphur* seede that ys ryght.
Of my Daughter wythowten dred,
Byn made Elyxirs whyte and redd,
Therefor of her draw a Water cler,
The *Scyence* yf thow lyst to leare.
Thys Water reduceth every thynge,
To tendernes and to fyxing:
It burgeneth growyth and gyveth fryght and lyght,
Ingression lyfe and lastyng in syght:
Alle ryghteous werkes sooth to say,
It helpeth and bryngyth in a good way:
Thys ys the Water that ys most worthy,
Aqua perfectissima & flos mundi:
For alle werkes thys Water makyth whyte,
Reducyng and schyning as Sylver bryght:
And of the Oyle greate marvell there ys,
For all thyngs yt bryngyth to rednes:
As Cytrine gold he ys full high,
None ye so redd nor none ys so worthy:

And in the Erth grete marvele ys hyd,
That ys first so black, and than so red:
And alle ys done in howres three,
Thys may be cleped *Gods Prevetie*;
Than the Erth shall torne red as blood,
Citrine Gold, naturall cleere and good,
And than the red Oyle to hem schall goe,
Red Ferment, and red Mercury alsoe,
And grow togeder weekes seaven,
Blessed be Almyghty God of Heven:
One Ounce of thys Medycine worthy
Cast upon two hundred ownces of Mercury:
Schall make Gold most royall,
And ever enduring to holde tryall;
Fyre and Hammer Tuch and Test,
And all essayes most and least.
And yt ys Medycen above common Gold,
To mans body as God yt would.
For Gold that cometh from the Oare,
Is nourished with fowle Sulphur:
And Engendered upon Mercury he ys,
And nouryshed by Erth and Sulphur I wys,
And our Gold ys made of thre pewre soules,
In the wych ys noe Corrupcyon foule:
But purged pewre as clene as Chrystall,
Body and Spyryt and Sowle wyth all;
And so they grow into a stone,
In the wych Corrupcyon there ys none;
And than cast hym upon *Mercury*,
And he schalbe Gold most worthy,
Now have you heard the makyng of our Stone,
The begynyng and endyng ys all one.

THE

THE WORKE OF *RICH: CARPENTER.*

OF *Titan Magnasia* take the cler light,
The rede Gumme that ys so bryght,
Of *Philosofris* the *Sulfer vife,*
I called *Gold* wythouten stryfe;
Of hem drawe owte a Tincture,
And make a matrymony pure:
Betweene the husband and the wyfe,
I spoused wyth the Water of lyfe:
And so that none dyvysion
Be there, in the conjunccion
Of the *Moone* and of the *Sonne,*
After the marriage ys begonne;
And that *Mercury* the planete,
In loef make hem so to mete:
That eyder wyth oder be joyned even,
As a Stone engendered sent;e down fro heven;
Of hem make water clere rennynge,
As any Chrystall bryght schynynge.
Drawen out of bodyes fyxed,
By Nature prively mixed
Within a vessal depured clene,
Of *Philosofris* bright and schene;
Beware the Fume escape the nowght,
And alleso marked well in thy thowght;
That of the Fire the quallitee,
Equal to *Phebez* bemes be;
In the moneth of *Iune* and *Iule,*
Understand me be not dulle;

For

For thou schalt see marveles grete,
Colures spring oute of the heate:
Fyrste Blakke and Whyte, and so Redde,
And after Setryne wythouten drede:
And so wythin howres thre,
That *Stone* schall thorowe perced be
Wyth Aier that schall upon hym lyght,
The wych ys a wonder syght:
Whenne the spiryt ys refreyned,
And wyth the Bodie so constrayned,
That hem asounder maye nothyng parte,
So Nature hem doth there so coart,
In matrise whenne they both ben knyte,
Lett never thy Vessel be unshytte;
Tyl thys ingendred have a stone,
That in thys world ys not suche on:
For hyt ys called Anymal,
Richer then the Mineral.
Wyche ys founden in every place,
Who foundeth hyt myght have grase:
In the and me and over alle
Both Vegetables and Sophisticall:
On Hilles hye and Valeys lowe,
He groweth who cowde hyt know,
Take thys for an informacion,
In Caryt and in Proporcion,
Lyth alle who so coude seke oute,
In *Bus* and *Nubi* ys alle the doute:
He that puttes hemself in pres,
To Genis and to Species:
Qualitas and every Quantite,
To mane a man hyt wol not be,
To brynge about thys tresure,
I mene owre *Stone* of suche valour;

And

And yet who coude wel understonde,
May fynde hit redy at hys honde,
For Fowles that in the Ayre done flee,
And. alſo Fiſches in the See:
The moyſter of the rede Grape
And of the whyte, who coud hym take:
Vertues of Erbes vegetyff,
And ſoules of Beſtes ſenſytyff:
Reyſons of Angels that doth diſcerne,
Goude and Yeul Man to governe,
All bryngs to thyn houſe
Thys noble *Ston* ſo preciouſe,
And Soverente of alle thys Werke,
Both to Lewd and to Clerke:
Lyth alle by diſcrecion,
In Fyre, and in Decoccion:
The craft recordeth yif he can rede,
How all and ſume who ſhal ſpede;
In Bokes cler as ye maye ſee,
Stat in Ignis regimine:
To brynge forth at my devys,
Thys ryche Rubye, thys *Ston* of prys:
Harde hevy and percyng,
Now ys thys a wonder thyng:
I coude never ſuche on a ſpye,
Save that I fynde howe on *Marie:*
Fyrſt founde hyt wythouten leſe,
The wyche was ſuſter to *Moyſez*:
But who hyt be that ſchall werke,
Let hem not begenn in the derke:
For he mai fayle for faute of lyght,
But the Sunne ſchyne full bright:
Avyſe the wel er thow begene,
Or ellſe lytel ſchalt thow wynne.

THE HUNTING OF THE *GREENE LYON.*

Written by the Viccar of MALDEN.

ALL haile to the noble Companie
Of true Students in holy *Alchimie*,
Whose noble practise doth hem teach
To vaile their secrets wyth mistie speach;
Mought yt please your worshipfulnes
To heare my silly soothfastnes,
Of that practise which I have seene,
In hunting of the *Lyon Greene*:
And because you may be apaid,
That ys truth, that I have said;
And that you may for suerty weene,
That I know well thys *Lyon greene*:
I pray your patience to attend
Till you see my short writt end,
Wherein Ile keepe my noble *Masters* rede,
Who while he lived stood me in steede;
At hys death he made me sweare hym to,
That all the secrets I schould never undoe
To no one Man, but even spread a Cloude
Over my words and writes, and so it shroud,
That they which do this *Art* desire,
Should first know well to rule their Fyre:

For

For with good reaſon yt doth ſtand,
Swords to keepe fro mad Mens hand:
Leaſt th'one ſhould, kill th'other burne,
Or either doe ſome ſore ſhroud turne:
As ſome have done that I have ſeene,
As they did hunt thys *Lyon greene*.
Whoſe collour doubtles ys not ſoe,
And that your wiſdomes well doe know;
For no man lives that ever hath ſeene
Upon foure feete a *Lyon* colloured *greene*:
But our *Lyon* wanting maturity,
Is called *greene* for unripenes truſt me,
And yet full quickly can he run,
And ſoone can overtake the *Sun*:
And ſuddainely can hym devoure,
If they be both ſhut in one towre:
And hym Eclipſe that was ſo bryght,
And make thys redde to turne to whyte:
By vertue of hys crudytie,
And unripe humors whych in hym be,
And yet wythin he hath ſuch heate,
That whan he hath the *Sun* up eate,
He bringeth hym to more perfection,
Than ever he had by Natures direccion.
This *Lyon* maketh the *Sun* ſith ſoone
To be joyned to hys Siſter the *Moone*:
By way of wedding a wonderous thing,
Thys *Lyon* ſhould cauſe hem to begett a King:
And tis as ſtrange that thys Kings food,
Can be nothing but thys *Lyons* Blood;
And tis as true that thys ys none other,
Than ys it the Kings Father and Mother.
A wonder a *Lyon*, and *Sun* and *Moone*,
All theſe three one deede have done:

The

The *Lyon* ys the Preist, the *Sun* and *Moone* the wedd,
Yet they were both borne in the *Lyons* Bedd;
And yet thys King was begott by none other,
But by *Sun* and *Moone* hys owne Sister and Brother.
O noble *Master* of pardon I you pray,
Because I did well-neere bewray
The secret which to me ys so deare,
For I thought none but Brothers were here:
Than schould I make no doubt
To have written plainely out,
But for my fealty I must keepe aye,
Ile turne my pen another way,
To speake under *Benedicite*
Of thys noble Company:
Wych now perceives by thys,
That I know what our *Lyon* ys.
Although in Science I am noe *Clerke*,
Yet have I labour'd in thys warke:
And truly wythouten any nay,
If you will listen to my lay:
Some thing thereby yow may finde,
That well may content your minde,
I will not sweare to make yow give credence,
For a *Philosopher* will finde here in evidence,
Of the truth, and to men that be Lay,
I skill not greatly what they say.
For they weene that our *Lyon* ys
Common Quicksilver, but truly they miss:
And of thys purpose evermore shall fayle,
And spend hys Thrift to litle availe,
That weeneth to warke hys wyll thereby,
Because he doth soe readely flie;
Therefore leave off ere thou begin,
Till thow know better what we meane;

Whan

Whych whan thow doest than wilt thou say
That I have tought thee a good lay,
In that whych I have said of thee before,
Wherefore lysten and marke well my lore.
Whan thow hast thy *Lyon* with *Sol* and *Luna* well fedd,
And layd them clenly in their Bedd;
An easie heate they may not misse,
Till each the other well can kisse;
And that they shroude them in a skin,
Such as an Egg yelke lyeth in:
Than must thow draw from thence away,
A right good secret withouten any nay:
Wych must serve to doe thee good,
For yt ys the *Lyons* Blood:
And therewith must the King be fedd,
When he ys risen from the dead:
But longe tyme it wilbe,
Or ere his death appeare to thee;
And many a sleepe thow must lack,
Or thow hym see of Collour black.
Take heede yow move hym not with yre,
But keepe hym in an easy fyre;
Untill you see hym seperate,
From hys vile Erth vituperate;
Wych wilbe black and light withall,
Much like the substance of a fusball:
Your magnet in the midst wilbe,
Of Collour faire and white trust me;
Then whan you see all thys thing,
Your fire one degree increasing;
Untill yow well may se thereby,
Your matter to grow very dry:
Then yt ys fit wythout delay,
The excrements be tane away;

Prepaire a Bed most bryght and shine
For to lodge this young Chylde in:
And therein let hym alone lye,
Till he be throughly dry;
Than ys tyme as I doe thinke,
After such drouth to give him drinke:
But thereof the truth to shew,
Is a greate secret well I know;
For *Philosophers* of tyme old,
The secret of *Imbibition* never out tould;
To create *Magnesia* they made no care,
In their Bookes largely to declare;
But how to order it after hys creacion,
They left poore men without consolacion;
Soe many men thought they had had perfeccion,
But they found nothing in their Projeccion:
Therefore they mard what they had made before,
And of *Alchimy* they would have no more.
Thus do olde Fathers hide it from a Clearke,
Because in it consisteth the whole subtill warke;
Wych if ye list of me to know,
I shall not faile the truth to shew.
Whan your pure matter in the glasse is fitt,
Before that you your vessell shitt;
A portion of your *Lyons* sweate
Must be given it for to eate:
And they must be grounded so well together,
That each fro other will flee noe whither;
Then must you seale up your Glasse,
And in hys Furnace where he was,
You must set them there to dry.
Which being done then truly,
You must prepare like a good Phisitian,
For another *Imbibition*:

But

But evermore looke that you dry
Up all hys drinke, that none lye by,
For if yow make hym drinke too free,
The longer will your workeing be,
And yf you let hym be too dry,
Than for thirst your Child may dye;
Wherefore the meane to hold is best,
Twixt overmoyst and too much rost;
Six tymes thy *Imbibitions* make,
The seaventh that Saboath's rest betake:
Eight dayes twixt ilke day of the six,
To dry up moist and make it fix;
Then at the nynth tyme thy Glasse up seale,
And let him stand six weekes each deale:
With his heate temperd so right,
That Blacknes past he may grow white;
And so the seaventh weeke rest him still,
Till thow *Ferment* after thy will;
Which if thow wilt *Ferment* for Whyte,
Thereby thow gainst noe greate profitt;
For I assure thee thow needest not dred,
To proceede with fire till all be Redd;
Than must thow proceede as did *Philosophers* old
To prepaire thy *Ferment* of peure Gold,
Which how to doe though secret that it be,
Yet will I truly teach it thee.
In the next *Chapter* as erst I did say,
That soe the truth finde yow may,
Therefore of Charity and for our Lords sake,
Let noe man from my writings take
One word, nor add thereto,
For certainely if that he doe,
He shall shew malice fro the which I am free,
Meaning truth and not subtilty;

Which I refer to the Judgement
Of those which ken the *Philosophers* intent:
Now listen me with all your might,
How to prepare your Ferment right.
O noble Worke of workes that God has wrought,
Whereby each thing of things are forth aye broght;
And fitted to their generacion,
By a noble fermentacion;
Which *Ferment* must be of such a thing,
As was the workes begyning;
And if thow doe progresse aright
Whan thow hast brought the worke to whight;
And than to stay is thy intent,
Doe after my Comandement;
Worke *Luna* by her selfe alone,
With the blood of the *greene Lyon*:
As earst thow didst in the begining,
And of three didst make one thing,
Orderly yeilding forth right,
Till thy Magnet schew full whyte;
Soe must thow warke all thy *Ferment*,
Both White and Red, else were yt shent.
Red by yt selfe and soe the White,
With the *Lyons* Blood must be deight;
And if thow wilt follow my lore,
Set in thy *Ferment* the same houre,
Of *Sol* for Redd, of *Luna* for White,
Each by himselfe let worke tight;
Soe shall thy *Ferment* be ready edress,
To feede the King with a good mess
Of meates that fitt for his digestion,
And well agreeing to his Complexion;
If he be of Collour White,
Feed hym than with *Luna* bright;

If

If his flesh be perfect Red,
Than with the *Sun* he must be fedd,
Your *Ferment* one fourth parte must be,
Into your Magnet made evenly,
And joyne hem warme and not cold,
For raw to ripe you may be bold
Have disagreement soe have heate and cold:
Therefore put hem warme into thy Glasse,
Then seale it up even as it was:
And Circle all till yt be wonne,
By passing degrees every each one:
Both black and whyte, and also redd,
Than of the Fire heere have noe dread;
For he will never dreade the fyre,
But ever abide thy desire.
And heere a secret to thee I must shew,
How to *Multeplie* that thow must know,
Or else it wilbe over micle paine
For thee to begin thy worke againe:
I say to thee that in noe fashion,
It's so well Multeplied as with continuall Firmentation:
And sure far it wilbe exalted at the last,
And in Projeccion ren full fast:
There for in fyre keepe *Firment* alway,
That thy Medicine augment mayst aye;
For yf the maid doe not her leaven save, (crave;
Then of her Neighbours sche must needs goe
Or sche must stay till sche can make more,
Remember the Proverbe that *store is no sore:*
Thus have I tought thee a lesson, full of truth,
If thow be wicked therefore my heart is reuth:
Remember God hys blessing he can take,
Whan he hath given it, if abuse any you make,
For surely if thow be a *Clerke,*

Thow wilt finde trewth in thys werke:
But if so be that thow be lay,
And understond not what I say,
Keepe Councell then and leve thy Toy,
For it befitts no Lymmer Joy,
To medle with such grete secresie:
As ys thys hygh *Phylosophye.*
My Councell take, for thow schalt finde it true,
Leave of seeking thys *Lyon* to pursue,
For hym to hunt that ys a prety wyle,
Yet by hys Craft he doth most Folke beguile,
And hem devour and leave hem full of care,
Wherefore I bidd thee to beware.
And Councell give thee as my frend,
And so my *Hunting* here I end.
Praying God that made us we may not myss
To dwell with hym in hys Hevenly blyss.

THE BREVIARY OF NATURALL PHILOSOPHY.

Compiled by the unlettered Scholar

THOMAS CHARNOCK.

Student in the most worthy Scyence of *Astronomy* and *Philosophy*. The first of *Ianuary Anno. Dom.* 1557.

Anno. Dom. 1557. *The first day of the new yeare*
This Treatise was begun as after may appeare.

The Booke Speaketh.

COme hither my Children of this Discipline,
Which in naturall Philosophy have spent so long time;
To ease your painfull Study I am well willed
And by the grace of God it shall be fulfilled;
If he in me (my *Author*) will shed one drop of grace,
The better he shall finish me and in shorter space.
And if you will know what I am surely,
I am named the *The Breviary of naturall Philosophy.*
Declaring all *Vessells* and *Instruments*,
Which in this *Science* serve our intents.
For moe things belong unto the same,
More then any *Author* hath written the Name;
Which hath brought many a one in great doubt,
What is the Implements that longeth thereabout;
Wherefore in good order, I will anon declare,
What *Instruments* for our *Arte* you neede to prepare.

THE

The Preface of the Author.

GOe forth little Booke *in volume but small,*
Yet hast thou in thee that is not in them All,
For satisfying the mindes of the Students in this Arte,
Then art thou worth as many Bookes, as will lye in a Cart :
Glad may he be that hath thee in his keeping,
For he may find through diligent seeking,
All things in thee which shall be neccessary,
As Vessells and Instruments belonging to Alchimy ;
Which would set many a Mans heart on fire,
To have the same knowledge they have so great desire.
And no mervaile though they be glad and faine,
For they have spent many a pound in vaine ;
In making of Vessells of many divers sorts,
And have brought them out of many strange Ports :
Because they did not well understand,
That all things we need we have in England.
Now think you that this will not save many a Marke,
Unto those that have wrestled so long in our Warke ?
Yes some would spend all the Money in their pouch,
If they knew but this or halfe so much.
Wherefore of pitty I will no longer refraine,
But declare all things their purpose to attaine.
Wherefore if you do happen on my Booke,
Either by Casualty, Hooke, or by Crooke :
Yet pray for my Soule when I am dead and rotten,
That of Alchimy Scyence *the dore hath let open ;*
Sufficient for thee if thou have any Braine,
Now sharpen thy wits that thou maist it attaine.

The

The first Chapter.

NOw will I declare all things at large,
Of *Implements* of this Work and what is the charge:
And first with the *Potter* I will begin,
Which cannot make that which he hath never seene;
Whether that thy Vessels be made to thy minde,
Stand by while he worketh more surety to finde,
And shew him what to doe by some signe or similitude,
And if his witts be not to dull nor rude,
He will understand what thou doest meane,
For I think few Potters within this Realme
Have made at any tyme such cunning ware,
As we for our *Scyence* doe fashion and prepaire;
And when he hath formed them unto thy purpose,
For what occasion thou needest not disclose:
But if he say unto you, Good Master myne,
Tell me for what purpose or what engine
Shall these Vessels serve that thou cause me to make,
For all my life hitherto I dare undertake
I never formed such, nor the like of them;
Yet are they but plaine without wrinkle or hem,
One within another, it is a pretty feate,
The third without them to guide up the heate:
Then say unto him to satisfie his minde,
That ye have a Father which is somewhat blinde,
Who if it please God you will indeavour,
To stil a water his blindnes to dissever:
Which is the *Elixir* of lyfe as wise men say,
And in this doing God send me my pray;

Then will he say this or the like,
I pray God to send yee that which you seeke,
And thus with the *Potter* thou hast now done,
Without thou breake thy Pots with the heate of the *Sun*:
Which if it doe it turnes thee to paine,
And there is no way but to make them new againe.
As soone as with the *Potter* thou hast made an end,
Then with a *Ioyner* thou must Condescend,
Who also must have this Councell and witt,
To make a Tabernacle the Vessell to fitt;
Which wilbe also in greate doubt,
For what purpose it will serve about;
In that he never made nor framed none such,
Although it be made like to a Hutch:
Then tell him a Tale of a roasted Horse,
Unto the which he will have no remorse:
And laugh and say it is a Borrough for a Fox,
Although it be made sure with Keys and locke,
And thus with the *Ioyner* thou hast made an end,
Without thou set it on fire as I did mine.
As for *Glassemakers* they be scant in this land,
Yet one there is as I doe understand:
And in *Sussex* is now his habitacion,
At *Chiddinsfold* he workes of his Occupacion:
To go to him it is necessary and meete,
Or send a servant that is discreete:
And desire him in most humble wise
Ito blow thee a Glasse after thy devise;
If were worth many an Arme or a Legg,
The could shape it like to an egge;
To open and to close as close as a haire,
If thou have such a one thou needest not feare.
Yet if thou hadst a number in to store,
It is the the better, for *Store is no sore*.

THE

The second Chapter.

NOw LORD of thy grace I beseech thee suffer me,
To finish my pretence in this rude Studie:
For this nor ought else without thy helpe can be done,
As neither the Conjuncion of *Sun* nor *Moone*:
Nor yet other *Planets* can motion themselves an houre,
Without thy providence and thy divine power:
Wherefore in all things that we doe begin,
Let us with prayer call for helpe of him:
That he bring our doings to effect,
Which must be done very Circumspect:
Wherefore if you thinke to obtaine your intent,
Feare God and keepe his Comandement:
And beware of Pride and let it passe,
And never be looking too much in thy Glasse;
Deceive noe man with false measure,
For truly that is ill gotten treasure:
But let thy weights be true and just,
For weight and measure every man must
Unto his Neighbour yeild uprightly,
And so must thou in the worke of *Philosophy*:
And also feede him which is hungry,
And give him drinke which is thirsty.
Give liberally I say as riches doe arise,
And from thirsty body turne not away thy Eyes.
What and two poore Men at one tyme come unto thee
And say, Master, for the love of God and our Lady,
Give us your Charity whatsoever you please,
For we have not one peny to do us ease;

And we are now ready to the Sea preſt,
Where we muſt abide three moneths at the leaſt;
All which tyme to Land we ſhall not paſſe,
No although our Ship be made but of Glaſſe,
But all tempeſt of the Aire we muſt abide,
And in dangerous roades many tymes to ride;
Bread we ſhall have none, nor yet other foode,
But only faire water deſcending from a Cloude:
The *Moone* ſhall us burne ſo in proceſſe of tyme,
That we ſhalbe as black as men of *Inde*:
But ſhortly we ſhall paſſe into another Clymate,
Where we ſhall receive a more purer eſtate;
For this our Sinns we make our Purgatory,
For the which we ſhall receive a Spirituall body:
A body I ſay which if it ſhould be ſould,
Truly I ſay it is worth his weight in Gold:
Son give theis two, one penny in their Journey to drinke,
And thou ſhalt ſpeede the better truly as I thinke.

The third Chapter.

NOw have I good will largely to write,
Although I can but ſlenderly indite;
But whether I can or cannot indeede,
With the Chapter of *Fire* I will proceede:
Which if thou knoweſt not how to governe and keepe,
Thou wert as good go to bed and ſleepe,
As to be combred therewith about,
And therefore I put thee moſt certainely out of doubt;
For when I ſtudied this *Scyence* as thou doeſt now,
I fell to practiſe by God I vowe:

I

I was never so troubled in all my lyfe beforne,
As intending to my *Fire* both Midday Eve and Morne:
And all to kepe it at an even stay;
It hath wrought me woe moe then I will say.
Yet one thing of truth I will thee tell,
What greate mishap unto my Worke befell;
It was upon a Newyeares day at Noone,
My *Tabernacle* caught fire, it was soone done:
For within an houre it was right well,
And streight of fire I had a smell.
I ran up to my worke right,
And when I cam it was on a fire light:
Then was I in such feare that I began to stagger,
As if I had byne wounded to the heart with a dagger;
And can you blame me? no I think not much,
For if I had beene a man any thing rich,
I had rather have given 100 Markes to the Poore,
Rather then that hap should have chanced that houre.
For I was well onward of my Work truly,
God save my Masters lyfe, for when he thought to dye,
He gave me his worke and made me his Heire,
Wherefore alwaies he shall have my prayer:
I obteyned his grace the date herefro not to varie,
In the first and second yeare of *King Phillip* & *Queene Mary.*
Yet lewdly I lost it as I have you tould,
And so I began the new and forgot the old,
Yet many a night after I could not sleepe in Bed
For ever that mischance troubled my head,
And feare thereof I would not abide againe;
No though I shoulde reape a double gaine,
Wherefore my charge rose to a greater summe,
As in hyring of a good stoute Groome;
Which might abide to watch and give attendance,
Yet often tymes he did me displeasaunce,

And would ſleepe ſo long till the Fire went out,
Then would the Knave that whorſon Lout,
Caſt in Tallow to make the fire burne quicker,
Which when I knew made me more ſicker;
And thus was I cumbred with a drunken ſott,
That with his haſty fire made my Worke too hott;
And with his ſloth againe he ſet my worke behinde;
For remedy thereof to quiet my Minde,
I thruſt him out of dores, and tooke my ſelfe the paine,
Although it be troubleſome it is the more certaine;
For ſervants doe not paſſe how our workes doe frame,
But have more delight to play and to game.
A good ſervant ſaith *Solomon* let him be unto thee,
As thyne owne heart in each degree.
For it is precious a faithfull ſervant to finde,
Eſteeme him above treaſure if he be to thy minde;
Not wretchles, but ſober, wiſe, and quiet,
Such a one were even for my dyet:
Thus having warn'd thee of an ill ſervant ſufficient,
But a good ſervant is for our intent.

The fourth Chapter.

WHen my Man was gone I began it anewe,
And old troubles then in my minde did renew;
As to break ſleepe oftentimes in the night,
For feare that my Worke went not aright;
And oftentimes I was in greate doubt,
Leaſt that in the night, my fire ſhould go out:
Or that it ſhould give to much heate,
The penſivenes thereof made me to breake ſleepe:

And

And also in the day least it should miscary,
It hath made my minde oftentimes to varie;
Wherefore if thou wilt follow my reade,
See thy fire safe when thou goest to Bed:
At Midnight also when thou dost arise,
And in so doing I judge thee to be wise:
Beware that thy Fire do no man harme,
For thou knowest many a mans House and Barne
Have byne set on fire by mischance,
And specially when a Foole hath the governance;
Our Fire is chargeable, and will amount
Above 3. pound a weeke, who hath list to cast account,
Which is chargeable to many a poore man,
And specially to me as I tell can:
And *Geber* bids poore men be content,
Hæc Scientia pauperi & agento non convenit
Sed potius est illis inimica, and bids them beware,
Because their mony they may not well spare;
For thou must have Fires more then one. or two,
What they be *George Ripley* will thee shew;
Above a hundred pounds truly did I spend,
Only in fire ere 9. moneths came to an end;
But indeede I begun when all things were deare,
Both Tallow, Candle, Wood, Coale and Fire:
Which charges to beare sometymes I have sold,
Now a Jewell, and then a ring of Gold:
And when I was within a Moneths reckoning,
Warrs were proclaimed against the *French King*.
Then a *Gentleman* that ought me greate mallice,
Caused me to be prest to goe serve at *Callys:*
When I saw there was none other boote,
But that I must goe spight of my heart roote;
In my fury I tooke a Hatchet in my hand,
And brake all my Worke whereas it did stand;

And

And as for my Potts I knocked them together,
And also my Glasses into many a shiver;
The *Crowes head* began to appeare as black as Iett
Yet in my fury I did nothing let:
But with my worke made such a furious faire,
That the *Quintessence* flew forth in the Aire.
Farewell quoth I, and seeing thou art gon,
Surely I will never cast of my Fawcon,
To procure thee againe to put me to hinderance,
Without it be my fortune and chaunce,
To speake with my good *Master* or that I dye;
Master *I. S.* his name is truly:
Nighe the City of *Salisbury* his dwelling is,
A spirituall man for sooth he is;
For whose prosperity I am bound to pray,
For that he was my Tutor many a day,
And understood as much of *Philosophie*,
As ever did *Arnold* or *Raymund Lullie*:
Geber, *Hermes*, *Arda*, nor yet King *Caleb*,
Understood no more then my good *Master* did.
I travelled this Realme Est and West over,
Yet found I not the like betweene the Mount and *Dover*:
But only a *Monke* of whome Ile speake anon,
Each of them had accomplished our *White Stone*:
But yet to the *Red Worke* they never came neere,
The cause hereafter more plainely shall appeare;
And thus when I had taken all this paines,
And then could not reape the fruit of my gaines:
I thought to my selfe, so to set out this Warke,
That others by fortune may hit right the Marke.

THE

The fift Chapter.

I am sorry I have nothing to requite my *Masters* gentle-
But only this *Boke* a litle short Treatise; (nes,
Which I dare say shall as welcome be to him,
As if I had sent him a Couple of Milch Kine:
And heere for his sake I will disclose unto thee,
A greate seacret which by God and the Trinity,
Since that our Lord this world first began,
Was it not so opened I dare lay my hand,
No, all the *Philosophers* which were before this day,
Never knew this secret I dare boldly say.
And now to obteyne thy purpose more rathe
Let thy Fire be as temperate as the Bath of the Bathe.
Oh what a goodly and profitable Instrument,
Is the Bath of the Bathe for our fiery intent!
To seeke all the World throughout I should not finde,
For profit and liberty a Fire more fitt to my minde.
Goe or ride where you list for the space of a yeare
Thou needest not care for the mending of thy Fire.
A *Monke* of *Bath* which of that house was *Pryor*,
Tould me in seacret he occupied none other fire,
To whome I gave credit even at the first season,
Because it depended upon very good reason:
He had our *Stone*, our *Medicine*, our *Elixir* and all,
Which when the *Abbie* was supprest he hid in a wall:
And ten dayes after he went to fetch it out,
And there he found but the stopple of a Clout.
Then he tould me he was in such an Agonie,
That for the losse thereof he thought he should be frenzie,

And a Toy tooke him in the head to run ſuch a race,
That many yeare after he had no ſetling place;
And more he is darke and cannot ſee,
But hath a Boy to leade him through the Country.
I hapned to come on a day whereas he was,
And by a word or two that he let paſſe,
I underſtood ſtreight he was a *Philoſopher,*
For the which cauſe I drew to him neare;
And when the Company was all gone,
And none but his Boy and he and I alone,
Maſter quoth I for the love of God and Charity,
Teach me the ſeacrets of *Naturall Philoſophy.*
No Son, quoth he, I know not what thou art,
And ſhall I reveale to thee ſuch a preciuos *Arte?*
No man by me ſhall get ſuch gaines,
No not my Boy which taketh with me ſuch paines,
That to diſcloſe it lyes not in my Bands,
For I muſt ſurrender it into the Lords hands,
Becauſe I heare not of one that hath the fame;
Which lifts up his minde and is apt for the ſame,
Which if I could finde I would ere I dye,
Reveale to him that ſame greate miſtery:
Yet one there is about the Citty of *Salisbury,*
A young man of the age of Eight and Twenty,
Charnock is his name of *Tennet* that *Iſle,*
His praiſe and Comendacions ſoundeth many a Mile;
That for a Younge man he is toward and apt,
In all the ſeaven liberall Scyences ſet none apart:
But of each of them he hath much or litle,
Whereof in our *Scyence* he may claime a title:
His praiſe ſpreads alſo for his good indighting,
And of ſome of his doings I have heard the reciting,
Both of Proſe and Meeter, and of Verſe alſo,
And ſure I commend him for his firſt ſhewe,

I

I thinke *Chaucer* at his yeares was not the like,
And *Skelton* at his yeares was further to seeke;
Wherefore for his knowledge, gravity and witt,
He may well be Crowned *Poet Laureat.*
Ceaſe Father quoth I and heare me ſpeake,
For my name is *Charnock* upon whome you treate;
But this which you ſay to me is greate wonder,
For theſe quallities and I am farr aſſunder;
I am no ſuch Man as you have made reckoning,
But you ſhall ſpeake for me when I go a wiving:
Your praiſe will make me ſpeede, though it be not true,
Nor yet my ſubſtance worth an old horſe ſhooe.
Is your name *Charnocke*, and the ſame Man?
Yea Sir quoth I: then ſtumbled he to give me his hand:
And talked an howre with me in the *Philoſophers* ſpeeche,
And heard that in no queſtion I was to ſeeche,
My Son quoth he let me have thy prayer,
For of this *Science* I will make thee myne heire;
Boy quoth he lead me into ſome ſecret place,
And then departe for a certaine ſpace,
Uutill this man and I have talked together:
Which being done, quoth he, now gentle Brother,
Will you with me to morrow be content,
Faithfully to receive the bleſſed Sacrament,
Upon this Oath that I ſhall heere you give,
For ne Gold ne Silver as long as you live,
Neither for love you beare towards your Kinne,
Nor yet to no great Man preferment to wynne:
That you diſcloſe the ſeacret that I ſhall you teach,
Neither by writing nor by no ſwift ſpeech;
But only to him which you be ſure
Hath ever ſearched after the ſeacrets of Nature?
To him you may reveale the ſeacrets of this *Art*, (depart.
Under the Covering of *Philoſophie* before this world yee

What anſwer will you give me: let me heare?
Maſter quoth I, I grant your deſire.
Then Son quoth he keepe thys Oath I charge thee well
As thinkeſt to be ſaved from the pitt of Hell. (cion
The next day we went to Church, and after our devo-
A *Preiſt* of his Gentlenes heard both our Confeſſions;
Which being done, to Maſſe ſtreight we went,
And he miniſtred to us the holy Sacrament;
But he never wiſt what we meant therein:
For with a contrary reaſon I did him blinde,
And ſo home to dinner we went to our hoaſt,
All which refeccion I paid for the Coſt.
When dinner was done I walked in the field
Large and plaine, where people paſſe by but ſield,
And when we were in the midds, Boy quoth he go pick a
And come not againe before I for thee whiſtle. (Thiſtle
Now *Maſter* quoth I the Coaſt from hearers is cleare,
Then quoth he my *Sonn* hearken in thyne Eare;
And within three or foure words he revealed unto me,
Of Mineralls prudence the greate Miſterie.
Which when I heard my Spirits were raviſhed for Joy,
The *Grecians* were never gladder for the wynning of *Troy*:
As I was then remembring my good *Maſter* thoe,
For even the ſelfe ſame ſecret he did me ſhew:
Nyne dayes and no more I tarried with him ſure,
But Lord in this tyme what ſecrets of Nature
He opened to me at divers ſundry tymes,
As partly I have told thee in my former Rimes:
The reſt is not to be written on paine of Damnacion,
Or elſe in this *Boke* truly I would make relation;
Now *Father* quoth I, I will depart you froe,
And for you I wil pray whether ſoever I goe;
Son quoth he Gods bleſſing goe with thee and thyne,
And if thou ſpeede well, let me heare of thee againe.

THE

The sixt Chapter.

WHen I was gone a mile or two abroade,
With fervent prayer I praised the Lord:
Giveing him thankes for that prosperous Journy,
VVhich was more leaver to me then an 100 l. in mony:
Surely quoth I my *Master* shall know all this,
Or else my Braines shall serve me amisse;
Which if they were so good as the *Monke* made mēciō,
Then would I write to my *Master* with a better invenciō,
O Lord quoth I what a solemne Oath was this given!
Surely in sheetes of Brasse it is worthy to be graven;
For a perpetuall memory ever to remaine
Among the *Philosophers*, for an Oath certaine:
And when I was two dayes Journey homeward,
To aske him a question to him againe I fared,
Which I had forgotten, and would not for my Land,
But that doubt truly I might understand.
I thought it not much to goe backe with all speede,
To seeke him out, & to the house where I left him I yed,
And there in a Chamber anone I founde him out,
Praying upon his Beades very devout:
Father quoth I a word with you I doe beseech:
Who is that quoth he? my *Son Charnock* by his speech:
Yea forsooth quoth I, I am come back to you,
Desiring you heartily to tell me one thing true:
Which is this. Who was in *Philosophy* your Tutor,
And of that Seacret to you the Revealer?
Marry quoth he and speake it with harty Joy,
Forsooth it was *Ripley* the Canon his Boy:

Then I remembred my good *Master* againe,
Which tould he did it never attaine
Of no manner of Man but of God, he put it in his head,
As he for it was thinking lying in his Bead:
And thus I tarried with him all that night,
And made him as good Cheere as I might.
In the morning I tooke my leave of him to depart,
And in the processe of tyme came home with a merry
But that mirth was shortly turn'd to care, (heart;
For as I have tould you so my Worke did fare.
Once I set it on fyre which did me much woe,
And after my Man hindred me a Moneth or two;
Yet the *Gentleman* did me more spight then the rest,
As when he made me from worke to be prest,
Then Bedlam could not hold me I was so frett,
But sowst at my worke with a greate Hatchett;
Rathing my Potts and my Glasses altogether,
I wisse they cost me more or I gott them thither:
The ashes with my stur flew all about,
One Fire I spilt and the other I put out:
All the Rubish to the dunghill I carried in a Sack,
And the next day I tooke my Coates with the Crosse at
And forth I went to serve a Soldiers rome (the back;
And surely quoth I, there shall come the day of Dome;
Before I practise againe to be a *Philosopher*,
Wherefore have me Commended to my good *Master*.
And now my students in this *Art*, my promise I have kept
(justly,
And that you shall finde true when you understand me
(truly;
Which before that day never thinke to speede,
For a plainer *Boke* then this never desire to reade:
And true it is also yf you can pick it out,
But it is not for every Cart-slave or Loute;

This

This to understand, no though his witts were fyne,
For it shalbe harde enough for a very good Divine
To Conster our meaning of this worthy *Scyence*,
But in the study of it he hath taken greate diligence:
Now for my good *Master* and *Me* I desire you to pray,
And if God spare me lyfe I will mend this another day.

Finished the 20th of JULY, 1557. *By the unletterd Schollar* THOMAS CHARNOCK, *Student in the most worthy* Scyence *of* ASTRONOMY *and* PHYLOSOPHY.

Ænigma ad Alchimiam.

When vii. tymes xxvi. had run their rase,
Then Nature discovered his blacke face:
But when an C. and L. had overcome him in fight,
He made him wash his face white and bright:
Then came xxxvi. wythe greate rialltie,
And made Blacke and White away to fle:
Me thought he was a Prince off honoure,
For he was all in Golden armoure;
And one his head a Crowne off Golde
That for no riches it might be solde:
Which tyll I saw my hartte was colde
To thinke at length who should wyne the filde
Tyll Blacke and White to Red dyd yelde;
Then hartely to God did I pray
That ever I saw that joyfull day.

1572. T. Charnocke.

when

Ænigma de Alchimiæ.

WHen vii tymes xxvi had runne their rase,
Then Nature discoved his blacke face.
But whith an C. and L. came in with great bloſt
And made Blacke nye to flye the Coſte:
Yet one came after and brought 30. off greate might,
Which made Blacke and White to flee quite;
Me thought he was a Prince off honor,
For he was all in Golden Armoure,
And one his hed a Crowne off Golde:
That for no riches it myght be solde,
And trewly with no *Philosopher* I do mocke;
For I did it my sellffe *Thomas Charnocke*:
Therefore God coomforte the in thy warke
For all our wrettinges are verye darke,
Despyse all Bookes and them defye,
Wherein is nothing but *Recipe & Accipe*;
Fewe learned men with in this Realme,
Can tell the aright what I do meane;
I could finde never man but one,
Which cowlde teache me the secrets off our Stone:
And that was a *Pryste* in the Close off *Salesburie*,
God rest his Soll in heven full myrie.

1572.

T. CHARNOCKE.

Bloomfields

BLOOMEFIELDS
BLOSSOMS:
OR,
The Campe of PHILOSOPHY.

WHen *Phœbus* was entred the signe of the *Ramme*,
In theMoneth of *March* when all things do spring;
Lying in my bed an old Man to me came,
Laying his hand on my busy head slumbering;
I am, said he, *Tyme*, The *Producer of all thing*:
Awake and rise, prepaire thy selfe quickly,
My intent is to bring thee to *the Campe of Philosophy*.

2. Bloomes and Blossomes plentifully in that field,
Bene plesantly flourishing dickt with Collour gay,
Lively water fountaines eke Beasts both tame and wild;
Over shaddowed with Trees fruitefull on every spraye,
Mellodiously singing the Birds do sitt and say:
Father Son and holy Ghost one God in persons three,
Impery and honor be to thee O holy Trinity,

3. Lo thus when he had said I arose quickly,
Doing on my Clothes in hast with agility,
Towards the *Campe* (we went) *of Philosophy*:
The wonderfull sights ther for to see;
To a large greate Gate father *Tyme* brought me,
Which closed was then he to me said,
Each thing hath his Tyme, be thou then nothing dismaid.

4. Then greate admiration I tooke unto my selfe,
With sore and huge perturbacion of minde,
Beholding the Gate fastned with locks twelve:
I fantised but smally that *Tyme* should be my frend:
Why studiest thou man, quoth hee, art thou blinde?
With a rodd he touched me, whereat I did downe fall
Into a strong sleepe, & in a Dreame he shewed me all.

1. *Igitur audite somnium meum quod vidi.* (seaven
In the thousand yeare of Christ five hundred fifty and
In the Moneth of *March* a sleepe as I did lye,
Late in the night, of the clock about Eleven,
In spirit wrapt I was suddainely into Heaven:
Where I saw sitting in most glorious Majestie
Three I beholding: adored but one Deitie.

2. A Spirit incircumscript, with burning heate incombustible,
Shining with brightnes, permanent as fountaine of all light.
Three knit in one with Glory incomprehensible;
Which to behold I had a greate delight:
This truly to attaine to, surmounteth my might:
But a voyce from that Glorious brightnes to me said,
I am one God of immensurable Majestie; be not affraid.

3. In this Vision cleere, that did it selfe soe extend
With a voyce most pleasant being three in one;
Peirced my Minde, and tought me to Comprehend
The darke sayings of *Philosophers* each one;
The *Altitude*, *Latitude*, and *Profundity* of the *Stone*,
To be three in Substance, and one in Essence;
A most Heavenly Treasure procreate by Quintessence.

4. Then studied I what this Quintessence should be,
Of visible things apparant to the Eye;
The fift being even a strange privetie,
In every substance resting invisibly;
The invisible Godhead is the same thought I;
Primer cause of being, and the Primer Essence:
And of the *Macrocosmy* the most soveraigne Quintessence.

5. This

5. This is that heavenly seacret potentiall,
That divided is, and resteth invisible
In all things Animall, Vigetall and Minerall;
Whose vertue and strength in them is indivisible:
From God it cometh, and God maketh it sensible,
To some Elect, to others he doth it denay,
As I sat thus musing a voyce to me did say.

6. Study thou no more of my Being, but stedfastly
Beleive this Trinity equally knit in One;
Further of my Secrets to muse it is but folly,
Passing the Capacity of all humane reason;
The Heavens closed up againe at that season:
Then Father *Tyme* set me at the Gate,
And delivered me a Key to enter in thereat.

7. The Key of knowledge and of Excellent Science;
Whereby all secrets of *Philosophy* are reserate;
The seacrets of Nature sought out by diligence;
Avoyding fables of envious fooles inveterate:
Whith *Recipe* and *Decipe* this *Scyence* is violate.
Therefore to me this Key he did dispose
The seacrets of this *Arte* to open and disclose.

8. Thus said Father *Tyme* this Key when he me tooke;
Unlock quoth he this Gate now by thy selfe,
And then upon him sorrowfully did I looke,
Saying that one Key could not undoe Locks twelve,
Whose Axe quoth he is sure both head and helve
Hold will together, till the Tree downe fall,
Soe open thou the first Lock and thou hast opned all.

9. What is the first Lock named tell me then
I pray thee, said I, and what shall I it call?
It is said he *the Seacret of all Wise Men*;
Chaos in the bodyes called the *first Originall:*
Prima materia, our *Mercury*, our *Menstruall:*
Our *Vitrioll*, our *Sulphur*, our *Lunary* most of price;
Put the Key in the Lock, twill open with a trice.

10. Then the Key of knowledge I busily tooke in hand
And began to search the hollownes in the Lock,
The words thereof I scarce did understand,
So craftily conveid they were in their stock;
I proved every way, and at last I did unlock
The crafty Gynns thus made for the nonce,
And with it the other Locks fell open all at once.

11. At this Gate opening even in the entry
A number of *Philosophers* in the face I met,
Working all one way the secrets of *Philosophy*
Upon *Chaos* darke that among them was set,
Sober men of living, peaceable and quiet;
They buisily disputed the *Materia Prima*,
Rejecting cleane away *Simul stulta & frivola.*

12. Here I saw the Father of Philosophers, *Hermes*,
Here I saw *Aristotle* with cheere most jocund;
Here I saw *Morien*, and *Senior in Turba* more or lesse,
Sober *Democritus*, *Albert*, *Bacon* and *Ramund*,
The *Monke* and the *Chanon of Bridlington* so profound,
Working most seacretly, who said unto me;
Beware thou beleeve not all that thou doest see.

13. But if thou wilt enter this *Campe of Philosophy*
With thee take *Tyme* to guide thee in the way;
For By-pathes and Broad wayes deepe Valies and hills high
Here shalt thou finde, with sights pleasant and gay,
Some thou shalt meete with, which unto thee shall say,
Recipe this, and that; with a thousand things more,
To *Decipe* thy selfe, and others; as they have done before.

14. Then Father *Tyme* and I by favour of these men
Such sights to see passed forth towards the *Campe*,
Where we met disguised *Philosophers* leene,
With Porpheries, and Morters ready to grinde and stampe,
Their heads shaking, their hands full of the Crampe:
Some lame with Spasmer, some feeble, wan and blind
With Arsnick and Sulphus, to this *Art* most unkinde.

15. These

15. These were *Brooke* the Preist, and *Yorke* with Coates gay,
Which robbed KING *HENRY* of a Million of Gold,
Martin Perien, Major & Thomas De-la-hay
Saying that the King they greatly inrich would,
They whispered in his Eare and this Tale they him tould.
We will worke for your highnes the *Elixer vitæ*,
A princely worke called *Opus Regale*.

16. Then brought they in the Viccar of *Malden*
With his *Greene Lyon* that most Royall seacrett,
Richard Record, and litle Master *Eden*,
Their Mettalls by Corrasives to Calcine and frett;
Hugh Oldcastle and Sir *Robert Greene* with them mett.
Roasting and boyling all things out of kinde,
And like *Foolosophers* left of with losse in the end.

17. Yet brought they forth things beautifull to sight,
Deluding the King thus from day to day,
With Copper Citrinate for the Red, and albified for the White
And with Mercury rubified in a glasse full gay,
But at the last in the fire they went away.
All this was because they knew not the verity,
Of *Altitude*, *Latitude* and *Profundity*.

18. Thence Father *Tyme* brought me into a Wildernes,
Into a Thicket having by-paths many one;
Steps and footeings I saw there more and lesse
Wherein the aforesaid men had wandred and gone,
There I saw Marcasites, Mineralls, and many a stone.
As Iridis, Talck, and Alome, lay digd from the ground
The Mines of Lead, and Iron, that they had out found.

19. No marvel I trow though they were much set by
That with so greate Riches could endue the King,
So many Sundry wayes to fill up his Treasury;
With filty matters greate charges in to bring,
The very next way a Prince to bring to begging;
And make a noble Realme and Common wealth decay,
These are Royall *Philosophers* the cleane contrary way.

20. From thence forth I went (*Tyme* being my guide,)
Through a greene Wood, where Birds sing cleerely,
Till we came to a field pleasant large and wide
Which he said was called *The Campe of Philosophy*;
There downe we satt to heare the sweete Harmony
Of divers Birds in their sweete Notes singing,
And to receive the Savour of the flowers springing.

21. Here *Juno*, here *Pallas*, here *Apollo* do dwell;
Here true *Philosophers* take their dwelling place
Here duly the *Muses* nyne drinke of *Pyrenes* Well,
No boasting broyler here the *Arte* can deface;
Here *Lady Philosophy* hath her royall Pallace:
Holding her Court in most high Consistory,
Sitting with her Councellors most famous of memory.

22. There one said to me, an ancient Man was hee,
Declaring forth the Matter of the *Stone*;
Saying that he was sent thither to Councell me,
And of his Religion to chuse me to be one;
A Cloath of Tisshue he had him upon,
Verged about with Pearles of Collour fresh and gay,
He proceedeth with his Tale, and againe he did thus say.

23. Here all occult seacrets of Nature knowen are,
Here all the Elements from things are drawne out;
Here Fire, Air and Water in Earth are knit together:
Here all our seacret worke is truly brought about,
Here thou must learne in thy buisines to be stoute,
Night and day thou must tend thy worke buisily,
Having constant patience never to be weary.

24. As we satt talking by the Rivers running cleere,
I cast myne Eye aside and there I did behold
A *Lady* most excellent sitting in an Arbour
Which clothed was in a Robe of fine Gold,
Set about with Pearles and Stones manifold.
Then ask't I Father *Tyme* what she should be?
Lady Philosophy quoth, he most excellent of beauty.

25. Then

25. Then was I stricken with an ardent Audacity,
The place to approach to where I saw this sight,
I rose up to walke and the other went before me,
Against the Arbour, till I came forth right,
There we all three humbly as we might,
Bowed downe our selves to her with humility,
With greate admiration extolling her felicity.

26. She shewed her selfe both gentle and benigne,
Her gesture and Countenance gladded our comming:
From her seate imperiall she did her selfe decline,
As a Lady loving perfect wisdome and Cunning,
Her goodly Poems, her Beauty was surmounting:
Her speech was decorate with such aureat sentence,
Far excelling famous *Tullies* Eloquence.

27. Then Father *Tyme* unto that *Lady* said,
Pleaseth it your highnes this poore Man to heare,
And him to assist with your most gratious aide:
Then she commanded him with me to draw neere
Son, said the *Lady*, be thou of good Cheere.
Admitted thou shalt be among greate and small
To be one of my Schollers principall.

28. Then she committed me to *Raymund Lullie*,
Commanding him my simplenes to instruct,
And into her Secrets to induce me fully,
Into her privy Garden to be my conduct:
First into a Towre most beautifull construct,
Father *Raymund* me brought, and thence immediately
He led me into her Garden planted deliciously.

29. Among the faire Trees one Tree in speciall,
Most vernant and pleasant appeared to my sight.
A name inscribed, *The Tree Philosophicall*,
Which to behold I had greate delight:
Then to *Philosophy* my troth I did plight
Her Majesty to serve; and to take greate paine,
The fruits of that Tree with *Raymund* to attaine.

30. Then

30 Then *Raymund* shewed me Budds fifteene
Springing of that Tree, and fruites fifteene moe,
Of the which said Tree proceedes that we doe meane;
That all *Philosophers* covet to attaine unto
The blessed *Stone*; one in Number and no moe:
Our greate *Elixer* most high of price,
Our *Azot*, our *Basaliske*, our *Adrop*, and our *Cocatrice*.

31. This is our *Antimony* and our *Red Lead*
Gloriously shining as *Phœbus* at midday,
This is our Crowne of Glory and Diadem of our head;
Whose beames resplendant shall never fade away;
Who attaines this Treasure, never can decay:
It is a Jewell so abundant and excellent,
That one graine will endure ever to be permanent.

32. I leave thee heere now our seacrets to attaine,
Looke that thou earnestly my Councell do ensue,
There needes no blowing at the Cole, bussines nor paine:
But at thyne owne ease here maist thou continue,
Old Antient writers beleive which are true:
And they shall thee learne to passe it to bring,
Beware therefore of too many, and hold thee to one thing.

33. This one thing is nothing else but the *Lyon greene*,
Which some Fooles imagine to be *Vitrioll Romaine*,
It is not of that thing which *Philosophers* meane,
For nothing to us any Corosive doth pertaine,
Understand therefore or else thy hand refraine
From this hard *Scyence*, least thou doe worke amisse,
For I will tell thee truly; now marke what it is.

34. Greene of Collor our *Lyon* is not truly
But vernant and greene evermore enduring
In most bitternes of death, he is lively:
In the fire burning he is evermore springing;
Therefore the *Salamander* by the fire living,
Some men doe him call, and some na other name,
The *Mettalline Menstruall*, it is ever the same.

35. Some

35. Some call it also a *Substance exuberate*,
Some call it *Mercury* of Mettaline essence,
Some *Limus deserti* from his body evacuate,
Some the *Eagle flying* from the North with violence:
Some call it a *Toade* for his greate vehemence.
But few or none at all doe name it in his kinde,
It is a *privy Quintessence*; keepe it well in minde.

36. This is not in sight, but resteth invisible;
Till it be forced out of *Chaos* darke,
Where he remaineth ever indivisible,
And yet in him is the foundacion of our warke,
In our *Lead* it is, so that thou it marke.
Drive it out of him so out of all other,
I can tell thee no better if thou wert my Brother.

37. This *Chaos* darke the Mettalls I do call,
Because as in a Prison it resteth them within,
The seacret of Nature they keepe in thrall:
Which by a meane we do warily out-twyne,
The working whereof the easier to begin.
Lift up thy head and looke upon the heaven,
And I will learne thee truly to know the *Planets* seaven.

The second parte of the BOOKE.

Saturne in all, to this *Arte* hath most respect,
Of whom we draw a Quintessence most excellent,
Unto our Magistery himselfe he doth connect,
United in quallitie, and also made equipolent
In strength and in vertue; who lists to be diligent,
Shall finde that we seeke an heavenly tresure
And a precious Jewell that ever shall endure.

2. *Jupiter* the gentle, endewed with Azure blew,
Examiner by Justice declareth true Judgement,
Altering his Colours ever fresh and new,
In his occult Nature to this *Arte* is convenient;
To *Philosophie* is serviceable and also obedient,
Joyned with *Lunary* after his owne kinde,
Conteyneth this *Arte* and leaveth nothing behinde.

3. *Mars* that is Martiall in Citty and Towne,
Fierce in Battaile, full of debate and strife,
A noble Warriour, and famous of renowne,
With fi e and sword defendeth his owne lyfe,
He staineth with blood and slaieth with a knife
All spirits and bodyes, his *Arts* be so bold,
The harts of all others he wyns to him with Gold.

4 The *Sun* most glorious shining with power potent,
Above all other faire *Planets* seaven,
Shedding his light to them all indifferent,
With his glorious Beames and glistering shine,
He lightneth the Earth and the Firmament of Heaven:
Who can him dissolve and draw out his Quintessence,
Unto all other *Planets* he shall give influence.

5. Lady *Venus* of love the faire Goddesse
With her Son *Cupid* apperteyneth to this *Arte*,
To the love of the *Sun* when she doth her addresse,
With her Darts of love striketh him to the hearte,
Joyned to his seede of his substance she taketh parte:
Her selfe she endueth with excellent Tissue,
Her corrupt nature when she doth renew.

6. *Mercury* this seeing begineth to be fugitive,
With his rodd of Inchantment litle doth he prevaile,
Taken often Prisoner himselfe doth revive;
Till he be snared with the *Dragons Tayle*
Then doth he on a hard Coate of Male,
Soudred together with the *Sunn* and *Moone*,
Then is he Mastered and his Inchantment done.

7. The

The *Moone* that is called the lesser *Lunary*,
Wife unto *Phœbus*, shining by Night,
To others gives her Garments through her hearb *Lunary*,
And from the North to the South shineth full bright,
If you do for her looke she hydeth from your sight.
But by faire intreaty she is won at the last,
With *Azot* and *Fire* the whole Mastery thou hast.

8. The Maistery thou gettest not yet of these *Planets* seaven,
But by a misty meaning knowne only unto us;
Bring them first to Hell, and afterwards to Heaven:
Betwixt lyfe and death then thou must discusse,
Therefore I councell thee that thou worke thus.
Dissolve and *Seperate* them, *Sublime*, *Fix* and *Congeale*,
Then hast thou all: therefore doe as I thee tell.

9. Dissolve not with Corrosive nor use Separacion
With vehemence of Fire, as Multipliers doe use,
Nor to the Glasse topp make thou Sublimacion;
Such wayes inordinate *Philosophers* refuse,
Their sayings follow, and wisely them peruse:
Then shalt thou not thy selfe lewdly delude
In this goodly *Scyence*: Adiew, I thus conclude.

Incipit Theorica.

WEE intend now through grace divine
In few words of *Chaos* for to write,
Light from Darknes to cause forth to shine,
Long before hidden as I shall recite,
In every thing unknowne it is requisite
A Seacret to search out which is invisible,
Materiall of our Maistry, a substance insensible.

2. Because I should not seeme to inclose
Long hidden seacrets unto me committed,
Of my Lord God. Therefore plainely of *Chaos*,
My purpose shalbe thereof to be acquitted,
For dangerous burthens are not easily lighted.
In faith therfore I shall my selfe endeavour,
Lightly to discharge me before God for ever.

3. Devotely therefore unto thee O Lord I call,
Send me thy Grace to make explicacion
Of *Chaos*: For thou art opener of seacrets all:
Which ever art ready to heare the Suplicacion
Of thy meeke Servants, which with hearty humiliacion
To thee do I apply: send me now thy grace
Of thy Secrets, to write in due order tyme and place.

4. *Chaos* is no more to say, this is doubtles,
(As *Ovid* writeth in his *Metamorphosin*)
But a certaine rude substance, *indigestaq; moles*,
Having divers Natures resting it within,
Which with the Contrary we may it out twyne.
By *Philosophers Arte*, who so the feat doth know
The foure Elements from *Chaos* to out draw.

5. This *Chaos* as all things hath Dimensions three,
Which well considered shall follow the effect,
That is *Altitude*, *Latitude* and *Profunditie*,
By which three all the Water is direct:
Unto these Dimensions who hath no respect
Shall never divide the *Chaos* in his kinde,
But after his labour shall finde fraud in the end.

6. *Chaos* is to us the Vine-tree white and red,
Chaos is each Beast, Fish and Fowle in his kinde,
Chaos is the Oare, and Mine of Tinn and Lead,
Of Gold and Silver that we out finde,
Iron and Copper which things do binde:
And hold our sights and witts unto them bound,
The seacrets hid in them which we ne understand.

7. Out

7. Out of this misty *Chaos*, the *Philosophers* expert,
Doe a substance draw called a *Quintessence.*
Craftily deviding the foure Elements by Art:
With great Wisdome study and Diligence,
The which high Seacreat hath a divine Influence;
That is supernaturall of Fooles thought impossible,
An Oyle or such like called Incombustible.

8. The Maystery of this plainely to shew thee,
In forme heareafter I will it declare:
Setting forth here the *Philosophers Tree*,
Wherein now the whole *Arte* I shall Compare:
In this faire *Tree* Sixteene frutes are,
More precious then Gold in the Stomake to digest,
Put thy hand thereto and take of the best.

9. And lest the fault imputed should be,
In me, or nothers that of this *Arte* doth write.
I set before thee the true figure of the *Tree*,
Wherein orderly the *Arte* I will recite;
Understand my Sentence that thou maist worke right,
Consider that I said that *Chaos* is all thing
That we begin of, the true way of working.

10. Put case thy *Chaos* be Animall, Vegitall or Minerall,
Let reason guide thee to worke after the same;
If thou workest out of kinde, then loosest thou all:
For Nature with Nature rejoyceth and maketh true game,
Worke Animall with his kind and keepe thee out of blame;
Vegetable and Minerall in their Order due,
Then shalt thou be counted a *Philosopher* true.

11. When thou hast found what it is indeede,
Then knowest thou thy forme by reason it must be,
Search it wittily and draw from him his seede:
Then is there thy *Altitude* superficiall to see,
The *Latitude* shall appeare anon beleeve me.
When thou hast divided the Elements assunder,
Then the *Profundity* amongst them lyeth hid under.

12. Here is *Materia Prima*, and *Corpus confusum*,
But not yet the *Matter* of which *Philosophers* doe treate,
Yet this one conteyneth the other in Somme:
For *Forma*, *Materia* and *Corpus* together are knit;
With the Menstruall Water first thou must them frett:
That the Body first be finely Calcinate,
After dissolved and purely evacuate,

13. Then is it the true *Mercury* of the *Philosophers*,
Unto the Maystery apt needefull and serviceable;
More of this thing I neede not much rehearse:
For this is all the Secret most Commendable;
Materia Prima it is called Multiplicable,
The which by *Arte* must be exuberate,
Then it is the *Matter* of which Mettalls were generate.

14. *Sulphur* of Nature and not that which is common,
Of Mettalls must be made; if that thou wilt speede,
Which will turne them to his kinde every each one;
His Tincture into them abroad he will spread,
It will fix *Mercury* common at thy neede.
And make him apt true Tincture to receive.
Worke as I have tould thee, and it shall not thee deceive.

15. Then of *Sun* and *Moone* make thou Oyle incombustible,
With *Mercury* vegetable or else with *Lunary*,
Inserate therewith and make thy *Sulphur* fluxible
To abide thy Fire and also thy *Mercury*
Be fixt and flowing, then hast thou wrought truly.
And so hast thou made a Worke for the nonce,
And gott a *Stone* more precious then all Stones.

16. Fix it up now with perfect Decoccion,
And that with easy heate, and not vehement,
For feare of Induracion, and Vitrificacion,
Least thou loose all and thy labour mispent:
With Eight dayes and nights, this *Stone* is sufficient,
The greate *Elixir* most high of price,
Which *Raymond* called his *Basiliske* and *Cocatrice*.

17. To

17. To this excellent worke greate Cost neede not be,
Many Glasses or Potts about it to breake,
One Glasse, one Furnace and no more of necessity,
Who more doth spill, his witts are but weake,
All this is stilled in a Limbeck with a Beake.
As touching the Order of Distillacion,
And with a blinde head on the same for Solucion.

18. In this thy *Mercury* taketh his true kinde,
In this he is brought to Multiplicacion;
In this made he his *Sulphur*, beare it well in minde,
Tincture he hath herein, and inceracion,
In this the *Stone* is brought to his perfect Creacion;
In one Glasse, one Thing, one Fire and no mo,
This Worke is Compleate. *Da gloriam Deo.*

Incipit Practica.

WE have sufficiently declared the *Theorique*,
In words misticall making declaracion.
Let us now proceede plainely with the *Practique*,
Largely of the Matter to make explanacion:
I will therefore that you marke well my Narracion,
As true Disciples my Doctrine to attend
My *Testament*, and last *Will* to you I do comend.

2. Be you Holy therefore, Sober, Honest, and Meeke;
Love God and your Neighbour, to the Poore bee not unkind;
Overcome Sathan, Gods Glory see you seeke,
My *Son* be gentle to all men, as a Frend;
Fatherles and Widdow have alwaies in thy minde,
Innocente love as Brothers, the wicked do eschew,
Let Flaschood and Flattery goe, least thou it rue.

3. De.

3. Devoutely serve God, call daily for his grace,
Worship him in Spirit with heart contrite and pure,
In no wise let Sathan thy prayers deface:
Looke thou be stedfast in faith and trust most sure,
Lay up treasure in heaven which ever shall endure:
In all Adversity be gentle in thy heart
Against thy Foe; so shalt thou him convert.

4. Most heartily therefore O Lord to thee I call,
Beseeching thee to ayde me with thy heavenly grace,
Lovingly thy Spirit upon me downe let fall;
Overshaddowing me that I at no tyme trespas,
My Lord and my God grant me to purchase
Full knowledge of thy Secrets, with thy mercy to wine,
Intending thy truth this Practise I begin.

5. Listen thou my *Son*, and thine Eares incline.
Delight have thou to learne this Practise sage and true,
Attend my saying, and note well this Discipline:
These Rules following do as it doth ensue,
This labour once begun thou must it continue
Without tedious sluggardice, and slothfull wearines:
So shalt thou thereby acquire to thee greate Riches.

6. In the name of God this *Seacret* to attaine,
Joyne thow in one Body with a perfect unity:
First the red Man, and the white Woman these twaine:
One of the Mans substance, and of the Womans three,
By Liquefaction joyned together must they be:
The which Conjunction is called Diptative,
That thus is made betweene Man and Wife.

7. Then after that they be one Body made,
With the sharpe teeth of a Dragon finely,
Bring them to Dust, the next must be had,
The true proporcion of that Dust truly,
In a true Ballance weighing them equally;
With three tymes as much of the fiery Dragon
Mixing altogether, then hast thou well done.

8. Thy

8. Thy Substance thus together proportionate,
Put in a Bedd of Glasse with a bottome large and round,
There in due tyme to dye, and be regenerate
Into a new Nature, three Natures into one bound,
Then be thou glad that ever thou it found.
For this is the Jewell shall stand thee most in stead,
The Crowne of Glory, and Diadem of thy head.

9. When thou hast thus mixt thy Matter as is said,
Stop well the Glasse that the Dragon goe not out;
For he is so subtile that if he be overlayd
With Fire unnaturall, I put thee out of doubt,
For to escape he will search all about;
Therefore with gentle Fire looke that thou keepe it in,
So shalt thou of him the whole Maystery winne.

10. The whole Maystery hereof duly to fulfill,
Set thy Glasse and Matter upon thine Athenor;
Our Furnace called the *Philosophers Dunghill*,
With a temperate heate working evermore;
Night and day continually have Fuell in store,
Of Turfe, of Sawdust, or dry chopped segges,
That the heate be equipolent to the Hen upon her Eggs.

11. Such heate continually loke thou doe not lack,
Forty dayes long for their perfect union
In them is made; For first it turnes to Black,
This Collour betokens the right Putrefaction,
This is the begining of perfect Conception
Of your Infant into a new generation,
A most pretious Jewell for our Consolation.

12. Forty dayes more the Matter shall turne White,
And cleere as Pearles; which is a declaration,
Of voiding away of his Cloudes darke night;
This sheweth our Infants full organization,
Our White *Elixir* most cleere in his Creation.
From White into all Colours withouten faile,
Like to the Rainebow or the Peacocks Tayle.

Uu 13. So

13. So forth augment thy Fire continually,
Under thy Matter easily they must be fedd,
Till these Collours be gone use it wisely;
For soone after appeareth Yellow the messenger of the Redd,
When that is come then hast thou well sped,
And hast brought forth a *Stone* of price,
Which *Raymund* calls his *Basiliske and Cocatrice.*

14. Then 40 dayes to take his whole Fixation,
Let it stand in heate most temperate,
That in that tyme thou spare thy Fermentation,
To increase him withall that he be not violate,
Beware of Fire and Water, for that will it suffocate.
Take one to a hundred of this Confection,
And upon *crude Mercury* make thou Projection.

15. One of thy *Stone* I meane upon an hundred fold,
After the first and second right Fermentation,
Of *Mercury crude*, turneth it to fine *Gold*,
As fine, as good, and as naturall in ponderation,
The *Stone* is so vehement in his penetrations,
Fixt and Fusible as the Gold smiths Souder is,
Worke as I have said, and thou canst not doe amisse.

16. Now give thankes to the blessed Trinity,
For the benefit of this precious *Stone*,
That with his grace hath so much lightned thee,
Him for to know being three in one,
Hold up thy hands to his heavenly Throne.
To his Majesty let us sing *Hosanna*,
Altissimo Deo sit honor & gloria.

The

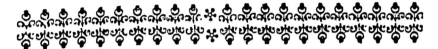

The Conclusion.

Our *Magistery is* Three, Two, *and* One:
The Animall, Vegitable *and* Minerall Stone.
First I say in the name of the holy Trinity,
Looke that thou joyne in One, Persons Three.
The Fixt, *the* Variable *and the* Fugitive,
Till they together tast Death and Live.
The first is the Dragon *fell,*
That shall the other twaine both slay and quell:
The Sun *and* Moone *shall loose their light,*
And in mourning Sables they shall them dight,
Threescore dayes long or neere thereabouts:
Then shall Phœbus *appeare first out,*
With strange Collours in all the Firmament,
Then our Joy is coming and at hand present:
Then Orient Phœbus *in his hemisphere*
To us full gloriously shall appeare:
Thus who can worke wisely
Shall attaine unto our Maistery.

FINIS.

SIR EDWARD KELLE'S WORKE.

ALL you that faine *Philosophers* would be,
And night and day in *Geber's* kitchin broyle,
Wasting the chipps of ancient *Hermes Tree*,
Weening to turne them to a precious Oyle,
The more you worke the more you loose and (spoile.
To you I say, how learned soever you be,
Goe burne your Bookes and come and learne of me.

Although to my one Booke you have red tenn,
Thats not inough, for I have heard it said,
The greatest Clarkes ar not the wisest men,
A Lion once a silly Mouse obeyd,
In my good will so hold your selves appaid:
And though I write not halfe so sweete as *Tully*,
Yet shall you finde I trace the stepps of *Lully*.

Yt doth you good to thinke how your desire,
And selfe-conceit doth warrantize vaine hope,
You spare no cost, you want no coals for fier,
You know the vertues of the Elitrope,
You thinke your selves farr richer then the Pope.
What thinge hath being either high or low,
But their *Materia prima* you do know.

Elixir vitæ, and the precious *Stone*,
You know as well as how to make an Apple;
If'te come to the workinge then let you alone,
You know the coullers black brown bay and dapple,
Controwle you once then you begin to fraple.
Swearing and saying, what a fellow is this?
Yet still you worke but ever worke amisse.

No

No no, my friends, it is not vauntinge words,
Nor mighty oaths that gaines that sacred skill;
It is obteined by grace and not by swords;
Nor by greate reading, nor by long sitting still,
Nor fond conceipt nor working all by will.
But as I said by grace it is obteined,
Seeke grace, therefore, let folly be refrained.

It is no costly thing I you assure,
That doth beget *Magnesia* in hir kind.
Yet is hir selfe by leprosie made pure:
Hir eyes be cleerer being first made blind:
And he that can Earths fastnes once unbind,
Shall quickly know that I the truth have tould,
Of sweete *Magnesia*, Wife to purest Gold.

Now what is meant by Man and Wife is this,
Agent and Patient, yet not two but one,
Even as was *Eva*, *Adams* Wife I wisse:
Flesh of his Flesh and Bone of his Bone,
Such is the Unionhood of our precious *Stone*.
As *Adam* slept untill his Wife was made,
Even so our *Stone*, ther can no more be said.

By this you se how thus it came to passe,
That first was Man, and Woman then of him:
Thus *Adam* heere as first and cheefest was,
And still remained a Man of perfect limme,
Then Man and Wife were joynd together trimme.
And each in love to other straight addressed them,
And did increase their kind when God had blessed them.

Even so the Man our *Stone* is said to sleepe,
Untill such time his Wife be fully wrought;
Then he awakes, and joyfully doth keepe
His new made Spouse, which he so dearely bought,
And when to such perfection they be brought,
Rejoyce the beauty of so faire a bride,
Whose worth is more then halfe the world beside.

I doubte as yet you hardly understand,
What Man or Wife doth truly signifie,
And yet I know you beare your selves in hand,
That out of doubt it *Sulpher* is and *Mercury*,
And so yt is, but not the common certeinly:
But *Mercury* essentiall is trewly the trew Wife,
That killes her selfe to bring her Child to life.

For first and formost she receaves the Man,
Her perfect love doth make her soone conceive:
Then doth she strive with all the force she can,
In spite of love, of life him to bereave,
Which being done, then will she never leave,
But labour kindly like a loving Wife,
Untill againe she him have brought to life.

Then he againe her kindnesse to requite,
Upon her head doth set a Crowne of glory,
And to her praise he Poems doth indite,
Whose Poems make each Poet write a story,
And that she slew him then she is not sorry.
For he by vertue of his loving Wife,
Not only lives, but also giveth life.

But here I wish you rightly understand,
How heere he makes his Concubine his Wife,
Which if you know not, do not take in hand,
This worke which unto fooles is nothing rife,
And looke you make attonement where is strife.
Then strip the Man into his shirt of Tishew,
And her out of her smock to ingender yssue.

To tell you troath he wanteth for no Wives
In Land, or Sea, in Water, Air, or Fire,
Without their deaths he waiteth not their lives.
Except they live he wants his cheif desire,
He bindes them prentice to the rightest Dier,
And when they once all Sorrowes have abidden,
Then finde they Ioyes which from them first were hidden.

For

For then they finde the Joy of sweete encrease,
  They bring forth Children beautifull to sight.
The which are able Prisners to release;
  And to the darkest Bodyes give true light,
  Their hevenly Tincture is of such great might.
Oh! he that can but light on such a treasure,
Who would not thinke his Joyes were out of measure?

Now by this question I shall quickly know
  If you can tell which is his Wife indeede:
Is she quick footed, faire faced yea or no,
  Flying or fixed as you in Bookes do reade?
  Is she to be fed or else doth she feede?
Wherein doth she joy, where's her habitation?
Heavenly or Earthly, or of a strange nacion?

What is she poore? or is she of any wealth?
  Bravely of her attyre, or meane in her apparrell?
Or is she sick? or is she in perfect health?
  Mild of her Nature? or is she given to quarrell?
  Is she a Glutton? or loves she the Barrell?
If any one of these you name her for to be,
You know not his Wife, nor never did her see.

And that will I prove to you by good reason,
  That truly noe one of all these is she,
This is a question to you that is geason:
  And yet some parte of them all she must be,
  Why then, some parte is not all you may see.
Therefore the true Wife which I doe meane,
Of all these Contraries is the Meane betweene.

As Meale and Water joyned both together,
  Is neither Meale nor Water now but Dow;
Which being baked, is Dow nor Water neither:
  Nor any more will each from other goe,
  The meane betweene is Wife, our Wife even so:
And in this hidden point our seacret lyes,
It is enough, few words content the wise.

Now

Now by this simile heere I do reveale,
  A mighty Seacret if you marke it well;
Call *Mercury* Water, imagine *Sulphur* Meale,
  What Meale I meane I hope the wise can tell:
  Bake them by craft make them together dwell,
And in your working make not too much hast,
For Wife she is not while she is in Paste.

This lesson learn'd now give me leave to play,
  I shall the fitter be to learne another,
My minde is turn'd cleane cam another way.
  I doe not love sweete secret thoughts to smother,
  It is a Child you know that makes a Mother.
Sith so it is then must we have a Childe,
Or else of Motherhood we are beguild.

What will you say if I a wonder tell you,
  And prove the Mother is Child and Mother too?
Do you not thinke I goe about to sell you
  A bargaine in sport, as some are wont to do?
  Ist possible the Mother, to weare her Infants shoe?
In faith it is in our *Philosophy*,
As I will prove by reason by and by.

Ripley doth bid you take it for no scorne,
  With patience to attend the true Conjunccion,
For saith he in the Aire our Child is borne,
  There he receiveth the holy Unction,
  Also with it a heavenly function.
For after death reviv'd againe to lyfe,
This all in all both Husband Child and Wife.

Whilst all is Earth *Conception* it is termed,
  And *Putrefaction* tyme of lying in,
Perfect *Conjunction* (by artes-men is affirmd)
  The womans Childing where doth all Ioy beg
  Who knowes not this, his witts are very thin.
When she is strong and shineth faire and bright,
She's tearm'd the VVife most beautifull to sight.

L

Loe thus you see that you are not beguil'd;
For if you marke it I have proved by Reason,
How both is one the Mother and the Child,
Conception, Breeding, Childing, every season:
I have declared to you without all Treason,
Or any false ambiguous word at all;
And hewn you worke then finde it true you shall.

This is that *Mercury* essentiall truly,
Which is the principall of the *Stone* materiall,
And not those crude Amalgames began newly;
These are but *Mercuries* superficiall,
This is that Menstrue of perfect tincturiall:
This is most truly that One thing,
Out of the which all profitt must springe.

If this content you not, abide displeas'd for me,
For I have done. If Reason take no place,
What can be said, but that there doubts will be,
Doe what one can, where folly wins the race.
Let it suffice, this is the perfect Base,
Which is the *Stone* that must dissolved be.
How that is done I will declare to thee.

This is the *Stone* that *Ripley* bidds you take,
(For untill thus it be it is no *Stone*)
Be rul'd by me, my councell not forsake,
And he commands, Let Crudities alone,
If thou have grace to keep thee free from moan.
Then stick to this, let Phansey not o'resway thee,
Let Reason rule, for Phansey will betray thee.

Take thou this *Stone*, this *Wife*, this *Child*, this *All*,
Which will be Gummous, crumbling, silken, soft:
Upon a Glasse or Porphire beat it small,
And as you grinde, with *Mercury* feede it oft,
But not so much that *Mercury* swim aloft,
But equall parts, nipt up their seed to save;
Then each in other are buried within their grave.

When thus and there you have it as is said,
Worke in all points as Nature wrought at first:
For Blacknes had thow needest not be afraid,
It wilbe White, then art thou past the worst,
Except th ou breake thy Glasse and beaccurst;
But if through Blacknes thou to Whitenes march,
Then will it be both White and soft as Starch.

This very place is cal'd by many names,
As *Imbibition*, *Feeding*, *Sublimation*,
Clyming high Mountaines, also *Childrens Games*;
And rightly it is termed *Exaltation*,
When all is nothing else but *Circulation*
Of the foure Elements whatsoere fooles clatter,
Which is done by heate upon Forme and Matter.

Earth is the lowest Element of All
Which Black, is exalted into Water,
Then no more Earth but Water wee it call;
Although it seeme a black Earthy matter,
And in black dust all about will scatter,
Yet when soe high as to Water it hath clym'd,
Then is it truly said to be *Sublym'd*

When this black Masse againe is become White,
Both in and out like snow and shining faire,
Then this Child, this Wife, this Heaven so bright,
This Water Earth sublimed into Aire,
When there it is it further will prepare
It selfe into the Element of Fire,
Then give God thankes for granting thy desire.

This Black, this White, doe we call *Seperation*,
Which is not manuall but Elementall;
It is no crude Mercuriall Sublimation,
But Natures true worke consubstantiall,
The White is called *Conjunction* naturall,
Secret and perfect Conjunction not grosse;
Which bringeth profitt all other losse.

When

When thrice yee have turned this Wheele about,
  Feeding and working it as I have said,
Then will it flow like Wax without doubt:
  Giving a Tincture that will not vade.
  Abiding all tryalls that can be made.
If wisely Project you can and keepe free,
Both profitt and creditt to you it wilbe.

Your *Medicine* fixed and perfectly flowing,
  White you must thinke will Whitenes increase;
So Red begets Red as Seede in the sowing
  Begetteth his like or as kinde doth in Beasse,
  And fire must be the true maker of peace :
For white or red *Ferment* your *Medicine* augmenteth,
And perfectly tinckteth and soone it relenteth.

That is to say, your *Medicine* ended,
  If White melt downe Silver and thereon Project it,
If Red melt downe Sol, for so it is intended;
  Like unto like in no wise reject it,
  And out of the purest looke you elect it.
Medicen one parte upon *Ferment* ten,
That One on one Thousand of *Jupiter* then.

Your *Jupiter* standing red hot on the fyre,
  So soone as your *Medicine* upon him is cast,
Presently standeth so hard as a Wyre,
  For then he is fixed and melteth by blast,
  And of all your working thisis the last.
Then let it by Test or strong water be tryde,
The best Gold or Silver no better shall bide.

Mercury crude in a Crucible heated,
  Presently hardeneth lik Silver anealed;
And in the high Throwne of Luna is seated,
  Silver or Gold as Medicine hath sealed:
  And thus our greate *Secret* I have reveled.
Which divers have seene, and my selfe have wrought,
And dearely I prize it, yet give it for nought.

FINIS. E. K.

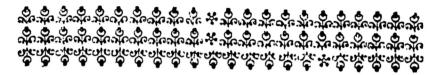

SIR ED: KELLEY *CONCERNING* the Philosophers Stone *written to his especiall good Freind*, G. S. *Gent*.

THe heavenly Cope hath in him Natures fower,
Two hidden; but the rest to sight appeare:
Wherein the Spermes of all the Bodies lower;
Most secrett are, yett spring forth once a yeare,
And as the Earth with Water, Authors are,
So of his parte is Drines end of care.

No Flood soe greate as that which floweth still,
Nothing more fixt than Earth digested thrise:
No Winde so fresh as when it serveth will;
No Profitt more, then keepe in, and be wise,
No better happ, then drie up Aire to dust,
For then thou maist leave of, and sleepe thy lust.

Yett will I warne thee least thou chauncé to faile,
Sublyme thine Earth with stinkeing Water erst,
Then in a place where *Phœbus* onely tayle
Is seene att midday, see thou mingle best:
For nothing shineth that doth want his light,
Nor doubleth beames, unlesse it first be bright.

Lett

Sr. Edw. Kelley to G .S. Gent.

Lett no man leade, unlesse he know the way
That wise men teach, or *Adrop* leadeth in,
Whereof the first is large and easiest pray;
The other hard, and meane but to begin.
For surely these and no one more is found,
Wherein *Appollo* will his harp-strings sound.

Example learne of GOD that plaste the Skyes,
Reflecting vertues from and t'every poynt,
In which the mover wherein all things lyes,
Doth hold the vertues all of every Joynt:
And therefore *Essence fift* may well be said,
Conteining all and yett himselfe a Maid.

Remember also how the *Gods* began,
And by Discent who was to each the Syre,
Then learne their Lives and Kingdomes if you can,
Their Manners eke, with all their whole Attire;
Which if thou doe, and know to what effect;
The learned *Sopheis* will thee not reject,

If this my Doctrine bend not with thy brayne,
Then say I nothing though I said too much:
Of truth tis good will moved me, not gaine,
To write these lynes: yett write I not to such
As catch at Crabs, when better fruits appeare,
And want to chuse at fittest time of yeare.

Thou maist (my Freind) say, what is this for lore?
I answere, such as auncient Physicke taught:
And though thou read a thousand Bookes before,
Yett in respect of this, they teach thee Naught:
Thou mayst likewise be blind, and call me Foole
Yett shall these Rules for ever praise their Schoole.

TESTAMENTUM JOHANNIS DEE PHILOSOPHI SUMMI

ad Johannem Gwynn, transmissum 1568.

THis *Letter* third and last I minde to make,
At your request for very vertues sake;
Your written panges, and methods set aside,
From that I byd, looke that you never slide.
Cut that in Three, which Nature hath made One,
Then strengthen hyt, even by it self alone,
Wherewith then Cutte the poudred Sonne in twayne,
By length of tyme, and heale the woonde againe.
The self same Sunne twys yet more, ye must wounde,
Still with new Knives, of the same kinde, and grounde;
Our *Monas* trewe thus use by natures Law,
Both binde and lewse, only with rype and rawe,
And ay thanke God who only is our Guyde,
All is ynugh, no more then at this Tyde.

Tho-

THOMAS ROBINSONUS
DE LAPIDE PHILOSOPHORUM.

THe Heavens, the Earth, and all that in them is,
Were in six Dayes perfected from Abisse:
From One sprung foure; from foure a second One;
This last a Gritt; that first the Corner Stone.
Without the First the Last may not be had;
Yet to the First the Last is too too bad.
When from the Earth the Heavens were seperated,
Were not the Heavens with Earth first cohobated?
And when the Heavens, and Earth and all were not;
Were onely Heavens create; and Earth forgott?
No: Heavens, and Earth sprung all from one at first:
Then who can say or Heavens, or Earth is worst?
Is not the Earth the Mother of them all?
And what the Heavens, but Earths essentiall?
Although they have in Heaven no Earthly residence,
Yet in the Earth doth rest their Heavenly influence:
Were not the Earth, what were the other Three?
Were not the Heavens, what on the Earth could be?
Thus as they came, so shall they passe together;
But unto Man not knowne from whence, or whither.
And for the tyme of Earths Heaven purifying,
Six thousand yeares they live, and have their dying:
Then all shall rest eternall and divine,
And by the Beauty of the Godhead shine.
I sweare there is noe other truth but this
Of that great *Stone*; which many seeke and misse.

FINIS.

EXPERIENCE AND *PHILOSOPHY.*

HAve you not heard yee Princes great, you Lords & Ladies all,
Of the mishap and heavy chaunce that now of late did fall?
A wofull Tale to tell
VVho could expresse it well:
Oh that some learned *Poet* had byne
With me, to se that I have sene:
Or else some other standing by,
That well could write a Tragidy
Of lasting fame and memory.
For yet not since this VVorld began,
Such cry, such clamour as was than
Heard never any earthly Man.

Experience that Princesse greate, I saw her in her Throne
Of glory, where her Majesty delightes to sitt upon;
And on her wayting by
A blessed Company
Of Virgins pure, that as I gesse,
VVere Children to that great Goddesse:
Their Princely port, their Comly grace,
Their pierles featur'd hands and face
Did shew them of most Noble race:
But of their prudent skill to tell,
In Artes where in they did excell,
No earthly Tongue can do it well.

And

And as I gazed thus upon that ſtrange and dreadfull ſight,
I ſaw how that *Experience* did teach theſe Ladies right,
The ſeven *Artes* Divine,
With deſent diſcipline,
By divers rules and orders grave,
As ſhe thought good for them to have.
But for to ſee how diligent
And buiſily their time they ſpent
To learne thoſe *Artes* moſt excellent,
The endleſſe travells that they tooke
From place to place, from booke to booke,
Amazed me on them to looke.

For ſome in divers Languages did reaſon and diſpute,
And other ſome did ſing and play on Organ,Harpe and Flute;
And ſome with Compaſſe found
All Meaſures ſquare and round:
And ſome by Cyphering could tell
Infinite Summes and Numbers well:
And ſome with Eloquence began
As Poets and Orators to ſcan
The Cauſes betweene Man and Man:
And ſome upon the Stars did gaze,
And other ſome ſat in a Maze,
To judge of Seacrets that there was.

Soe that nothing created was under the Firmament,
That hath a Being or Life by any Element,
No Simple nor Compound
In all the World is found
Under the Sky, or Clouds that fly,
But they ſought out the privity:
This Rocky Earth, this heavy Maſſe,
This Articke Virgin, this let not paſſe
To ſeeke the thing that therein was:
But put themſelves in preſſe to creepe
Into the Center of the Deepe,
Where ſundry Soules and Spirits doe ſleepe.

This thing *Experience* gan prudently to debate,
VVith cheerefull looke and voyce full mylde, as seemed to her (state.
And soone decreed she
Of her benignity:
Not for their sundry paines I take,
But only for her Glory sake,
That all these Ladies in a row
Should further of her Secrets know,
That from her Majesty did grow;
VVherewith to Councell called shee
A Lady grave of greate degree,
That named was *Philosophy*.

And after their discourse and talke, that *Lady* fell downe flatt
On hands & knees before the *Queene* in heaven where she satt.
And looking upon her face
Did say unto her grace:
Blessed be thou *Experience*,
Full mighty is thy Influence;
Thy wondrous workes records full well
In wordell of wordels where thou doest dwell,
In Earth, in Heaven, and in Hell;
That thou art now the very same,
That of Nothing All things did frame,
VVherefore now blessed be thy Name.

Wherewith the Heavens opened, and fiery flames did fall
Downe from the Throne of endles Joy and seate imperiall,
Where Angels infinite
Like glistering Starrs did sitt:
So pure and simple was the Light,
As all the World had burnt bright;
The flames and floods began to roare,
And did present their hidden store,
Of Spirits that sing for evermore,
All glory and magnificence,
All humble thankes and reverence
Be given to *EXPERIENCE*.

Then

Then sylence fell upon the face of Heaven Christalline
Where all the Powers mustered full ready to encline;
To that most Sapient,
The high Omnipotent:
That said *be it*, and it was don,
Our Earth, our Heaven were begun;
I am said it the most of might,
In worde in lyfe and eke in light.
I am Mercy and Judgment right,
The Depth is myne so is the Hight:
The Cold, the Hot, the Moyst, the Dry,
Where All in All is there am I.

What thing can tell when I began, or when I make an end?
Wherewith I wrought, and what I mought, or what I did intend?
To doe when I had done
The worke I had begun.
For when my Being was alone
One thing I made when there was none,
A Masse confused darkely clad
That in it selfe all Nature had
To form and shape the good and bad;
And then as Tyme began to fall,
It pleased me the same to call
The *first Matter*, Mother of all.

And from that Lumpe divided I foure sundry Elements,
Whom I commanded for to raigne in divers Regiments:
In Kinde they did agree,
But not in Quality.
Whose simple Substance I did take,
My seate invisible to make:
And of the Qualites compound,
I made the Starry Sky so round
VVith living Bodyes on the ground;
And blessed them infinitely,
VVith lyfe and long prosperity,
And bad them grow and Multiply.

Respecting these divided things so created by me,
Their light and lively spreading forth of them in their degree;
Retourning to the Masse,
VVhere there begining was,
And saw the refuse of the same,
How Voyd and Empty it became,
All darke, and nothing to remaine,
I put with wrath and greate disdaine,
My only Curse there for to raygne;
For I the Author of all Light
Did banish Darknes from my sight,
And blessed all things that shined bright,

So that I mard nothing I made, for that I made is still,
And so shalbe unto the end, only to worke my will:
One thing was first imployd,
And shall not be destroid,
It compasseth the VVorld so round,
A Matter easy to be found:
And yet most hardest to come by:
A Secret of Secrets pardye,
That is most vile and least set by,
And it my Love and my Darling,
Conceived with all living thing,
And travells to the VVorlds ending.

What neede have I of mans Devise of Peny or of Pound,
Of Gold or Silver, Lead or Tynn, or Copper in the ground,
Iron or Silver Quick,
Whereat the blind do prick;
Of Cankered Corosives that rust,
By Salts and sulphurs all to dust?
Seeke out therefore my darling deare;
For unto me it is most neere,
My spouse my Love and my Compeare:
And unto it looke thou direct
My seaven Children long elect,
That all things else they might reject.

A

A Child begetting his owne Father, and bearing his Mother,
Killing himselfe to give lyfe, and light to all other:
Is yt that I do meane,
Most myld and most extreame.
Did not the Word that dwelt in me
Take forme and walked visibly;
And did not I then dwell in it,
That dwelt in me for to unite
Three powers in one seate to sit?
And then *Experience* did say
Now knowest thou all, heere lyes the Key,
And then she vanisht cleane away.

There with arose *Phylosophy* as one filled with grace,
Whose looks did shew that she had byne in some Heavenly place:
For oft she wipt her Eyes,
And oft she bowd her knees.
And oft she kist the Steps with dread,
VVhereon *Experience* did tread;
And oft she cast her Head on high
And oft full low she cast her Eye
Experience for to espy:
But when she saw that she was gon,
And that her selfe was left alone:
I never hread thing make such mone.

FINIS.

THE MAGISTERY.

THrough want of *Skill* and *Reasons* light
  Men ſtumble at *Noone day*;
Whilſt buiſily our *Stone* they ſeeke,
  That lyeth in the *way*.

Who thus do ſeeke they know not what
  Is't likely they ſhould *finde*?
Or hitt the *Marke* whereat they *ayme*
  Better then can the Blinde?

No, *Hermes Sonns* for *Wiſdome* aske
  Your *footeſteps* ſhee'le direct:
Shee'le *Natures* way and *ſecret Cave*
  And *Tree of lyfe* detect.

Son and *Moone* in *Hermes* veſſell
  Learne how the *Collours* ſhew,
The *nature* of the *Elements*,
  And how the *Daiſies* grow.

Greate *Python* how *Appollo* ſlew,
  Cadmus his *hollow-Oake*:
His *new-rais'd-army*, and *Iaſon* how
  The *Fiery Steeres* did yoke.

The *Eagle* which aloft doth fly
  See that thou bring to *ground*;
And give unto the *Snake* ſome *wings*,
  Which in the *Earth* is found.

Then

Then in *one Roome* ſure *binde* them both,
To *fight* till they be *dead*;
And that a *Prince* of *Kingdomes three*
Of *both them* ſhalbe *bred*.

Which from the *Cradle* to his *Crowne*,
Is *fed* with his owne *blood*;
And though to ſome it ſeemeth ſtrange,
He hath no other *Foode*.

Into his *Virgin-Mothers* wombe,
Againe he *enter* muſt;
Soe ſhall the *King* by his *new-byrth*,
Be *ten times ſtronger* juſt.

And able is his *foes* to *foile*,
The *dead* he will *revive*:
Oh happy man that underſtands
This Medicen to atchive!

Hec opus exigium nobis fert ire per altum.
DECEMBER, 1633.

W. B.

ANONYMI:

OR,

SEVERALL WORKES OF *unknowne Authors.*

NOw I schall her be gynne,
To teche the a Conclusion;
In the name of the Trenete
Send us grace that well hit be;
Now take two Onces as mych of anoder,
And dyssolve on ther with the toder,
Y tel the trowthe as my broder,
Put in to a Glas wyth owtten oder:
Than take three Onces of the bytter,
And meng hym with the swetter;
And put them than into a Glas,
Even right as the toder was:
Than take a unc of the best,
And do with hym as thou didst erst,
In a Glas than thou him put,
And loke thy mowth be wel I shut;
Now thow hast here Glasses thre,
Even lyke unto the Trynete,
Than hem stop these everychon,
Even a sute as thow hast on:
About thy Glasses a wal thow make,
Last the wynde ham al to crake,

Than

Than thy Glaſſys now all I thre,
With yn that grave they ſchal be;
Now thys I fed with moyſty hete,
To make that Glaſſys ſwynke and ſwete,
Then let hem ſtonde thus wekys thre;
And wel the beter they ſchal be.
Than put hem all now into on,
The wich ys lyke than be a ſtone;
Than let hem ſtonde ſo theryn,
Whan thou haſt made thy Conjunction:
Tyl ſevyn dayes be al I don,
Much the better woll be thy Ston;
Than upon thy Glas thow ſett
A fayre heed and wel I mette,
Draw up thy water with eſy fyre,
Within a Rotunde good and cler,
Tyl thi Mater wol ſtyl no mer,
Than ſet thow hem in dry Fyr,
Than ſe thow ſtyl with reaſonabyl hete,
Tyl thy Mater wol no more lete.
Whan he ys ther both good and dry,
Ful fayne wolde he than be moyſty;
Than wey that Stone within the Glas,
And put hym hys Lecur has it was;
Now whan thys fryſt drawte ys don,
Thow muſt Embybe with good proporciun:
Now looke thow wel what ys hys whyght,
And wyth the fourth part than hym dyght,
And evermore wyth partys fowr,
Now tyl he be of Whyte colowr;
And thus loke thow make good wache,
Tyl the Body thy Spirit can cache;
And alſo thy Sowle ſo muſt he,
Than underſtand thow haſt thre.

Z Now

Now schyt thy Glas as hyt was er,
And worke hyt forthe on thys maner;
Whan tho thre to gedur ben knyte,
With moch joy than thow mayst sitte.
For than art thou ricchar than the *King*,
But he have the same thyng.
Thus is alle thy Medcyn wroght,
Evyn after thin owne thoght;
How thys Medcyn thow schalt encres,
And make hyt mor tyll thow lyst sees;
The trowth I schall now the certefie,
How thow schalt hyt thus Multyply:
Loke as thow did thy Werke befor,
Encres hit forth with mor and mor:
As thow did at the begynnyng,
So continu forth to the endyng:
Thus for soth infynytely
Thou mayst this craft forth Multiply:
Lyke as a man hath lytil Fyr,
And mor to make ys hys desyr;
He be hovyth this ys no nay,
More Wode or Cole ther to lay:
And thus he may hys Fyr encres,
That he schall never be fyreles.
One the same wise thou understande,
Ever thy Medcyn must be growande;
And whan the lyst Projecciun make,
Loke to this lesson good tent thou take;
Whan thy Medcyn is very parfit,
Thow schalt hym cast on hys lyke;
Als evyn than as thow can gese,
On part on Ten looke thow not messe,
The trowthe yf thow wil wete,
Than ys thy Lexer evyn complete;

And than of that On part thow take,
The trew Projeccion thus schalt thow make;
Cast that on Ten of Tyn or Leede,
Or Coper or Mercury ther in that steede,
Into fine Lun hit schal be broght,
Or into Sol evyn after thi thoght:
After that thy Lexer ys,
Be hit White or Rede I wys,
If thow hit cast on Iren alſo,
If it schal be Lun or Sol ther to:
Thys ar the Secrets of *Phylosophie*,
I councel the keepe hit secretlye;
And serve thy God both nyght and day,
The better thou shalt speede, thys ys no nay.
Now I have taught the how thow schalt do,
The blys of hevyn God bryng hus to.

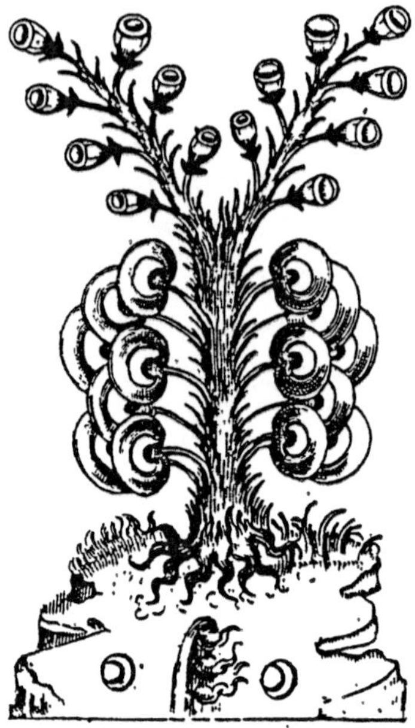

HER ys an Erbe men calls *Lunayrie*,
I bleſſet mowte hys maker bee.
Aſterion he ys, I callet alle ſo,
And other namys many and mo;
He ys an Erbe of grete myght,
Of Sol the Sunn he taketh hys lyght,
He ys the Fader, to Croppe and Rote;
Wyth fragrant Flowris that ben ſote,
Flowrys to bere in that ſtede,
Swm ben Whyte, and ſwin ben Red:
Hys Lewys grwyth, both day and nyght,
Lyke to the Ferment that ys ſo bright:
I ſhall declare, thys Erbe ſo lyght,
To many a man hyt ys a fayre ſeyght;
Friſt at the Rote I wolle be gynne,
That cawſyth alle thing for to ſprynge;

A growyth a pon a Mowntayne brym,
Where *Febis* hath grete dominacion:
The Sune by day, the Mone by nyght,
That maketh hym both fayre and bryght,
The Rote growyth on stonns clere,
Whyte and Rede, that ys so peyre:
The Rote ys blacke, the Stalke ys red;
The wyche schall ther never be dede,
The Lewis ben rownd, as a Nowbel son,
And wexsyth and wanyth as the Mon:
In the meddes a marke the brede of a peni,
Lo thys is lyke to owre sweght Lunayre:
Hys Flowrys schynith, fayre and cler,
In alle the Worlde thaye have non pere,
He ys not fownde in no maner wyse,
But of a Schepeherd in Godis servyse:
The good Schepeherd that I her mene,
Ys he that keepeth hys Sowle clene:
Hys Flowrys ben gret and sum ben small,
Lyke to hem that growyth in Dale;
With many a vertu both fayre and cler,
As ther ben dayes in alle the yere,
Fro fallyng Ewel and alle Sekeneys,
From Sorowe he brengyth man to Bles;
Unto that blese that wee maye come,
Byth the help of Marys Sonne:
And of hys Moder that ys so fre,
Amen good Lord for cherite.

I Schal yow tel wyth hert mode,
Of thre Kynggys that ben so goude,

And how thaye cam to God almyght,
The wich was ther a sweet syght.

I figure now howr besset *Stone*,
Fro Heven wase sende downe to *Solomon*:

By an Angele bothe goude and stylle,
The wych wase than Christis wylle.

The

The preſent of hem in Bedlem than,
To Cryſt brwght Aurum Tus & Myrham.

Owre Sol and Sulphir wyth his Mercuri,
Both Bodi and Soule wyth oure Luneyre.

Aurum betokeneth heer, owre Bodi than,
The wych was brwght to God and Man.

And Tus alleſo owre Soule of lyfe,
Wyth Myrham owre Mercurye that ys hys Wyfe.

Here be the thre namys fayre and good
And alle thaye ben but one in mode.

Lyke as the Trenite ys but on,
Ryght ſo conclude the *Phyloſofeers Stone.*

Thow mayſt a ſe her now in ſyght,
Off owre *Stone* figuriet a right.

How ſende he waſe out of Heven,
By an Angele wyth mylde Stefyn.

And by hys fygure thow mayſt ſe
That hyt ys lyke to perſonis Thre.

To Fader and Sonne and holi Goſt,
The wych was and ys of mytis moſt;

Into hys blyſe now come wee,
Amen goud Lord for cheyte.

I shew you here a short Conclusion,
To understand it if ye have grace,
Wrighten without any delusion;
Comprehended in a litle space.
All that in this Booke wrighten is,
In this place comprehended is,
How Nature worketh in her kinde,
Keepe well this Lesson in your minde:
I have declared micle thing,
If you have grace to keepe in minde,
How that our Principle is One thing,
More in Number and One in kinde;
For there ben things Seven
That in a Principle doe dwell,
Most precious under Heven,
I have so sworne I may not tell.
In this Booke I shew to you in wrighting,
As my Bretheren doe each one,
A similitude of every like thing,
Of the which we make our *Stone.*
Our *Stone* is made of one simple thing,
That in him hath both Soule and Lyfe,
He is Two and One in kinde,
Married together as Man and Wife:
Our Sulphur is our Masculine,
Our Mercury is our Femenine,
Our Earth is our Water cleere;
Our Sulphur also is our Fier,
And as Earth is in our Water cleare,
Soe is Aer in our Fier.
Now have yee Elements foure of might,
And yet there appereth but two in sight;
Water and Earth ye may well see,
Fier and Aer be in them as quality:

It

Thys *Scyence* maie not be taught to every one,
He were acurst that so schould done:
How schould ye have Servants than?
Than non for other would ought done,
To tyl the Lande or drive the Plough,
For ever ech man would be proud enough;
Lerned and leude would put them in Presse,
And in their workes be full busie,
But yet they have but little increse,
The writings to them is so misty.
It is full hard this *Scyence* to finde,
For Fooles which labour against kinde;
This *Science* I pray you to conceale,
Or else with it do not you meale,
For and ye canot in it prevaile,
Of much sorrow then may you tell:
By suddain mooving of Elements Nature may be letted,
And wher lacks Decoction no perfection may be,
For some Body with leprosy is infected;
Raw watery humors cause superfluity:
Therefore the *Philosopher* in his reason hath contrived
A perfect Medicine, for bodyes that be sick,
Of all infirmetyes to be releeved,
This heleth Nature and prolongeth lyfe eak;
This Medicine of Elements being perfectly wrought,
Receypts of the Potecary we neede not to buy,
Their Druggs and Dragms we set at nought,
With *quid pro quo* they make many a ly.
Our *Aurum potabile* Nature will increase,
Of Philosophers Gold if it be perfectly wrought,
The Phisitians with Minerall puteth him in prese:
Litle it availeth or else right nought.
This *Scyence* shall ye finde in the old boke of *Turb*;
How perfectly this Medicine *Philosophers* have wrought,

Rosary with him also doth record,
More then four Flements we occupie nought;
Comune Mercury and Gold we none occupie,
Till we perfectly have made our *Stone*,
Then with them two our Medicine we Multiply,
Other recepts of the Potecary truly we have none.
A hundred Ounces of *Saturne* ye may well take;
Seeth them on the fire and melt him in a mould,
A Projection with your Medicin upon hem make,
And anon yee shall alter him into fine Gold;
One Ounce upon a hundred Ounces is sufficient,
And so it is on a thousand Ounces perfectly wrought,
Without dissolucion and Subtillant;
Encreasing of our Medicine els have we nought.
Ioy eternall and everlasting blisse,
Be to Almyghty God that never schal miss.

In some Copies I found these following Verses set before this Worke.

EArth out of Earth clensed pure,
By Earth of himselfe through his nature,
Rectified by his Milke who can it tye, (truly:
And afterward united with Water of lyfe
A Dragon lying in his deepe denne,
Rotting in Water to Putrefie then:
Leprouse huge and terrible in sight,
By bathing and balning the Dragon cometh to light;
Evermor drowned in the bottome of his Well,
Tyl all his Leprousie will no longer dwell,
In his owne Nature he altereth cleane
Into a pure substance, ye wat what I meane.
I shew you here a short Conclusion, &c.

Why

WHy art thou so Poore and I so Rich,
Aboundance of Tresure in me thow maist
In all the World I am nothing so liche;
As Man that is so proginitous to my kynde,
The Rych man on the Poore hath no pity,
In me therefore have thow affiance,
It is oft tymes seene in Towne and Cittie:
He is evyll at ease that hath no Craft nor Scyence.
The Ryche men of the Poore now have greate dispight,
That they should wyth thyr cunyng any good thing wyn;
And to give to the Poore almes they have no delight,
Lytle is the Charity that is them within,
And Ensample of *Dives* as the Scripture can tell,
Poore *Lazerus* at his Gate for default dyed;
Had he given him Almes he had not gon to hell,
Now for to repent him truly it is too late.
Man thou hast no goods but God doth them send,
Departe with thy Brother as God doth thee Comand.
Thy lyfe that wyll the better amend,
Death will with thee make a suddaine hand,
Thy worldly goods thow schalt forsaken:
Give every Beast againe his due,
And than schall thy body be full naked:
Death on the will nothing rue.
Why so far and I so neare?
Hast thou no grace Man me to meete,
So oftyn as I to the do appeare;
And yet of me thou takest no keepe,
In common Mercury thou doest me seeke:
In Alkali and in Alembroke,
In common Sulphur and Arsenick eke,
Which makes many a man to dote.
Common Mercury is not good,
It bringeth many a man to care;

It makes his Haire grow through his hood,
And his Purse both thin and bare.
Mercury and I are of allye,
But she with me may not compare;
In nature she is both cold and dry,
Therefore I councell thee to beware:
Many a man she makes full bare,
Because she lacks humidity,
On her to spend they would spare,
She brings many a man to poverty.
I am she which wise men seeke,
Mercury which is most of might;
Hot and moyst, light and weake,
Of the Elements I am full right,
Water, Earth, Aire and Fire,
Quality, and Quantity, you can never have your desire,
Without Concoction perfectly,
Great riches in us be,
Who hath grace us for to know,
By vertue of her humidity,
In the Fire our *Stone* doth grow.
Thou needy man, where is thy minde?
I councell thee this lesson leare:
Our Mercury is but of one thing,
In our Vessell thin and cleere.
Common Mercury in him is none,
Neither Gold nor Silver in him none is;
Of Mettalls we make not our *Stone*,
By proportion more or lesse,
All manner of Mettalls we deny,
Untill the time our *Stone* be wrought;
All other Receipts we defie
That of the Potecaryes be bought,
With all Spices, save onely Mercury.

Gould

Gould with him ſtands us in ſteed,
Our Medicine for to Multiplie,
After our Phiſicks Stone be Red.
A true Leſſon I have thee tought,
Pray for me and forget it nought:
Many Bookes mayſt thou ſee,
That is not writ ſo openly.
And as I am true Chriſtian man,
A truer Booke findeſt thou none;
And thou wilt of this *Scyence* leare
In riches thou ſhalt have no peare;
He that made this Booke hath it well preved,
The better therefore he may be beleived;
Therefoee I pray you for charity,
To keepe this Booke very ſecretly.
If any man this *Science* of you will crave,
Know he be Sapient that the Coppy ſhall have
I made it not for every man,
Neither for them that lirle good can,
But for me and for my Brother,
Such as have Reaſon and no other;
Keepe this Leſſon well in minde,
Beware thou worke not againſt Kinde;
And in thy Worke make no greate haſt,
That thou labour not in waſt:
Worke in light and not in darke,
And ask Councell of a Clerke:
Elſe may you both lightly fayle,
Without you have both good Counſayle.

TAke our Rose with the red Flower,
Which thou maist know by his Colour;
And him knock into Plates small,
A like thin beate over all.
And with a Corosive good and fine,
Forthwith drawe the same tyne;
Of things that be new and good,
And diverse in Nature and one in Moode,
And put together with strong grinding,
In Horse wombe ever abiding;
In a Vessell good and strong,
Thou so it rule and thinke it not longe,
For within a Moneth or litle moe,
And with his might the Body slo;
Thy Corrosive will thy Rose so frett,
Till he be thin as Milke in Meate.
But how the Corrosive made shalbe,
I will it shew plainely to thee;
As I said to thee before,
Elss knowest thou litle of this lore.
Take Maidens Urine younge of age,
Ashes, Salt, and Lyme,
Of him together make a mariage.
Then the Corrosive is both good and fine:
For without this Corrosive shortly said,
Well compound together in One,
All your Worke is but voyd;
As *Philosophers* write every ech one:
For Doctors both to lay and Clearke,
Written that our first Warke
Is to bring our Body all and some;
And him to reduce in Mercurium.
Then is our Worke well begun,
If the first love be thus wone.

Now

Now ſay *Philoſophers* much more,
Our ſecond Worke if thou wilt know,
Labour with paine and travell therefore:
And God is ready thee it to ſhew,
To bring our Water into Air,
Of *Philoſophers* the ſecond verſe,
Spare not to worke and be not afraid;
For ſo it will be without leſe,
But yet be wiſe in the Warke,
For haſty men never lack woe:
And aske the Councll of a Clarke,
For ſober thrift is beſt thereto,
And ſo Continue night and day
I thee charge, and ſleepe thee not,
For in ſix Weekes truly in ſay,
All into Earth it wilbe brought:
So the Fyre continued be,
Every Decoction to even meaſure,
And after that fyre his quality,
Thou muſt all the Worke rule,
For when it is in Earth full black,
Then is it our black Stone,
He is ſo ſtrong he may not lack,
Tyll all thy Worke be y done.
The third degree as I thee ſay,
Of our Stone now black as pitch,
Thou muſt him waſh with waters gay;
And make him white for ſo did Ich;
And when thou haſt waſht him cleane,
Then is his blacknes gone;
Then is he bright and ſhine,
As Carbuncle or Beril ſtone:
But ere he come to that degree,
It wilbe labour but thinke not long,

For

For many a Colour change will he,
Browne, Red, Ruſſet, ever amonge:
After that to many other mo,
Greene, Blew, Pale and Whyte,
But all theſe let them goe,
They are not to thy profit,
And when thou haſt thus wrought,
By ſix weekes and a day,
Then is the Earth truly ſought,
A white powder collor'd in ſay:
But then ſpare the fyre,
And bate him even to meaſure;
And within a month and litle mo,
The Whyte Stone hath nigh ſure done,
Which will ſhine and melt as wax,
He muſt needes Maſteries do,
The Spirit and Soule make him ſo lax;
That all other kindes he tourne him to.
Then Ferment him with his like,
By joyning of true Decoction,
And feede him forth by litle and lite,
That both together be brought in one,
In Colour ſight and Demeane,
That there be no diviſion:
As thou haſt wrought ſo will it prove,
Take heede how thou haſt done
In this worke of Conjunction;
Thou ſhalt ſe marvells greate,
Both going up and coming downe,
Of Colours ſpringing by the heate:
For the ſoule that is ſo withheld,
Andthe ſpirit that is ſo bright,
I me n it ſeene ſay they would,
Certaine it were a wondrous ſight,

And

And all this is paſt,
That God and Kinde hath done his cure,
Of the Whyte Stone be not agaſt,
He will not flee but bide the Fyre.
Now farther if thou wilt Worke,
To have the ready way,
Take good heede and be not dull,
For ile tell thee the truth in fay:
Hold alwaies as thou did
Before in the other Stone,
Thou cannot faile God be thy ſpede,
As Clerkes write every one,
For your Fyre will him dere,
So it be dry and laſtingly;
Save other while the changing cheare,
Till he have ſottill faſting and ſlye.
Firſt I wot well change he woll,
Into Citrine and pure degree;
And after that Colour is full,
He ſhall never but be White ay,
After that Tawny and Colour de Pale,
He changeth often in ſuch lay:
Till he be Red withouten faile,
As good Coroll or Roſe in May.
Then dread he nothing I wis,
Of this Worlds adverſity,
An Emperour of conqueſt then he is,
The *Philoſophers* ſayne worthy to be:
And when thou haſt thus done,
And thereof ſeene the privity,
Thanke God and Chriſt his only Son.
Together with our bleſſed Lady.

TAke of the eger bloud that is ſo Red,
And diſtill that by Lymbick till it be bright,
Therewith diſſolve the Philoſphers lead,
Filtering it till it be cleere in ſight,
Evaporating it if ye do right.
And from the Medicine with ſtrong Fier,
D ſtill our Mercury moſt of myght,
Rede as blood and ſtrong of Eyre,
And there you have your Stone I wyſſe,
Conteyning in them all that you neede,
The Erth thereof true Ferment is.
Of our purpoſe yf you will ſpeede,
In other Bokes whatſoever you Reede,
From this Doctrine you never flitt,
But further with theſe Stones proceede;
Into foure Elements dividing it,
Ayre, Water and Oyle well rectified,
The Earth by boyling make white as Whale bone,
Againe together them neately joyne,
And of them make a precious ſtone;
The matter goeth to the White alone,
This *Ariſtotle* tought *Alexander* his lore,
The Stone thus fixed make fugitive,
Againe with Aer reſerved in Store;
And then againe make fix belyve:
Multiply it in one and more,
With Nature and Oyle reſerved in ſtore,
Both white and red as you did firſt,
This ſecret made me ſtudy full ſore,
Many a night ere I it wyſte;

For

For my Maſter from me it hidd.
Now is one point yet behind,
With this Stone that muſt be done:
Ingendering him of Water, Ayr and Winde,
The Red on Sun the White on Moone,
Molten looke thow caſt full ſoone;
And Multiply in them their Tincture,
And then take of the powder with a ſpoone,
And ſtraine it on Mercury hott and pure;
And a marvelous Battell thow ſhalt ſe ſoone
Betweene that and the ſaid Mercury,
Either it will turne it Sun or Moone,
And then thou ſhalt the Maſtery unfold,
And thus proceeding Multiply,
In every thing as I have tould;
And thus endeth our *PHILOSOPHY.*

THe World is in a Maze, and wot you why?
Forſooth of late a great rich Man did dye;
And as he lay a dying in his Bed,
Theſe words in ſecret to his Son he ſaid.
My Son quoth he, tis good for thee I dye,
For thou ſhalt much the better be thereby;
And when thou ſeeſt that lyfe hath me bereft,
Take what thou findſt, and where I have it left
Thou doſt not know, nor what my riches be,
All which I will declare, give Eare to me.
An Earth I had all Venome to expell,
And that I caſt into a mighty Well;
A Water eke to clenſe what was amiſſe,
I threw into the Earth and there it is;
My Silver all into the Sea I caſt,

My Gold into the Air, and at the last
Into the Fyre for feare it should be found,
I threw a Stone worth forty thousand pound:
Which Stone was given me by a mighty King,
Who bad me weare it in a fore-fold Ringe:
Quoth he this Stone is by that Ring found out,
If wisely thou canst turne this Ring about:
For every Hoope contrary is to other,
Yet all agree and of the Stone is Mother.
And now my Son I will declare a wonder,
That when I dye this Ring must breake assunder:
The King said so, but then he said withall,
Although the Ring be broke in peeces small;
An easy Fire shall soone it close againe;
Who this can doe he neede not worke in vaine.
Tyll this my hidden Treasure be found out
(When I am dead) my Spirit shall walke about;
Make him to bring your Fier from the Grave,
And stay with him till you my Riches have;
Theis Words a wordly man did chance to here,
Who daily watcht the Spirit but nere the neere;
And yet it meetes with him and every one,
Yet tells him not where is this hidden *STONE*.

A

A
Dialogue *betwixt the* Father *and the* Sonne,
Concerning the two Principles *of the* Blessed Stone.

MY *Sonne* if that *Sulphur* be absent away, *Father.*
Our worke is reproved what ever they say,
And it is Water & Fire as tru as your Creed
Which constraineth a Body till it be dead:
Of him shalt thou never have your desire,
Till he be blew as Lead through his owne Fire,
I do liken our *Sulphur* to the Magnet Stone,
That still draweth to her Naturally,
So with our *Sulphur* the firey Woman Mercury,
When she would from her husband flye.
Father I pray you for Charity, *Son.*
Where shall I this *Sulphur* finde?
For I never did him se with Eye;
Nor never knew him in his kinde.
In our Water my *Sonne* keepe it in your minde, *Father.*
Where he will appeare so white as any snow,
Grammercy *Father* ye be full kinde, *Son.*
For through your teaching full well I know.
Now teach me the Red stone when it is in minde,
How it is made by Natures Law.
The White and Red be both of one kinde, *Father.*
Now hast thou my *Son* all thy desire,
Whose tincture by growing thou shalt it so finde,
Through vertue of the Sun and regiment of Fire
His riches there he doth increase,
Farre passing all that I can name,
If they in Fire shall come in presse:
Gune is their glory but he the same,

For the vertues of the *Planets* ſeaven
Shall have, and alſo from the Pole of heven,
Since the VVorld began noe Gemme is found
Equall him till in vertues all,
The Saphir, nor the Diamond,
The Ruby rich behind ſhall fall,
So ſhall the Turkie and Carbuncle:
If they in fire togeather ſhall fight,
All One except ſhall looſe their might,
The fire on him hath power none,
His Elements be ſo coequall,
An Incombuſtible Oyle is this our Stone
In power farr paſſing others all.

Son. In what Element *Father* is our Sulphur bright?
Is it in all, or is it in one?

Father. In all *Sonne* he muſt need be of right,
For Seperacion of Elements we make none:
And yett in them we can it not ſee,
For ſenſuall matter is he none,
But equallitie only intellectuall,
Without which our *Stone* never fixt be ſhall.
Qualitie *Sonne* alſoe groweth in the fire;
Betwixt the White ſtone and the Read,
For Colours many to you ſhall appeare,
Untill the tyme the Woman be dead:
The which things if ye ſhall not ſee,
Red ſhall your *Stone* at noe time bee;
For where the Woman is in preſence,
There is much moyſture and Accidence:
Watry humors that in her bee
Will drowne and devoure our qualitye,
Remember and thinke of *Noahs* flood,
For too much Water was never good:
And yet as qualitie is hid in quantitie,

So

So must in Water our Earth be:
Riches in him thou shalt much finde,
After alteracions all due to his kinde;
When Oyle in him is coagulate,
Then is our *Stone* body made liquefact:
When Sulphur Water and Oyle be one,
Indued with riches then is our *Stone*.
I cannot thee tell a richer thing;
Then is our *Stone* when he is fire dureing,
Our Fire maketh her so strong.
Father how to make our *Stone*, *Son.*
Fayne would I knowe that have we done;
My Sonne with lent and easie heate, *Father.*
The Elements togeather will kindly meate:
Haste not to fast whilest they be rawe,
Keepe well the Fie beware of the lowe.
Shutt well the Vessle least out passe the Spirit,
So shall you all things the better keepe;
For if the Spiritts doe passe you from,
Remedy to gett them againe have you none:
And how marveillous it is the Elements to meete
Keepe this as your principall secrete,
At your begining give God the prayse;
And keepe your Matter in heate forty dayes,
But so that all things be made cleare,
Or else you are never the neare:
And within this tyme itt wil be Black;
And oft chainge colour till it be White,
There you may cease and further proceede,
By mendinge the heate to your mesure indeed;
And there withall now will I end,
And to God onely thee Commend.

JOHN

JOHN GOWER

CONCERNING

The PHILOSOPHERS STONE.

AND also with great diligence,
Thei fonde thilke Experience:
Which cleped is *Alconomie*,
Whereof the Silver multeplie;
Thei made, and eke the Gold also.
And for to telle howe itt is so:
Of bodies seven in Speciall,
With fowre Spirites joynt withall;
Stant the substance of this matere,
The bodies which I speke of here,
Of the Plannets ben begonne,
The *Gold* is titled to the Sonne:
The *Moone* of Silver hath his part,
And Iron that stonde uppon *Mart*:
The Leed after *Saturne* groweth,
And *Jupiter* the Brasse bestoweth;
The Copper sette is to *Venus*:
And to his part *Mercurius*
Hath the Quicksilver, as it falleth,
The which after the Boke it calleth,
Is first of thilke foure named
Of Spirits, which ben proclaymed,
And the Spirite which is seconde,
In *Sal Armoniake* is founde:

The

The third Spirite *Sulphur* is,
The fourth Sewende after this,
Arcennium by name is hotte
With blowyng, and with fires hote:
In these things which I say,
Thei worchen by divers waye.
For as the *Philosopher* tolde,
Of Gold and Sylver thei ben holde,
Two principall extremitees,
To which all other by degrees,
Of the mettalls ben accordant,
And so through kinde resemblant:
That what man couth awaie take,
The rust, of which they waxen blake,
And the savour of the hardnes;
Thei shulden take the likenes;
Of Gold or Silver parfectly,
Bnt for to worche it sykerly;
Betweene the Corps and the Spirite,
Er that the Metall be parfite,
In seven formes itt is sette
Of all, and if one be lette,
The remnant may not avayle,
But otherwise it maie nought fayle;
For thei by whome this Art was founde,
To every poynt a certayne bounde,
Ordeinen that a man may finde,
This Craft is wrought by wey of kinde;
So that there is no fallace in;
But what man that this werke begyn;
He mote awaite at every tyde,
So that nothynge be left asyde.
Fyrst of the Distillacion,
Forth with the Congelacion,

Solucion, Disscencion,
And kepe in his entencion,
The poynt of Sublimacion,
And forthwith Calcinacion,
Of very Approbacion,
So that there be Fixacion,
With temperate hetes of the fyer,
Tyll he the perfite Elixer,
Of thilke *Philosophers Stone,*
Maie gette, of which that many one
Of *Philosophers* whilome write:
And if thou wolt the names wite,
Of thilke *Stone* with other two,
Which as the Clerkes maden tho;
So as the Bokes itt recorden,
The kinde of hem I shall recorden.
These old *Philosophers* wyse,
By wey of kynde in sondry wise;
Thre *Stones* made through Clergie,
The fyrst I shall specifie,
Was cleped *Vegetabilis*;
Of which the proper vertue is,
To mans heale for to serve,
As for to keepe, and to preserve,
The body fro sicknes all,
Till death of kinde upon hym fall.
The second Stone I the behote,
Is *Lapis Animalis* hote:
The whose vertue, is proper and couth,
For Eare and Eye, Nose and Mouth;
Whereof a man may here, and see,
And smell and tast, in his degree,
And for to feele and for to goe,
Itt helpeth a man of both two:

The

The witts five he underfongeth
To keepe, as it to hym belongeth.
The third Stone in ſpeciall
by name is cleped *Minerall*,
Which the Mettalls of every myne,
Attempreth, till that thei ben fyne;
And pureth hem by ſuch a wey,
That all the vice goth awey,
Of Ruſt, of Stynke, and of Hardnes:
And when they ben of ſuch clennes,
This minerall ſo as I fynde,
Transformeth all the fyrſt kynde,
And maketh hem able to conceive,
Through his vertue and receive
Both in ſubſtance and in figure,
Of Gold and Silver the nature.
For thei two ben the extremitees,
To which after the propertees,
Hath every mettall his deſire,
With helpe and comforte of the fyre.
Forth with this Stone as it is ſaid,
Which to the Sonne and Moone is laide:
For to the Red, and to the White,
This Stone hath power to profite;
It maketh Multiplicacion
Of Gold and the fixacion,
It cauſeth and of this babite,
He doth the werke to be parfite:
Of thilke *Elixer* which men call
Alconomy, as is befalle
To hem, that whilome were wiſe;
But now it ſtant all otherwiſe:
Thei ſpeken faſt of thilke *Stone*,
But how to make it now wote none.

After the sooth Experience,
And nathles greate diligence,
Thei setten up thilke dede,
And spillen more then thei spede;
For alwey thei fynde a lette,
Which bringeth in povetee and Dette;
To hem that rich were to fore,
The Losse is had the Lucre is lore:
To gette a pound thei spenden five,
I not how such a Craft shall thrive:
In the manner as it is used,
It were better be refused,
Then for to worchen upon wene,
In thinge which stant not as thei wene:
But not for thy who that it knew,
The Science of himselfe is trew:
Uppon the forme as it was founded,
Whereof the names yett be grounded;
Of hem, that first it founden out:
And thus the same goth all about,
To such as soughten besines,
Of vetue and of worthines,
Of whom if I the names call,
Hermes was one the first of all,
To whom this Art is most applied,
Geber thereof was magnified,
And *Ortolane* and *Morien*,
Among the which is *Avicen*.
Which founde and wrote and greate partie,
The practicke of Alconomie,
Whose bokes plainlie as thei stonde,
Uppon this Crafte few understonde.
But yet to put hem in assay,
There ben full manie now a day,

That

That knowen litle that thei mene,
It is not one to wite and wene,
In forme of words thei it trete;
But yet thei failen of beyet.
For of to much, or of to lite,
There is algate found a wite:
So that thei follow not the line,
Of the perfect Medicine,
Which grounded is upon nature;
But thei that writen the Scripture;
Of Greke, Arabe, and Caldee,
Thei were of such Auctoritee,
That thei firste founden out the wey,
Of all that thou hast herd me sey,
Whereof the Cronicke of her Lore,
Shall stonde in price for evermore.

THE

VISION OF

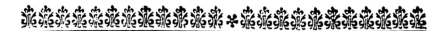

Sr: GEORGE RIPLEY:

CHANON of BRIDLINGTON.

When busie at my booke I was upon a certeine night,
This Vision here exprest appear'd unto my dim-
(med sight,
A *Toade* full rudde I saw did drinke the juce of
grapes so fast,
Till over charged with the broth, his bowells all to brast;
And after that from poysoned bulke he cast his venome fell,
For greif and paine whereof his Members all began to swell,
With drops of poysoned sweate approaching thus his secret Den,
His cave with blasts of fumous ayre he all be-whyted then;
And from the which in space a golden humour did ensue, (hew:
Whose falling drops from high did staine the soile with ruddy
And when this Corps the force of vitall breath began to lacke,
This dying *Toade* became forthwith like Coale for colour blacke:
Thus drowned in his proper veynes of poysoned flood,
For tearme of eightie dayes and fowre he rotting stood:
By tryall then this venome to expell I did desire,
For which I did committ his carkase to a gentle fire:
Which done, a wonder to the sight, but more to be rehear'st,
The *Toade* with Colours rare through every side was pear'st,
And VVhite appeared when all the sundry hewes were past,
Which after being tincted Rudde, for evermore did last.
Then of the venome handled thus a medicine I did make;
VVhich venome kills and saveth such as venome chance to take.
Glory be to him the graunter of such secret wayes,
Dominion, and Honour, both with Worship, and with Prayse.

AMEN.

VERSES

VERSES BELONGING TO *AN EMBLEMATICALL* SCROWLE:

Suppofed to be invented by GEO: RIPLEY.

I Shall you tell with plaine declaracion,
Where, how, and what is my generacion:
Omogeni is my Father,
And *Magnesia* is my Mother:
And *Azot* truly is my Sifter,
And *Kibrick* forfooth is my Brother:
The *Serpent* of *Arabia* is my name,
The which is leader of all this game:
That fomeryme was both wood and wild,
And now I am both meeke and mild;
The *Sun* and the *Moone* with their might,
Have chaftifed me that was fo light:
My Wings that me brought,
Hither and thither where I thought
Now with their might they downe me pull,
And bring me where they woll,
The blood of myne heart I wiff,
Now cauleth both Joy and bliffe :

And

And dissolveth the very *Stone*,
And knitteth him ere he have done;
Now maketh hard that was lix,
And causeth him to be fix.
Of my blood and water I wis,
Plenty in all the World there is.
It runneth in every place;
Who it findeth he hath grace:
In the World it runneth over all,
And goeth round as a ball:
But thou understand well this,
Of the worke thou shalt miss.
Therefore know ere thou begin,
What he is and all his kin,
Many a Name he hath full sure,
And all is but one Nature:
Thou must part him in three,
And then knit him as the Trinity:
And make them all but one,
Loe here is the *Philosophers Stone*.

THe *Bird* of *Hermes* is my name,
Eating my wings to make me tame.

IN the *Sea* withouten lesse,
Standeth the *Bird* of *Hermes*:
Eating his Wings variable,
And thereby maketh himselfe more stable;
When all his Fethers be agon,
He standeth still there as a stone;
Here is now both White aud Red,
And also the Stone to quicken the dead,

All

All and sume withouten fable,
Both hard, and nesh and malliable
Understand now well aright,
And thanke God of this sight.

TAKE thou *Phœbus* that is so bright,
That sitteth so high in Majesty;
With his beames that shineth soe light,
In all places where ever that he be,
For he is Father to all living things,
Maynteyner of Lyfe to Crop and Roote,
And causeth Nature forth to spring;
With his wife being soote,
For he is salve to every sore,
To bring about thys precious worke;
Take good heede unto his lore,
I say to learned and to Clerk,
And *Omogeny* is my Name:
Which God shaped with his owne hand,
And *Magnesia* is my Dame;
Thou shalt verily understand,
Now heere I shall begin,
For to teach thee a ready way:
Or else litle shalt thou wyn,
Take good heed what I say;
Devide thou *Phœbus* in many a parte;
With his beames that byn so bright,
And thus with Nature him Coarte,
The which is mirrour of all light:
This *Phœbus* hath full many a Name,
Which that is full hard for to know;
And but thou take the very same,
The *Philosophers Stone* thou shalt not know,

Therefore I councell ere thou begin:
Know him well what it be,
And that is thick make it thin;
For then it shall full well like the.
Now understand well what I meane,
And take good heed thereunto,
The worke shall else litle be seene:
And tourne thee unto mikle woe,
As I have said in this our Lore,
Many a Name I wiss it have,
Some behinde, and some before;
As *Philosophers* of yore him gave.

ON the *Ground* there is a *Hill*,
Also a *Serpent* within a *Well*:
His Tayle is long with Wings wide,
All ready to fly on every side,
Repaire the Well round about,
That the *Serpent* pas not out;
For if that he be there agone,
Thou loosest the vertue of the *Stone*,
What is the *Ground* thou mayst know heere,
And also the *Well* that is so cleere:
And eke the *Serpent* with his Tayle
Or else the worke shall litle availe,
The *Well* must brenne in Water cleare,
Take good heede for this thy Fyre,
The Fire with Water brent shalbe;
And Water with Fire wash shall he;
Then Earth on Fire shalbe put,
And Water with Air shalbe knit,
Thus ye shall go to Putrefaccion,
And bring the *Serpent* to reduction.

First

First he ſhalbe Black as any Crow,
And downe in his Den ſhall lye full lowe:
I ſwel'd as a Toade that lyeth on ground,
Burſt with bladders ſitting ſo round,
They ſhall to braſt and lye full plaine,
And thus with craft the *Serpent* is ſlaine:
He ſhall ſhew Collours there many a one,
And tourne as White as wilbe the bone,
With the Water that he was in,
Waſh him cleane from his ſin:
And let him drinke a litle and a lite,
And that ſhall make him faire and white,
The which Whitnes is ever abiding,
Lo here is the very full finiſhing:
Of the White *Stone* and the Red,
Loe here is the true deed.

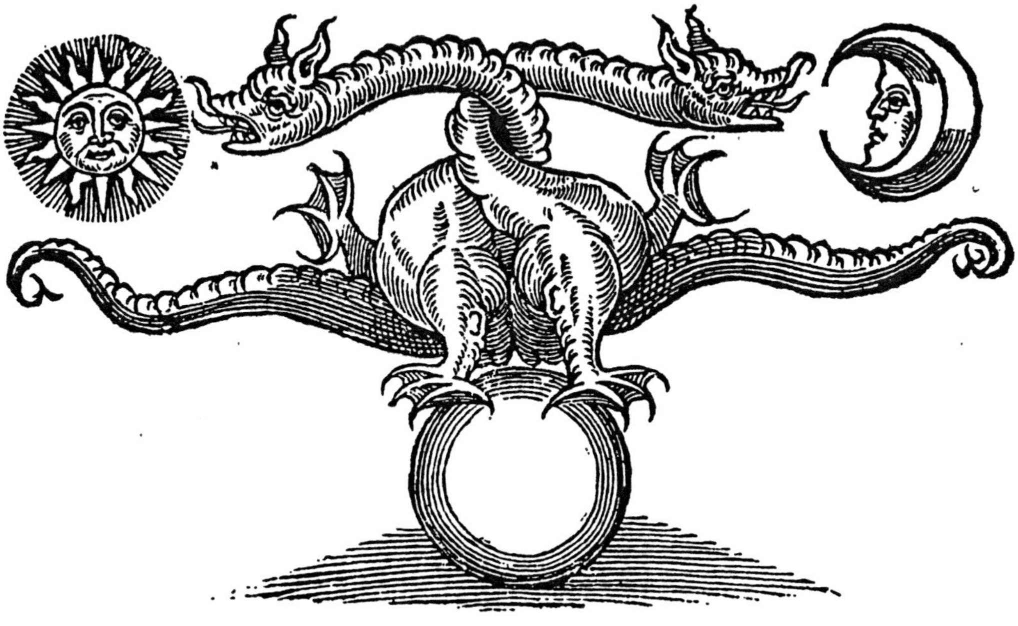

THE MISTERY *OF ALCHYMISTS,*

Composed by Sir Geo: Ripley Chanon of *Bridlington.*

WHen ☉ in ♈ and Phœbus ſhines bright, (ing
The Elements reviving the new Year ſpring-
The Son by his vertue gives Nature & Light,
And moyſture refreſheth all things growing:
In the ſeaſon of the Yeare when the Sun waxeth warme,
Freſhly and fragrante the Flowers doe grow,
Of Natures ſubtill working we cannot diſcerne,
Nor yet by our Reaſon we can it not know,
In foure Elements is comprehended things Three,
Animalls, Vegetabills, Mineralls muſt be,
Of this is our Principle that we make our *Stone,*
Quality and Quantity is unknowne to many one.

Son. Quality (*Father*) would I faine know,
Of what nature it is and what it hath in his kinde.

Father. As Colours divers which on the ground do grow,
Keepe well this ſecret (*Son*) and marke it in thy minde.

Son. Without Proportion (*Father*) how ſhould I it know,
This working now is far from my minde.

Father. Nature and kinde (*Son*) together do grow,
Quality by waight (*Son*) ſhalt thow never finde.

Son, To ſeperate Elements (*Father*) I muſt needes know,
Either in Proportion which be more or leſſ.

Out

Out of our Principle foure Elements thou shalt draw, *Father.*
Thou shalt neede nothing else that needefull is;
Our Principle in quality is so perfectly mixed,
By vertue of the Son and his quality,
So equaly Joyned, so throughly fixed,
As nothing so well mixed may be.
This Principle (*Father*) is but one thing, *Son.*
Good (*Father*) tel me where it doth grow.
In every place (*Son*) you shall him well finde; *Father.*
By Tast and by Colour thou shalt him well know;
Fowles in the Ayer with it doe fly,
And Fishes doe swim there with in the Sea,
With Reason of Angels you may it diserne,
Both Man and Woman to governe,
With our fixed Body (*Son*) we must thus begin.
Of him make Mercury and Water cleare,
Man and Woman is them within,
Married together by vertue of our Fire,
The Woman in her working is full wild,
Be well aware she goe not out;
Till she have conceived and borne a Chylde,
Then all his Kin on him shal lout;
In their workes they be unstable,
The Elements they be so raw;
And in their Colour so variable,
As sometyme like the head of a Crow,
When he is black ye may well like,
Putrefaction must go beforne,
After Blacke he wilbe White,
Then thanke ye God the Chyld is borne.
This Child is both King and Emperour,
Through his region both far and neere;
All the World doth him honour,
By the vertue he hath taken of the Fire:

His first Vesture is White and pure,
As any Christall shining cleere,
Of White tincture then be you sure;
By verture taken of our Fire,
His first Vesture that is so White,
Betokeneth his Virginity,
A similitude even thereto like,
And according to the Trinity:
Our Medicen is made of things Three,
Against which the *Philosophers* cannot say nay,
The Father, the Son in one degree,
Corpus, *Spiritus* & *Anima*.
When Nature is with Nature, thou mayst fruite finde,
By proportion more or lesse,
In practise hereof many men be blinde,
Because they understand not what Nature is;
His second Vesture as Gold is Red,
In his Vessell bright shining,
A Diadem set on his head,
Richer then any earthly thing.
His third Vesture is Purple pure,
Like Sun-beames he shineth bright and clere,
Of Red tincture then be you sure:
By the vertue he hath taken of our Fire.
My beloved *Son* I commande thee,
As thou wilt have my love and blessing,
That thou to God kneele on thy knee,
Unto him give laude and thankeing;
For theis guifts of grace geven unto thee,
To have trew knowledge of this worthy *Scyence*,
That many men seeke by land and sea,
And cannot finde it for any expence:
I shall shew thee my *Son* here a hid S ecret,
Because thou art vertuous in thy living,

Of

Of me elſe ſhouldſt thou never it weet,
And for thou art wiſe in thy Councell keeping,
And therefore I charge thee on my bleſſing,
Not to ſhew it to any man living,
For it is the firſt Principle of our bleſſed *Stone*,
Through which our noble worke is releeved,
Note well that I ſhew now to thee my *Son*,
If Sulphur be abſent our worke is deprived;
Our Sulphur my *Son* is Water and Fire,
Conſtraining the Body till it be dead,
Of hem thou haſt never thy deſire,
Till he be bloe as any Lead,
After all this he doth revive,
That in his Veſſell before was dead;
I can no better in my reaſon contrive,
Then to figure him to the greate God head.
For as there dyed no more then One,
Howbeit that there be perſons Three,
The Father, the Son by might is one:
The holy Ghoſt make our full Trinity:
A ſimilitude like unto our *Stone*,
In him ben things three which be concluded all in one,
Our Sulphur is likened to the holy Ghoſt,
For he is quick, called the Spirit of Slyfe,
In his working of might he is moſt.
He raiſeth our Body from death to lyfe,
Many (my *Son*) with him do riſe,
The holy Goſpell therein is expert,
The number my reaſon cannot contrive,
Multum & quantum fructum adfert:
I liken our Sulphur to the AdamantStone,
That Steele drawes to him naturally,
So doth our Sulphur the woman,
When ſhe from her husband would flye.

I

Son. I muse greatly (*Father*) and mervaile in minde,
Whereof this *Stone* is ingendered,
And also of what manner of kinde,
For I have traveled many a Country,
In vallies low and on hills high,
And spurred therefore of foes and freind,
Yet could I never that Sulphur see,
Nor in any place wat I where him to finde.

Father. *Son* he is made of the Elements,
That God hath given both soule and lyfe,
From Mettall he may never be absent,
For he rules both man and wife.

Son. *Father* I pray you for charity,
Where shall I this Sulphur finde,
For perfectly I know him not by quality,
Nor yet to fore know him by kinde.

Father. In our Water *Son* keepe this in minde,
For there he will appeare as white as snow.

Son. Gramarcy *Father* to me ye be full kinde,
For through your teaching full well I it know,
Now *Father* I pray you for charity,
The while it is in your minde,
To ken the red Sulphur that you will teach me,
And then I trust your Doctrine to finde.

Father. White and Red Son be both one in kinde,
Now hast thou all thy desire,
Keepe well this secret and close it in thy minde,
His tincture and growing is by vertue of our Fire,
For in our Fire our *Stone* will grow,
And there his riches he doth encrease,
And so doth no *Stone* that I do know,
That in the fire will put him in prease;
We liken him therefore unto the Sun,
That to all Elements giveth light.

Nevre

Never sith the World was begun,
Was any but he of so much might,
Were he never of so high degree,
Saphir, Diamond or Emarald Stone,
The Turcas, or the rich Ruby,
Of all vertuous Stones set ower alone,
The greatest Carbuncle that is full of light,
May not with our *Stone* Compaire,
For if they in the Fire should fight,
The Carbuncle of vertue should be full bare,
To destroy our *Stone*, *Son* that will not be,
The Elements in him be so equall;
He is an Oyle incumbustible,
And of all things most imperiall.
In which Elements (*Father*) is our Sulphur in? *Son.*
Is he in all, or in any one?
In all (*Son*) he needes must be, *Father.*
For Seperation of Elements make we none,
Sulphur in Elements *Son* we may not see,
By Nature in them he is so privily mixed,
In Elements he is a quality,
Our *Stone* will never else be perfectly fixed.
Quality (*Son*) growes also in fire,
Betwixt the White Stone and the Redd,
For many Colours there will appere,
While the tyme the Woman be dead.
Father must the Woman needes be dead? *Son.*
Our *Stone* else my *Son* will never be Redd; *Father.*
For whereas a Woman is in presence,
There is much moysture and accidence,
Wetnes and humours in her be,
The which would drown'd our Quality;
Perceive well (*Son*) by *Noahs* flood,
To much moysture was never good.
Like as quality is hid in quantity,

So must our Erth in Waters be,
The riches in him thou shalt finde,
After alteration of kinde,
His Oyle in him is congelate,
This makes our Body liquefact,
Sulphur and Oyle all of one kinde,
Which makes our *Stone* rich and couloring;
I cannot tell thee *Son* a richer thing,
Then he is in the Fire during,
The Fire to him may do no wrong,
Sulphur of Nature makes him so strong.

Son. How to make our *Stone* (*Father*) I would faine know.

Father. In soft heates my (*Son*) Elements will meete,
Hast not to fast whilst they be rawe,
In the Vessell (*Son*) the better thou shalt him keepe,
Rule well the Fire and and beware of the Lawe,
Shut well the Vessell for going forth of the Spirit;
Soe shall you all things the better keepe;
For how to get him againe it is strange to know,
It is hard for some men to make Elements meete,
Keepe well this Secret *Son* and God daily praise,
Put into thy Vessell Water cleare,
And set it in Fire full forty dayes,
And then in the Vessell blacknes will appeare,
When that he is black he will change tyte,
Many Colers in him then will appeare,
From coulour to colour till it be white,
Then it is tyme *Son* to change the Fire,
And melt the heat to your desire;
And if you will have him White still,
Then must you your Medicine apply,
A dry Fire put him till,
And a moyst Fire naturally,
Till he be made fixed,
For to take Mercury before his flight,

As

As he is by nature privily mixed,
Of fusion then he shalbe light,
And if you to his proportion take,
Fine Luna then will he make,
So micle of piercing will he be,
Both fluxible with penetrabilitie;
And (*Son*) if thou wilt have thy Medicine Red,
In a dry Fire thou shalt him keepe,
Ever still in one steed,
That never your Vessell come to wet.

So hard, so heavy and so peircing, *Son.*
(*Father*) this a wonderous thing,
So hot, so moyst, so light, so wet,
This greate Secret *Father* will I keepe,
So white, so red, so profitable,
Of all Stones most incomparable.

He may do more then any King, *Father.*
He is so rich *Son* in his working,
Gould and Silver men would faine have,
Poore and rich for it do crave,
They that of it have most aboundance,
Of the people have most obaisance,
To serve them both day and night,
And in the feeld will for it fight,
Therefore *Son* upon my blessing,
Keepe secretly this precious cunning,
Of thy Councell make neither King nor Knight,
If they knew they would set it light;
For when they have what they will,
God's curse wil come they say the untill,
For had I wist and had I wend,
That commeth evermore behinde,
Our Mercury my (*Son*) is white and thin,
In our Vessell shining bright and cleere,
Our Sulphur is in him within,

Burning him more then our dry Fire,
He fixes him more in one yeare,
By his naturall working I understand,
Then doth the Sonne by his dry Fire,
In yeares a long thousand,
In short space we may have done,
When our Medicine thou wilt assay,
Thou maist make both Sol and Lune.
In lesse space then in one day.

Son. *Father* is it Water in the well springing,
Or is it Water in the river running?
Other Water(*Father*) can I not finde.

Father. Noe(*Son*) it is of another kinde,
Howbeit it is Water cleere,
Our Sulphur in him is soe cleving,
He may not be departed by any fire,
I tell thee the throath in this thing.

Son. By no fire(*Father*) how may that be?

Father, Fire he is ever brenning,
Our Sulphur is made of the Sun and such humi-
That in the Fire he is ever during. (dity

Son. The tyme of our working would I know,
In what space might be made our *Stone*,
By Corne and by Frut (*Son*) thou maist it wel
Once in a yeare it is afore thee done; (know.
The Sun in the Zodiack about doth gonne,
Through the twelve Signes once in a yeare,
Soe long it is ere we can make our *Stone*,

Father, Haste not to fast but rule well thy Fire,
The vertue of our *Stone* few men can tell,
The Elements in him be so mighty,
Aboundance of treasure in him do dwell;
For in riches all Stones exceeds he.

FINIS.

The

The Preface prefixt to Sir *Geo: Ripley's* *MEDULLA;* *Which he wrote* Ann. Dom. 1476. *and Dedicated to* Geo: Nevell *then Arch-Bishop of* Yorke.

RIGHT *noble* Lord, *and* Prelate *Deere,*
Vouchsafe of me these Verses take,
Which I present unto you heere,
That mencion of the Stone *doth make,*
Of Wise men meetered for your sake.
For which of you thus much I crave,
Your gentle favour for to have.

2. *This* Stone divine *of which I write,*
Is knowne as One, and it is Three;
Which though it have his force and might,
Of Triple nature for to be,
Yet doe they Mettalls judge and try.
And called is of Wise men all,
The mighty Stone *that Conquer shall.*

3. *Disdaine you not nor yet refuse,*
To learne the vertues of them now,
By which you may if you them use,
Your selfe preserve and eke know howe,
Old age to hide, and Youth outshewe.
And Brasse by them transmuted is,
And eger Bodyes clensed I wis.

4. *Fined also and made full pure,*
And Aurified be at the last.
The first of these I you assure,
Right hurtfull is for Man to tast,
For Life it will resolve and wast.
Of Corrosives made corrupting all,
And named is the Minerall.

5. *But* Animall *the second is,*
The third forsooth the Vegitable,
To cure all things their vertue is,
In every cause what soe befall,
Mankinde in health preserve they shall:
Reneweth Youth and keepeth it sound,
As trew by proofe the same is found.

6. *And here I will teach you plaine,*
How for to make their Mixtures pure:
In order faire without disdaine.
I will tell you no Dreame be sure,
Beleeve me while my life may dure.
Looke what with mouth to you I say,
My deedes shall prove it true alway.

7. *Yett shall some Figure my Meeter hide,*
Least the Arte with wings should fly away,
And soe as vile abroad to slide,
Whose sence, or Truth cannot decay,
And without fraude I will display
The matter plaine on every side,
And true likewise what soe betide:

8. *Although ere this you have heard say,*
That such as practice doth this Arte,
Their thrift in Ashes seeke alway:
And learne at length with heavy heart,
Not more but lesse to make their part,
Yet be not you dismayed therefore;
Ne feare nor shrinke for it the more.

9. *But trust the words which I you tell,*
For truly I doe flatly say,
I have both seene and known it well,
And wittnesse will the same alway,
This the Marrow *called is I say,*
A truer Text full well I wote,
In all this World finde shall you not.

10 *Then*

10. *Then as this Writing of our Wine,*
Whereof I bring you here a taste;
Whose heavenly Water pure and fine,
Doth all things Worke withouten Waste,
To your desire the bodyes fast
It doth dissolve, make light and open
With other things, not yett of spoken.

11. *Against Nature yet is it not,*
But naturall as may men trow,
Which being cleansed from his spott,
There Phœbus *splendor shall forth shewe,*
And cause it fragrantly to grow;
For how more fragrant it shalbe,
Soe much of Valor more is hee.

12. *For* Phœbus *nature doth surpasse,*
And bodyes pure, and eke the sky,
It doth beshine both Corne and Grasse,
The Sonn reneweth from on hye,
And causeth things to fructifie.
Doth mix, and fix, and natureth,
Drives plagues away and nourisheth.

13. *Abandoneth, draweth, and clenseth the Aire,*
Maketh dews sweete, floods and humors dry,
Maketh softe, hard, sweete and fayre;
And purifieth Natures perfectly,
By his Working incessantly;
It maketh all things to grow I say,
And chaseth Ugly things away,

14. *In Laurell Tree, it is full greene,*
In Gold it lodgeth glistringly;
It decketh Stones with brightnes sheene,
The shinening bodyes are made thereby:
But if you will more certeinly,
Of Phœbus *vertue have knowledging,*
Then Saturns *Chyld must yssue bring.*

15 O

15. O Pastor meeke draw Water cleere,
From buds of Vynes out of a Glasse,
As red as blood as Gold it were;
Which will you give a Gummy Masse,
As pretious as ever was.
Thus without fraude made open is by wyse,
The Arte which you shall not dispise.

16. It multiplyeth and maketh also,
Gold Potable know this for trewe,
By it are things increased soe,
That health thereby you may renewe,
To learne those Secreats dayly sue,
Which formally prolong well may
Your Life in joy from day to day.

17. For although many hate this Arte,
Yet it is precious over all;
Try and discerne within your hearte,
By all the Lessons misticall;
A Gift it is Cœlestiall
Which here is taught to you him by
That prov'd it hath Assuredly.

18. This have I written for your sake,
Not in vaine stile, but order plaine,
This little Booke of him you take,
Which frankly doth bestowe his paine.
To God committinge you againe,
And all that doth wish well to thee,
In any place wheresoever they bee.

19. If you unbroken long would keepe,
In perfect health, your Vessel still;
Then for your Cannon looke you seeke,
Remembring him that hath good will,
By your assistance to fulfill:
And in such sort your Worke display,
As sound may to your lawd alway.

A

SHORT WORKE

That beareth the Name of the aforesaid

Author,

Sir G. RIPLEY.

TAke *Heavy*, *Soft*, *Cold*, and *Drye*; (ly:
Clense him, and to Calx grind him subti-
Dissolve him in Water of the Wood;
If thou can do any good
Thereof, take a Tincture
And Earthy Calx good and pure.
Of this maist thou have with thy travaile,
Both Mercury, Water, and Oyle;
Out of the Ayre with Flames great,
Fire into the Earth doth Creepe;
In this Worke if thou wilt winn,
Take heed wherewith thou dost begin,
And in what manner thou dost work,
For loosing thy way in the darke;
And where, with what, and how, thy matter shal
I tell and Councell thee as my Frend: (end;
Make Water of Earth, and Earth of Water;
Then art thou well onward in the matter.

For thou shalt find hid in the myre,
Both Earth, Water, Ayre, and Fire:
I tell thee my Brother, I will not flatter,
Of our Earth is made our Water:
The which is cleere white as Snow;
And makes our Earth Calcine and growe.
Blacknesse first to thee doth shew,
As by thy practise thou shalt know:
Dissolve and Calcine oft, and oft; (brought:
With Congelation till the Body to whitnes be
Make the Body fluxible, and flowing;
With the Earth, perfect, and teyning.
Then after Ferment is once done;
Whither thou wilt with Sunne or Moone,
Dissolve him with the Water of life,
Ycalled Mercury withouten strife:
Put the Soule with the Body, and Spirite
Together in one that they may meete;
In his Dammes belly till he wax great,
With giving Drinke of his owne sweate:
For the Milke of a Cow to a Child my brother
Is not so sweete as the Milke of his Mother:
This Child that is so marveilously wrought,
Unto his Heritage must be brought:
His livelyhood is so worthy a thing,
Of abilitye to spend with a King:
He that beareth all this in minde,
And understandeth these Parables all;
With Seperation he may finde,
Poore and Rich, great and small;
With our Sulphur we make our Antimony, White and
And thereof we make our Mercury quick, & dead. (Red;
This is a Mettall that I speake of one of the seaven,
If thou be a Clerk read what I meane.

There

There is no Plannet of six neither great nor small,
But if he be put to them, he will Calcine them all.
Unto red blood he must be brought;
Else of him thou gettest right nought:
Reach him then with the Wood Water,
Man, and Woman Clothed under one hatter,
In and of them is conceived a Child
Lovely of beauty, meeke and mild;
Out of the Earth with dropps strong,
Nourish the Child in his Mothers wombe;
Till he be come to full age;
And then make thou a Mariage,
Betweene the Daughter, and the Sonne,
And then thou hast the Mastery wonn.
The beginning of this Worke, if thou wilt crave,
In holly Writ thou shalt it have:
Both in Masse Booke and in Psalter
Yea wrighten before the Preest at the Alter:
And what is Antimony that thou shalt worke,
I have written to thee if thou be a Clerke;
Looke about before if thou canst finde
Plainely written, which maketh men blind:
Our Werke is bringing againe our Mercury,
And that *Philosophers* call Solucion;
And if thou loose not the uncleane body,
Thou werkest without discretion;
The Inbibition of Water, is not the loosing;
But bringing the Body into water againe turning:
That is to say into such water,
That is turning the Body into his first Matter:
The second Werke is to bring,
Earth and Water to Congealing;
The cleansing of the Third is another
Unto Whitenes; my owne Brother;

With this Water of his owne,
That is full marvalous to be knowne:
The fourth werke is distilling
Of Water, and Earth upsweating.
And thus hast thou by one assent,
Earth, Ayre, Water, and Fire; the foure Elements:
The Ashes that are in the bottome of the Vessell,
Looke thou dispise them not though left,
For I tell thee right well,
There is the Diadem of our Craft.

FINIS.

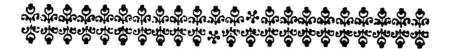

JOHN LYDGATE
MONKE OF
St. EDMUNDS BURY,

In his Translation of the second Epistle that King Alexander *sent to his Master* ARISTOTLE.

WHan *Alysaundre* as is Rehersyd heer
This *Phylosophre* for vertues manyfoold,
Sent unto hym a secret Messengeer,
Without exskus to come to hys housoold,
But he ageyn for he was feeble and old,
And impotent on the tother syde,
And unweldy for to goon or ryde.

But chiefe cause why *Alysaundre* sente,
A purpoos take and a fantasye,
To declare pleynly what it mente;
He wyst in sooth that in *Philosophye*,
Wyth other secrets of *Astronomye*:
He was experte and mooste cowde understonde,
Thys was in cheefe Cause of the Kynges sonde.

Powder of Planetys and mevyng of all Sterrys,
And of every heavenly Intelligence;
Dysposicion of Pees and ek of Werrys,
And of ech othyr straunge hyd Scyence,
As the sevene Goddys by theyr Influence
Dyspose the Orders of Incantacions,
Or of sevene Metallys the Transmutacions.

With othir Craftys which that be secre,
Calculacion and Geomancye,
Dyfformacions of *Circes* and *Meed*:
Lokynge of Facys and Pyromancye,
On Lond, and Watir, Craft of Geometrye.
Heyghte and Depnesse with all Experyence,
Therefore the *Kinge* desires his presence.

But for all this within himselfe a thing
There was a Secre he kept not to disclose;
Nor to publishe opynly to the *Kynge*,
Takeyng Example by two things in a Roose,
First how the Flower greet sweetnesse doth dispoose:
Yet in the Thorne men finde great sharpnesse,
And thus in Konnyng there may been a lykenesse.

In Herbe and Flour, in Writeing, Word and Stoon,
Ech hath his vertue of God and of Nature,
But the knowyng is hyd froo many oon:
And not declaryd to every Creature,
Wherefor he cast twen Reason and Measure:
To shape aweye both the *Kyng* to plese,
Somewhat to unclose and set his herte at ese.

There

There is of ryght a greete difference,
Tween a Princes royall Dignite,
And a twen Commons rude In telligence,
To whom nat longeth to meddle in no degre,
Of Konnynges that should be kept secre,
For to a Kynges famous magnificence,
And to Clerkys whiche have Experience.

Itt cordeth well to search out Scripture,
Mysteries hid of Fowlys, Beeste, and Tree,
And of Angellys moost sotyl of Nature;
Of Mynerålls, and Fysshes in the See,
And of Stonys specially of Three.
Oon *Myneral* another *Vegetatyff*,
Partyd on Foure to lengthe a Mannys lyffe.

Off whych I radde oonys among othir Stonys,
There was oon calyd *Anymal*;
Foure Elements wrought out for the noonys:
Erthe, Watir, and Ayre, and in especyall,
Joyned with Fyre proporcyon maad egal.
I dar seyn breefly and not tarye,
Is noon swych *Stoone* found in the Lapidarye.

I rad Oonys of a *Phylosophre*,
Ageyn ech syckenesse of valew doth moost cure,
All the Tresure and Gould in *Crasus* Coffre;
Nor all the Stoonys that grow by Nature,
Wrought by Craft or forgyd by Picture.
Lapis & non Lapis, Stoon of greetest fame,
Aristotiles gaff it the same name.

And

And for I have but little rad or seyne,
To write or medle of so high mateerys,
For presumcion some would have disdeyn;
To be so bold or clymbe in my desires:
To scale the Laddere above the nyne Speerys,
Or medle of Rubyes that yeve so cleere a light,
On hooly shrines in the dirk night.

I was nevir noon expert Jowelcere,
In suych mateerys to put my sylfe in prees,
With *Philosophres* myn Eyen wer nat cleer,
Nowthir with *Plato* nor with *Socratees*:
Except the Prynce *Aristotilees*.
Of Philosophres to *Alisaundre* Kyng,
Wrott of this *Stone* the mervaylle in all werking.

In prevy wyse lych to hys Ententys,
Secretys hyd cloos in *Phylosophye*,
Fyrst departyng of the foure Elementys;
And aftyrward as he doth speceffye,
Every ech of hem for to recteffye.
And after thys lyk hys Oppynyon,
Of thys foure to make a Conjunccyon.

In suych wyse performe up thys *Stoon*,
Seene in the joynynge there be noone outrage
But the fals erryng hath founyd many one;
And brought hem aftyr in full greete rerage,
By Expensys and outragyous Cóstage.
For lak of brayn they wern maad soe wood,
Thyng to begynne whych they not understood.

For

For he that lyst putte in Experience,
Forboode secrees I hold hym but a foole,
Lyke hym that temptyth of wylfull neglygence,
To stonde up ryght on a three foote stoole,
Or sparyth a stewe, or fyssheth a bareyn poole.
Whan all is doon, he get noon othir grace,
Men wyl skorne hym and mokke hys foltish face.

Itt is no Crafft poore men t'assayle,
It causeth Coffers and Chestys to be bare,
Marryth wytts, and braynes doth affray;
Yit by wryting this booke doth declare,
And be Resons lyst not for to spare,
Wyth Golden Resouns in taast moost lykerous,
Thyng *per Ignotum* prevyd *per Ignocius*.

Title of this Booke *Labor Philosophorum*,
Namyd alsoe *De Regimine principum*,
Of Philosophres *Secreta Secretorum*,
Tresour compyled *omnium Virtutum*;
Rewle directory set up in a som,
As Complexions in helthe and sekenesse,
Dyspose them sylf to mornyng or to gladnesse.

The whych booke direct to the Kyng
Alysaundre both in the werre and pees,
Lyke hys request and royall commanding,
Full accomplished by *Aristotiles*,
Feble for Age and impotent doubtles,
Hoole of corage and trew in his entent;
T'obeye his byddyng this booke he to hym sent.

How Aristotle *declareth to King* Alysaundre *of the Stonys.*

TOwching the *Stone of Philosophres Oold,*
Of which they make moost Sovereyn mencyon ;
But there is oon as *Aristotle* toold ,
Which alle excelleth in Comparison,
Stoon of Stoonys moost Sovereyn of renoune ;
Towching the vertue of this rych thyng,
Thus he wrote to the most sovereyn King.

O *Alysaundre* grettest of dignite,
Of al this World Monark and Regent,
And of al Nacyons hast the Sovereynte ;
Echoon to obeye and been obedyent,
And to conclude the fyn of our entent,
All worldly Tresure breefly shet in oon,
Is declaryd in vertue of this *Stoon.*

Thou must first conceiven in substance,
By a maneer uncouth dyvysion ;
Watir from Eyr by a disseverance :
And fyr from Eyr by a departicion,
Echoon preservyd from all Corruptyon.
As *Philosophres* a forme have specefyed,
Which by Reason may not be denyed.

Watir from Eyr departyd prudently,
Eyr from Fyr and Fyr from Erthe don,
The Craft conceyved devyded truly ,
Withouten Errour or Decepcyon,
Pure every Element in his Complexion.
As it perteyneth pleynly to his parte,
As is remembryd perfyghtly in this Arte.

This

This *Stone* of Colour is ſometyme Citrynade,
Lyke the Sonne ſtremyd in his kynd,
Gold treſſyd maketh hertes full glade;
With more Treſour then hath the Kyng of *Inde*,
Of pretyous Stoonys wrought in their kynde.
The Cetryn Colour for the Sonne bryght,
Whyte for the Morne that ſhyneth all the nyght.

This *Philoſophre* brought forth in *Paris*,
Which of this Stoonys wroot fully the nature,
All the Dyvyſion ſet by grett advys;
And thereuppon did his beſy cure,
That the perfeccion long ſhould endure,
Lyke the entent of *Ariſtotles* ſonde,
Which none but he cowd well bryng on honde.

For though the mateer opynly nat toold,
Of this Stoonys what *Phyloſophres* mente,
Ariſtotiles that was experte and Oold;
And he of *Paris* that forth this preſent ſent,
And in all hys beheſte feythfull true of Entent:
With Circumſtances of *Araby Inde & Perce*,
Towching the Stoonys that Clerkys can reherſe.

Hermogenes hadde hymſelfe alloone,
With the ſeyd *Phelip* that with him was ſecre,
Knewh the vertue of every prevy Stone;
As they were diſpooſyd of Degree,
From him was hyd noon uncouth prevyte.
This *Hermogenes* and he knewh every thing,
Of alle ſuych vertues as long to a Kyng.

THE FIRST CHAPTER.

IN the name of the holy Trinitie,
I will write of this Worke breiflie;
Leaving matters of circumstance,
And promise the truth to advance:
I will not write Figuratively,
But declare the Matter plainely,
And how things must be made to accord,
By Natures true worke and the helpe of our Lord:
The World is but one inclosed with heavens round,
Though divers matters and formes be therein found:
The Earth this worlds Center borne up by the Aire,
In kinde hath noe more but being baire,
And neerest to not being, *Philosophers* have told,
In kinde of Complexion is full dry and cold;
And now for my Figure of rotundity,
I will shew how Elements accord and disagree:
And though the Elements be so contrary,
Yett by heavens Influence they are brought to unite,
And when once togeather a body they binde,
Nought may them loosen without wrecke to the kinde.
First Fire in Nature is hott and dry,
Aire differs from Fire in moisture only:
Earth only for coldnesse from Fire disagrees,
This Concord and discord every man sees:
Aire hot and moist of complexion and kinde,
Water differs from Aire but in heate we finde:

Soe

Soe that in moysture we finde them both one;
Naturall heate in Water we finde none;
Water cold and moiste of Complexion is,
Earth differs from Water in drynes I wis:
Earth agrees with Fire in drynes noe doubte,
Thus one in another the Wheele turnes about.
From this round Circle proceeds a quadrant,
Each line unto another an equall distant:
And as the round Figure concludes all in One,
Soe the Quadrant of foure things makes distinction.
From this Quadrant a Fire must proceed,
Which is *Animall, Vegitable* and *Minerall* we reede:
And with the Fire I will begin;
Pray God I be not too bold therein.
The whole Composition of this world is fram'd,
Of the Three things which before I have nam'd:
Now to make things of Excellencie,
We must take things neerest Nobilitie;
And as this greate Masse conteines things Three,
Soe Blood, Flesh and Bone in the least World we see;
Yett lesse World and greate World is all but One;
Thus still we keepe an Unyon:
Whatsoever itt is that is alive,
Without Blood they may not thrive.
Sperme is Generacion of each thing,
Of what kinde soever itt bene;
Blood is Sperme be itt White or Redd,
For without Blood each thing is dead:
Blood conteineth the three things I have told,
And in his Tincture hath Nature of Gold:
Without Gold noe Mettle may shine bright,
Without Blood noe Body hath bene fitt of light:
Thus doth the greate and lesse World still,
Hold the Union according to Gods will:

Now of all things Blood Noblest is,
For nothing in the World may itt misse,
Blood hath true proporcion of the Elements foure,
And of the three species I spoke of before:
The Blood must be the principall matter of each thing,
Which hath any manner of increasing:
Mercury in Mettalls is the Blood certeine,
Sperme in Animalls getts the like againe;
Vegetable moysture from heaven so good,
Yett all these three are but Blood:
Then Blood in procreation is neerest of kinde,
This Secrett good *Brother* keepe close in thy mynde:
And uppon that Condition,
Which Blood thou shalt take I will make repeticion;
The true Blood of Mettalls is hard to have,
And long tyme of getting itt doth crave:
Blood of Vegetables hath moysture greate store,
And therefore to have itt requireth much labour:
The true Blood to finde without labour and cost,
Thou knowst where to have it ere thy witts be lost.
Seeke out the noblest as I said before,
For now of the Matter I dare say noe more.
This Secrett was never reveal'd till this tyme,
By any Mans writings that ere I could finde,
But I which by practice have found itt true,
Knew how things caused things to renew:
God grant noe *Alchymists* meete with my Booke,
For they would have *Elixir* by hooke or by crooke;
And he would spend what his Freinds wan,
And be as neere at the last as when he began,
And would promise to give men Gold greate store,
But beware thou of Expence, as I said before.

CHAP.

CHAP. II.
Of the manner of the Worke.

NOW after the Matter the Manner compute,
How to bring this our Worke aboute:
First take the Matter crude as itt is,
Which will cost you little or nought I wis:
Searce it soe cleane as it may be,
Untill from filth itt is all free,
Which wilbee done in houres three or foure,
Then will it be cleare from his ill humour:
Then take the Faces which you shall finde,
In the same which the Matter left behind:
Purge him also with the noblest Element,
Untill that he to Earth be brent:
Then have you a *Stone* of wonderfull might,
With small Cost a secret right.
Take ye this *Stone* and use Millers Craft,
Till it be fine powder and made very soft:
Then give him the moisture which from him ye tooke,
Then use him as ye shall finde in this booke.
But give him noe other Drinke but of his owne kinde,
For elce you doe not after my mynde.
Let him drinke noe more then will suffice,
Beware of Floods I you advise:
Then search him twice againe as you did before,
And still put uppon his owne liquor:
Thus their first Order to passe is brought,
And your foulest Worke fully wrought.

CHAP.

Chap. III.
Of the second Order.

NOW the second Manner I will shew plaine,
How you shall worke it with little paine:
When your three searsings be done after my lore,
Then breake the *Stone* as you did before:
Then must you have one Veschell,
Which must be made like an Eggshell,
Into the which Vessell the Matter you must putt,
Then see that itt be well closed upp:
The Vessells divided in parts three,
Whereof two still voyde must bee:
This Vessell must be set in a kinde heate,
That the Matter may kindly sweate;
The Spiritts must not be opprest with Fire,
For then thou shalt never have thy desire;
Neither must thy Vessell have cold,
For then itt will spoile as *Philosophers* have told;
But keepe itt in a temperate heate alwayes,
For the space of fortie dayes:
Then Blackesse will appeare to sight,
That Blacknesse thou must bring to be White.
ake out t he Glasse at the forty dayes end,
And se that from cold thou doe itt defend;
And set itt in a Furnace with dry fire,
Till itt be White after thy desire,
Which wilbe done in Weekes three,
And dryed from his moysture utterly:

Then

Then with the first Water thou first didst imbibe
Againe thou maist feede it att this tyde,
But give itt noe more, nor you doe thinke
May suffice at once for itt to drinke,
This done putrefy as you did before,
Even in the very selfe same maner,
And in the said tyme which it stoode before,
Itt will becom of blacke Colour,
And in the same Order if it congeale White,
Then is your Worke both perfect and right;
Now you must goe lerne the Bakers occupacion,
How he Leavens Bread by Fermentacion;
And truly to Ferment take noe plate of Gold,
But parte of that the plates doe hold.
You know that if *Sol* shew not a faire Tincture,
Itt will be had but in little honour,
Then Tincture of Gold is a most noble thing,
With a grace to noble men of our workeing,
For that true proverbe doth well accord,
Base things befitt not a noble Lord.
Now have I told you what Ferment is,
To teach you to Ferment I will not misse;
This Chapter is now brought to an end,
And now the third Order to shew I intend.

Chap. IV.
Of the third Order of this Worke.

RECIPE *Sol* that is pure and good,
And see that from him you take his pure blood,
Your *Stone* you must divide in parts three,
And the fourth of the Ferment must be.

If you will have for Red, and White too,
To Red after this Order you must doe,
And the White after the same,
Must be ferment with *Lune* by name,
And the matter equally divyde
One for the Red, the other for the White.
Another like Vessell for the White you must looke,
As before is taught you in this Booke.
When your Ferments to your matters be put,
Then your Vessell close you must shut;
And sett it to Putrifye as you did before,
The full tyme as I said of yore:
And use itt in every degree,
As in the next Chapter before you may see.
But looke that you knowe your two Ferments assunder,
Or elce of your folly itt were great wonder:
And when from his Blacknesse you have brought itt White,
Then have you *Elixir* of wonderfull might:
Your Red to his perfection is not fully brought,
But your White is perfectly wrought.
Your Red with most strong heate must be fedd
In a close Furnace untill itt be Redd:
When itt is Redd and will melt like waxe,
Then of all that should be nothing laxe.
Now have you a *Stone* of wonderfull might,
Which will take Mercury before his flight,
And command him to stay, and cause him to bring
All Mettalls unto him, and call him their Kinge,
And make such obedyence without Digression,
That of him they shall all take Impression;
Now have you a *Stone* of wonderfull power,
Which conteineth the three Species and the Elements foure:
Fire in Colour, Water by Effusion,
Earth to sight without delusion,

Aire

Aire is in Water all men doe knowe,
And thus the foure Elements accordeth nowe:
As for the three Species I will ſhewe,
How in your *Stone* you may them knowe:
Tincture for Blood perteineth to the Animall,
Moyſture the Vegetable part poſſeſſe ſhall;
All Earth is Minerall without any doubt,
Thus keepe we in one Circle and never goe out.
Now have I my *Figure* perfectly wrought,
Yett of the Center I have ſaid right nought.
A Center is a pricke of whatſoever itt be,
Without any manner of diviſibilitie;
And made as Nature doth well provide,
So as no Accident may itt divide:
Only by hand but in the Quantitie,
But by noe Element ſeperate the Qualitie;
If in greate Fire you ſett it downe,
A true Salamander itt wilbe found;
If in the Water thou throwe I wis,
It will live there as doth a Fiſh;
If in the Aire you caſt it up hye,
There will it live, and never dye:
If in the Earth thou bury itt faſt,
Then will it remaine there, and ever laſt.
Thus can no Element divide without doubt,
The Center which our Wheele turnes about:
Now how to Multiply your Medicine I trow,
Would doe you much good for to knowe;
For unleſſe you know howe to Multiply,
Your Medicine will be ſpent quickly:
Then would itt put thy minde to much paine,
To thinke that thou muſt make itt againe:
Therefore the next Chapter ſhall teach thee right,
To Multiply this *Stone* of wonderfull might.

Chap. V.
How to Multiply.

NOW in this Chapter I meane to ſhewe,
How to Multiply that thou may knowe:
If Iron to the Load-ſtone be not put certeinly,
Itt will decreace wonderfully;
The Species of all things both more and leſſe each one,
Are mainteyned by reaſon of Multiplication;
Then if they be not Multiplyed they decay,
But Multiplication makes them be all away.
All things after Conception receive naturall Food,
To mainteine their kind as Nature ſeeth good:
Soe likewiſe our *Stone* muſt needs Multiply,
Or elce the Species of that *Stone* will dye:
And Multiplication muſt needs be of ſuch thing,
As the thing multiplied takes beſt likeing.
Fire which burneth perpetually,
If Matter want Fire will dye;
But for to feed our *Stone* rightly,
The way I will ſhewe preſently.
Take your Glaſſe and Medicine withall,
And in a warme Fire ſett itt you ſhall;
And when itt begins to liquefy,
Put common Mercury to itt by and by;
And itt wilbe devoured anon
By vertue of heate that is in our *Stone*,
And as much as you putt in quantitie,
Soe much doth your Medicine augment truly:
Yett you muſt have reaſon not for to cloye,
With overmuch cooling, kind heate thereby:

And

And as of a Dragme you will make a Pounde,
You may well do itt, if you keep round;
And when it is Multiplied sufficiently,
Then from the Fire set it by.
A man in this Land once I knewe,
That marred that he made, and so may yowe;
Except ye doe as I have taught,
And then neede you to feare nought.
Another I knewe which wanted good direccion,
And at once spent all at one projection.
These knew not howe itt should be multiplyed,
Which things I have taught you at this tyde;
But see that the Mercury wherewith ye Multiply,
Be made soe cleane as itt may be.
Now to make him extend his perfection,
It is needfull to know how to make projeccion:
Whereof in the next Chapter I will treate,
For of Multiplicacion I will noe more speake.

Chap. VI.
Of Projection.

NOw lacke we but onely this Lesson to take,
Perfectly projection for to make:
Take one parte of the Medicine, and of ☿ ♄ or Tinn,
But see that you make them exceeding cleane;
And when your Mettall doth Liquefy,
Then cast in your parte of Medicine quickly.
Then will it be brought to such a passe,
That all will be as brittle a glasse;
Take the brittle substance as it is,
And upon an (100.) to take doe not misse.
That 100. uppon 1000. soe still increase you may,

And project noe more when your Tincture doth decay.
This projection is sure without any doubt,
Thus is our Wheele turned round about.
In what Vessell to project I need not to tell,
For a Maister of his Arte knoweth it very well;
To project on Mettalls nowe you knowe,
And to project on mans body nowe will I shewe.
First the Body must be purged well,
And by swetting and bathing be made suttell.
And when you are cleane according to your minde,
Take a dragme of your Medicine with the Quintessence of Wine;
Such a suddeine alteration itt will showe,
As you need not to feare Corruption noe moe:
Nowe of his Vertues I need not to declare,
They are fully shewne by others elce-where.
Now to the holy Trinitie I thee commend,
Thankeing him my Worke is at an end:
Chargeing thee this Secret from bad men to keepe,
Though with greate Importance of thee they itt seeke;
And beware itt goe not from thy hand,
Except to a perfect honest man.
By Bookes the true Worke I could never finde,
Therefore left I this Booke behinde,
That to whose share soever itt might fall,
By itt they might know our Secretts all.
God grant noe *Multiplyer* meete with my Booke,
Nor noe sinister Clerkes thereon to looke;
Then will they pay their debts surely,
And build Churches, and Steeples very hye;
Keepe itt from these folkes I thee pray,
As thou wilt answere before God att last day:
For whatsoever hath bin said to our worke doth accord,
Therefore give honour, praysе, and thankes to our Lord;
Holy and Reverend be his Name,
Which to me vile Synner hath revealed the same.

THE

THE

HERMET'S TALE.

IN Pilgrimage one onely thing I found
Of worth in *Lemnes* nere to *Vulcan*'s ſhopp,
A Chriſtall founteine running under ground,
Between a Vally and a Mounteines topp.
Pleas'd with this ſight, I bid a *Hermite* tell
The ſtory of the place, who there did dwell.

Within this Vale a hallowe dusky Cave
There is (quoth he) of greate Antiquity,
Where plumes of *Mars* blew greene and red you have:
Torne from his creſt for his Iniquity.
The Troope of Smiths, as he for *Venus* lay,
Surpris'd and tooke him, yett he gett away.

For as the *Cyclops* him in tryumph brought,
To halting *Vulcan* to receive his doome,
They lifted up his beaver, and found nought
But vacant place and Armour in the roome.
Of th'armour then they thought they had good prize,
But working it they found itt ſcyndarize.

The Smiths amaz'd finding themſelves deluded,
Satt all in Counſaile in their Maſters Denne,
Deliberating well, at length concluded,
There is no equall War twixt Godds and men,
Lett's finde the Angry God and pardon crave,
Lett's give him *Venus* our poore ſelves to ſave.

They

They sought in Heaven *Mars* knew his fact so bad,
He came out there, then one began to tell,
Saturne turn'd from his Throne, a Place had
Not far from thence, hard by this Christall Well.
Thither they wen, and found two Gods alone,
Sitting within a darke, but glittering throne.

Downe fell old *Vulcan* on his crooked knee,
And said forgive, O mighty God of Warr,
My servants and my selfe (once God as yee)
Then use thy will with *Venus* my faire starr.
Saturne (quoth *Mars*) and I must not yet part,
Though shee for whom th'art pard'ned hath my heart.

With this the Cuckold with his sweaty Troope
Went to his Forge and seem'd to make a legg,
Att every steppe, where halting made him stoope,
In thankes to *Mars*, granting what he did begg;
In whose remembrance you shall ever have
Syndars, and fetters in that hollow Cave.

But lett me tell you all that then befell,
Iove seeing this, meaning the Smith to right,
Sent downe a winged God, he trusted well,
Disguis'd in habitt of a shineing light,
Which to the Vally from the Hill's high topp,
Affrighted all the smiths in *Vulcans* shopp.

A voyce was heard from *Ioves* Embassadour,
To summon *Mars* t'appeare before the Gods:
With *Saturne* forth came *Venus* Paramour:
Thinkeing with might to gett of right the odds:
Downward came he 9. myles, they upward fower,
All mett in mist, he fledd, they nere went lower.

Vulcan

Vulcan came hobling up to se what's done,
He findes nor light, nor Gods, but other shape;
To witnesse of this fact he calls the *Sonne*,
Who streght cryes Murther,and made hast to scape:
Some dyeing Soule groan'd forth, *Apollo* stay,
Helpe wise *Apollo* ere thou goest away.

With this *Apollo* lookeing round about,
Espies this fountaine knowes the voice was here,
And boweing downe to finde the party out,
Himselfe unto himselfe doth streyght appeare.
There gaz'd he till a sturdy showre of rayne
Tooke wise *Apollo* from himselfe againe.

Farewell *Apollo* then *Apollo* sayd,
To morrow when this storme is fully past,
Ile turne and bring some comfortable ayd,
By which Ile free thee ere the latter cast.
Then did itt cry as if the voyce were spent,
Come sweete *Apollo*, soe itt downwards went.

Vulcan went to his Forge, the *Sonne* to bed,
But both were up betimes to meete againe;
Next morne after the storme a pale soule dead
Was found att bottome of this faire Fountaine.
Smith (said *Apollo*) helpe to lade this spring,
That I may raise to life yonder dead thing.

Then *Vulcan* held *Apollo* by the heele,
While he lades out the Waters of the Well;
Boweing and straining made *Apollo* feele
Blood from his nose, that in the fountaine fell.
Vulcan (quoth he) this Accident of blood
Is that or nought must doe this Creature good.

He ſpake the word, and *Vulcan* ſawe itt done,
Looke *Sol* (ſaid he) I ſee itt changeth hue,
Fewe Gods have vertue like to thee ô *Sonne*,
From pale itt is become a ruddy blue;
Vulcan (quoth *Phœbus*) take itt to thy forge,
Warme it, rubb it, lett itt caſte the Gorge.

Thus *Vulcan* did, itt ſpued the Waters out,
And then itt ſpake and cry'de itt was a cold;
Then *Vulcan* ſtuft and cloath'd it round about,
And made the *Stone* as hott as ere itt would.
Thus fourteene dayes itt ſickly did indure,
The *Sonne* came every day to ſe the cure.

As itt grewe well the Colours went and came,
Blew, Blacke, White, Redd, as by the warmth & heate,
The humours moved were within the ſame,
Then *Phœbus* bid him put it in a ſweate;
Which *Vulcan* plyde ſoe well, it grue all Red,
Then was itt ſound, and cald for drinke and bread.

Stay (quoth *Apollo*) though itt call for meate,
Diſgeſtion yett is weeke, 'twill breede relapſe,
By ſurfett, therefore ere you lett itt eate,
Some little exerciſe were good perhapps,
Yett had itt broath alowde the ſtrength to keepe,
But when 'twas on his leggs it would ſcarce creepe.

Sol ſawe ſome reliques left of th'ould diſeaſe,
A ſolutine (quoth he) were good to clenſe,
With which the ſickneſſe he did ſo appeaſe,
Health made the Patyent ſeeke to make amenſe;
Who went away three weekes, then brought a *Stone*,
That in projection yeelded ten for one.

This

This did he lay downe att *Apollo*'s feete,
And said by cureing one th'hast saved three:
Which three in this one present joyntly meete,
Offring themselves which are thine owne to thee.
Be our Physitian, and as we growe old,
Wee'le bring enough to make new worlds of Gold.

With that this *Hermite* tooke me by the hand
And ledd me to his *Cell*; Loe here (quoth he)
Could'st thou but stay, and truly understand
What thou now seest, thou knowst this Mystery.
I stayd, I saw, I tryde, and understood,
A Heav'n on Earth, an everlasting good.

A DISCRIPTION of the STONE.

THough *Daphne* fly from *Phœbus* bright,
Yet shall they both be one,
And if you understand this right,
You have our hidden *Stone*.
For *Daphne* she is faire and white:
But Volatile is she;
Phœbus a fixed God of might,
And red as blood is he.
Daphne is a Water Nymph,
And hath of Moysture store,
Which *Phœbus* doth consume with heate,
And dryes her very sore.
They being dryed into one,
Of christall flood must drinke,
Till they be brought to a white Stone:
Which wash with Virgins milke,
So longe untill they flow as wax,
And no fume you can see,
Then have you all you neede to aske,
Praise God and thankfull be.

The standing of the Glasse for the tyme of the Putrifaction, *&* Congelation *of the* MEDICINE.

THe *Glasse* with the Medicine must stand in the fyre
Forty dayes till it be Blacke in sight; (desire,
Forty dayes in the Blacknesse to stand he will
And then forty dayes more, till itt be White,
And thirty in the drying if thou list to doe right;
And then is the Sulphur perfectly Calcinate,
To drinke up his moysture for him, being preparate.

In this tyme the *Glasse* neither open nor shutt,
But still let him stand all the aforesaid dayes,
Not once from the Furnace that ye take him upp:
For by Cooling the Matter the Medicine decayes,
Therefore you must Fire continue alwayes,
In one measure and temperatenes of heate,
Untill all be White, and the Sulphur compleate.

This heate sufficeth for this principle one,
Which is the cheife ground of our Secretts all,
Without which Knowledg thou must not make the *Stone*,
If thou labour thy lyfe tyme, not prosper thou shall,
Therefore merry beware thou doe not fall.
But first truly learne, before thou beginne,
And so to true workeing thou shalt the better wynne.

 Follow

Follow this Booke, and wander not aſide
Out of the way, to the left hand, nor the right,
But ſtreight betweene both direçtly you guide
Thy Worke, ſoe as I to thee doe write,
For in this Booke I will thee plainely excite,
How thou ſhalt make the Philoſophers Lead,
That is *Elixir* to the White and the Redd.

And then the Golden Oyle called *Aurum potabile*,
A Medicine moſt mervelous to preſerve Mans health,
And of Tranſmutation the greateſt that can bee,
For in the ſame Oyle is nothing but wealth;
Then glorious he is in the power of himſelfe:
For noe ſickneſſe can ſtand where he is in place,
Nor povertie dwell in the pleaſures of his Face.

Ænigma

Ænigma Philosophicum.

THere is no light, but what lives in the *Sunne*;
There is no *Sunne*, but which is twice begott;
Nature and *Arte* the Parents first begonne:
By *Nature* 'twas, but *Nature* perfects not.
Arte then what *Nature* left in hand doth take,
And out of *One* a *Twofold* worke doth make.

A *Twofold* worke doth make, but such a worke
As doth admitt *Division* none at all
(See here wherein the *Secret* most doth lurke)
Unlesse it be a *Mathematicall*.
It must be *Two*, yet make it *One* and *One*,
And you do take the way to make it *None*.

Lo here the *Primar Secret* of this *Arte*,
Contemne it not but understand it right,
Who faileth to attaine this formost part,
Shall never know *Artes force* nor *Natures might*.
Nor yet have power of *One* and *One* so mixt,
To make by *One fixt*, *One unfixid fixt*.

D. D. W. Bedman.

FRAGMENTS COPPIED From THOMAS CHARNOCK'S owne hand writing.

When an hundreth & fourscore had run their
Then sone after in short time & space, (race
Blacknes began to shew his Face, (in syght
But when a C. and L. had overcumde hym
He made him wash his Face white & bright
Which unto me was a joyfull syght.
Yet xx. at last came in with greate bost,
And made both Black and White to fly the Cost.

Written by T. Charnock *at the end of* Scotus de Bufone.

Here in Gods name take thy rest,
Quietly in thy warme nest,
For so *Charnocke* thinks it best,
Tyll the *Sune* hathe runne West,
Seaven tymes 600. and 16. just,
Then this *Chyld* awake thou must.

Written

Written at the end of RIPLYE'S *Cantalena.*

ABowte *653*. I dare be bold,
This *Chyld* shall put on a Crowne of Gold;
Or at *656*. at the moste,
This Chyld shall rule the roste.

O*Ther Fragments scattered in the wast places of an Old Manuscript, written with* T. Charnock's *own Hand.*

WE worke this Worke of wonder,
By Wayght, Measure and Number.
Quoth THOMAS CHARNOCK.

WHen he is full Black then take some payne,
To wash him 7. tymes in the water of Jourdayne.

CHARNOCK.

FRo the tyme that he be Black and Ded,
Wash him 7 tymes, or he be perfect Red.

ANd when he is full Black then take some payne,
To wash hym 7. tymes in the water of Jourdayne.

ANd when you see hym perfect Redd,
Then take a stone and knock him on the hedd.

Id est.

ANd when this Woman is brought a bed,
Take the *Chyld* and knock hym on the hedd.
CHARNOCKE, 1573.

PErfect Whyte will not be accomplished,
Untill it hath byne twelve tymes circulated,

Id est.

Six tymes Black, and vi. tymes Whyte.

BEtwixt true Black, and true Whyte;
Wyll appeare many Collers to syght. } T. C.

BEtwixt Purgatory and Paradyse,
The Raigne-bows Collers will arise. } T. C.

BEtwixt Black and Whyte sartayne,
The Pekokes fethers wyll appeare plaine. } T. C.

LOoke you conceive my words aright,
And marke well this which I have sede;
For Black is Ferment unto the Whyte,
And Whyte shalbe Ferment unto the Rede:
Which I never saw till I had whyte heres upon my head.

T. C. 1574.

The 50 yeare of my age.

IN

In some Coppies I have found these Verses placed before Pearce the Black Monk, *upon the* ELIXIR.

MAN and Woman God hath wrought,
And full mykle fruite forth they brought,
So multiplyeth the workes of our heaven
And yet come they but of one thing. (King
Now quod *Marlin* what may that be?
The slithe of the Yearth so say we:
Yearth it was, some Men would say nay,
And yet was it nether cleane yearth sand ne clay,
But the feces of yearth it was of Colour grey,
Which then turned to yearth as it on yearth lay.
The Water turned to blude to make man stronge,
The Ayre and Fire was medled theare amonge.
How be Ayre and Fire quod *Marlin*?
Through the workes of our Lord quod *Martin*.
For the brightnes of the holy Ghost is the Aire,
And the lightnes that gafe lyfe is Fyre.
Wheare hast thowe goe too Scolle to learne all this?
For that thou sayest is right true I wisse;
And I suppose it in thie thought,
That with iiii. Spirits it must be wrought.
Nay your Spirits are too wilde quoth *Marlin* againe,
Therefore I will not medle with them certaine:
I will have a Spirit made by kinde naturally,
That will abide with every body kindly;
Such a Spirit could I macke quod *Marlin*,
And yet men would hold yt but in veyne.

And yet of all workes it is the best,
Lest of Cost and most surest:
For if it should faile then were we done all,
And therefore for the most parfitest worke we it call;
It is so rich when it is wrought,
Though all the world were turned to nought:
As mennye rich bodyes agayn make would he,
As ever were or ever should be.
Take Earth of Earth, Earths Brother, &c.

I have seene an old Coppy of the said work of Pearce the Black Monk, *to the end of which these following Verses were joyned.*

NOW of this *Matter* derke and nothing clere,
An Exposicion I doe mack here;
Wherein I charge you secre to be,
That frend ne foe doe yt se;
Erth hyd within the bodies center is most fine,
Water of Wood Essell of Wine,
For by the moyster of the Grape,
This centrall Earth who can it take;
It and *Sercion* do our Maistry make,
For it shall become Mercuriall,
And after that Essentiall.
But now beware that you not faile,
For then you loose your greate travaile,
Whan you have drawne owte of the Gum,
All the *Mercury* that wyll come,
Understand that Lycowres three
In that *Mercury* conteyned be;

The

The first is the Watur of lyfe Ardent,
By Bath departed that is most lent;
It burneth as Aquavite by live,
And is called our *Mercury* attractive,
Wherewith is made Earth Christalline,
Out of all Collours Metallyne:
I speke no more thereof as yet,
For in this worke we neede not it.
Then runneth a Water after thilke,
Litle in quantity white as mylke;
Whych ys sperme or nature of our *Stone*,
That is earnestly sought of many one:
For of Man, Beste, and every thynge,
Sperme is there begynyng,
Therefore we our *Mercury* do it call.
Whych ys found here and there and over all,
For wythout yt ys nothyng lyvyng,
Wherefore yt ys in every thyng:
As well in thyngs most preciouse,
As in thyngs most vyle and odious;
Of yt they have there first nature,
Thys moyster to you as now is clere,
Thys ys the *Mercury* that we call
Vigetable, Minerall and Animall:
Our Quicksilver and our *lac Virginis*,
Our Water permanent forsooth yt ys;
Wyth thys Water Mercuriall,
We wasch the fylth Originall
Of our Erth tyll yt be whyte,
Lyke a Gumm that floweth lyte,
By dry fyre after that schale cume
Oyle wherewyth we make red Gumm:
Wych ys our Tincture and our Sulfur vive,
The soule of *Saturne* the Golde of life.

Our Tincture and our airy Gould,
Wych before was never so plainely tould;
God graunt that I do no displeasure
To hym in fulfillyng your desire.
Now Elements be divided every one,
Wyth thys Oyle make red your *Stone*;
Owre Gumms two then have schall ye,
Wythout the wych no *Elixir* may be.
They go the Body and the Spirits betwixt,
Wythowte the wych our *Ston* cannot be fixt,
And makyth of hym in a lytle space,
Two *Elixirs* by Gods Grace:
Whereby are trewly alterate,
All Metalline Bodies into a better state,
Wyth *Sol* and *Luna* equall to be,
To helpe us in our necessitie.
Now thanked be God most gracious,
Wych hath this Secret lent to us,
Hys grace therewyth to us he leave,
To our Soules helth us for to meve.

This following Fragment *in some copies I have found placed at the end of the aforegoing Exposition of* Pearce the Black Monke. *In others, immediately before* ——With *Hic* and with *Hæc*, &c. *and bearing this Tytle,*

A CONCLUSION.

TAke Wynde and Water, white and greene,
And thereof draw a *lac Virgine*;
Where some it call a water cleere,
The which water hath no Peere;
And then make your Fier stronger,
When the white fume doth appeare;
Chaunge your Receiver and continue longer:
And then shall you see come a Fire,
Red as blood and full of Yre.
Quod dicitur menstruum fætens, & sol philosophorum,
In quo fit nostra dissolutio, & congelatio.
Sublimatio, attractio, & etiam fixatio,
Et Sulphuris nostri, sive foliati creatio.

WIth *hic* and with *hac* thus may ye do,
As Husband and Wife togeather them wed;
Put them in a chamber both two,
And shet fast the dore when they be a bed.
The woman is both wanton and wilde,
With her husband she cannot rest,
Till she have conceived a Child;
Of all his kin he shall be best.
He is a Childe of the Elements
Both by Father and by Mother,
None so worthy in presence,
Not perfect *Sol* his owne Brother.
Sol and *Luna* owe unto him obedience,
And all that him needes they to him bring,
Saturne doth to him obesance,
Howbeit he is next of his kinne:
There is neither Emperour or Kinge,
But of his presence they would be glad,
If he from them were one yeare wanting;
In their hearts they would be full sad.
In riches he exceedeth all other,
The Elements in him are so even,
Luna is his Sister, and *Sol* is his Brother,
His Father dwelleth among the planets seaven.
Nulla virtus minerabilus where shall we him seeke,
Sit tibi principium principale Councell we must it keepe;
Reperitur ubiq; localis by way in every streete.

An

An other Conclusion.

FIrst Calcine and after Putrefie,
Dissolve, distill, sublime, discend and fix
With *Aquavitæ* oftymes wash and dry;
And make a marriage of Body & Soul the Spirit betwixt.
Which thus together naturally if ye cannot mix,
Then shall the Body utterly dye in the flix.
Bleeding and changing Collours as ye shall see,
In *bus* and *nubi* he shall uprise and descend;
First up to the Moone and after up to the Sun,
Onely shipped within a litle glasen Tunne.
When he commeth thether, then is all the Maistry wonne,
About which Journey great goods ye shall not spend,
And ye shall be Glad that ever it was begun;
Patiently if ye list, to your worke to attend.
Who so shall our Pearle and our Ruby make,
Our Principle let him not forsake.
For at the beginning if his Principle be trew,
And that he can by craft so him bake;
Trewly at the end his Worke shall him not rew.

The whole Scyence.

THere is a bodi of a Bodi,
And a Soule and a Spryte,
Wyth two Bodyes must be knete.

There ben two Erthys as I the telle,
And two Waters wyth hem do dwelle;
The ton ys Whyte the tother is Red,
To quick the Bodies that ben ded.

And oon Fyre in Nature y hydd,
And oon Ayre with hem that doth the dede.
And all hyt commeth out of onn kynde,
Marke thys well Man and beare yt yn mynde.

TAke *Mercury* from *Mercury* which is his wyfe,
For *Mercury* wife to *Mercury* maketh greate stryfe:
But *Mercurys* wyfes Wyfe,
To *Mercury* maketh no stryfe.

AND thou wed *Mercury* to *Mercury* with her wyfe,
Then shall *Mercury* and *Mercury* be merry with-
(outen stryfe:
For *Mercuries* Wyfe to *Mercury* maketh greate stryfe,
But *Mercuries* wyfe's wyfe to *Mercury* maketh no stryf.

A

A Ridle to you I will propose,
Of a Comon thing which most men knowes,
Which now in the Earth very reefe doth grow,
But is of small Price as all men know;
And that without roote, stalke or seede,
Wherewith of his kinde another to breede:
Yet of that nature, that it cannot cease,
If you plant it by peeces it selfe to increase,
Right heavy by kinde, yet forced to fly,
Starke nought in the purse, yet good in the Eye,
This something is nothing which seemeth full strange,
Having tasted the fire which maketh the change:
And hath many Collours yet sheweth but one,
This is the materiall of our *STONE.*

I Asked Philosophy how I should
Have of her the thing I would,
She answered me when I was able,
To make the Water malliable,
Or else the way if I could finde,
To mesure out a yard of Winde:
Then shalt thou have thyne owne desire,
When thou canst weigh an ounce of Fire:
Unlesse that thou canst doe these three,
Content thy selfe, thou get'st not me.

LEt the old man drinke wine till he pisse:
The meanes to the *blest Stone* is:
And in that menstrous water drowne,
The radiant brightnes of the Moone,
Then cast the Sun into her lapp,
That both may perish at a clapp.
Soe shall you have your full desire,
When you revive them both by Fire.

IF ye wolle to hys Medycyn aplye,
Make furst hevy, hard, hotte and drye:
Nesshe, lyght, cold and wete,
Put ham togeder and make ham mete,
Thus may ye spend mor thann the King,
Yf ye have connyng of suche a thynge.

IF thou the Fixid can dissolve,
And that Dissolv'd doest cause to fly,
That Flying then to Fixing bring,
Then maist thou live most happily.

R. B.

ANNO-

ANNOTATIONS AND DISCOURSES, UPON *Some part of the preceding* VVorke.

Pag.6.lin.1. TO the honor of God——

FRom the *first word* of this *Proeme*, and the *Initiall letters* of the *six* following *Chapters* (discovered by *Acromonosyllabiques* and *Sillabique Acrostiques*) we may collect the *Authors* Name and place of Residence: For those *letters*, (together with the *first line* of the seventh *Chapter*) speak thus,

Tomas Norton of Briseto;
A parfet Master ye maie him trowe.

Such like *Fancies* were the results of the *wisdome* and *humility* of the Ancient *Philosophers*, (who when they intended not an absolute concealement of *Persons, Names, Misteries,* &c.) were wont to hide them by *Transpositions, Acrostiques, Isogrammatiques, Symphoniaques*, and the lyke, (which the searching *Sons* of *Arte* might possibly unridle, but) with designe to continue them to *others*, as concealed things; And that upon the Question no other Answer should be returned, then the like of the (a) *Angell's* to *Manoah*. [*His name was Peli*, to wit, *admirable* and *secret*.] (a) *Judg.* 13. 18.

In imitation of whome, tis probable our *Author* (not so much affecting the *vanity* of a *Name* as to *assist* the lovers of *Wisdome*) thus *modestly* and *ingenuously* unvailes himselfe; Although to the generality of the world he meant to passe *unknowne*, as appeares by his owne words:

(b) For that I desire not worldly fame,
But your good prayers unknowne shall be my name. (b) *Nort. Ordinall.* pag. 6.

(c) *Iohn Pitts* from *Iohn Bale*, and (d) he from *Robert Record*, relates, that this *Thomas Norton*, was *Alchymista suo tempore peritissimus*, and much more curious in the Studies of *Philosophy* then others, yet they passe some undecent and abusive *Censures* upon him, with referrence to this *vaine and frivolous Science*, (c) *De illustr. Angl. Script.* pag. 666. (d) *De Script. Br. Cent.* 11. f. 67.

Science, as they are pleas'd to tearme it, (and a better opinion I find not they had even of the *Hermetick learning* it selfe.) Indeed, every one that is educated a *Scholler*, is not borne to affect or be happy in every *Art*, some love one, some another, but few *All*. And this ariseth from the various *Influences* of the *Starrs*, which beget sundry *Inclinations* and *Affections* in Men, according to the different *Constitutions* and *Temperatures* of their *Bodies*; so that commonly what either a man does not *affect*, or *know*, he *despises* or *condemnes*, yet seldome with any shew of *Reason*. But it is no good *Conclusion* for *Blinde men* to affirme the *Sun* has no *light*, because they were never so happy as to see it. For though thy selfe (saith *Conwrath*) art ignorant of a *Matter*, 'tis not denied to others to know the same. However, our *Author* was so happy as to become a *Master* of this *Science* very early: which he learned in (e) *forty dayes*, and when he was

e) *Ord*.p.33.

(f) Scantly of the age of twenty eight yeares,

f) *Ordin*. p. 88.

He earnestly moved his *Master* (who is generally thought to be *Ripley*) to communicate the *Red Medicine* to him, which after some tyme (finding him capable of it) he accordingly did.

Much more might be said in *Honour* of this *Author*, but I refer the *Reader* to the *Ordinall* it selfe, which will abundantly satisfie.

Besides this worke (which is called both by *Pitts* and *Bale*, *Epitomen Alchymiæ*, but by himselfe

(g) Named of Alkimy the Ordinall,
The Crede mihi, the Stantard perpetuall)

g) *Ordinall*. pag.9.

He wrote another Booke *De transmutatione Metallorum*; and to these (h) *Pitts* adds a third *De Lapide Philosophico*.

h) Pag.666.

In the time of *Hen* 8. there flourished Nyne Brothers of the family of the *Nortons* and all *Knights*, one of them (viz.) *Sir Sampson Norton*, *Master* of the *Ordnance* to the said *King* (an *Office* of greate *Honour*, and not usually confer'd but upon Men very *eminent*) lyes buried in (i) *Fulham Church* nere *London*, whose *Tombe* was adorned with severall *Hermeticke*, *Hieroglyphicall* paintings, which have lately perisht by the *Ignorant zeale* of those that understood them not.

i) *Wever's fun. Mon.* fo.526.

The *Epitaph* this.

Of your cherite pray for the Soule of Sir Sampson Norton
Knight, late Master of the Ordinance of warre, with King
Henry the 8th and for the Soule of Dame Elizabyth hys wyff.
Whych Sir Sampson decessyd the eyghth day of February
one thousand five hundred and seventeen.

Pag.11.l.7. That no Man, for better ne for worse,
Chaunge my writing for drede of Gods curse.

Doubtlesse *Norton* was truly sensible of the high injuries done to *learned men* through the *Erronious Transcriptions* of their *Bookes*, and had shared in the unimaginable *misfortune* which thereby befell the then *Students* in *Philosophy*, for he lived in those tymes that could not afford him the use of any other Bookes

Bookes save onely *Manuscripts* (*Printing* having not served an Apprentiship to *England*(k) when he wrote this *Oridinall*) & in that regard he layes this weighty charge upon unfaithfull *Scribes* who *negligently* or *wilfully* alter their *Copy*, whereby the wariest *Students* are encombred with *doubts*, and misled, or plunged into unhappy *Errors*.

k) The first *Printing-Presse* was set up in *Westmin. Abbey* by *Symon Islip*, An.1471 and *William Caxton* the first that practised it there. See *Stowes Surv.* 525.

How ordinary a fault this was amongst the *Transcribers* of former times may appeare by *Chaucer*, who (I am confident) tooke asgreate care as any man to be served with the best and heedefullest *Scribes*, and yet we finde him complayning against *Adam* his *Scrivener* for the very same:

(l) So ofte a daye I mote thy worke renew,
It to Correct and eke to rubbe and scrape,
And all is thorow thy neglegence and rape.

l) *Chaucer to his Scrivener.*

But as in other *Artes* and *Sciences* the fault is scarce pardonable, so cheifly in *Hermetique learning*, where the Injury may prove *irreparable*.

(m) And chaunging of some one Sillable,
May make this Boke unprofitable.

m) *Ord.* p.11.

Pag.33.l.13. If I shulde write I shulde my fealty break
Therefore Mouth to Mouth I must needes speake.

THis is part of the *Letter* which *Norton's* Master wrote when he invited him to come and receive the *Secret* by *word of Mouth*, for without *breach* of his *Oath* he durst not commit it to *writing*, lest he might *cast the Childrens Bread to Doggs*.

In like manner *Aristotle* refused to communicate to *Alexander* by *Letter*, things apperteyning to this *Mistery*, untill a *personall meeting* might allow him to do it *viva voce*: for thus writes *Lydgate* out of *Aristotles Secreta secretorum*.

There be Secrees of Materis hih and lowe,
Hyd in Nature concelyd and secree,
Which Alysandre desired for to knowe;
By Aristotles a certyn prebitee,
Nat specified cloos in hym sylff kept he,
Which was delayed of grete providence,
Tyll he hymsylff came to his presence.

And this was for fear his *Writings* should come to the view of such whose *Eyes* were not worthy the perusall of so *sublime Secrets*, and thereby suffer under the contempt of the prophane *Vulgar*, or by *wicked men* be abused to *wicked uses*. (For *a Secret discovered* will not faile of doing *Injury* to one party or an other) which (if by his meanes it should happen) might render him *Criminall* before *God*, and a *presumptuous violator* of the *Calestiall Seales*.

Cap 2.

However the auncient *Philosophers* have used *writings*, and they as well *obscure as obvious, whereby the* Ignorant *might be more Ignorant, but the* Wise *understand and profitt, the one be deceived, the other alured*: And like *Aristotle* who (publishing his *Acromaticall Discipline* and) being therefore taxed by *Alexander* (because he alone had learned them of him) answered *Se scripsisse, &*

G.br.

non scripsisse; edidisse quidem sed legentibus non intelligentibus. They have taken much paines by *Ænigmaticall* and *Parabolicall* discoveries (according to their affected *Ideoms*) to point out the *Philosophers Mercury,* and (with an *univocall* consent) asserted the wonderous operations of an *Agent* and *Patient* united but *we must not looke for the Name of that in plaine words which hitherto never, any man durst name:* For that they have lockt up *in scrinio pectoris,* and purposely deprived of *light.*

Anonymi.

Their chiefest study was to wrap up their *Secrets* in *Fables,* and spin out their *Fancies* in *Vailes* and *shadows,* whose *Radii* seems to extend every way, yet so, that they all meete in a *Common Center,* and point onely at One thing.

o) *Chauc. Prol.* to his owne *Tale.*

o) And thus ye wote that every Evangelist,
That telleth us the pains of Jesu Christ.
Ne sayth not al thing as his fellow dothe,
But nay the lesse her Sentence is all soth.
And all accorden in her Sentence,
Al be therein her telling difference.
For some of hem saine more and some lesse,
When thei his piteous passion expresse.
I meane of Mark Mathew Luke and John,
But doubtlesse her Sentence is all one.

p) *De chim. Mir. secunda pars* Pag. 28.

And to this effect is that of *Count Trevisan.* (p) *He that well understands the* Philosophers *shall finde they agree in all things, but such as are not the* Sonns *of* Art *will think they clash most fouly.*

Pag. 33. l. 15. —— Myne Heire unto this Art
I will you make ——

THere has ever beene a continued *Succession* of *Philosophers* in all *Ages,* although the *heedlesse world* hath seldome taken notice of them; For the *Auncients* usually (before they dyed) *Adopted* one or other for their *Sonns,* whom they knew well fitted with such like *qualities,* as are sett downe in the *letter* that *Norton's Master* wrote to him when he sent to make him his *Heire* unto this *Science.* And otherwise then for pure *vertues* sake, let no man expect to attaine it, or as in the case of *Tonsile.*

q) *Ordin.* Pag. 41.

q) —— For Almes I will make no store,
Plainly to disclose it, that was never done before.

r) *ibid* pag. 35.

Rewards nor *Terrors* (be they never so *Munificent* or *Dreadfull*) can wrest this *secret* out of the *bosome* of a *Philosopher:* amongst others, witnesse (r) *Thomas Dalten.*

Now under what *Tyes* and *Ingagements* this *Secret* is usually delivered, (when bestowed by *word of mouth*) may appeare in the weighty *Obligations* of that *Oath* which *Charnock* tooke before he obtained it, for thus spake his *Master* to him:

Will

q) Will you with mee to Morrow be content
Faithfully to receive the blessed Sacrament
Upon this Oath that I shall here you give,
For ne Gold ne Silver as long as you live,
Neither for love you beare towards your Kinne,
Nor yet to no great Man preferment to winne,
That you disclose the Secret that I shall you teach,
Neither by Writing, nor by no swyft Speeche;
But onely to him which you be sure,
Hath ever searched after the Secrets of Nature,
To him you may reveale the Secrets of this Arte,
Under the Covering of Philosophie before this World yee (depart. q) *Brev. of Phi. los. cap. 5.*

And this *Oath* he charged him to keepe *Faithfully* and without *Violation*.

r) As he thought to be saved from the pitt of Hell. r) Chap. ibid.

And if it so fell out, that they met not with any, whome they conceived in all respects worthy of their *Adoption*, (s) *they then resigned it into the hands of God*, who best knew where to bestow it. However, they seldome left the *World* before they left some *written Legacy* behind them, which (being the *issue* of their *Braine*) stood in roome and place of *Children*, and becomes to us both *Parent* and *Schoolmaster*, throughout which they were so universally *kinde*, as to call all *Students* by the deare and affectionate Tytle of *Sons (t)* (*Hermes* giving the first President) wishing all were such, that take the paines to tread their Fathers stepps, and industriously follow the Rules and Dictates they made over to posterity, and wherein they faithfully discovered the whole *Mystery*; s) *Ord:* pag. 37. t) *in Pimend.*

u) As lawfully as by their fealty thei may,
By lycence of the dreadfull Judge at domes day. u) *Ordin.* pa. 10.

In these *Legitimate Children* they lived longer then in their *Adopted Sons*, for though these certainly perished in an *Age*, yet their *Writings* (as if when they dyed their *Souls* had been *Transmigrated* into them) seemed as *Immortall*, enough at least to perpetuate their *Memories*, till *Time* should be no more. And to be the *Father* of such *Sons*, is (in my Opinion) a most noble happinesse.

w) *Let Clownes get Heires, and Wealth; when I am gone,*
And the greate Bugbeare grisly death
Shall snatch this Idle breath,
If I a Poem leave, that Poem is my Son. w) *Rand. Poems* pag. 63.

Pag 34. li. 33. I made also the Elixir of lyfe,
Which me bereft a Marchaunt's Wyfe.

THe *Conjecture* has much of probability in it which speakes this the *Wife* of *Will. Cannings*, who was 5. tymes *Major* of *Bristoll*, contemporary with *Norton*, and whose *wealth* was farr beyond the best of those tymes, as appeares

Mmm by

" by that notable Worke of his in building *Saint Mary of Radcliff* without the
" *Walls* of *Bristoll*, into which *Church* there is a Stately ascent upon many
" *Staires*, so large withall, so finely and curiously wrought, with an arched
" *Roofe* over head of stone, artificially Imbowed; a *Steeple* also of an exceeding
a) *Brit.* fo. 237. " height, that all the parish *Churches* in *England* which hitherto I have seene
" (saith judicious (a) *Camden*) in my judgement it surpasseth many degrees.

b) *Camb. Brit.* fo. 238. c) *Chron.* fo. 467. d) *Godw.* pag. 367.

The said *William Cannings* also (b) *Instituted*, (*Isaacson* saith very much (c) *augmented*) the *Colledge* of *Westbury* neere *Bristoll* (not long before (d) founded by *John Carpenter, Bishop of Worcester*) and in his old age tooke upon him the *Sacerdotall function* and became *Deane* thereof.

Pag. 38. li. 4. **And Delvis at Teuxbury lost his head**

e) 4. *May* 1471

VVIthin two dayes after the (e) *Victory* which *Edw*, *the fourth* obteyned over *Queene Margaret* and *Prince Edw* (the *Wife* and *Son* of *Henry the sixt*) at *Teuxbury*; This (f) *Delvis* (the *Sonne* of Sir *John Delvis* then slaine) was *beheaded*: Notwithstanding a *Pardon* granted unto him and others by the *King* at the earnest solicitation of a *Priest* who withstood his entrance into a *Church*, whither *Hee* and many more were fled for *Sanctuary*, till the said Pardon was obteyned. A just punishment for betraying so honest a *Philosopher* as *Dalton* into the hands of so imminent danger, as the *Story* at the latter end of the *second Chapter* mentions.

f) *Stow.* Ann. fo. 424.

Pag. 39. li. 1. Tonsile **was a Labourer in the Fire.**

THe great *Letter T.* set in *pa.* 6. wherein the *Gryphon* is cut, should have been placed the first *Letter of* the *Line*: But this mistake was comitted in my absence from the *Presse*, for which the *Printer* beggs pardon, as also the *Engraver*, for giving the *Gryphons* hinder *Feete*, those *cloven ones* of a *Hogg*, instead of the *ungued pawes* of a *Lyon*.

What was contained within the lower compasse of the said *T.* which in the *Originall Manuscript* was like a *Capitall Secretary* T. seemes (in my judgement) a *Coate* of *Armes*, for although it was not drawne in the forme of a *shield* or *Scucheon*, yet within the compasse of the *Letter* (which I take to be the *field*) was *Azure*, a *Gryphon Rampant*, with *Wings displayed*, *Argent*. But to what *Family* it belongs I cannot yet learne.

Pa. 52. l. 1. Brise **whose Surname when the change of Coyne was had.**

g) *An.* 1465. h) *Stow Annal.* 418, *Surv.* 46.

THis alteration of our *English Coyne* was in the (g) 5th. of *Edward* the 4th. the value of Money at one rise was never so great before or since; for he made of an (h) *old Noble* of *Gold* a *Ryall*, and from the value of 6 s. 8 d. with adding 8. d. in *allay* raised it to 10 s. (and so other *Coynes* in like *proportion*) and yet that *Noble* was by *H.* 4. made 4 d. in value lesse then the *Rose Noble*

of

of *Edw*: 3. coyned Anno 1351. the (*i*) Gold whereof as is affirmed (by an unwritten-verity) was made by *Projection* or *Multiplication Alchimicall* of *Raimund Lully*, in the *Tower* of *London*, and besides the *Tradition*, the *Inscription* is some proofe, for as upon the one side there is the *Kings Image* upon a *ship*, to notifie that he was *Lord* of the *Seas*, with this title set upon the *reverse*, a *Crosse floury* with *Lioneux*, inscribed, *Iesus autem transiens per medium eorum ibat*, that is, as Jesus passed invisible and in most secret manner by the midst of *Pharises*, so that *Gold* was made by *invisible* and *secret Art* amidst the *Ignorant*, *Mayerus* confirmes this, and saith (*k*) *Raymond* made most pure *Gold* in the *Tower* which is yet called *Raymonds noble, obrizi summæq; indicaturæ*, some of which himselfe had seen. Tis also worth observing that (*l*) there was no *Gold* coyned in *England* before the said *Edward the third's Reigne An.* 1443. & *Raymond Lully* was long in *England* before that, for (*m*) *An.* 1332. he wrote his *Testamentum Novissimum* in St. *Katherins Church* neere the *Tower* of *London*, and *Dedicated* it (with other of his *Workes*) to *Edward the third*, and it may be presumed he was some while there before he wrote the same: For, that he was brought over by *Cremer Abbot* of *Westminster*, afterwards made knowne to the *King*, and did furnish him with much *Gold*, as shall appeare hereafter in the *Annotations* upon **Hermes Bird.**

(i) *Camb. Rem.* pag. 172.
k) *Simb. aur.* pag. 418.
l) *Camb. Rem.* pag. 172.
m) See the latter end of his *Test. Nov.*

Pa. 61 li. 7. **But the cheife Mistris among Sciences all For the helpe of this Arte, is Magick naturall,**

IUdiciall *Astrologie* is the *Key* of *Naturall Magick*, and *Naturall Magick* the *Doore* that leads to this *Blessed Stone*.

Howbeit, the *Ignorance* and *Malice* of some times, and the common *Custome* of ours has most falsly and abusively called *Necromancy* (and what other *Arts* are raised from the Doctrine of *Divels*,) *Magick*; without affording that just and due distinction which ought to be made betweene them: and what greater Injury to learning then without Distinction to confound *Laudable knowledge*, with what is *Impious* and *Devilish*? For, if there be any thing in (what we call) *Magick*, other then *a searching into those hidden vertues which God has been pleas'd to bestow upon created things* (though closely lockt up by the generall Curse) *whereby we may aptly and naturally apply* Agents to Patients, I say, if in it there be any thing else, they are only subtill *falsehoods* that shelter and shroud themselvs under that *Tytle*, and which would gladly be esteemed *Leaves* of that *Plant*, from whose *Root* they never sprung. And therefore is it not lesse absurd, then strange, to see how some Men (who would have the World account them learned, and whome I beleive to be so learned, as to have read and found what Latitude is due to the word *Magus*, how it is accepted by the *Judicious*, and what a vast difference there is, betweene the *Doctrine* of a *Magician*, and the abuse of the *Word*) will not forbeare to ranke *True Magicians* with *Conjurers*, *Necromancers* and *Witches* (those grand *Impostors*) who (*n*) violently intrude themselves into *Magick*, *as if Swine should enter into a faire and delicate Garden*, and (being in league with the *Devill*) make use of his Assistance in their *workes*, to counterfeit and corrupt the admirall *wisdome* of the *Magi*, betweene whom there is as large a difference as betweene *Angels* and Devils

n) *Paracel. de. occult Phil.* cap. 11.

The *Magick* here intended, and which I strive to Vindicate, is, *Divine*, *True*, of the *Wisdom of Nature*, & indeed comprehēdeth the whole *Philosophy of Nature*, being (o) a *Perfect Knowledge of the works of God, and their Effects.* It is that, which (p) *reduces all* naturall Philosophy *from variety of* Speculations *to the* magnitude of workes, and (q) *whose* Misteries *are far greater then the* naturall Phylosophy *now in use and reputation will reach unto.* For by the bare application of *Actives* to *Passives* it is able to exercise a kind of *Empire* over *Nature*, and worke *wonders*: and 'tis from the ignorance of such marvelous *Operations* that the *Ignorant*, (viz the most *learned* in other things (as well as the *Illiterate*) if they be not learned in this,) either by an unwarrantable *adoration* esteeme them as *Miracles*, which onely are the *workes* of *Naturall* or *Mathematicall Philosophy*: or else (which is an *Errour* as wide on the left hand) forthwith censure and slander those truly *Naturall* as *Diabolicall*, because wonderfull *strange* and beyond the *randome* of their *Apprehensions*. The latter of which might as well say (r) *Jacobs* practising to make his *Lambs* of a *Py'd Colour* was performed by the assistance or ministry of the *Devill*, and as well condemne the use of *Phisick*, because the *Devill* has taught *Witches* divers harmfull and uncharitable uses of *Herbs*, *Mineralls*, *Excrements*, &c.

o) *Gaff.Curios.* pag.66.
p) *Bac.adv.* fo. 33.
q) Dr.*Gells* *Serm.*1650.
r) *Gen.*31.37.

And as in some *dull ages*, and among some *Grosse Spirits* it has proved dangerous to be *Learned*, Witnesse our Renowned *Roger Bachon*, whom (Together with *Artepheus*, *Arnold*, *de villa nova*, who were *Philosophers* of known reputation & credit) (s) *Wierus* reckons among the *Deplorati ingenii homines* (t) *all whose Workes fairely written and well bound, were by Religious pretending Sciolists dam'd as Devilish, with long Nailes through them fastned to desks in the Franciscan Library at Oxford*, and there *with Dust and Moths cousumed*: Even so our other famous Country-man [*Profound Ripley*] was also abused, (u) *who after his death is said to have been branded with the name of a* Necromancer. *Pope Silvester* the *second* pas'd for a *Magician* (in the worst sence) because he understood *Geometry*; and about 150. yeares agoe (so blind an age was it,) that to know *Greeke* and *Necromancy* were one and the same thing, in opinion of the *Illiterate*. However, let the *Ignorant* scoffe and attribute that to *Deceipt* and *Illusion* which is the proper worke of *Nature* produced by exquisite knowledge, I am confident the ingenously learned will approve and admire it.

s) *De Prestigiis Dæm.* li.2.ca.4. pag.140.
t) *Selden pref. to Hopt.Concord*
u) *Bale Cent.*8. fol.633.

But to teare off that ugly *vizard* which *Envy* has placed before the *Face* of so *Divine* a *Beauty*, and to make way for the meaning of our *Author*, I thinke it necessary (in the first place) that I touch upon the *Word*, that gives a name to the *Professors*;

And that is *Magus* (primitively a *Persian* word) which onely signifies or imports a *Contemplator of Heavenly and Divine Sciences*, *a studious Observer*, *an expounder of Divine things*, *a name* (saith (w) Marcellus Ficinus) *gratious in the Gospell, not signifying a Witch or a Conjurer, but a wise man and a Priest.* And in truth a true *Magician*, acknowledges *God*, to be the true *Cause* and *Giver of life* and *vertue* to *Nature*, and all *Naturall* things, of the *Causes* of which things (*as also of* (x) *Divine*) is the whole scope and effect of all their *Writings* and *Discourses*:

w) *Par:prim.fo.* 573.
x) *Magia præcipua est pars Theologiæ.*

In the Next place, that I give the *Definition* of *Magick* (because as (y) *Myrandula* sayes) *it is an Art which few understand and many reprehend*, and therefore of necessity to be clearly evinced:) Receive it from a learned hand: youle finde it worth your observance.

y) *Pic.Mir.*fo. 81.

Ma-

Magick, is, the Connexion of naturall Agents and Patients, answerable each to other, wrought by a wise Man to the bringing forth of such effects as are wonderfull to those that know not their causes. Thus Hee. *Paracelsus* called it (z) *a most secret and hidden Scyence of supernaturall things in the Earth, that whatsoever is impossible to be found out by mans Reason may by this Art.* And shortly after to cleere it from imputations adds, *that tis in it selfe most pure and not defiled with Ceremonies nor Conjurations as Necromancy is.*

z) *De Occult. Phil.*cap.11.

Agreeable to both (but more copiously delivered) is that of *Corn: Agrippa*, who affirmes, (a) *Magick to containe the profoundest Contemplation of most secret things, together with the nature, power, quality, substance, and vertues thereof, as also the knowledge of whole nature:* That *instructs us concerning the difference and agreement, of things amongst themselves, whence it produceth its wonderfull effects, by uniting the vertues of things through the application of them one to the other, and to their inferiour sutable Subjects, joyning and knitting them together throughly by the powers and vertues of superiour Bodies.* This briefly is an account of that *Learning*, whose *Operations* and *Effects* (being full of *Misteries*) was by the Ancients esteemed as the highest and sacred *Phylosophie*, the *fountaine of all good doctrine: Animadverto* (saith *Pliny*) *summum Literarum claritatem, gloria nque, ex hac scientia antiquitus, & penes semper petitam.*

a) *De Occult. Phil.*lib.1.ca.2.

What hath been hitherto said, will not (I presume) offend the *Eares* of the most *Pious*, for here is no *Incantations*, no *Words*, no *Circles*, no *Charmes*, no other fragments of invented *Fopperies*; nor needs there any: *Nature* (with whom true *Magicians* only deale) can worke without them, she findes *Matter*, and they *Art*, to helpe and assist Her, and here's *All*.

To instance the *Generation* of *Froggs*, *Lyce*, *Wormes*, *Insects*, &c. The worke of a *Philosopher* is therein onely to (b) strengthen the *Seeds* of *Nature*, (for she alone Workes) and so to quicken them that they hasten the worke of *Generation* (and by such meanes *Tho. Aquinas* supposes *Pharo's Magitians*, produced *Froggs*) insomuch as it seems to the *Ignorant* not to be the *Worke* of *Nature*, (that usually operates more leasurely,) rather the *Power* of the *Devill*. But they who are learned in those *Arts*, marvell not at such working, but Glorifie the *Creator*. To whose *Honour* alone these Operations must chiefly tend, *for* (c) *he is best praised in his workes*, and we knowing him in and by these visible things, may through such knowledge understand his more *Secret* and *Invisible* things, and thereby be better inabled to *Glorifie* him, then men otherwise can.

b) *Guli. Par. de. leg.* cap.24.

c) Dr. *Gells Serm.*1650.

Now I deny that any measure of understanding, in *naturall Magick*, how large soever, or the utmost and farthest search we can possibly make into that pure and primitive knowledge of *Nature*, to be a prying into those *Hidden Secrets*, which *God* would have concealed and ranked among the number and nature of those things he has prohibited us to search into, (as I know there are that will tell you it is, and they such as weare the *Coat*, and would be loath to want the reputation of *Schollars*) And this is fully manifested from *Adam*, who (d) before his *Fall* was so absolute a *Philosopher*, that he fully understood the true and pure knowledge of *Nature* (which is no other then what we call *Naturall Magick*) in the highest degree of Perfection, insomuch, that by the light thereof, upon the present view of the *Creatures* he perfectly knew their *Natures*, and was as able to bestow names sutable to their *Qualities* and *Properties*,

d) Gen.2.v.19. 20.

For, This was a larger and cleerer *Ray* of the *Light* of *Nature*, then all the industry of man (since the *Fall*) was able to hope for or attaine unto, and (to attest the allowance) bestowed upon him by *God* himselfe: Nor was it this *Naturall* knowledg that introduced his Fall, or can be any *Offence* or *Sin* in us (were it possible) to arrive at his *Perfection*. No certainly; *Adams* transgression (for which he fell) was of a higher *Nature*, [even *that* proud inquiry into the (e) *knowledge of good and evill, with no lesse intent then to make a totall defection from God, and depend wholly upon himselfe and his free will.*]

e) Bac. advancement; *fol.* 5. and 43.

Besides, tis worthy Observation, that *God* in constituting *Moses* to be a *Governor* over his owne people, seemed as willing to make choyce of such a one for that high *Office*, as was (f) learned in all the *Sciences*, then in request with the *Egyptians*, among whom *Magick* was the chiefe. And we find that upon *Salomon's* Prayer to *God* for *Wisdome* he granted him *a Heart as large as the Sea*, and therein lodged so greate knowledge of *Humane* things, that he penetrated whatsoever the understanding of *Man* might comprehend: and (to manifest the inoffensivenesse of *Naturall Magick*,) never reckons it up in all his *Retractations* Though he throughly understood it, and in his *practise* attempted the highest Experiments, which had it been *unlawfull*, certainly he would not have omitted.

Thus much for a *Preparative*. And now that I may come closer to what *Norton* intends, and bring *Magick* neerer to our purpose; We must understand that the *Order* and *Symmetry* of the *Universe* is so setled by the *Lawes* of *Creation*, that the lowest things [the *Subcelestiall* or *Elementary Region*] should be immediately subservient to the *Midle*; the *Midle* [or *Celestiall*] to those above; and these [the *Supercelestiall* or *Intelligible*] to the *Supreame Rulers* becke. With this it is further to be knowne that these (g) *Superiours* and *Inferiours* have an *Analogicall* likenesse, and by a secret *Bond* have likewise a fast " *coherence* between themselvs through insensible *Mediums*, freely combining " in *Obedience* to the same supreme *Ruler*, and (also to the) benefit of *Nature*: Insomuch, that if we take the said *Harmony* in the *Reverse*, we shall finde that things *h Supercelestiall* may be drawne down by *Celestiall*, and *Supernaturall*, by *Naturall*. For this is the *Maxim* of old *Hermes*, (i) *Quod est superius, est sicut id quod est inferius.*

f) Act. 7. v. 22. Ench. Phis. Rest. Can. 11.
g) Canon. 3.
h) Cor. Agr. de oc. Phil. *l.* 1. *cap.* 38.
i) Tab. Smaragd.

And upon this ground (k) *Wisemen* conceive it no way *Irrationall* that it should be possible for us to ascend by the same degrees through *each world*, to the very *Originall world* it selfe, the Maker of all things and first *Cause*.

k) Cor. Agr. de Occult. Philos. *lib.* 1. *cap.* 1.

But how to conjoyne the *Inferiours* with the *vertue* of the *Superiours* (which is marrying *Elmes* to *Vines*) or how to call out of the hidden places into open light, the dispersed and seminated *Vertues*, (i e. *Virtutes in centro centri latentes*,) is, the work of the *Magi*, or *Hermetick Philosophers* onely; and depends upon the aforesaid *Harmony*. For,

They know that the *Production* of things is *Naturall*, but the bringing forth of the *vertue* is not *Naturall*: because the things are *Create*, but the *Vertues Increate*.

Hence it is that the *Power* and *Vertue* is not in *Plants*, *Stones*, *Mineralls*, &c. (though we sensibly perceive the *Effects* from them) but 'tis that *Universall* and *All-piercing Spirit*, that *One operative Vertue* and *immortall Seede* of *worldly things*, that *God* in the beginning infused into the *Chaos*, which is every

where

where *Active* and still flowes through the *world* in all kindes of things by *Universall extension*, and manifests it selfe by the aforesaid *Productions*. Which *Spirit* a true *Artist* knowes how-so to handle (though its *activity* be as it were dul'd and streightly *bound up*, in the close *Prison* of *Grosse* and *Earthie bodies*) as to take it from *Corporiety*, free it from *Captivity*, and let it *loose* that it may freely *worke* as it doth in the *Ætheriall Bodies*.

But the *meanes* whereby it is to be done (which is the *first Preparation*) all *Philosophers* have hitherto *concealed*. For,

l) To (m) Create Magnesia they made no care,
In their Bookes largely to declare.
But how to Order it after its Creation,
They left poore Men without Consolation.

l) Hunt. Green Lyon.
m) *i.e.* To tell what it is, though Ænigmatically.

And unlesse *God* please to *reveale* it, (like the *Iewish Fire*) it must be kept *hidden*, and till he doth there is no *humane industry* can forcibly *wrest* the *knowledge* thereof out of the *Almighties hands*.

n) *Si te fata vocant, aliter non.*

n) Augurel.

Looke not then for it at the *hand* of *Man*, for tis the *Gift* of *God* onely.

o) A singular gift and grace of th'Almighty.

o) Ordin. *p*. 13.

Nil dat quod non habet, Man has it not, (*that is*,) he has it not to bestow where he will.

p) The Philosophers were y sworne eche one,
That they shulde discover it unto none,
Ne in no Boke it write in no manere,
For unto Christ it is so lefe and deare:
That he wol not that it discovered be,
But where it liketh to his deite:
Man to inspire and eke for to defend,
Whan that him liketh: lo this is his end.

p) Chan. Yeom. Tale.

In fine, if any man be so blest as to discover and unvaile our *Diana*, he shall finde and confesse that he was beholding to *Naturall Magick* for directions at the *Beginning*, *Midle*, and *End*; and when it is wrought up to his *highest degree of Perfection*, he shall see things not fit to be written; for (may I aver it with awfull Reverence) *Angelicall wisdome* is to be obteyned by it.

Pag. 72. li. 25. Tasted our White Stone a parte.

UNlesse the *Medicine* be qualified as it ought, tis *death* to tast the least *Attome* of it, because its *Nature* is so highly Vigorous and strong above that of *Man*; For if its least parts are able to strike so fiercely and throughly into the *Body* of a base and corrupt *Mettall*, as to *Tinge* and *Convert* it into so high a degree as perfect *Gold*, how lesse able is the Body of *Man* to resist such a

force.

force, when *its* greatest strength is far inferiour to the weakest Mettall? I doe believe (and am confirm'd by severall *Authors*) that many *Philosophers* (having a desire to enjoy perfect *Health*,) have destroyed themselves by adventuring to take the *Medicine* inwardly, ere they knew the true use thereof, or how to qualifie it to be received by the *Nature* of *Man* without *destruction*.

Pa.88.li.15. ——**The Red Stone is preservative,
Most precious thing to length my lyfe.**

THis is the Stone which some builders up of life *have refused*, when in truth it was the *cheife Stone in the Corner*; It being produced from that undefiled *vertue* which is yet left with the *Creature* (as a small remainder of the *First Blessing*) and able to make a (q) perfect *union* betweene the *Body*, *Soule* and *Spirit*, whilst our lively *Fire*, (that *Medium* between the *Body* and *Spirit*) by receiving this *Ætheriall Medicine* consisting of heavenly *vertues* (that consume the *Impurities* and *Superfluities* of the *Body*) is delivered from all *Impediments*, and the Body forced to agree with that incomparable *Nature* into which it is changing by so sweete and powerfull *Compulsions*, and consequently life Prorogued.

q) R. Bost. Phis. cap. 3.

As touching the *Prolongation* of *life*, wee meete with some *Presidents* in *Histories*, and they not *Fables*, where by the *Applicaticn* of things inward or outward, the *Spirit* hath beene renewed, the *Body* strengthned the *Vitall* and *Animall* faculty quickned, *decrepid* and *withered Age* renewed, & *Life* inlarged. Besides these *Relations*, we perceive *Nature* is so curteous to some kind of *Creatures*, as the *Hart*, *Eagle*, and *Serpent*, that she affords them meanes to obteine the benefit of *Renovation* (here Nature teaches them *Naturall Magick*, for tis no other) and why then may it not be granted to Man if sought after? Nay the (r) consideration of this *Favourable Blessing* afforded to *Animalls* has been the principall ground whence many *Philosophers* have addicted themselves to the search "of this Mistery, hoping that might not be denyed to Man, upon his search, "which is bestowed gratis upon the Creature.

r) R. Bach. Ep. De Secret. Natur. cap. 6.

It is apparent that our (s) *Diseases proceed chiefly from Transplantation* (though I deny not but some *Hereditary Corruption is intail'd* upon *Posterity*, from the decaying, mouldering, and rotten *Natures* of our *Ancestors*) for, by what we *Eate* or *Drinke* as *Nourishment*; the corrupt and harmfull, nay deathfull qualities; which the (t) *Divine malediction* lodged in created things, is removed from them into our *Bodyes*, and there grow up and multiply till (having heightned the *Sal*, *Sulphur* and *Mercury*, into an irreconcileable *Contestation*, through the impurities wherewith they are loaded and burthened) they introduce a miserable *decay*, which consequently become a *Death*: and this is the sooner hastned if thereunto we adde the heavy *loade* of *Luxuriousnesse* and *Glutony*. Yet is not this *Death Naturall* but *Accidentall*, and (as may appeare by what has been said) a (u) *Death arising out of the fruits of the greate World* which *growes up by Transplantation*, the *Rebellious Disobedience* of man provoking *God* to *plant* a *Death* in every thing that he had made, by the *Curse* wherewith he had *cursed the Earth*. And to this the Doctrine which the (w) *Angell* taught *Esdras* is agreeable.

s) Severin. Idea Med. Philos. cap: 12.

t) Sir W. Raw. Hist. fol. 65.

u) J W. Epist.

w) 2 Esd. cap. 7. v. 11. 12. 13.

And though it is appointed *all must dye*, against which *Decree* no *Elixir* has power

power to resist, yet this *Medicine* is a remedy for the particular *corruption* of *Man*, to keep back those *greifes* and *diseases* which usually accompany & molest *Old Age*; insomuch, that that *Death* which man eates in his *Bread* may be brought to a *Seperation*, and consequently (in the comfort of an *Uninterrupted Health*) spin out his *thread* of *life* to the longest end of that *Nature* fallen from *Originall Justice*. For tis a certaine truth that what we receive into our *Bodies*, of that, *Nature* findes two *Substances*, the (one with a Gladsome appetite,) she retaines to feede *Vitality*, the other (with an abhor'd dislike) she expells, as not onely uselesse but *Putrefactive* and *Dangerous*: and if thereupon we throughly advise with our selves we must needes confesse *Her* way is best to be imitated, in seperating the *Pure* from the *Impure*, (which are joyned together in every thing) before we make use of them, and where *she* does manifestly *Substract* and *Divide*, let us not there *add* and *multiplie*; for doubtlesse the *Faeces* (y) profit nothing, nay in sick persons they plainely *oppresse* the penetrating vertue of the *Spirit* it selfe, and commit that *seperating Art* to the diseased *Body*, which through *weaknesse* is not able to performe the *Taske*. y) *Rothm. Comment.*

The *Brevity* of *Life* came in with the *Fall* of *Adam*, and though some of the *Autients* before the *Flood* lived almost a thousand yeares, yet certainely their lives were *prorogued* by the use of this *Medicine*, with which they well knew how to *seperate* and *correct* the obnoxious *Qualities* of all things, and I much question whether the *generality* of Persons then lived *so long*, or onely *those* who were the (z) *true Ancestors*; of *Abraham*, they not being alwaies the *eldest* and *first begotten* of the *Patriarks*, but such as *God* chose out of the *Family* to continue the *line*, and had (by the permission of *God*, as a singular and peculiar *blessing*) this *Secret Traditionally* committed to them. x) Sir *W. Raw. Hist.* fo. 64.

Pa. 89. li. 27.———— **I never made assay**
Of the Red worke before this day.

HEnce some affirme that *Norton* neither had nor knew how to make the *Red Medicine*, but that's not so, for to the time of publishing his *Ordinall*, 'tis true, he had not a *second time* gon about to make it, and why?

(a) **The cause appeareth in this Boke before,**
When Hee was robbed then Hee would no more. a) *Ord.* pag. 89.

Yet that he was *formerly* at *worke*, *made* it, and was *robb'd* thereof appeares also (b) before, where he saith the (c) *Merchants Wife* stole it from him, and that the misfortune thereof deterr'd him from making further progresse therein. Besides, he avers his *Master* taught it him, and that he fully nw how to make it, for so himself witnesseth. b) *Ord.* pag. 34. c) See Anota. upon pag. 34.

d) *Ord.* pag. 89.

(d) **I had with Grace the true Doctrine**
Of Confection of the Red Medicine.

And lastly, in the latter end of the 5. *Chap.* of the aforesaid *Ordinall*, *Norton* truly and cleerely declares how it is made; unto which *I* refer the *Reader*.

Pag. 99. li. 31. **Wherefore they being in warke of Generacion, Have most obedience to Constellation.**

Here our *Author* refers to the *Rules* of *Astrologie* for *Electing* a time wherein to begin the *Philosophicall* worke, and that plainly appeares by the following lines, in which he chalkes out an *Election* fitly relating to the Businesse.

In the *operative* part of this Science the *Rules* of *Astronomie* and *Astrologie* (as elsewhere I have said) are to be consulted with.

e) Pat. Sapient.

(e) **For in Astronomie thou must have right good feeling,**
Or else in this Worke thow schalt have simple beleving.

So that *Elections*, (whose *Calculatory part* belongs to *Astronomie*, but the *Judiciary* to *Astrologie*) are very necessary to begin this worke with; and the paines that *Norton* hath taken manifests no lesse, most Authors hinting the same, although we take but little notice thereof. For

f) Ord *pag.* 60.

(f) **Such simple kindes unformed and unwrought,**
Must craftily be guided till the end be sought.
All which season they have more obedience,
Above formed Natures to Sterrs Influence.

g) Mar. Ficinus.

Generally in all *Elections* the *Efficacy* of the *Starrs* are used as it were, by a certaine *application* made thereof to those unformed *Natures* that are to be wrought upon; whereby to further the working thereof, and make them more available to our purpose. (g) *For since both inferiour and superiour Causes concur to every effect, it followeth that if the one be not considered as well as the other, this Negligence will beget Error.* And by such *Elections* as good use may be made of the *Celestiall influences*, as a *Physitian* doth of the variety of *Herbes*. Agreeable to which is that of *Ptolomy Aphor.* 8. *A Juditious man helpes forward the Celestiall operation, even as a discreet Husbandman assists Nature in his plowing and preparing the Ground.* But *Nativities* are the Radices of *Elections*, and therefore we ought chiefly to looke backe upon them as the principall *Root* and *Foundation* of all *Operations*, and next to them the *quality* of the Thing we intend to fit, must be respected: so that by an apt position of *Heaven*, and *fortifying* the *Planets* and *Houses* in the Nativity of the Operator, and making them agree with the thing signified; the *Impression* made by that *Influence*, will abundantly augment the Operation.

h) Sir *Chr: Heyd.* Def. of Astrol. *pag.* 363.

And this is upheld by very evident reason of Nature, (h) *for* (saith *a learned Gent.* whose *Defence of Judiciall Astrologie* (so long since published) stands hitherto firme & unconfuted, notwithstanding all the whifling Assaults of any *Adversary*) *the Celestiall Influences never cease to flow into us, and therefore not unlikely that the like position or Configuration to that under which we are borne, may by like impression and influence increase and strengthen the operation of the former, more then it would if the Nativity were considered alone.* And upon these grounds *Norton* advises to make *Elections* like those he layes downe.

i) **Unlesse**

i) Unlesse then your Nativity pretend infection,
In contrarietye to this Election.

i) Ordin p. 100

Which is the same in effect with that of (k) *Ptolomy*, where he saith to this purpose, *viz.* "Though an *Election* of a *Day* or *houre* be well made, yet "will it prove of little *advantage* unlesse sutably *constituted* to the *scheame* "of the *Nativity*, because else it cannot divert that *evill* which in the *Nativity* "the *Planets* threatned: and hence it comes that *Actions Thrive* or *Miscarry* (though begun at one and the same time,) according as the position of *Heaven* then agrees with the *Nativity* of the *Persons* that manage them.

k) Aphor. 6.

As touching the *Necessity* of *Elections*, to be used in *Dyet*, *Building*, *Dwelling*, *Apparell*, and the severall *Actions* of our *Life*, let any that would be satisfied, read *Marcellus*, *Ficinus*, *Hesiode*, *Cato*, *Virgil*, *Varro*, *Columella*, *Pliny*, who (and generally all *Philosophers*) ordered their affaires of planting, sowing, lopping, &c. by them.

For in those things (here below) which have no sence (as well as those that have) the *Heavenly Influences* alwaies make *Impression* according to the measure and Capacity of the *Subject*, and doe evidently manifest their *Dominion* in them, (l) for *nothing is more powerful then their Influences*, when Impressiō is once made. Witnesse their power in *Plants*, *Herbes*, *Corne*, and what is *Vegitable*, whose *Seeds* diversly prosper, or decay, according to the state of the ☽ with the ☉ at the time of their *sowing*. This the *Husband-mans Experience* can tell the world, and the *Sun's Annuall Accesse* and *Recesse* makes manifest to the sence.

l) *Gaff. Curios.* pag. 219.

And great Reason there is in *Nature* why the *Moons* condition ought chiefly to be observed, for she is the *Planet* neerest the *Earth*, and appointed as it were the *Vehiculum* of all other heavenly *Influences* unto what is *Sublunary*, and in that regard she is properly called (m) *An Instrument of the Armies from above*: according to whose present *Condition* things are steered; for if she be *Fortunate* by good *Aspects*, *happy* by *Position*, *swift* of *Course*, and increasing in *Light*, things *thrive* apace and *flourish*; But the contrary if she suffer *Impediments*. We may ordinarily observe how *poorely* and *slowly* the *Seeds* of *Plants* grow up, nay many times *languish* and *degenerate* into an unkindly *Quality* and *Tast*, if sowne in the *Waine* of the Moone, and the Reason is because the *Moysture* and *Sapp* that should feed them is exceedingly diminished; yet it is the fittest tyme for cutting downe *Timber*, or what else we would preserve from decaying.

m) Eccl. 43. 8.

(n) *Thurneisserus* (among many other admirable and usefull *Observations*) gives us the *Position* of *Heaven* under which severall *Plants* are *Impregnated* with the greatest *vertue*, the gathering of which at such times, for *Phisicall* uses, deserves to be taken notice of; for the notable difference that evidently appeares betwixt their *virtues* and the vertues of such as are gathered without that Consideration. In a word, by *Elections* we may *Governe*, *Order* and *Produce* things as we please: *Faber quisq; Fortunæ propriæ.*

n) Hist. Plant.

Pag. 100. li. 1. **Is a direct and firie Ascendant.**

IN this and the first *Ten* following *lines*, are laid downe the *Authors Rules* for framing an *Election* by, agreeable to which he erects you *Scheames* (about the *Latitude* of 51. degrees) that are placed before the sixth Chap. which I have caused to be exactly *Copied* from the *Originall*, though some *Planets*, I must acknowledg, are not placed in that exact order (for *houses* and *signes*) as *Astronomicall Rules* direct, and the *Doctrine* of *Astrologie* requireth. For Example, In the first *House* of the first *Figure* you have ☿ in 7. *degr.* of ♐, the *Ascendent* in 2. *degr.* of ♐, and then the ☉ in the 18. *Degr.* of the same *signe*; whereas the 2. *degr* of ♐ being fewer *degrees* of that *Signe* then 7. (wherein ☿ is placed) should Antecede it. Againe in the second *Figure* you have both ☿ and the ☽ in the 11th *House* thereof, who should of Right be posited in the 10th. because the 20th *degree* of ♎ is the Cuspe of the 11th, and therefore all *Planets* in lesser *degrees* of that *Signe* are falling into the 10th. Besides you have ♀ placed in every *Figure* so remote from the ☉, that *Astronomers* must count it absurd, since she is never above 48. *degr. Elongated* from him; and yet in the third *Figure* she comes not within the compasse of a ⚹ *Aspect*, nay in the second she is almost in ☍ to him.

For their *Position*; I could have placed them in Houses according to *Art*, but I rather let them stand as I found them in the *Originall*, being well assured they were thus Posited by *Designe*, and not through *Ignorance* or *Mistake*; for our *Author* manifests himselfe a learned *Astrologian*, and too wary a *Pen-man* to be guilty of either. And though it may seem contrary to *Art* for the Position of ♀ to be so far distant from the ☉, yet tis agreeable to his *Rule* of *Election* that she is so often placed in the 4th *House* (especially seeing the *Signe* falls out to be there in which she is exalted) because he appoints the *Lord* thereof to be fortunate,

o) *Ord.* pag. 100. (o) **For this is Thesaurum absconditum of old Clerks.**

Withall, the *Planets* as they stand here placed in *Signes* and *Houses* are not so as that these *Figures* were the *Elected* times for the *Authors* owne *Operations* (or any others in that *Faculty*) but are rather *fained* and invented, onely to bring them within the compasse of his *Rules*. And to satisfie my selfe herein, I have taken some paines to *Calculate* the places of the *Planets* for severall years about the *Authors* time, but cannot finde the three *Superiors* and place of the ☉ to be in those Signes wherein he has posited them.

It is also worthy of our Observation to see how the *Author* continues his *Vailes* and *Shadows*, as in other parts of the *Mistery*, so likewise in the very *Figures* of some of the *Planets*, for he does not exhibite them under the Characters commonly now (or then) used, but Hieroglyphically in Figures agreeable to their Natures, yet (p) diversitie of *Names* (or *Figures*) makes no diversitie in the things they signifie: For ♄ is pointed out by a *Spade*, ♃ by a *Miter*, ♂ by an *Arrow*, ♀ by a beautifull *Face*, ☿ by the figure (in those daies) usually stamped upon the Reverse of our *English Coyne*: Onely the ☉ and ☽ are left us in that fashion the *Auncients* bestowed upon them.

p) *Aristotle.*

Pag.

Pag.100.li.32. **Trust not to all Astrologers, I saie whie:
For that Art is as secret as Alkimie.**

ASTROLOGIE is a profound *Science*: The depth this *Art* lyes obscur'd in, is not to be reach't by every vulgar *Plumet* that attempts to sound it. Never was any *Age* so pester'd with a multitude of *Pretenders*, who would be accounted (and stick not to style themselves) *Masters*, yet are not worthy to weare the Badge of illustrious *Urania*. And (oh to be lamented!) the *swarme* is likely to increase, untill through their Ignorance they become the ridiculous object of the *Enemies* to *Astrologie*; (would that were all,) and *Eclipse* the *glory* of that *light*, which if Judiciously *dispens'd* to the *World* would cause *admiration*; but *unskilfully expos'd*, become the scorne and contempt of the *Vulgar*.

He that understands no more of *Astrologie* (nor will make a further use of it) then to quack with a few *Tearmes* in an *Horary Question*; is no more worthy to be esteemed an *Astrologian* then Hee who hath onely learnt *Hebrew* may be accounted a *Caballisticall Rabbi*. Tis true, he may be so fraught with *words*, as to amuse the unlearned, with the *Canting* noyse thereof, but what is that if compared to the full and intire knowledge of the *Language*? Yet of this sort at present are start up divers Illiterate *Professors* (and *Women* are of the Number) who even make *Astrologie* the Bawd & Pander to all manner of Iniquity, prostituting Chast *Urania* to be abus'd by every adulterate *Interest*. And what willbe the issue (I wish it may prove no *Prophesie*) ere long *Astrologie* shall be cried down as an *Impostor*, because it is made use of as a *Stale* to all bad *Practises*, and a *laudable Faculty* to bolster up the *legerdimane* of a *Cheate*. And besides having now growne famous by the true *Predictions* of some of her able and honest *Sons*, shall grow into as much disgrace and infamy, by the unskilfull *Prognosticks* of ignorant Illegitimate *Bastards*: who rather then they will accuse themselves when they faile of truth in their *Judgments*, will not stick to condemne *Astrologie* it selfe as defective and lame, in what their slothfull negligence or ignorant blindnesse was not able to finde out. And therefore *Norton* here speaks truly, that *Astrologie* (take it with all its Comprehensions) is as *Secret* or *Misterious* as *Alchimy*, and as difficult to be throughly and perfectly understood.

There are in *Astrologie* (I confesse) shallow *Brookes*, through which young *Tyroes* may *wade*; but withall, there are deepe *Foards*, over which even the *Gyants* themselves must *swim*. Such is the Doctrine of *Nativities*, *Directions*, *Annuall Revolutions* and what else depends thereupon, belonging to *Man*, the *litle World*: and beyond these, those of *Comets*, *Eclipses*, *Great Conjunctions* and *Revolutions*, that refer to the greate *World*. These are subjects of *Eminency*, and being judiciously handled, Magnifie the *Art*. But,

q) **Many men weene which doth them reade,
That they doe understande them when they do not indeede.** q) *Ordin*.cap. 5.pag.60.

I know some few *Artists* have satisfactorily manifested what *excellency* of *Skill* there is in Judging an *Horary Question*, and how much of *truth* may be

 drawne

drawne from that branch of *Art*; But they are those that are throughly read in all other parts of *Astrologie*; for such only are able to give a true *Resolution* to the *Querent*, and from the events of their considerate *Predictions*, bring *Honour* to the *Art*, and gaine *Reputation* to *Themselves*.

Pag. 104. li. 20. **Ordeine therefore to fetch breath from your Foote.**

IN regard of the *violent Nature* of the *Medicine* which is *deadly* indeed, because its *Nature* is so infinitely *strong* above *Mans*, that it overcomes his *Spirits* and *poysons* him; *Norton* therefore lets fall a hinte, what Parts an *Operator* ought to Arme, and whence to fetch *Breath*: Meaning thereby, that those *Orifices* of the *Body* be closely stopt (through which there is so open a passage, that a *Strong vapour* would fly as speedily as *lightning* into the *inmost parts*) while the *Vessell* is opening. But how to *breathe* the while is the *Difficulty*. We have *Practises* something neere it, as of those who attempt to lye long under *Water*, &c.

And therefore let this be a *Caution* sufficient to young *Practisers* in this *Science*, that when they worke upon a *Matter*, and bring it (as they suppose) to some *perfection*, if they can indure the *opening* of their *Vessell* without being Armed, they may rest satisfied that nothing is more certaine then that their *Matter* is not the *Philosophers Mercury*, and their *Practise* erronious.

Pag. 105. li. 17. **Now have I taught you every thing by Name.**

r) *Hor.*

———r) *Hoc tibi dictum*
Tolle memor:

THis Verse ought to be heedfully observed by the Student in this *Science*, for he speaks a reall truth, *Nihil prætermissum quod à quovis dici posit.* Nothing being *wanting*, nor nothing *left out* that is *needfull* to be knowne to compleate this greate *Worke*: which many have not the happinesse to *apprehend*, though it should be more *plainely* discovered unto them. Much alike unfortunate as those that *Sandivogius* speaks of, (s) to whom he had intimated the *Art* from *word to word*, but they could by no meanes understand him, yet would be accounted *Philosophers*.

s) *Præf. in Ænig. Philos.*

Seeing then a *Man* may be in the true *Path* and not know it to be so, it behove's the serious *Student* earnestly to desire of *God* to (t) "remove from his "Mind al thoughts without understanding, to make him a (u) Child of the light "as of the Day, that his (w) Eyes may behold the right, and his Eye-lids di-"rect his wayes. That his Dayes be not spent in vanity, nor his Yeares wast "doing nothing: but that (y) one Day may teach another, and one Night "add knowledge to another, And then he shall find that though this *Author* has opened his *Mouth* in a *Parable*, yet he hath declared [or made plain] hard *Sentences* of Old.

t) *Wisd.* 1. 5.
u) 1 *Thes.* 5. 5.
w) *Prov.* 4. 25.
y) *Psa.* 19. 2.

z) *Ord.* pa. 106.

z) **For in this Ordinall (he sets you out of doubt,)**
Is nothing set wrong, nor no point left out.

Pag.

Pag.106,li.21. **In the yeare of Christ MCCCCLXXVII. This Worke was begun ——**

IN the *search* I have made after *Authentique Manuscripts* to compleate this *Worke*, a private *Gentleman* lent me a very faire one of *Norton's Ordinall*, which I chiefly followed; yet not admitting to compare it with fourteen other *Copies*. It was written in *Velame* and in an auntient *sett Hand*, very exact and exceeding neate. The *Figures* (whence I caused these herewith printed to be *Graved*) being also most neatly & exquisitely *lym'd*, and better work then that which was *Henry the seaventh's* own *Booke*, (as I am informed by those that have seene both.) It had placed in the midle and bottome of the *Compartiments* of *Flowers, Birds* and *Beasts*, the *Nevell's* Coate of *Armes*, with others which that *Family* quartered. This induced me to believe it to be the *Originall* (or one exactly *Copied* from it) presented by the *Author* to *George Nevell* then *Arch-Bishop of Yorke*, who was a most wealthy and *Magnificent Bishop*; as appeares not onely by the rich (*a*) *Iewell* he offered at *Becketts Tombe*, but for the greate and stately *Entertainment* he provided at *More* in *Hartfordshire* for *Edward the* 4th: to make which more Magnificent he brought forth a (*b*) vast *Treasure* of *Plate*, that he had hid during the distractions of former *yeares*, all which the *King* seised upon with his *Money* and *Goods* then valued at 20000 l. (a farre more considerable sum of *Money* in those *dayes*, then *now*;) and made of the *Arch-Bishops Mitre* (set with precious *Stones*) a *Crowne* for himself.

a) Isaac. Chr. *fo.*468.

b) Stow. Ann. *fo.*426.

I have beene informed that there was greate *Correspondency* betweene this *Arch-Bishop* and the *Hermetique Philosophers* of his time, and this is partly confirmed to me from *Ripley's* (c) *Dedication* of his *Medulla* to him, *Ann.*1476. as also the presentation of this of *Norton's Ordinall*; for though I finde the said *Arch-Bishop* dyed the same yeare this *Ordinall* was begun to be written, yet the certaine time of that yeare I cannot yet learne; But it was towards the latter end thereof, when his Successor (*Lawrence Booth*) was *Consecrate*, viz. (d) 25. *Sept.* Besides, in all probability he lay not long *sick*, because he dyed (at *Blithlow*) upon a (*e*) *Iourney* from *Yorke*: So that the *Booke* might be finished and *presented*; (or if not presented, yet *intended*) before he dyed, though begun but the same yeere.

c) See the Preface.

d) Godw. Succ. *p.* 481.

e) Godw. *pag. ibidem.*

Pag.107. **The Compounde of Alchymie, &c.**

THis *Worke* (which is also called the *Twelve Gates*) was pen'd by Sir *George Ripley*, and formerly (*f*) set forth in print by *Ralph Rabbards*; I have compared it with severall other *Manuscript Copies*, amongst which I happily met with one written neere about the time that *Ripley* lived, (and in these Streames of *Learning* the more clearest and without the least of *Mixture* is to be found neerest the *Spring-head*,) the which I most relyed upon. Yet where they differ, the *Reader* (if this *Copy* please not) may make use of the former.

f) An. 1591.

It appeares at the end of this (*g*) *Worke*, that it was written in the yeare 1471. which I the rather take notice of, because I have met with a kind of *Retractation* of *Ripley's* beginning,

g) Pag. 193.

Fœlix

Fælix quem faciunt aliena pericula cautum.

Wherein he beseeches all men, wheresoever they shall meete with any of his *Experiments* written by *Him*, or that go under his *Name*, (from the yeare 1450. to the yeare 1470.) either to *burne* them or afford them no *Credit*; being written according to his *esteeme*, not *proofe*; and which (afterwards upon *tryall*) he found *false* and *vaine*: for soe long was he seeking the *Stone*, but in the truth of *practise* had not found it, till towards the end of that yeare, and then (saith He) *Inveni quem diligit anima mea.*

So that this *Treatise* of the 12. *Gates* being wrote the yeare after, is unquestionably to be *relyed upon*, because pen'd from a grounded *experimentall Practise*, as himselfe Testifies in his *Admonition*,

h) *Ripl.* Admonition.

h) I never saw worke truly but one,
Of which in this Treatise the truth I have told.

In which (for the Students safeguard) he gives an account of his own *Erronious Experiments*, therein following *Chaucer*, *Richardus Anglicus*, *Dionisius*, *Zacharius* the noble *Trevisan*, and divers other honest and Consciencious *Philosophers*.

i) Anno 1649.
k) *Pref. ad Oper.* G. Rip.

Ludovicus Combachius (who hath (*i*) lately set forth divers of *Ripley's Works* in *Latin*) tells us (*k*) that he then had in his hands these *Twelve Gates* rendred in most pure *Elegiaque verse*, by one *Nicholas May* upon the Command of the *Emperour Rudolph* the *second*, and that he could willingly have added it to that he *published*, (which was *translated* out of *English* into *Latine verse* by Sir *Edw: Kelley*) for the better understanding thereof, but that the *Copy* was none of his owne.

l) *Printed at* Tolouse.

The learned *Faber*, (1646.) bestowed much Paines and Cost in publishing to the world (*l*) *Basilius Currus Triumphalis*, and others, in one *Volume*. In the *Argument* of which *Booke Georgius Riplæus Canonicus Anglus doctissimus & mirandus in quo nihil falsi & supervacui ad metallorum omnium proprietates, & naturas manifestandas*, is thus Ingeniously acknowledged. He further assures us that his *Workes* are worthy to keep pace with the best *Philosophers*; and knowes that Policie in *Printing* is surest, and takes well with the *Iudicious*, to begin with a good *Worke*, and end with the best; to which place he refers ou *Ripley*. But I must needs tell the *Reader* that in *pag.* 338. and so to the end, he is by *mistake* called *Triplanus* instead of *Riplæus*. There are other the like notorious faults which the *Printer* (most likely) is guilty of, as giving *Isaac Holland* the name of *Irsacus*. *Cornelius Drebble* he prints *Tornelius*, (and sometimes *Fornelius*) *Trebellianus*; and besides these, further causes of *Exception* to other parts of the *Worke* (too many to be mentioned here) amongst the rest where *Faber* sayes they were all rendred into *Latin* out of *Dutch*, and that this peece of *Ripley's*, which he there calls *Triplanus de lapide Philosophorum* (but is indeed an *Epitomy* of these 12. *Gates*) was by one *Nicholas Barnard* a *Philosopher* Translated out of *Dutch* into *Latin*, intimating withall that it was *Originally* written in the *Germain Tongue*; which is very *false*, injurious to our *Author*, and dishonourable to our *Nation*.

Thus much for the *Worke*, and now to say something touching our *Author*.

Philemon Holland in his *Translation* of *Cambden's Britania* Printed 1636. is is pleased to take the liberty to tell us that the place of his *Nativity* was *(m)* *Ripley*, a *Village* in the *County* of *Surrey*, and calls him a *Ring-leader of our Alchimists, and a mysticall Impostor.* This Imputation of *Mysticall Impostor* smells more of *Envious dislike* then *faithfull Account*, and therefore I'le passe it by. But as to the place of his *Birth*, I am induced to believe it to be about *Yorkshire*, (not that he was a Foundling at *Ripley* in that *County*, or of so obscure *Parents*, that the name of the place of his *Nativity* must be impos'd upon him in defect of, a better) No certainly, his *Name, Relation*, and *Kindred* discover him to be the Sonne of a *Gentleman*; and though I cannot exhibite his *Pedigree*; yet it appeares in some ancient *Manuscript Copies* of his (n) *Medulla* (which I have seene) that his Relation of *Kindred* lay in the *Northerne parts*, where (he saith) "he had divers Kindred, Gentlemen of "Yorkshire and Lincolnshire, as *Tevarsall, Ripley, Medlay, Willoughbie, Burham,* "*Waterton, Flemming* and *Talboyes*, who (as he there complaines to the *Arch-*"*Bishop Nevell*, to whom he dedicated that Worke) were by the Conquering "Sword of *Edward* the *fourth*, (*God* so permitting) lamentably destroyed. 'Tis also considerable that his *Ecclesiasticall Promotion* hapned to be at *Bridlington*, a (o) *Towne* in the *East Riding* of *Yorkshire*.

m) fol. 195.

n) *towards the end thereof.*

o) *Camb. Brit.* fo. 714.

——p) **According to my Profession,**
In Order Chanon Regular of Bridlington.

p) *Pref. to his 12. Gates.*

And probably such his *Advancement*, might be procured rather in that *Country* where his *Kindred* and *Friends* lived, and himselt that *Country-man*, then if he had been a *Stranger*.

I determine not whether *Holland* has done the learned *Antiquary* or profound *Philosopher* the greater *Injury*, in what he puts downe concerning the place of his *Birth*; for I must let the *world* know, 'tis not to be found in the *Originall Latin* which *Cambden* published *Anno* 1607. nor can I learne that there was any other *Impression*, to the time of *Translation*, nor in probability could there be when *Holland* (q) fell to worke immediately upon the coming out of the said *Impression* in 1607. and set forth his *Translation* within foure Yeares.

q) *Postscript to Camb. Brit.*

So that I cannot but wonder at the Boldnesse of this *Translator*, not onely in *adding* many things of his owne score, but for abusing so learned a *Philosopher* with the Tearme of *Mysticall Impostor*, and putting it upon the Account of an *Author*, who should he thus vilifie one of so cleere a *Reputation*, ingenious *Schollars* might have just cause to question the *Candidnesse* of his *Pen* in other things. But this kind of liberty I finde *Holland* hath taken in other parts of that worthy *worke*, The effects whereof, hath rendred *Banbury* (amongst others) much beholding to him for an eminent *Flout*: For, where *Cambden* fames it for (r) *Cheese* onely, he addes *Cakes* and *Zeale*: Neither of which are to be found in the *Originall*, though doubtlesse both in the *Towne*, and for better purpose then to be *boasted* of.

r) *Nunc conficiendo Caseo notissimum* fo. 266

But to leave this *Digression* & returne to *Ripley*. *Pitts* tells us, "He was a Man "of a *Quick*, & (more then can be expressed) curious *Wit*, and that *Totam ferè* "*suā ætatē in perscrutandis rerū Naturaliū occultis & abstrusis Causis & effectibus* "*consumpsit*; He wasted almost his whole *Life* in searching out the occult and "abstruse Causes and Effects of *Naturall things*. And that he might more

s) *Pitts de illustr. Ang. Scrip.* pag. 677.

"copiously and plentifully study *Philosophy*, and accomplish what he conceived "his *mind*, he boldly travailed through *France*, *Germany*, and *Italy*, where he "grew into familiarity with severall of the most *Learned men*.

t) *Bale Cent.* 8. fo.622.

Leland saith truly, that he (t) laid the foundation of his Studies in *Italy*, for there indeed he had the *blessing* first to see *Projection*.

u) *Cantalena* G. Ripley.

(u) *In Romanis partibus nuptiis Mercurii,*
Accidit post studium semel quod interfui.

w) *Pitts* p. 677

'Tis further testified, that He alwayes either (w) *Writ*, or *Learnt*, or *Taught* something; He was perfectly *learned* in *all* the liberall *Arts*, and well red in all manner of *Philosophy*; a most famous *Mathematitian*, a *Rhetoritian* and *Poet*, (x) *per eam ætatem, non vulgaris effectus. Combachius* styles him (y) *Author procul dubio dignus, qui ab Amatoribus Chemiæ sedulo evolvatur, cum in sermone apertus sit, rotundus & planus, nec ullis spinis aliorum more obsitus:* A worthy *Author* without exception, who is diligently studyed by the lovers of *Chimestry*, forasmuch as he is *open, well compast*, and *plaine of delivery*, and not wrapt in any Thornes, after the custome of others. *Habet insuper* (saith the same *Author*) *cum Lulii scriptis magnam affinitatem, ut unus alterum explicet, &c.* Besides, he hath great Affinity with the Writings of *Lully*, insomuch that the one explaineth the other.

x) *Bale.* fo.622

y) *Præf. ad oper* C. Rip.

Amongst other parts, abroad, he visited the *Isle of Rhodes*, and resided there for some time with the *Knights* of the *Order* of *Saint Iohn of Ierusalem*. An *Acquaintance* of mine hath in his *custody* certaine private *Observations* of an *English Gentleman* of good quality and credit, who in his *Travells* abroade, *Observes* (amongst other things) that in the *Isle of Malta* he saw a *Record*; which declares that this Sir *George Ripley* gave yearely to those *Knights* of *Rhodes* 100000l. towards maintaining the *war* (then on foot) against the *Turks*.

But at length, that he might bid his farewell to the *World*, and wholly consecrate himselfe to *God*, and betake him to his private *Studies*, upon his (z) returne into *England* he obtained an *Indulgence* of *Pope Innocent* the *eighth*, that for the future he might be

z) *Bale Cent.* 8.

a) *Tit. oper.*

a) **Exempt from Claustrall Observance,**

and alwaies discharged and freed from the burthen of the *Ceremonies* and *Observancy* of his *Order*; but in regard the *Chanons* admit no such things, he became a (b) *Carmelite* in the *Monastery* of Saint *Butolph*, which (saith *Leland*) is a famous (c) *Mart Towne* nigh the *Banks* of the *River Lindus*: This *River* I take to be the *River Witham* in *Lincolnshire* (anciently called (d) *Lindis*) which passing from *Lincoln*, runs towards the maine *Sea* by *Boston*, more truly called (e) *Butolphs Towne*, (for it carried that name from *Butolph*, a most holy and devote *Saxon*:) And if you observe *Cambdens Map* of *Lincolnshire*, you shall see St. *Butolph* stands neere to *Boston*. So that in all likelyhood this was the *place* of *Ripley's Retirement*, where he continued an *Anchorite* untill his *Death*, and was there *Buried* Anno 1490.

b) An. 1488.

c) *Bale* fo.622.

d) *Camb. Brit.* fo.538.

e) *Ibid.* fo.532.

The probability whereof, may be further confirm'd from his *Medulla*, where it appeares he had then (f) a great desire to return into *England*, and to that end therein became a *Suter* to the *Archbishop of Yorke*, that by his meanes he might obtaine an *abiding place* in some *Religious house*, within his *Dioces*. Which *Arch-*

f) See the latter end of that worke.

Archbishop presently after dying, he could not performe, but not unlike *Ripley* having still an earnest *longing* thereto, (because it was his *native Countrey*,) might without doubt otherwise effect.

And whereas *Bale* saith he obteined *Pope Innocents* Indulgence upon his returne into *England*, and thereupon became a *Carmelite*, *An.*1488. It is manifest from the aforesaid *Medulla*, that at the writeing thereof, which was in 1476. (at least 12. yeares before the time *Bale* makes him to enter into that *Order*) he had this *Dispensation*, for so he tells the *Archbishop*: And if so, then it must be either (g) *Sixtus* the fourth, or *Paul* the second (his *Predecessor*) that must grant it unto him.

(g) *Isaac. Chron.* fo. 366.

He wrote divers *Bookes* worthy of perusing, but amongst those which *Bale* Registers, I shall onely cull out these, *viz.*

1. *Compendium Alchimiæ, seu Castellum Duodecim Portarum.*
2. *Concordantias Guidonis & Raymundi.*
3. *Secreta Philosophorum.*
4. *Alcumistarum Misteria.*
5. *Artem brevem vel Clangorem.*
6. *Practicam Ceremonialem.*
7. *Dictata Ægri.*
8. *De Magia Naturali.*
9. *De lapide Philosophico, latinè Tractatum rythimicum.*

All which *Pitts* recites, and to them adds the following *workes*.

10. *Medullam Philosophiæ.*
11. *Pupillam Alchimiæ.*
12. *Terram Terrarum.*
13. *Experimenta Philosophica.*
14. *De rerum temperaturis.*

What followes *Ludov: Combachius* has lately printed, and added to some of the aforementioned *Peeces*.

15. *De Mercurio & lapide Philosophorū.*
16. *Philorcium Alchimistarum.*
17. *Clavis Auræ Portæ.*
18. *Viaticum seu Varia Practica.*
19. *Accurtationes & practicæ Raymundinæ.*
20. *Cantalena.*

And *lastly* take into the *Number* the small *Peeces* published in this *Theatrum*: *viz.* His

21. *Epistle to* Edw. *the fourth*, pag. 109.
22. *Vision*. pag. 374.
23. *Verses belonging to his Scrowle*——— Pag. 375.
24. *Preface to his* Medulla, 389.
25. *A short worke supposed to be his*, Pag. 393.

Pag. 177. lin. ult. **A Quintessence this Water we call,**
In Man, which helpeth Diseases all.

PHysick is a *divine Science*, even *Gods Theologie*; for the *Almighty* wrote his *Scripture* in that language, before he made *Adam* to reade it. The *Ten Fathers* before the *Flood*, and those that followed, together with *Moses* and *Salomon*, were the great *Physitians* in former *Ages*, who bequeathed their heavenly knowledges of *naturall* helpes to those they judged as well *worthy* in honesty and industry, as capable thereof: and from their piercing *Beames* all *Nations* enlightned their *Tapers*. *Abraham* brought it out of *Chaldea*, and bestowed much thereof upon *Egypt*, and thence a refulgent *Beame* glanced into *Greece*. The *Coäcks* and *Æsculapian Family*, &c. *God* greatly incouraged to serve that *Age*. *Democritus* and *Hypocrates* supported *Ruinous Mankinde*, with their *Phisicall* administrations, and *Schollers* successively supplyed their places for at least 400. yeares, untill *Galen* undertooke by his strong *Abilities* and incessant Paines to vivifie the then dying *Genius* of *Phisick*: which hath since most nobly beene Augmented, by the stupendious paines of *Arabians* and *Europeans*

And in the *Progresse* this *Science* has made into severall parts of the *World*, we may finde, that *God* hath evermore been pleas'd to call upon the *stage* thereof in sundry Ages, some choyce and eminent *Men*, whom (by the *Illumination* of his *blessed Spirit*) he hath furnished with ability to reade the *Characters* of his blessed will, writ in that ample and sacred *Volume* of the *Creation*, and the severall *Pages* of individuall *Natures*. And further, to testifie his care of his *Creatures*, hath also given them *Balme* in their hands to stoppe the over-spreading contagiousnesse of bainefull *Diseases*. But to contract the Rayes of my Prospective to our owne *homes*, the *Phisitians Colledge* of *London* doth at this day nourish most noble and able Sons of *Art*, no way wanting in the choycest of Learning; And though we doe not, yet the World abroad has taken notice of sundry learned *Fellowes* of that *Societie*, as *Linacres*, *Gilbert*, *Ridly*, *Dee*, *Flood*, &c. and at present *Doctor Harvey*, who deserves for his many and eminent *Discoveries*, to have a *Statue* erected rather of *Gold* then of *Marble*.

Neverthelesse, it has beene observed in other *parts* that we *English* will sooner abuse and detract from the worth of any of our owne *Nation* (though never so well deserving) then render them what they justly merit by a worthy *Applause*: And rather cry up a Frie of *Illiterate Quacks*: (for every *Galen* hath his Plague, [a mounting ignorant *Thessalus*] that cheate the *poore* and *simple* of their Money, and (I wish they did not) often in Conclusion murder their over-credulous *Patients*;) then give the learned *Phisitian* the due (*b*) *Honour* (b) *Eccles*. 38. *God* has appointed us to pay him.

Now as *God* hath formerly shed most eminent *Beames* of the *first light* upon a few particular *Men* (as it were to gratifie the deserving Labourers at all times of his day;) So I am confident there are yet most noble *seeds* of that *light* of *Nature* appointed to spring up for the Benefit of *Posterity*. The *Glory* whereof we see hath shin'd in other *Horizons*, shortly it will draw neere to *ours*; and that which with incessant *Toyle* cannot yet be *Discovered*, shall in those dayes be freely *Revealed* to some that little dreame of it. I am more then Confident *Succession* will meete with many *advantages* and *helpes*, which this corrupt and ingratefull *Age* deserves not, nor shall have; because we deride, what *Posterity* will adore with a lasting admiration: The *Circuit* of that great and *Sabbathicall* Conjunction of the two *Superiour Planets* which began An. 1603. in the *Fiery Triplicity*, will *Illustrate*, *Enlarge*, and *Refine* Arts like the tryed *Gold*, It shall produce more pregnant and famous *Philosophers* by *Fire*, (I meane such as is *Etheriall*) then yet the *world* ere saw; and so purifie some inge-

ingenious *Inquisitors*, as to make them fit *Mettall* for *Angells* to Project on. This *Fiery Trigon* shall not passe, before that *God* make *manifest* what he commanded former *Ages* to keepe *Secret*, Where old *Hermes* his *Ætheriall Phisick* (*viz*. this **Quintessentiall Water** which *Ripley* here speakes of, and which is

(i) **Such as auncient Phisick taught,** i) Sir E.K. to G S.

shall be *Restored*; whose *perfect* and *incorruptible Qualities* of *Heate*, *Cold*, *Moisture* and *Drinesse* are able not onely to *Nourish*, *Fortifie*, and *Encrease* the *Vitall Spirits*, but *Digest*, *Correct* and *Consume* all *Impediments* and *Corruptions*, those hurtfull and Impure *Seeds* which crept in with the *Curse*, (and joyning themselves with the *Good*,) have ever since (like a growing *Tyde*) encroached so far upon the *Body* of *Man*, till he is almost *overwhelm'd* and ready to *Perish*.

But it is to be acknowledged that those *Chemists* deserve a considerable share of *Honour*, who, for want of this *Ætheriall* and *Universall Medicine* (which *God* hath hitherto granted to few) zealously apply themselves to finde out a *Particular* one, (that *sedulous Industry* may afford to more) and to raise up a *Body* of *Phisick*, from those (*k*) *Three Principles* which are to be found in every *Body*, because compounded of them; (though strongly lockt up) namely *Sal*, *Sulphur*, and *Mercury*: (to which *De Clave* of late adds two more, *viz*. *Earth* and *Phleagme*) and so comfortably relieve decaying *Mortality*, and heale *Diseases* by the meanes they are Cured. k) *Bost. Phis.* cap. 4.

In the painefull and curious *search* of which *Experiments*, where there is more of *Nature* that still lyes hid, (yea she is as Infinite in her *Productions*, as the *Minde* of *Man* can be *Unsatiable*, in the *search*) let the satisfaction the Ingenious *Artist* findes in one *Truth*, leade him cheerfully on to make *Inquisition* after a further, perhaps the *Event* of his *Labours* may discover a *Perfection* iu the *knowledge* he hunts after, and *Providence* may be as kinde to so diligent an *Inquisitor*, as *Nature* is to the *Ant*, who bestows *Wings* on her in her *declining Age*, as a reward for her former *Labours*.

And albeit I magnifie *Chemicall Phisique*, yet I do not lessen the due commendations that belong to *Galenicall*: nor dare I, when so great an *Hermetick Philosopher* as *Arnoldus de villa Nova* has taken so much paines to Joyne them together. And besides him, it has been the worke of *Maierus*, *Faber*, and many other conscientious *Philosophers*, to reconcile them. Who laying aside (indeede abhorring) all thought of *Faction*, conceive nothing to come neerer the *Divinity* of *Nature*, or be any way more gratefull to *God* and *Good men*, then to help the *Afflicted*, and relieve the *Sick*; nor greater *Charity* then to bestow *health*, and support *dejected Nature*. Nor is *Galenicall Phisick* hard to come by, it being at all times easy to be met with, the *Superficies* of the *Earth* never denying us some thing or other for *Medicine*, and they, *Milde*, *Gentle*, and *Safe* for weake and tender *Natures*. Moreover, it is observed by *Nollius* and others, that where *God* strikes with any *Disease*, in those parts he also sends forth a *Plant* that he endowes with vertue to cure it. And truly I cannot but admire at those snarling *humours*, who make it their *Taske* to disparage what they affect not, (nay oftentimes what is beyond their owne worth) and rent those noble parts of *Art* asunder, which *Nature* has conjoyned in an harmonious *Agreement*, and whose wide breaches, honest hearted *Philosophers* endeavour to make up by a friendly Reconciliation, it being not to be denyed, but that each hath their peculiar *Eminencies* for which they deserve both *Praise* & *Honour*. For my owne part, I am none of the *Detractors* from *Learning*, but beare an Universall affection to *Arts*, and am in freindship with each of their particular *Branches*; Nay even in those I understand not, for I am perswaded by the satisfaction I have received in things which before time I knew not, that there may be something deserving of my faire Opinion, in what I am yet to know.

l) *Bac.adv.* pag. 37.

It has proved a great (l) *Errour* in some *Practitioners*, who (tumbling up and downe their owne *Speculations*) seeke out for *Truth* in the *Little world*, and withdrawing themselves too much from the *Contemplation* of *Experimentall Naturall Obsevations*, neglect to looke for it in the *greate* and *common World*: When certainly such may far sooner arrive at that *Truth* they seeke for in *Man*, if they would but observe the Beginnings, Change, declination, and death of all things, in and upon this inferiour *Globe*, and compare their vertues with our owne internall *Natures*, for they are certainly (*m*) united by a Noble, excellent, and secret Harmony and Relation.

m) See Davison's Curic. Chemic.

n) De occult. Phil. *cap.* 3.

And having found the true *Originall* and *Cause* of *Diseases*, then further to search after a proper remedy; for all *Diseases* are not cured by one sort of *Physick* (save that which is *Ætheriall* and *Incorporeall*) And therefore according to the Doctrine of (n) *Paracelsus*, such as are bred from so light a cause as the impure *Seeds* of *Vegitables*, viz. *Meate*, *Drinke*, *Fruits*, *Herbes*, and the like *Elementary* things, may be very easily cured with the *Secrets* of *Hearbes*, *Roots*, and such like mild and tender *Medicines*, of which sort *Galenicall Physick* is more plentifully furnished then any of the rest. Those that are produced from the more rude and knotteer *Qualities* of *Mineralls*, and what is cast within the Compasse of that *Tribe*, the *Chemicall Phisitian* must expell by the power and force of his *Metalline Sulphurs*, &c. *Vegitables* being (in this Case) too weake to *Master* and *Dissolve* their tenacious and coagulated *Spirits*: Those which are derived from the *Influences* of *Heaven*, must be removed by *Plants*, &c. *Magically* gathered and prepared, or by *Sigills*, &c. framed or made under sutable *Positions* and *Aspects* of the *Planets*, and impregnated with the rayes of *Celestiall Vertues*, for without opening the *Bodyes*, Infusing superiour *Influences*, and (by an additionall Artifice) *fixing* them to the said *Bodies*; their own ordinary *vertue* (be *Elections* never so propitious) hath not strength enough to conquer *Diseases* of that *Nature*: and severall of these choice *Secrets* (of *Nature* and *Art united*) I my selfe have *prepared*, *made* and Experimentally *verified*. Finally, where *Diseases* happen by *Supernaturall* meanes, as by *Inchantments*, &c. none of the other three are able to remedy the same, save onely *Magicall* and *Supercelestiall* meanes, by and through the Vertues of particular *Intelligences*, Or the *Red Medicine* wrought up to the highest degree of *Perfection*. And in such cases the *Hermetique Philosopher* must apppeare, who

o) *Anonymi.*

o) ——In his Reason hath contrived
A Perfeit Medicine, for Bodies that be sick
Of all infirmities to be releived,
This heleth Nature, and prolongeth lyfe &c.

Therefore

Therefore let all men cease to wonder why so many *Diseases* seeme *incurable*; when many times being *Supernaturall* we judge them *Naturall*, and the true *Causes* unknowne, no sutable *Medicamen* is administred.

And whereas I have toucht upon *Sigills*, I thinke it will not be remote from this *discourse*, if I give a little satisfaction to my *Reader* therein; Though perhaps it may be esteemed as a thing of too daring a *Nature* for my *Pen* Nor am I ignorant how some, most learned Men, have extremly suffered under the heavy and sharp *Load* of unworthy and rash *Calumny*, for manifesting or defending this *Doctrine*; but it hath only beene (such is their *Glory*) by those that could never sufficiently *Answer* their *Arguments*.

The framing of *Sigills*, *Lamels*, *Talesmes* (for all depend upon one *Radix*) is a piece of *Learning* as (p) Ancient as the *Babilonians* and *Caldean Magi*, (who first found out the Secret power of *Figures*) a chiefe part of their *Magick*, And practised by the greatest *Philosophers* in the *Easterne World*; Where remaine to this day, (as evident Testimonies of their first *Invention*) very many and ancient *Talesmes*, the miraculous effects whereof were admired and approved throughout all *Ægipt* and *Persia*: although (I confesse) their *Name* and *Use* be yet scarce knowne in these parts of the *World*; Or if, onely to such whose *Wisdome* thinkes fit to conceale and preserve the *knowledg* thereof, from the hands of the senslesse and profane.

p) See R *Moses*, his *Doctor dubiorum*.

Among all other *Philosophers* (famous for this kinde of knowledg) *Apolonius Tyaneus* was the (q) mightiest, and his *Workes* (in my Opinion) most *Stupendious*: Who though the Envious and Ungratefull *World*, has throwne some dirt upon him, to blemish the Innocency of his *Operations*, yet he never deserved other then well; all He did being for the (r) *good* thereof, and not for *hurt*; He was no lesse a *Pious* then *Illustrious Philosopher*, His whole *Life* being strict and vertuous, and his *Death* not blasted with any scandalous *Exit*. And for a justification of his *Praxis*, take this Testimony of *Justinus*, who, saith (s) that he was a Man skillfull in the " *Dissent* and *Consent* of all *naturall Powers*; and who wrought wonderfull things by the meanes of this *Science*; " (which were only *Naturall* and not *Miraculous*:) For which purpose, he " made choyce of such fit *Subjects*, as might conduce to the perfection of " what he intended to Effect: And indeed *God* did not withstand those " *Workes* of his, in regard they were done by the knowledg of *Naturall things*, " for the use and benefit of *Man*.

q) *Greg. Observ.* pag. 36.

r) *Mayerus Sym. Aur. Mens.* pag. 127.

s) *In quest. ad Orthod: quæst.*

What I have further to say, shall onely be to shew what *Naturall powers*, *Sigills*, &c. *Graved* or *Imprest* with proper *Characters* and *Figures*, and made under certaine peculiar *Constellations* may have. *Albumazar*, *Zahel*, *Haly*, *Albategnus*, and divers other *Arabians*, give us severall examples of such as have been cured of the biting of *Serpents*, *Scorpions*, *Mad dogs*, &c. by *Talismaticall Figures*: And in other *Authors* we meete with a world of (t) *Stories* which tell what Admirable effects they have *wrought* being rightly prepared, (which should I here mention, would swell beyond the limits of my *Discourse*) But this peece of *Art* is of extreme difficulty, and not to be performed by every one that takes it in hand.

t) *See Greg. Observ. Gaff. Curos.*

As for the use of such *Characters*, *Letters*, *Words*, *Figures*, &c. Formed or Insculped upon any *Matter* we make use of, we are led to it by the president of *Nature*, who *Stampes* most notable and marvelous *Figures* upon (u) *Plants*, Roots

u) *See Crolius de signat. inter. rerum.*

Roots, *Seeds*, *Fruits*, nay even upon rude *Stones*, *Flints*, and other inferiour *Bodies*.

Nor are these remarkable *Signatures* made and described by Chaunce, (for there is a certaine *Providence* which leades on all things to their end, and which makes nothing but to some purpose,) but are the *Characters* and *Figures* of those *Starrs*, by whom they are principally governed, and with these particular *Stamps*, have also peculiar and different *vertues* bestowed upon them. What *Artists* therefore doe in point of *Character*, is onely to pursue the Track, that is beaten out by *Nature*; And by how much the more the *Matter* whereupon such *Impressions* are made, is sutable to the *Qualities* of those *Starrs* whose *Characters* it is signed with: By so much more apt and inclineable it will be to receive those *vertues* that shall impower it to produce an *Effect*, in things whereunto it's applyed.

Neverthelesse, this is not all, for this *Body* must have as it were a *Soule* infused, and be *Impregnated* with a *Celestiall vitality*, or else it remaines *Ineffectuall* and *Dead*. In which respect other meanes must be found out before we can obtaine that Effect. And therefore we are to Consider, that the *Soule* of the *World* is not confined, nor the *Celestiall Influences* limited, but doe indifferently emit and communicate their *Vertues* alike, as well to things *Artificially made*, as to those that are *Naturally generated*, though sometimes they are more, at othertimes lesse vigorous and powerfull, according to the different *Aspects* under which they are wrought: In which regard a fit *Election* must be built up from the foundation of *Astrologie*, sutable to the *Nature* of the *Operation* proposed, which being effected, and the *Stars* finding a *figure* aptly disposed for receiving them, they forthwith *Impresse* their *vertue*, which they retaining doe afterwards *operate* in that they finde to be *semblable*. And this is not strange if we reflect upon the Vulgar experiments of the *Loadestone*, who communicating its vertue to a peece of *Iron* (a thing made fit by *Nature* to attract and reteine) that *Piece* thereby becomes of strength to communicate this vertue to a *third*. But if we should consider the *Operations* of this *Magnet* throughly (which proceeds onely from a *Naturall Principle*) there is no other *Mystery*, *Celestiall*, *Elementall*, or *Earthly*, which can be too hard, for our *Beliefe*.

Moreover, these *Celestiall vertues* and *peculiar Gifts* are not infused into *Individuall* and *particular things*, by the *Idea*, and by meanes of the *Soule* of the *World* alone, But also are invited thither, through the *Obedientiality* of their *Matter*, and a certaine aptitude and likenesse that these *Inferiours* beare to their *Superiours*; which being once taken in, they thereupon contract and reteine (besides such as they receive from their owne *Species*) those naturall *Vertues* and Roots of the *Starrs*, wherewith they suscitate and stir up the *Influences* of the Celestiall *Bodies*; who are (as it were by compact when *United*) Obliged to *Operate* in and for that purpose, which the *Artist* appoints them: And more especially if the Minde of the *Operator* be vehemently inclined towards the same. For *that* through the strength and Efficacy of the *Imagination* and *Passion*, (being seriously intent upon any *Operation*) is joyned with the Minde of the *Starrs* and *Intelligences*, and as sodainly fitted with *Vertues*, as if it were the proper Receptacle of their *Influences*, and consequently helpes more effectually to infuse their *Vertues* into our *Workes*: And the reason is, *because there is an apprehension and power of all things in the* Minde: Whereupon all things

having

having a naturall *Obedience* to it, have also of necessity an *Efficacy*; and more to that which desires them, with a strong and intent Desire.

Notwithstanding, all these *Wonders* are not wrought but by the Cooperation of *second Causes* disposing of the *Corporall Matter*, *God* (the first cause of all things) having variously distributed these *vertues* to every one as he pleaseth, who by his Command and appointment are necessitated to produce their *Effects*.) Which *Matter* (by reason of its *Purity* or *Inequality* may cause the *Celestiall vertues* to erre in their *Actings*, (for certainly *Influences* may be hindred, and prove ineffectuall through the indisposition or insufficiency of the *Matter*.) And therefore it is no ordinary *Speculation* to awaken the *sleeping Spirit* which lyes bound up in the straight Prison of the *Body*; to invite and allure that propitious *Spirit* to descend from *Heaven*, and unite it selfe with that which is *Internall*; and there withall to convey a *Vinculum* thereinto, that is of power to hold fast and fix the *Celestiall Influencs*, from recoyling back into their *united Centers*.

This is the *Series* and *Order* of *Nature* conjoyn'd with *Art*: and this, and all this must be effected, before one true *Magicall Operation* can be performed.

Pag. 194. **Liber patris Sapientie.**

THough I cannot yet satisfie the *Reader* who was the *Authour* hereof, and therefore must *Register* it, (together with **Experience and Philosophy**, the **Hermets Tale**) amongst the *Anonymi*: yet I can assure him *He* gives exceeding good advice to the *Student* in this *Science*, where he bids him be *Secret* in the Carriage on of his *Studies* and *Operations*, and not to let any one know of his *Undertakings*, but his good *Angel* and *Himselfe*: and such a close and retyred *Brest* had *Norton's Master*, who

w) **When Men disputed of Colours of the Rose,**
He would not speake but keepe himselfe full close. w) *Ordin*. p. 32

Privacy will (questionlesse) prove an unimaginable benefit to him, whereas on the contrary *Apertnesse* exposeth a true *Philosopher* to a multitude of Misfortunes. Witnesse Sir *Ed. Kelley*, whose immoderate *Ambition* of spreading his *Name*, lifted him up even to a *Madnesse* of *publique Carriage*; which not correcting in Time, he most miserably *fell*, through the fatall *Virtego* of imprudent *Glory*. To such therefore I shall only adde *Chaucers* Councell which may prove of no litle advantage if they remember it.

x) **Make privy to your dealing as few as you maie,**
For three may keepe Councell if twaine be awaie. x) *Tea Commis. of Love*.

THe *Figure* cut in *Brasse* and placed in *Page* 210. is an Hieroglipicall device of *Cremer* somtime *Abbot* of *Westminster*, and *Scholler* (in this *Science*) to *Raymond Lully*, which he caused to be painted upon an *Arched Wall*

 in

in *Westminster Abbey*, where now the *Statues* of our *Kings* and *Queenes* are set in their respective *Habits*.

I met with it *Limned* in a very *Ancient Manuscript*, before the old *Verses* that (y) follow, which there seemed to serve as a *Preface* to that *Worke* which beares the Tytle of **Hermes Bird**. In it is conteyn'd the Grand *Misteries* of the *Philosophers Stone*, and not more *Popish* or *Superstitious* then *Flamell's Hieroglyphicks* portraid upon an *Arch* in St. *Innocents* Church-yard in *Paris*; Notwithstanding it has pleased some, to wash the *Originall* over with a *Plasterer's* whited *Brush*. As also (of late) to breake in Pieces the *Glasse Window* behinde the *Pulpit* in St. *Margarets* Church at *Westminster*, wherein was fairely *Painted* (but unhappily mistaken for a *Popish Story*) the whole *Processe* of the *Worke*, in this manner.

y) See pag. 211.

The *Window* is divided into three *Parts*: In the Outermost whereof upon the right hand was drawne a *Man* holding a *Boy* in his hand, and a *Woman* with a *Girle* in hers, all standing in *upright*, *naked postures*, upon a *greene foliate earth*: The *Man* and *Woman* had *Fetters*, wherewith their *Feet* seemed to be *chained* to the *ground*, which *Fetters* were presented as falling from off their *Legs*. Over the *heads* of these *persons* were the *Sun* and *Moone* placed, and painted of a sad darke red *Colour*.

Within the *Left* side of the *Window* was a Beautifull *Young man*, clad in a Garment of *various Colours*, bearing a *Yellow Crosse* upon his *Shoulders*, his *Body Encircled* with a *Bright Glory*, which sent forth *Beames* of divers Colours, He stood upon an *Earth* intimating *Oculus Piscium*.

At the *Foote* of the Midle Part of the *Window* was a faire large Red *Rose* full spread, which issued *Rayes* upward, and in the Middle an exceeding bright *Yellow Glory*. Above the *Rose* was the *Figure* of a *Man* rising with *Beames* of *Light* spread about his *Head* (somwhat like the Posture used to expresse *Christ's* rising from his *Sepulchre*) He had a *Garment* of a *Reddish Colour*, deepned with *Red* and heightned with *Yellow*; In his left *Hand*, a *White Stone*, which he held towards the Persons arising in that part of the *Window* on the *Right Hand*; and in his *Right Hand* he held forth a Red *Stone* towards Him, whose *Garments* was of *various Colours*.

In the uppermost part of this *VVindow* over the *Figures* was *Transversely* written as followeth:

In the *first* part of the *Left Hand*,

Omnes gentes adepti plaudite quia dominus frater bester.

In the *Middle* Part.

S. . . . at mittens spiritum suum, ecce nova facio omnia celum & (z) t . . .

In the *Third* on the *Right Hand*.

Factus quasi unus ex . . . . . is . . . . angelis tibi———.

z) In this place tis probable the word to be supplyed is *terram*.

Under these *Figures* in the *Left side* of the *VVindow* were the *Stawels* and the *Martyns* Coates of *Armes* quartered; And at the bottome of the *Right side* thereof, was this *Coate of Arms* placed, (*viz.*) *Argent, a Chevoron * Embattelled, Gules, & Vert*; which for the rarenesse of *Bearing* I thought fit to *Blazon*, and withall (because upon very diligent search among the *Records* of *English Coats* of *Armes* it is not to be found) in hope it may come to the view of such, who (if not at home) may from abroad produce the *Bearer*, and consequently bring

* Elements of Armor. p. 95.

to

to light the *Person* that design'd these *Hieroglyphicks*, and caused them thus to be *Painted*.

Pag.213. **Hermes Bird.**

WHich *Piece* (as 'tis thought) was written *Originally* by *Raymund Lully* (or at least made *English* by the afore mentioned *Cremer*) and that upon this Occasion.

Cremer travelling into *Italy* fell into the acquaintance of *Lully*, and so exceedingly wrought upon him by his perswasions that he (*a*) brought him over into *England*, where within *two yeares* (but after *thirty yeares* erronious *Experiments*) he obteyned the *Secret* from him. And afterwards bringing *Lully* to the sight and knowledge of *Edward* the *third*, upon some deepe *Ingagements* and *Promises* that the *King* entred into, *to prosecute a VVarre against the Turkes in person, to bestow somwhat on the House of God, but nothing in Pride or VVarring against Christians,*) he was content *permissione Divina Regem sua Arte divitem facere*. Which when the *King* had obtained, he brake his *Promise*, turned his *Designe* against *France* (the first *Expedition* being (*b*) Anno 1337.) and finding that *Lully* (after he had seene him violate his faith in destroying *Christians* in stead of *Mahumetans*) refused to further his Ambition with new *supply* of *Gold*, He clapt him up in the *Tower*, where he lay a long time, and seeing no possibility of *Release*, begun to study his *Freedom*, and to that end made himselfe a *Leaper*, by which meanes he gained more Liberty, and at length an Advantage of escaping into *France*, where in all probability he pen'd this *Piece*.

(*a*) Vide Testament. Cremeri.

(*b*) Stow. Ann. fo. 234.

The whole *Work* is *Parabolicall*, and *Allusive*; yet truly *Philosophicall*: and the *Bird* (that intitles it) the *Mercury* of the *Philosophers*, (whose *vertues* and *properties* are therein largely described,) By the word *Chorle*, is meant the Coverous and Ignorant *Artist*, the *Garden* is the *Vessell* or *Glasse*, and the *Hedge* the Furnace.

Pag.233. **The Tale of the Chanon's Yeoman.**

ONe Reason why I selected out of *Chaucer's Canterbury Tales*, that of the *Chanon's Yeoman* was, to let the *VVorld* see what notorious *Cheating* there has beene ever used, under pretence of this true (though Injur'd) *Science*; Another is, to shew that *Chaucer* himselfe was a *Master* therein.

For, in this *Tale Chaucer* sets forth the deceipts in *Alchimy* to the life, and notably declaimes against all such villanous *Pretenders*, who being wholly ignorant of *Art*, have notwithstanding learnt the *Cunning*, to abuse the World; And this paines he tooke (as himselfe professeth) meerly

c) **To the intent that men maie beware thereby,**
And for no other cause truly.

c) *Chau. Yeom. Tale.*

Herein following the *President* of all sincere and conscientious *Philosophers*, then whom, the *Injur'd world* cannot more condemne the abuses of these *Impostors*

postors that disgrace the *Art*, in that they are continually *advising* to shun them as spreading *Infection*; and setting out *Lights* and *Directions*, that may serve as so many *Land marks*, (if we will but take notice of them) to make us avoyd the *Rocks* of their *Fraud* and *Deceipt*, which will otherwise split us.

The famous *Art* of Physick is not more abused, with *Quacking Mountebanks*; nor that other of *Astrology* more injur'd by some nibling *Sciolists* and ignorant *Juglers*: then this *Divine Science* hath suffered by the *Legerdemaine* of some *Pretenders*. What though some Moderne *Chemists* rove beyond the *Latitude* of their *Profession*, (being hurried on by a Covetous thirst, to obteyne this *Arcanum Dei*, this *Thesaurus incomparabilis*;) and by operating in strange *Matters*, & torturing of various *Bodies*, bring *Disparagement* upon this worthy *Science*; yet we ought not therefore to confound praise-worthy *Arts*, with the *Abuses* which *Impostors* shuffle into them; or for the falsenesse or corruption of the bad, condemne the pure and good: If so, *Religion* it selfe (as well as other *Learning*, and *Professions*) would scarce be exempt from the like blemishes, and wounds, if not destroyed and buried in scornfull *Ignorance*.

This is the *Misery*, (and tis not *ultra Caduceum* for me to speake it) that there are a Generation of *People* that rush headlong into the acquaintance of such *Men*, there's nor staviug them off, much like the doting *Idiotts* which so eagerly courted *Chaucer's Chanon*, after whom

d) Chan. Yeom. Tale.

——d) Men riden and gone full many a Myle
Him for to seeke and have acquaintance,
Not knowing of his false governance.

Let *Philosophers* say what they can, and *wise men* give never so good Counsell, no warning will serve, they must be Couzened, nay they have a greedy appetite thereunto; but it has beene ever so, and we are told of old, that

e) Ordin. *pag.* 7

e) Many Artificers have byne over swift,
With hasty Credence to fume away their thrift,

so strong and powerfull a misleader is *Covetousnesse*.

f) Ord. *pag.* 17.

g) Chap. of Putresac.

f) *Norton* describes these *Cheats* exactly, and give as ful an account of their *Subtilties* as he dare, for feare of incouraging such as bend their *VVitts* that way. (g) *Ripley* dissects them to the *Bone*, and scourgeth them naked to the view of *all*; the like doth many other *Philosophers*: *Bloomefield* gives us a *Catalogue* of the cheife of this *Tribe* in his time, and I may safely tell the *Reader* he shall gaine much benefit by this *Worke*, if he pick but out what is said concerning them, and study that *First*.

In some darke *Passages* tis as greate a Curtesie to be taught to know *Blocks*, as to be directed which way to avoyd and get beyond them, and being soe thanke *Ripley* for this his following Cautionary advice.

h) Chap. of Putresac.

h) Beware therefore for Jhesus sake,
And medyll with nothing of greate Cost,
For and thou doe, yt is but lost.

As also *Norton*,

> i) Cease Laymen cease, be not in lewdnesse ever,
> Lewdnesse to leave is better late then never.

i) Ord. *p.* 126.

I wish I could say this *Age*, this *Nation*, the *World*, were not alured and infected with the *Cyrene* notes of some grand, and notable *Impostors*, or that the too too *Credulous* had not met with the same misfortune which *Story* tells us others have undergone, even to *Ruine*. Yet to those that have been Decoy'd into the *snare*, and would gladly for the future pursue a more hopefull *Course*, let them heare *Richard Carpenter*.

> k) Abyse the well ere thou begin,
> Or else lytel schalt thou wynne.

k) See Carpent. worke.

And with him *Chaucer*,

> l) If that your Eyne cannot seene right,
> Loketh that your Minde lack not his sight.

l) Chan Yeom. Tale.

And againe,

> Let no man busie him this Arte to seche,
> But he that the entention and Speeche
> Of the Philosophers understand can,
> And if he doe he is a lewde man.
> For this Scyence and Connyng quod (m) he,
> Is of the Secre of Secrees parde.

m) Arnold. de villa nova.

Let me tell them they may become *happier* and expect a *Blessing* in what they seeke; If with *Job* they can thus throughly purge themselves and say, *If I have made Gold my Hope, or fine Gold my Confidence*, &c. that is, if they can study this *Science* and not pursue it for Transmutation of Metals sake onely,

> n) For Covetous men that findeth never
> Though they seke it once and ever,

n) Pearce Black Monke.

and certainly the lucre of that will fix a *Curse* upon their *Endeavours*, and plunge them headlong into an unfathom'd depth of *Misfortune*.

If what hath been delivered be not of force to make men watch over their *undertakings*, and heedfully avoid the *Springs* and *Ginns* that are ordinarily laid to intrap them into *Ruine*; but that on the contrary they carelesly slide into a *Venture* upon any *Tearms*, Ile leave them with this incouragement,

> o) Who soe that lysteth to utter his folly,
> Let him come forth and learne to Multiplie;
> And every man that hath ought in his Cofer,
> Let him appeare and were a Philosopher.

n) Chan. Yeom. Tale.

 Now

Now as Concerning *Chaucer* (the *Author* of this *Tale*) he is ranked amongst the *Hermetick Philosophers*, and his *Master* in this *Science* was Sir *John Gower*, whose familiar and neere acquaintance began at the *Inner Temple* upon *Chaucer's* returne into *England*, for the Troubles of the *Times* towards the latter end of *Rich: the second's* Raign had caused him to retire out of their *Danger* into *Holland*, *Zeland*, and *France*.

He is cited by *Norton* for an *Authentique Author*, in these words;

p) Ord. *pag.* 42.

p) And Chaucer rehearseth how Tytans is the same.

Besides he that Reads the latter part of the *Chanon's Yeoman's Tale*, wil easily perceive him to be a *Iuditious Philosopher*, and one that fully knew the *Mistery*.

Master *Speght* (in that commendable Account he gives of *Chaucer's* life,) is perswaded he was borne in *London*, from something intimated in his *Testament of love*. But *Bale* saith, He was (*q*) *Nobili loco natus*, and that neere unto *Oxford*, for (saith he) *Leland* had *Arguments* which made him believe he was borne either in *Oxford-shire* or *Bark-shire*. But what those *Arguments* were we now know not, yet may believe them to be of considerable *weight*, because they were doubtlesse such as he gathered in his *6. yeares* laborious search into the *Libraries* of our *English Monasteries* and *Colleges*, being furthered by the liberall *Encouragement* and *Commission* of *Hen.* 8. And had it not been for his indefatigable *paines*, *All* that was notable in this *Nation* (r) *had in all likelyhood beene perpetually obscured, or at best, but lightly remembred, as uncertaine shaddowes.* Neverthelesse the *fruits* of this famous *Antiquaries* labours, are no where now intirely to be seene, unlesse dispersed through the *workes* of some other men, who have most arrogantly and unworthily made them their owne: amongst the rest I perceive *Polid. Virgil* stole much *Tymber* from this worthy *Structure*, with part whereof he built up his *Worke*, the rest be enviously burnt, for thus I finde *Lelands Ghost* Complaining.

q) Bale Cent. 7. *fol.* 525.

r) See his Newyeares gift to *H.8.*

s) Lelands Ghost.

s) Am I deceiv'd? or doth not Lelands Spirit,
Complaine with Ghosts of English Notaries;
Whom Polidore Virgill robb'd of merit,
Bereft of Name, and sackt of Histories,
While (wretch) he ravisht English Libraries.
Ah wicked Booke-theefe whosoever did it:
Should one burne all, to gett one single Creditt.

Am I deceiv'd? or doth not Lelands Spirit
Make Hue and Cry, for some Booke Tresure stelth;
Rifling his Workes, and razing Name and Merit;
Whereby are smothered a Prince-given Wealth,
A learned Writers Travaile, wits, and Health:
All these he spent to doe his Country pleasure,
Oh save his Name, the World may know his Treasure.

But

But begging *Pardon* for this *Digression*, (being on the behalf of so deserving a *Schollar*) I return to *Chaucer*. *Pitts* Positively saies he was born in *Woodstock*, of *noble Parents*, and that *Patrē habuit Equestris Ordinis Virū*, his *Father* was a *Knight*. And this may not be unlikely if we Consider, that not onely the *Name* is as *Auncient* as (t) *William* the *Conqueror's* time, but that some of the *Family* have beene both of large *fortunes* and good *quality*. For we finde (u) that *Edw the* 1. heard the *Complaint* of *John Chaucer* in the *Damage* of 1000 l. And also, that there was in the *Raigne* of *H.* 3. and *Ed.* 1. one *Elias Chaucer*, of whom (w) ——*Edwardus dei gratia, &c. liberate de Thesauro nostro Eliæ Chausecir' decem Solid*: With which (x) *Characters* our *Geffrey Chaucer* is written in the *Records* of *Ed*. 3. and *Rich. the second*.

But wheresoever he was *Borne*, his *Education* was chiefly in the *University* of *Oxford* in *Canterbury-Colledge*, (y) (suppressed by *H.* 8. and now joyned to *Christchurch*) though for some time he studied at *Cambridge*.

t) Roll. of Battell Abby.
u) Record in Tur. Lond.
w) Record in Scacc:
x) Speght in vit. Chaucer.
y) Stow. An. fol. 957.
z) Court of Law. Chap. 2

z) Of Cambridge Clarke.——

He quickly became a Witty *Logitian*, a sweet *Rhetoritian*, a pleasant *Poet*, a grave *Philosopher*, a holy *Divine*, a skilful *Mathematitian*, his Tutors therein were Frere John Son, and Frere N. Lenne, (a) (Friers *Carmelites* of *Lynne* remembred with honour in his *Treatise* of the *Astrolabe*) and moreover (I may safely adde) an able *Astrologian*, for almost in every Worke he inter-weaves most sound and perfect *Astrologie*. In Brief, he was *Universally learned*, and so affirmes his Scholar *Tho. Occleve*.

a) Bale f. 525.

b) O Universall Fadre of Science.

b) Prolog. to H. 5. while Prince.

Pitts stiles him (c) *Vir Belli Pacisq; Artibus mirè Florens*. A Man that excelled in *Arts* both of *Warre* and *Peace*, and a little after, *Nam jam antequam virilem ætatem attigisset, erat Poeta Elegans, Et qui Poesim Anglicam ita illustravit, ut Anglicus Homerus merito haberetur*: For ere he came to *Mans Estate*, he was an *Elegant Poet*, and one, who illustrated *English Poesy*, that he might have beene deservedly accounted the English Homer. *Lidgate* the *Monke* of *Bury* calls him the (d) *Load star* of our *Language*, and tells us that it was he, that

c) Pag. 472.
d) Pref to Bochas.

e) Made first to distill and Raine
The Gold dew dropps of Speech and Eloquence,
Into our Tongue through his Excellence.
And found the Floures first of Rhetoricke,
Our rude speeche onely to inlumine,
That in our Tonge was never non him like.

e) Jo. Lidgate de Nativ. Mar.

For indeed in his time all good Letters were laid asleep in most parts of the *World*, and in *England* our *Tongue* was exceeding wild and rude, yet (through his *refining* and *polishing*) it became more sweet and pleasant, in which regard he is stiled

f) The first finder of our feire language.

f) Occl. de Reg. Princ: cap. de Concill.

He

He spent many of his yeares in *France* and *Flanders*: severall *Preferments* he had at *Court*, for he was (g) *Armiger Regis* to *Ed.* 3. (a place of very good *Reputation*) (h) *Valectus Hospitii*, viz. *Groome* of the *Pallace*, and after in *R.* 2. time (i) *Controuler* of the *Custome-house London*; With these he had severall *Annuall pensions* during his *Life* granted from *R.* 2. and *H.* 4. His *Abilities* for *Forraigne Imployments* were so farre taken notice of, that he was twice or thrice sent abroad into other *Countries*, and thought fit to be one of the *Embassadors* into *France* to move a *Marriage* betweene *Richard* the second (while *Prince* of *Wales*) and the *Lady Mary*, *Daughter* to the *French King*. His *Revenue* was 1000l. *per annum*, a very plentifull *Estate*, the times considered.

g) Pat. Rot. first parte of 50. *Ed* 3. *M.* 5.
h) In Pellis Exitus Scacc.
i) Anno 8. R. 2

He dyed at *London* 25. *Octob. Ann.* 1400. as appeares by the *Inscription* upon his *Tombe* at Saint *Peters* in *Westminster Abby*, in an *Isle* on the *South* side of the *Church*.

Mr. *Nicholas Brigham* built this *Marble Monument* to his *Memory*, the true *Pourtraicture* whereof I have caused to be exactly graved in *Brasse*, and placed in *page* 226. There was formerly round the ledge of the *Tombe* these following *Verses*, but now no remainder of them left.

Si rogites quis eram, forsan te fama docebit:
Quod si fama negat, mundi quia gloria transit,
Hæc monumenta lege.

The *Picture* of Chaucer is now somwhat decay'd, but the *Graver* has recovered it after a *Principall* left to *posterity* by his worthy Schollar *Tho. Occleve*, who hath also these *Verses* upon it.

k) Occl. de Regem. Princ: *cap. de Concilio.* Upon the figure of *Chaucer.*

k) And though his life be queinte the resemblaunce,
Of him hath in me so fresshe liknesse,
That to putte other men in remembraunce
Of his persone, I have here the liknesse
Do make, to this ende in sothfastnesse,
That thei that have of hem lost thoute and mynde,
By this Peinture, may ageine him fynde.

Before Mr. *Brigham* built the aforesaid *Monument* it seemes Chaucer had a *Stone* layd over his *Grave* upon which was ingraved this following *Epitaph*.

Galfridus Chaucer *Vates & fama Poesis,*
Materna hac sacra sum tumulatus humo.

Pag 257. **Dastin's Dreame.**

I Am perswaded this *Worke* called by the Name of *Dastin's Dreame*; has beene turned into *English Verse* by some later *Philosopher*; for in his *dayes* we meete with no such refined *English*, and in *Latin* we have his *Vision* with which (in effect) this agrees.

The *Time* he liv'd in is not certainely knowne; I finde none that mention it; but tis beleeved it was long since. Our Country man (*l*) *Bale* speaks of him yet,

l) Cent. 10. *pag.* 49.

yet throwes at him and this *Science* some uncomely abuses: Neverthelesse he calls him *Alcumisticæ artis ætate sua primus & in Anglia Magister unicus*; the *Prime Alchymist* of his *Age*, and the only *Master* thereof in *England*; A *Producer* and *Foreteller* of things which (it seemes in his apprehension) he could not attaine to by *Nature*; He made a diligent search into all things that might possibly be found out in *Chemistry*, insomuch that he boldly *wrote* and *published* severall *Experiments*.

And though (*m*) *Pitts* renders him a very *Poore man*, and layes the blame upon his owne *Artifice*; (being so much addicted to *Alchymie*,) yet questionlesse (if he were *Master* of such *learning* as they confesse him to be, and his *Poverty* were not *voluntary*;) he might have advanced himselfe to riches when he pleased. He wrote these following *Bookes*, m) Pag. 871.

1. *Super Arte Alcumistica.*
2. *Visiones ad huc alias.*
3. *Secreta Secretorum.*
4. *Speculum Philosophorum.*
5. *Sapientum Aurinum.*

(n) *Maierus* saith he left behind him a considerable *Chemicall Tract*, which *Janus Lacinius* hath put in his *Collections*. Not unlike but this may be in *Lacinius* his *Pretiosa Margarita novella de Thesauro, ac preciosissimo Philosophorū lapide*; but the *Booke* I have not yet seene, and therefore cannot tell whether what is there published of *Dastin's*, be any of the before mentioned *Workes*. n) *Symb. Aur. Mens.* pag. 458.

Pag. 269. **Take Erth of Erth, Erths Moder.**

Ludovicus Combachius in his late *Collections* of some of *Ripley's Workes*, put this of *Pearce* the *Black Monk's* among them under the Title of *Terra Terræ Philosophicæ*; and publishes it as *Ripley's*: and withall that Tytle [*Terra Terrarum*] which (o) *Pitts* also gives to one of his *Workes* may seeme to insinuate this; But I conceive all are not *Ripley's* which walk under his *Name*, for questionlesse, many *Pieces* are (of late *Tymes*) fathered on him which he never wrote; *Bale* has not this at all among the *Catalogue* he delivers of what was *Ripley's*. And I have met with it in so old a *Manuscript* under the tytle of *Pearce* the *Black Monke*, that the *Hand* (as I Judge) speakes it to be antienter then *Ripley's* Time. o) Pag. 677.

Pag. 275. **Of Titan Magnesia take the cleere light,**
The Redd Gumme that is so bright:

Some Ancient Copies have it also thus,

Of Spaine take the cleere light,
The Red Lion that is so bright.

WHo to pitch upon for the *Author*, I was a long time ignorant of, yet at length I happily met with an old *Manuscript* (and it was the ancientest *Hand-writing* I ever saw this *Piece* written in) to which was affixt the

Name of *Richard Carpenter*; and thereupon I have *Intitled* it, **Carpenter's Worke.**

p) *Issac.Chron.* fo.467. I finde that in *Anno* 1447. *John Carpenter* then *Bishop* of *Worcester* (p) founded the Colledge at *Westbury* neere *Bristoll*, (mentioned (q) before to be Augmented by *William Cannings*: (r) by " pulling downe the old *Colledge*, and in " the new Building inlarged it very much, compassing it about with a strong " *Wall*, Embattaled; adding a faire *Gate*, with divers *Towers*, (more like un-"to a *Castle* then a *Colledge*,) and lastly bestowed much good *Land* for augmenting the *Revenue* thereof. Besides this he built the *Gatehouse* at *Hartleborough*, a *Castle* neere and (s) belonging to the *Bishop of VVorcester*; and did severall other *VVorkes* of *Piety* and *Charity*.

q) Pag.442.

r) *Godw*.p.367.

s) *Camb.Brit.* fo.574.

This *Bishop Carpenter* is supposed to be *Brother*, or neere *Kinsman* to *Richard Carpenter* our *Author*, and accounted an *Hermetique Philosopher*. He was *Contemporary* with *Norton*, and *Cannings*; and for the most part lived neere unto them, at the aforementioned *VVestbury*; nay he had so great Affection to that *Place* (not unlike for the *Societies* sake of *Norton* and *Cannings* or for some speciall Blessing he met with there) that (t) he intended to have it honoured with a part of his *Style*; and to have taken upon him the *Name* of *Bishop* of *VVorcester* and *VVestbury*, which though he could not effect, yet chose it for his *Buriall place* where he lyes *Inter'd*.

t) *Godw*.p.442.

In another old *parchment Manuscript* (and that a very faire one) I met this *VVorke*, *Prefaced* with what followes.

Aske ye of the Clerkes that holden them so wise, what is the Whete that most be sowen in the Erth, and whedere it is norshed forth hot or cold. For if it were in heate, it scholde never rote without cold and moysture. Also sey to hem alle, al that ever was comen of on, but it is dissevered in thre, as Fadere, and Sone, and Holy Ghost, One way there is, and no moo. Also loke which is the Fader and Modere of alle Metalles, For if thou drawe or take eny other manner thinge than his owne kynde, thou losest all thy werk: For looke whennys he cometh, and in his owne Moderes bely norshe him forth, and when he is of age norsh him forth with his owne Moders mylke, and gif him is owne Moders mylke.

Pag.278. **The Hunting of the Greene Lyon.**

IN the *Campe of Philosophy*, *Bloomefield* reckons up a *Worke* that beares the *Title* of the *Greene Lyon*, and amongst other *Impostors* (of his Tyme) calls the *Vicar* of *Maldon*, (but in some *Copies Vicar* of *Walden*) the *Author*; and consequently esteemes the *Worke* spurious,

u) Bloomf. Blos. *first part*.

u) **Then brought they in the Vicar of Maldon,**
With his Lyon Greene, that most royall Secret;

But what *Piece* soever that was I know not: I am confident this, that I here present my *Reader* with under that *Title*, is a perfect *Worke*, and truly

Philo-

Philosophicall; besides some Copies owne *Abraham Andrewe* for their *Author*, and is so confirm'd to me by the *Testimony* of a credible *Philosopher*.

Pag.293.l.20. God save my Masters life———

THomas Charnock (the *Author* of the *Breviary* of *Naturall Philosophy*) had the happinesse to have *Two Masters* that made him inheritor of this *Secret*; The first was he, whom here he Mentions, and it seemes

w) Was a Priest in the Close of Salisburie. w) Ænigm. de Alch.

This he further confirmes in his Breviary, thus:

x) Master J. S. his name is truly,
Nigh to the Citty of Salisbury his dwelling is,
A Spirituall man forsooth he is. x) Brev. of Phil. *Cap*. 4.

It seemes he had some *acquaintance* with this *Priest*, and in that time bent his *Studies* this way, Insomuch that the *Priest* falling *sick* (whilst his *VVorke* was a going) thought *Charnock* deserving of it; for *He*

———y) When he thought to dye,
Gave him his Worke and made him his Heire. y) Chap 3.

This *VVorke Charnock* continued going, till unhappily it perisheth by *Fire* upon a *Newyeares* day at *Noone*; probably it might be *An*. 1555. for that fell out in the *first and second of Phil.* and *Mar.* and in those yeares of their *Raigne* (which was parte in the yeare 1554. and parte in 1555.) he (z) received the *Secret* from the aforesaid *Priest*, as himselfe Testifies. At which time he was about 30. or 31. yeares of *Age* (though he intimates he was about 28. yeares old when he first met with the *Prior of Bath*) for *Ann*. 1574. he was 50. yeares old, as appeares at the end of his (b) *Fragments*, which I Coppied from his owne *Hand*. z) Chap. ibid. a) Chap. 5. b) See *pag*. 426

Pag. 296 lin 23. Only a Monke of whom I'le speake anon.

THis *Monke* was *Charnocks* other *Master*, into whose Company he (c) accidentally happened, his *Name* was *William Bird*, and by his *Function*, *Prior of Bath*, at the Dissolution of that *Abbey*;

This *Bird* (while *Prior*) expended much *Money* by (e) *endeavouring what he might to finish the Abby Church of Bath* (the (f) foundation of which sumptuous *Building* was begun by *Oliver King*, but he dying left it unperfect:) *and had brought it to a perfection, when the Dissolution of the Abbey, had once overthrowne what before was set up.*

It seemes this *Prior* had the *Elixir* upon the *Suppression* of the *Abby*: he hid it in a *VVall*.

c) Chap. 5. d) Chap. ibid. e) Godw. Succ. pag. 308. f) Cambd. Brit. 234.

g) Chap. 5.

g) And Ten dayes after he went to fetch it out,
And there he found but the stople of a Cloute.

For it was taken away; It made their Hearts *light* who found it, but his so *heavy*, and the losse so discontented and afflicted him,

h) Chap. ibid.

h) That many yeare after he had no setling place.

and (losing his *Eyes* soone after his *Ecclesiasticall preferments*) was quite deprived of attempting to make the *Elixir* againe. Whereupon he liv'd *obscurely*, and grew very *poore*; and not able to give *Charnock* entertainement, but his owne *Purse* paid for it, both times he was with him.

Pag. 298. lin. 25. Charnock is his name, of Tenet that Isle.

TEnet or *Tainet* is an *Isle* that lies in the *East* part of *Kent*, and the *Birth-place* of *Charnock*; however though he might be born there, yet he dwelt about (*i*) *Salisbury*, when he first met with his *Master Bird*. He cals himselfe the *Unlettered Schollar*, and by severall *Fragments* and *Notes* that I have seene of his owne *VVriting*, it does not appeare, that he understood much *Latin*, or knew how to write true *English*; yet though he wanted the *Shell* he obteyned the *Kernell*, and had the good fortune to meete with that in plaine *English*, which many (who have the assistance of other *Languages*) goe without; Thus we see by him, that *God* hath not excluded all who are *Masters* of no other then their own *Language*; from the happinesse of *understanding* many Abstruse and subtill *Secrets*; I could instance severall in this *Science*: and this very Consideration invited that noble *Fraternity* of the *R.C.* to publish their *Fame* and *Confession* in Five severall *Languages*, to the end the *unlearned* might not be deprived and defrauded of the *knowledge* thereof. Nor was the *Processe* (which all Students may take notice of) tedious or long in delivering to *Charnock*. For thus he saith,

i) Chap. 5.

k) His Master Birde.

Within three or foure words (k) he revealed to me.
Of Minerall Prudence the greate Misterie.

He lived in the *Ranke* of an *Ordinary man*, else I presume his *Quality* might have priviledged him from being *Prest* for a *Common Souldier*. And from a *Memorandum* of his owne hand, it may be gathered, that he practised *Chirurgery*; for thereby it appeares *He* bargained to have *Five Markes* for healing the *Leg* of one *Richard Deane*, for the payment of which one *Iohn Boden* and *VVilliam Lawly* became Suretyes.

Pag.

Pag. 300. li. 23.——— Remembring my Master tho.
Pag. 301. li. 5.——— My Master shall know all this.
li. 8. Then would I write to my Master———
Pag. 302. li. 1. Then I remembred my good Master againe.

IT is S. J. the *Priest* of *Salisbury* whom *Charnock* means in these severall places, and whose *Christian Name* was James: for in another private *Memorandum*, written by *Charnock*, I finde thus much;

> Memorand' that Sir Robart which did confer with my Tutor Sir James, in King Edwards dayes, dwelleth now in the Savoye in London, and hath it a Working there, as Harry Hamond told me at Saint James Faire.
>
> Anno Domi: 1566.

Page 301. li. ult. Forsooth it was Ripley the Chanon his Boy.

SOme will have this to beare a double *Construction* (either that *Ripley* was *Boy* or *Servant* to a *Chanon*, as being bred up under a *Chanon* while a *Boy*; or that it was one who was *Ripleys Servant*, and brought up with him when *young*; to whom *Ripley* (finding him faithfull) might commit the *Secret*) and so leave it uncertaine whether *Ripley* or his *Scholler* was Master to the aforesaid *William Bird*. But I rather conceive the latter most probable; for, *Ripley* *(l)* dyed about the yeare 1590. and the time that this *Bird* communicated this *Secret* to *Charnock*, was at least 64. years after. So that questionlesse this *Bird* was too young to be acquainted With so weighty a *Mystery* at the time of *Ripley's* death. However *VVilliam Bird* had a *Master*, though Sir James the *Priest* of *Salisbury* had none; but received it from Gods hands by inspiration: for *Charnock* sayes he tould him

l) *Bale Cent* 8. *fo*.623. *Pitts*. pag. 678.

> ———m) He did it not attaine,
> Of no maner of Man but of God, he put it into his head
> As he for it was thinking, lying in his bed.

m) Cap. 6.

Pag. 302. lin. 13. Yet the Gentleman did me more spight then the rest,
As when he made me from my worke to be Prest.

CHarnock was much hindred in the Course of his *Practise* by the Malice of this *Gentleman*, who it seems was some ill *Neighbour*, that bore him a *Grudge*, and executed it in as bad a time for the honest *Philosopher* as possible might be; [even then when he was neere finishing his worke,

> ———n) Within a Moneths reckoning.]

n) Cap. 4.

causing

causing him to be prest for a *Souldier* upon the Designe of relieving of *Calis*, (which was the (o) beginning of *Iannary Anno* 1558. and almost six *Moneths* after he had finished the *Breviary* of *Philosophy*,) whereupon in a *Discontent* he destroyed *All*.

o) Stow. An. 632.

Pag. 303. li. 6. **And if God spare me lyfe I will mend this another day.**

THe *Breviary* of *Naturall Philosophy* was begun to be written within two or three yeares after he was *Master* of the *Secret*, and though he seeme to promise some other *VVorke*, yet I could never learne that he wrote any thing afterwards, save onely His two *Ænigmaes*, (the which I have Marshald after his *Breviary*) and the *Fragments* incerted, Pag. 424. What time he dyed, is uncertaine, but after the yeare 1577. I meete with nothing under his owne *Hand*, although severall yeares before that, his *Pen* lay not still; for in divers spare places of his *Bookes* he inserted sundry *Notes*, to the which most commonly he affixt a *Date*; some whereof I have published in this *Theatrum*.

Pag. 305. **Bloomefield's Blossomes.**

THe *Author* himselfe also calls this *VVorke* the *Camp of Philosophy*, and the *Practick* thereof he styles by the *Name* of his *last VVill and Testament*. It was written by *VVilliam Bloomefield* (some Copies have called him Sir *William Bloomefield*) a *Bachellor* of *Physick*, admitted by *H*. 8.

I have seene a faire *Manuscript* of *Norton's Ordinall*, wherein (at the toppe of the *Leafe*, that begins every *Chapter* and some other Eminent places,) is a *Scrowle*, and in the first fold thereof is written [*Myles*] in the midle of it, the Number of the *Chapter*, and in the third fold [*Bloomefield*] which *Myles Bloomfield* I take to be the Owner of the *Booke* (and perhaps some *Brother* or *Kinsman* to our *William Bloomefield*:) Neverthelesse by at Note in that *Booke* (of an indifferent antient hand) I afterwards found this *Myles* is called the *Author* of

Blosmefields Blossomes.

Pag. 324. **Sir Edward Kelle's Worke.**

I Cannot give my *Reader* an Account of Sir *Edward Kelley*, but I must also mention that famous *Artist*, Doctor *John Dee*; (whose *last VVill and Testament* followeth Sir *Edw. Kelle's* Worke) He being sometime his Intimate *Friend*, and long *Companion* in *Philosophicall Studies*, and *Chemicall Experiments*: Till at length the worthy *Doctor* (leaving him in *Germany*) returned for *England*, and so by *Providence*, escaped from being his further *Companion*; in that straight *Confinement* which Sir *Edw. Kelley* suffered, (by *command* of *Radulph* the 2. *Emperour* of *Germany*) at Prague.

Touching

Touching Sir *Edward Kelley*, he was borne at *VVorceſter*, the *Scheame* of whoſe *Nativity (Graved* from the *Originall Calculation* of Doctor *Dee*, and under his *Hand)* I here Exhibite.

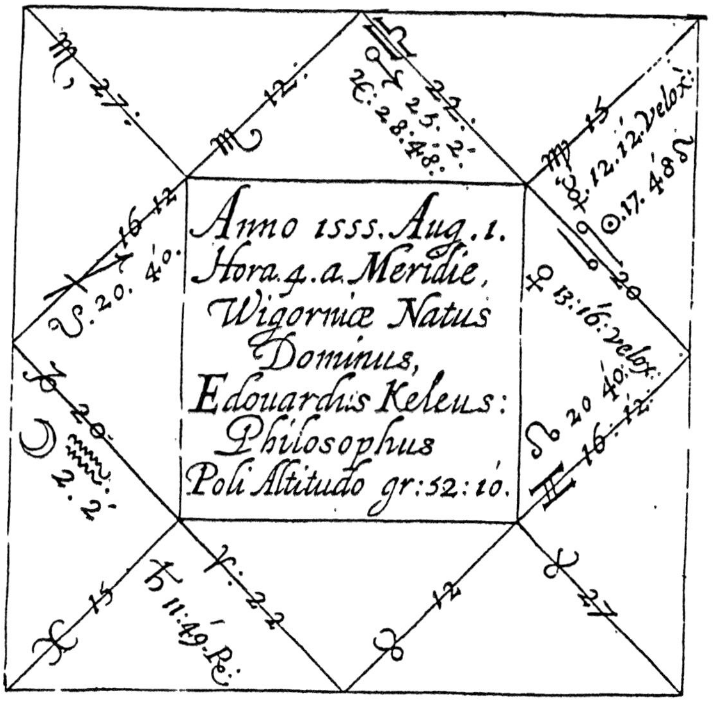

Which may be gratefull and acceptable unto ſuch that can read the *Language* of the *Heavens*: Inſomuch, that therein they ſhall finde out more concerning him, then *Story* has left us. For, whereas he by ſome is called *Philoſophus Dubius*, ſomewhat a better *Opinion* might be hence *Collected*, and that from the *Poſition* of *Mercury Lord* of the *Ninth*, (the *Houſe* of *Knowledge*, *Wiſdome* and *Science*;) and who is placed upon the *Cuſpe* thereof in *Virgo*, where he is exceeding Strong, and Fortunate, in *Dignities*; *Eſſentiall* and *Accidentall*, [viz. in his owne *Houſe*, and *Exaltation*, *Direct*, and *Swift* of *Courſe*, free from *Combuſtion*, and in the *Tearme*, and *Face* of *Venus*; to whom he applies by a *partile Sextile*.] *Venus* alſo is *Angular*, and beholding the *Cuſpe* of the *Ninth Houſe*, by a *Sextile*; All which (with Conſideration that the *Degree Aſcending* is in the *Tearmes* of *Mercury*,) doe truly render him a *Man* of cleere *Underſtanding*, quick *Apprehenſion*, an excellent *Wit*, and of great propenſity to *Philoſophicall Studies*. And indeede, by all Reports he was very *Ingenious*, and a continuall *Searcher*, in the abſtruſe and difficult *Secrets* of *Philoſophy* and *Chemiſtry*.

Yet for all this, he could not eſcape the hard *Cenſures* and *Scandalls* of thoſe that underſtood not what he did; which the *Dragons Tayle* in the *Aſcendant*, was

was at all times ready to further and promote, and from whose *Position* the *Nature* of those abusive *Aspersions* may be *(Generally)* gathered: and partly from a *story* which *VVever* in his *Funerall Monuments inserts*, where, though he make him an *Actor* in the worst part of *Conjuration*, and backs his *Relation* with some *Formall Circumstances*; Yet that nothing was done in the *Nature* he *Relates*, good and sound *Reasons* (too tedious to be touched here) induce me to believe.

As touching *Doctor Dee*, he chiefly bent his *Studies* to the *Mathematicks*; in all parts of which he was an absolute and perfect *Master*. Witnesse his *Mathematicall Preface* to *Euclids Elements*, wherein are enumerated many *Arts* of him wholly invented (by *Name*, *Definition*, *Propriety*, and *Use*) more then either the *Grecian* or *Romane Mathematitians* have left to our knowleage: with divers and many *Annotations*, and *Inventions*, *Mathematicall*, added in sundry places of the said *Booke*: Together with severall *Pieces* of *Navigation*, *Perspective*, and other rare *Mathematicall* works of his in *Manuscript*.

His Epistle prefixed to *Iohn Field's Ephemerides* 1557. *De usu Globi Cœlestis* to Ed. 6. *De Nubium solis lunæ ac reliquorum Planetarum*, &c. *Distantiis*, &c. to Ed. 6. *Astronomicall* and *Logisticall Canons* to *Caculate* the *Ephemerides* by; *De stella admiranda in Cassiopeæ Asterismo*. An Advise and Discourse about the *Reformation* of the *Vulgar Yeare*, speake him a learned *Astronomer*.

And lastly, that he was a good *Astrologian*, and a studious *Philosopher*, his 300. *Astrologicall Aphorismes*, His 120. *Aphorismes De præstantioribus quibusdam naturæ virtutibus*. *Monas Hieroglyphica*. *Speculum unitatis*, (being an *Apologie* for our famous *Frier Bacon*) His *Cabalæ Hebraicæ compendiosa Tabula*, with many others, afford no small *Evidence* to the *VVorld*.

All which and many more (in severall other kinds of learning) as *History*, *Heraldry*, &c. written by him before the year 1583. Some time He bestowed in
p) 28. Dec. 1579. *vulgar Chemistry*, and was therein *Master* of divers *Secrets*, amongst others he (p) revealed to one *Roger Cooke*, the *Great Secret* of the *Elixir* (as he called it) of the *Salt* of *Metalls*, the *Projection* whereof was *One* upon a *Hundred*.

His great *Ability* in *Astrologie*, and the more secret parts of *Learning* (to which he had a strong propensity and unwearyed *Fancy*,) drew from the *Envious* and *Vulgar*, many *rash*, *lewd*, and *lying Scandalls*, upon his most *honest* and *justificable Philosophicall Studies*; and many times forced him out of the *bitternesse* of his *Soule* (which was even *Crucified* with the malice of *Impudent Tongues*) most seriously and fervently to *Apologize*. Nor could he enjoy *Tranquility* in his *Studies*, but was oftentimes disquieted and vexed with the sower *dispositions* of such as most Injuriously *Scandalized* both *him* and *them*,
q) An. 1583. Insomuch that the (q) yeare he went beyond *Sea* his *Library* was seized on, wherein was 4 ·oo. *Books*, and 700. of them *Manuscripts* (a Caveat for all *Ingenious* and *eminent Philosophers* to be more *wise* then to keep any dear or *Excellent* Books in their own *Houses*.) And tis most probable that at this *time* his before mentioned *Speculū unitatis*, might fall into those *hands*, that would never since suffer it to see the *Light*, which might occasion the Learned *Selden* to say, this
r) Seld. Pref. to (r) *Apologie* was long since *promised* by him; but intimating it was never *VVrit*.
H ·pt. Concor. *An.* 1591. (s) Master Secretary *VValsingham*, and Sir *Tho: George* were sent to
s) Nov. 9. his then dwelling house at *Mortlack* by vertue of a *Commission*, to understand the

the *Matter* and *Causes* for which his *Studies* were *Scandalized*. And for some other thing in the like *Nature*, was he necessitated to send his (*s*) *Apologeticall letter* to the *Archbishop* of *Canterbury*. s) Jan.6. 1595.

These kind of *Persecutions* were stil Multiplyed upon him, and he sometimes Personally agreeved by them: for about the yeare 1594. he was under a kinde of *Restraint*, which occasioned him to (*t*) write to the *Lady Scydmore* to move the *Queene* that either he might declare his *Case* to the *Body* of the *Councell*, or else under the *Broade-seale* have *liberty* to goe freely where he pleased. t) 28. Oct. 1594.

And thus much concerning these two famous men in severall; now shall I give the *Reader* an *Account* of their *joynt Actions* abroad, as also what relates to *Doctor Dee* after his returne into *England*: which I shall doe from an unquestionable *Authority*, even *Doctor Dee's Diary*, all written with his owne hand; where I shall take the larger Field to walke in, because I move upon so certaine ground: some of which passages may please (if not concerne) the *Reader*. For I think it not fit to suffer such *Eminent lights* longer to lie in *Obscurity*, without bringing them forth to the view of the *VVorld*.

'Tis generally reported that *Doctor Dee*, and Sir *Edward Kelly* were so stangely fortunate, as to finde a very large quantity of the *Elixir* in some part of the *Ruines* of *Glastenbury-Abbey*, which was so incredibly *Rich* in *vertue* (being one upon 272330.) that they lost much in making *Projection*, by way of *Triall*; before they found out the *true height* of the *Medicine*.

And no sooner were they *Masters* of this *Treasure*, then they resolved to *Travell* into *Forraigne Parts*, where falling into acquaintance with one *Albertus Laskey* a *Polonian Prince* (which came into *England* the beginning of *May*, *An*. 1583.) on the 21. of *Sept*. following, They, their *VVives*, *Children*, and *Families*, went beyond *Sea* with the said *Prince*.

And whether they found it at *Glastenbury* (as is aforesaid) or howsoever else they came by it, 'tis certain they had it: for at *Trebona* in *Bohemia* (whither they were come to (*u*) *dwell*) Sir *Edward Kelley* made (*w*) *Projection* with one small *Graine* thereof (in proportion no bigger then the least graine of Sand) upon one *Ounce* and a Quarter of *Common Mercury*, and it produced almost an *Ounce* of most pure *Gold*. This was done to gratifie *Master Edward Garland* and his Brother *Francis*, and in their presence; which *Edward* was lately come to *Trebona*, being sent thither to *Doctor Dee*, from the *Emperour* of *Muscovia*, according to some *Articles* before brought, by one *Thomas Symkinson*. I also finde this *Note* of *Doctor Dee's*, Jan. 5. 1586. *Donum* Dei 2. ounces. E. K. Moreover, for neerer and later *Testimony*, I have received it from a credible *Person*, that one *Broomfield* and *Alexander Roberts*, told him they had often seen *Sir Ed: Kelly* make *Projection*, and in particular upon a piece of *Metall* cut out of a *Warming pan*, and without *Sir Edwards* touching or handling it, or melting the *Metall* (onely warming it in the *Fire*) the *Elixir* being put thereon, it was *Transmuted* into pure *Silver*: The *Warming-pan* and this piece of it, was sent to *Queen Elizabeth* by her *Embassador* who then lay at *Prague*, that by fitting the *Piece* into the place whence it was cut out, it might exactly appeare to be once part of that *VVarming-pan*. The aforesaid *Person* hath likewise seen in the hands of one *Master Frye* and *Scroope*, *Rings* of Sir *Edward Kellyes Gold*, the fashion of which was onely *Gold wyre*, twisted thrice about the *Finger*: and of these fashioned *Rings*, he gave away, to the value of 4000l. at the *Marriage* of one of his

u) Sept. 4. 1586
w) Dec. 9. 1586

his *Servant Maides*. This was highly *Generous*, but to say truth he was openly *Profuse*, beyond the modest *Limitts* of a *Sober Philosopher*.

During their abode at *Trebona*, they tried many *Chymicall Experiments*(to see whether they could make that *Iewell* they possest, (the particular account of their *operations* I neede not here relate) yet I cannot heare that ever they accomplished any thing; onely I finde the 27. *of Aprill* noted by *Doctor* Dee with severall expressions of *Ioy* and *Gladnesse*, as ——*Hæc est dies quam fecit Dominus*. Againe ——*Misercordia* Dei *magna*, and lastly,——*Omne quod vivit laudet* Dominum. And to testifie what they meant, he writes upon the 30. *day* following, *Master Edward Kelley did open the Great secret to me. God be thanked.*

Whiles they lived at *Trebona*, *Sir* Edward *Kelley* went dives times to *Prague*, and the 15. *of Ian.* 1587. he went into *Poland*, but returned the 9 of *Febr*. after, And 'tis probable these *Iourneys* were made in quest after some famous *Chemists* Things were not carried here so privately, but *Qeene Elizabeth* had notice given her of their *Actions*, whereupon she used severall meanes by *Letters* and *Messages* to invite them back into *England*, where it was believed she had so far prevailed that *Master Simkinson* and *Master Francis Garland's Brother*
x) 8. Dec. 1587 *Robert*, coming from *England* to (x) *Trebona* supposed they had beene ready to come over to *England* upon the *Queenes Letters* formerly sent them. And
y) 1 May 1589. though *Sir* Edward *Kelley* staid behinde, yet *Doctor Dee* (y) left *Trebona* and and came for *England*. But whether occasioned by some unkindnesse received from *Sir* Edward *Kelley* or falling out of their *Wives*, or the *Solicitation* of *Queene* Elizabeth (or all these concurring) I am not yet certaine, not unlike but each of them might contribute to their *Seperation*.

For that there was some *Greate* and *Wonderfull* unkindnesse past from *Sir Edward Kelley*, appeares, by his sending for Doctor *Dee*, the beginning of *Ian*. 1588. under shew of *Reconciliation*, and discovering more then an Ordinary *Intimacy* and *Compliancy* about that time, which *faire shewes* the *good Doctor* notes with this *prayer*. *God leade his heart to all Charity and Brotherly love*: As also by *Letters* sent from Doctor Dee to Sir Edward *Kelley* and his *Wife* the end of *March* following, requiring at their hands *Mutuall Charity*, which
z) May 9. (z) after upon *Mistris Kellys* receiving the *Sacrament* she gave her hand to *Doctor Dee* and his *VVife* in *Token* of *Charity*. But it seemes these things were not cordiall but onely outward; for 9. *Sept*. following, (the Lord *Chancellor* coming to *Trebona*) the *Rancour* & *Dissimulation* was more evident to him, and it seemes grew up to a greater height then he could beare. And thereupon he thought wisely to avoid the further *Danger* by leaving *Germany* which occasi-
a) 4. Jan. 1589. oned him to (a) deliver to Sir Edward *Kelley the Powder, the Bookes, the Glasse, with some other things*, and thereupon received his *Discharge* in *writing* under his *Hand* and *Seale*.

While these *Discontents* continued, severall Letters past betweeen *Queene Elizabeth* and Doctor *Dee*, whereby perhaps he might promise to returne; At
b) 1. Mar. 1589 length it so fell out, that he (b) left *Trebona* and took his *Iourney* for *England*.

The ninth of *Aprill* he came to *Breame* and had not stayed there three dayes, but the *Landtgrave* of *Hesse* sent *Letters* of *Civill Complements* to him, and within three dayes after, Doctor *Dee* presented him with his *Twelve Hungarian Horses*

Horses, that he bought at *Prague* for his *Journey*. (c) Here that famous *Hermetique Philosopher*, [Doctor *Henric Kunrath* of *Hamburgh*] came to visit him: The 16. of *Nov.* he went thence to *Stade*, where he met with Mr. *Edward Dyer* going *Embassador* for *Denmarke*, who the yeare before had beene at *Trebona*, and carried back *Letters* from the *Doctor* to Queene *Elizabeth*; He was a great Corespondent of Doctor *Dees*, and as earnest a *Searcher* after the *Stone*. c) 27 June 1589.

The 23. of *Novemb.* following, he arrived at *Graves end* having beene out of *England* 6. yeares 2. *Moneths* and 2. *Dayes*, and the 9th of *Decemb.* presented himselfe to the *Queene* at *Richmond*, where he was favoured with a kinde *Reception*.

Being setled againe at *Mortclack*, the *Queene* used to call at his *House* to visit him, and shewed her self very Curteous to him, upon all Occasions. Against *Christmas* 1590. she sent him *Two hundred Angels* wherewith to keep his *Christmas*, and a *hundred Markes* against *Christmas* 1592. she likewise sent him word by Mr. *Thomas Candish*, to doe what he would in *Alchymie* and *Philosophy*, and none should controule or molest him: and not unlike by the *Queenes example*, divers *Personages* of *Honour* at *Court*, frequented his *Company*, and sent him many *Guifts*, from time to time. Amongst others Sir *Thomas Jones* most nobly offered him his *Castle* of *Emlin* in *Wales*, to dwell in, free with all *Accomodations*.

His *Favour* was faire at *Court*, the *Queene* her selfe bad him finde out something for her to bestow; yet all the preferment he gain'd was the (d) *Grant* of the *Chancellorship* of St. *Pauls*, and the 27 of *May* 1595. his *Patent* past the great *Seale*, for the *Wardenship* of *Manchester*, whither *He*, his *Wife*, *Children*, and *Family* came the 14. of *Feb.* 1596. and the 20. day following was *Installed*, and in this *Wardenship* (wherein he had the unhappinesse to be often vext with the *Turbulent Fellowes* of that *Colledge*) dyed, deserving the *Commendations* of all *Learned* and *Ingenious Schollers*, and to be remembred for his remarkable *Abilities*, d) 8. Dec. 1594.

After Doctor *Dee* came into *England* (as is before remembred) *Correspondency* was still maintained betweene him and Sir *Edward Kelley*, in Letters sent by Mr. *Francis Garland* and others; (and some expectancy of Sir *Edwards* comming over: (e) Mr. *Thomas Kelley* (his Broher) putting the *Doctor* in hopes thereof likewise) but at length Sir *Edward* was clapt up *close Prisoner* by the *Emperour* (for he had so unwarily and openly managed the *Secret*, that it had given the *Emperour* occasion to carry a strict *Eye* over all his *Actions*, out of a desire to be sharer, with him in his good fortune) yet it seemes the *Emperour* set him at (f) *Liberty*, and Doctor *Dee* had notice of it the 5. of *Decemb.* after. And though he began to grow into the *Emperours favour*, in hopes to be entertained into his *Service* (for so he certified Doctor *Dee* by Letters in *August* 1595.) Neverthelesse he was clapt up againe into *Prison*, and attempting to make his *Escape* out of a high *Window*, by the teering of his *Sheetes*, which were tyed together to let him downe, he (being a weighty Man) fell and broke his *Legg*, and thereof *dyed*: (The *Ascendent* then coming by Direction to the place of the (g) *Moone* with *Latitude*, she being *Lady of the* 8th. house in the *Radix* and posited in *Aquarius*.) And this is one report of his *Death*; others there are, but Doctor *Dee* mencions none at all of the manner e) 23. Dec. 1589. f) 4 Oct. 1593 g) See the Scheme of the Nativity.

 thereof

h) Anno 1595. thereof; onely this, (h) *Novemb.* 25. Newes that Sir *E. K.* was slaine.

Pag. 365. **A Dialogue betwixt the Father and the Sonne.**

i) Placed in pag. 338.

THis *Dialogue* is there placed among the *Anonymi*, in regard I then knew not the *Author*, but afterwards I met with the intire (i) *Worke*, and found it to be that of *Ripley's*, which is called the *Mistery of Alchymists*, and that this *Fragment* was but drawne out of it, only drest up with another *Tytle*; which if the *Reader* compare he shall readily finde.

For the want of *Sense* in some parts thereof, as also in other *Elder Pieces*; I hope the *Dimnes* of the *Taper* will be excused where there was no *clearer light* to be found. For though (like the *Sun*) they may seeme to have some *Spots*, yet the candid Peruser must confesse they are not without their peculiar *Glories*. The truth is, some Passages through them were so obscure and dark, and the *Paths* I followed so rugged and uneven, that I could neither stay in them without manifest *disparagement*, or goe out of them without some *Danger*: and from my *discoveries* fraught thence, I am well assured I might have more contented the *Reader*, could I have satisfied my *Self* better. However, I durst not adventure to *Rectifie* what I found *amisse*; but thought it better to leave it to the *Judgement* of each that takes the paines to *study* them, then obtrude my owne *sense*, lest what I judge an *Emendation*, others may censure as a *Grosse fault*: and withall ever remembring the strict *Charge* the generality of *Philosophers* have continually given to *succession*, not to *meddle* or *alter* any of their *Workes*; I, (even in what I feare are manifest *Imperfections*) dare not but most inviolably observe them, and amongst them all this *Credible* and *Trusty Philosopher* is not unworthy of our taking notice of, who thus requires the same.

k) Hunt. green. Lion.

k) **Therefore in Charite and for the Lords sake,**
Let no man from my writing take
One word, or add thereto,
For certainely if that he do,
He shall shew malice fro which I am free,
Meaning Truth and not subtilty.

Pag. 368. lin. 5. **And also with grete diligence.**

l) Lib 4. fo. 76.

THis *Piece* is the *Worke* of Sir *John Gower*, and Collected out of his *Booke* (l) *De Confessione Amantis.* He is placed in the *Register* of our *Hermetique Philosophers*: and one that adopted into the Inheritance of this *Mistery*, our famous *English Poet, Geoffry Chaucer*. In this litle *Fragment* it appeares he fully understood the Secret, for he gives you a faithfull account of the *Properties* of the *Minerall, Vegitable*, and *Animall Stones*, and affirmes the *Art* to be true.

This

This Craft is wrought by wey of kinde,
So that there is no fallace in.

And againe,

The Scyence of himselfe is trew,
Upon the forme as it is founded.

He was an eminent *Poet*, and hath (*m*) written the story of the *Golden Fleece*, like an *Hermetique Philosopher*: which *Philosophicall* veine is to be traced through severall other parts of his *Works*. The first acquaintance betweene *Him* and *Chaucer* began at the *Inner Temple*, where Sir *John Gower* studied the *Lawes*, and whither *Chaucer* came to follow the like course of studies upon his returne out of *France*. He was (saith *Pitts*) a (*n*) noble and learned *Man*, *Galfrido ferè per omnia similem*, *quique eundem prorsus habuit omnium studiorum suorum propositum finem*, resembling *Geoffry* almost in every thing, and who had surely the same proposed end of all their *Studies*; they soone perceived the similitude of their manners, quickly joyned in *Friendship* and *Labours*; they had dayly meetings and familiarity, and all their endeavour was to refine and polish their *Mother Tongue*, that there might appeare the expresse footesteps of the *Roman Eloquence* in our *English Speech*.

m) *Lib.* 5.

n) *pag.* 573.

This appeares by *Chaucer's* sending to *Gower* his *Troylus* and *Cressida* after he had finished it, for his perusall and amendments.

o) O Morall Gower, this Booke I direct
To the, and to the Philosophicall Strode
To vouchsafe, ther neede is, to correct,
Of your Benignitees and Zeles good.

o) See the end of Troylus and Cres.

And surely these two added so much of splendour and ornament to our *English Idcome*, as never any the like before them: for they set foote to foote, and lovingly contended, whether should bring most *honour* to his *Country* both endeavouring to overcome, and to be overcome each of other, they being not only the *Remembrancers* but *Imitators* of him,

Quod lingua Catonis *&* Enni,
Sermonem patrium ditaverit, & nova rerum
Nomina protulerit,

p) *Stow* Margens it, that he was no *Knight*; yet we have it (*q*) from *Bale* that he was *Vir Equestris Ordinis*, of the Order of *Knighthood*, and *Leland* sayes that *Ab illustri stemmate originem duxit*, that he had his Originall from an *Illustrious Pedigre*.

p) Surv. *fo.* 450.

q) Cent. 7. 524.

He (r) built a great part of St. *Mary Overies Church* in *Southwarke*; and when *death* had snatcht out of his bosome his deare Companion *Geoffry Chaucer*, he then prepared a resting place for his owne *Body* in the *Chapell* of Saint *Iohn* in the said *Church* where he founded a *Chauntry*. He was very *old* and *blind* when he *dyed* and *lived* but two yeares after *Chaucer*. He had a stately *Monument* erected, wherein was his whole *Portraicture* cut in *Stone* in the *Wall* on the

r) Stow. Ann. p. 326.

North side of the said *Chapell*. The *Haire* of his *Head* Aburne long to his Shoulders, but curling up, and a small forked *Beard*; on his *Head* a *Chaplet*, like a *Coronet* of foure *Roses*, a habit of *Purple*, (Mr. *Speght* sayes *Greenish*) *Damaske* downe to his *feete*, a *Coller* of *Esses* of *Gold* about his *Neck*, the *Ornaments* of *Knighthood*, under his head the likenesse of three *Bookes* which (amog severall others) he compiled, the first *Speculum Meditantis*, written in *French*, the second *Vox Clamantis* written in *Latin*, the third *Confessio Amantis*, pen'd in *English*, which last was printed the 12. of *March* An. 1554. His *Armes* were these, *Argent*, a Chevoran *Azure*, three *Leopards heads* thereon *Or*, their *Tongues Gules*, two *Angels Supporters*, and on the *Crest* a *Talbot*.

His Epitaph

Armigeri Scutum nihil a modo fert sibi tutum,
Reddidit immolutum morti generale tributum,
Spiritus Exutum se gaudeat esse solutum,
Et Ubi virtutum Regnum sine labe statutum.

——*Deus nobis hæc Otia fecit.*

A

TABLE OF

The severall Treatises, with their Authors Names, contained in this WORKE.

A

A *Table* explaining the *Obſcure*, *Obſelete*, and miſ-ſpell'd *words* uſed throughout this VVORKE.

A

Abowen above.
Abrayde, aroſe, recovered, upſtart.
Agone, gone, fled.
Alconomie, Alchemie, Chemiſtrie.
Algates, Notwithſtanding, ever, forſooth, even now, altogether.
Allebiate, Elevate, lift up.
Alle, all.
Als, alſo, as well.
Ana, of each, a like quantity.
Anoder, another.
Annuellere, ſecular.
Appale, decay.
Appearage, appearing.
Appetible, deſireable.
Askaunce, as though, as if, aſide.
Askys, aſhes.
Auctors, Authors.

B

Baines, Bathes.
Bale, ſorrow.
Balne, Bainea Maria.
Behite, or **Behoote**, promiſe.
Belive, anon.
Ben, **byn**, be.
Beyet, begotten.
Blent, blind, turned back.
Blive, quickly, gladly.
Bloe, blew.
Blynne; ceaſe.
Boote, helpe.
Bawne, ready.
Brast, breake.
Brede, bredth.
Breve, **brevely**, briefe, ſhort.
Brenning, burning.
Broder, brother.
Browzt, brought.
Burbeley, bubling.
Burgeon, bud.
Byforne, before.
Byth, by.
Bythe, be.

C

Certes, undoubtedly.
Cheese, chuſe.
Cheepys, ſheepes.
Cheve, thrive.
Chorle, ſlave, clowne.
Chrystis Chriſt his.
Chyte, chiteth.
Clatter, brable.
Clapp, prate.
Clot leafe, Bardana, or greate Burdock leafe.
Clypses, Eclipſes.
Coart, inforce.
Convenable, Convenient.
Coude, could.
Couthe perfectly, know.
Cowlys, Monkes hoods.
Crop, topp.
Croslets, Crucibles.

D

Debonair, Humane, civil, meeke,

humble, gentle.
Delen, deale.
Demyd, demeth, Judged.
Denigrate, make black.
Depured, clensed.
Derke, darke.
Disceber, spend.
Dight, made ready, handled, used.
Dole, grieve, sorrow.
Done, doth.
Doncle, douce, sweet.
Draff. filth.

E

Emprisse, interprise, fashion, order.
Engluting, stopping.
Engine, witt, device.
Er, untill.
Erbe, Hearbe.
Erst, earnest.
Esell, Viniger.
Every eche, every one.
Eyre, wrath.

F

Fader, Father.
Fagg and faine, glose and flatter.
Fals false.
Fallacie, Deceipt.
Fanels, fanes.
Fastlely, firmly.
Faute, want, lack.
Fay, truth.
Fayne, glad.
Febis, Phæbus.
Fecis, dreggs.
Federis, fethers.
Fet, fetched.
Fende, Devil.
Ferle, strange.
Feynein, faineth.
Flewme, phlegme.
Foemen, Enimies.
Foltish, fullich, fully.
Folys, fooles.
Foyson, plenty.
Frape, Company, a rable.
Fright, fruite.
Frist, first.
Froze; frozen.
Fructuous, fruitfull.
Fychyes, Fishes.

G

Gafe, gave..
Gayer, Gaudier, Braver.
Geason, strange, rare.
Goude, good.
Gownds, gownes.
Gleire, white.
Godleech, kinde, respective.
Growyth, groweth.
Guerdon, reward.
Gyse, manner.
Gynns, snares.

H

Halse, Neck.
Hallow, hollow.
Haunt, use.
Hause, imbrace.
Haubergeon, a Coate of Male.
Height, called.
Hem, them.
Hende, gentle.
Henting, catching.
Herdy deed, stout act
Hernes, vallies, corners.
Hert, Hart.
Hestys, wills, promises, commandements.
Heyle, health.
Heyne, labourer, drudge.
Hing, hang together.
Hole, whole.
Hos, who so.
Hyr, their.
Hyt, it.

I.

Jape, Jest, yet by abuse drawne into a more wanton sense.
I cleped, called.
Ich, I.
I deale, meddle.

Jette,

Fette, device.
Ilke, same.
Ilyche, alike.
Engine, wit, devise.
I nowe, enough.
I not, I know not.
Intreate, handle.
Interdite, prohibited.
Iren, Iron.
Itake, taken.
Iwys, verily.
Iyfe, if.

K.

Keele, coole.
Keepe, care.
Ken, know.
Kid, made knowne.
Kidles, Kindles, i. e. fœtus, young ones.
Kythe, made known, shew. acquaint.

L.

Latt, let, hinder.
Laude, praise.
Laber, rather.
Laurer, lawrell.
Lay. law, song.
Cease your Lay, hold your Tongue.
Laysir, leasure.
Leare, learne.
Leasings, lyes.
Leese, loose.
Lech, Chirurgeon.
Lefe, left.
Leife, deare.
Leman, Concubine.
Lente, gentle.
Lettrure, a Booke of learning.
Lewde, ignorant.
Lewys, leaves.
Lexer, Elixir.
Lyken, affect.
Lite, little.
Lix, soft, plyable.
Longith, belongeth.

Losells, Crafty fellowes.
Losen, lesyth, loseth.
Loze, lost.
Lore, Doctrine, learning, knowledge.
Loef, love,
Loute, kneele, honour.
Lyche, like.
Lygg, lye.
Lysten, liketh, pleaseth.
Lyfelode, livelyhood.

M.

Maden, made.
Malison, curse.
Maugre, despite.
Maser, a broad drinkng-bowle.
Mede, mete, reward, help.
Medled, mingle.
Meger, leane.
Mele, meddle.
Menge, mingle.
Merds, Turds.
Mere, merry.
Meveth, moveth.
Micle, much.
Mo, more.
Moder, Mother.
Mollock, Earth, Dung.
Mote, must goe.
Mought, mowte, might.

N

Nas, was not.
Nathlesse, neverthelesse.
Ne, not.
Nere, were not.
Nemene, name,
Neshe, Tender.
Wilde Nepe, Catmint.
Nis, is not.
Nones, condition, purpose.
Nould, nolde, could not.
Nowbelson, Rose noble.
Nowther, neither.
Nye, is not
Nythe, neere.

O

Oder, odther, other.
Oft sythes, oughteſt.
Onychyne, Onix.
Ornate, decked.
Outwyn, depart, ſeperate.
Owthtys, oughteſt.

P

Panter, pitfall.
Parde, truly.
Parfite, perfect.
Pawkners, purſes.
Pleſaunce, delight.
Plyte, condition.
Plyght, turned, catched.
Pome-lgryſe, daple-grey.
Porpheries, Marble mingled with red.
Poyetes, Poets.
Prease, ſubjection.
Prefe, preve, proofe.
Preked, ridden faſt.
Previtie, ſecret.
Prolle, to prole after a thing.
Prawe, profit, honour.
Pyght, caſt, ſetled, propped.

Q

Queinte, ſtrange.
Quall, daſh, deſtroy.
Quyte, requite.

R

Rache, a litle cur Dog.
Rad, reade.
Ragounce, a kinde of precious ſtone.
Rath, quickly.
Recorden, recordeth.
Recure, recover.
Rede, meaning.
Rede, help, advice, ſpeeche, arte.
By Rewe, in order.
Ribaudry, baudry.
Ryghtfull, Juſt.
Rowe, ugly, blodily.
Rowne, whiſper.
Ruſe, red.
Rumbled, made a noyſe.
Ruth, lamentation.
Ryſe, frequent.
Ryve, rende.

S

Salew, honour.
Samples, ſorts.
Sans peere, without Fellow.
Sauter, Pſalter.
Scolys, ſchooles.
Schalt. ſhalt.
Sche, ſhe.
Schould, ſhould.
Schrevy, ſhreve.
Scuche, ſuch.
Seech, ſeeken, ſeeke.
Secree, ſecret.
Seild, ſeldome.
Sembleabyl, like.
Sewend, followes.
Shene, ſchine, ſhining.
Sh. nt, harmed, infected.
Shrewes, Infortunes.
Shrap, ſc·ape.
Sith, by and by.
S'ot lyche, ſlovenly.
Slypped, burniſhed.
Some dele, ſomewhat, ſomething.
Soote, ſweete.
Soothfaſtly, inſooth, truly, truth.
Sours, ſpring.
Spray, ſprig, bough.
Spurred, enquire.
Squames, ſtales.
Stabull, ſtable.
Stante, ſtand.
Steven, Stefen, ſound, alſo time.
Stillatorie, Alembick.
Stounde, time, moment, dumpe.
Strande, a banke.
Stynt, ceaſe, ſlacke.
Subſtray, ſubſtract.
Succended, inflamed.
Suffren, ſuffer.
Suſter, ſiſter.
Swezte, ſweete.
Swm, ſome.

Swych,

Swych, such.
Swynke, labour.
Swythe, swiftly.
Syker ynow, sure enough.
Sykerly, assuredly, stedy.
Syken, certain.

T

Tallages, payments, customes, taxes.
Taunte, a reprochfull Checke..
Temps, times.
Tente, .heede.
Teyne, an Ingot of Mettal.
Test, a device to try Gold with.
Tho, although some.
Threpe, affirme.
Titled, intitled.
Toder, the other.
Tofore, heretofore.
Togedur, together.
Trenete, Trinity.
Tristy, sad.
Trowe, trust.
Trowys, suppose.
Trusten, confidence.
Twayne, two,
A Twin, in two seperated, parted.
Twenes, Tunes.
Twifolde, double.
Tyte, handsome.

V

Vade, fade.
Vere, spring:
Unbound, delivered.
Uncoud, uncouth, strange.
Underfongeth, taketh in hand.
Unnethe, scarce.
Unwist, unwitting, unknowne.
Uphelyche, earnestly heartily.

W

Walken, walke.
Warke, worke.
Wastle bread, *libellus* fine Cimnell.
Wex, Wix increase.
Weerish, waterish.
Weene, thought, doubt.
Weening, thinking.
Wellid, riseth, springeth.
Wende, goe.
Wit, understanding.
Werne, were.
Whilome, ere while, sometimes.
Wile, deceipt.
Wist, kn owne.
Wall, will.
Wame, wombe.
Wanne, dwell plenty.
Woode, made.
Woorche, Swoorchen, worke.
Wolbig, thinking, judging.
Wose, was.
Waulden, would.
Wreach, wreake, revenge, wrath.
Wrenches, trapps.
Wrighten, written.
Wych, which,

Y

Ybore, borne.
Ydo, stayed.
Yef, Yeabe, gyf, give.
Yefet, fetched.
Yern, Iron.
Yllumine, enlighten.
Ynawe, sufficient.
Ynde, Indie.
Yode, yede, went.
Yrs, erewhile.
Ythe, thrive.
Ybel, apaid.

FINIS,

It will concerne the Studious Reader to Correct the faults escaped in this Worke, The most materiall whereof follow.

PAg.2.l.19.r. *uolunt* Pag.21.l.4.r. *like a* l.5.r. *did* l.25.r. *was a* pag.22.l.19.r. *scan* pag.30.l.22.r. *parte* pag.32.l.7.r. *the Motion* pag.37.l.12. *Troy :. trie* pag.45.l.17.r. *his* pag.46.l.17..*dele* [*I*] l.33.r. *ultimum* pag.56.l.7.r. *made* pag.63.l.19.r. *know* pag.66.l.14.r. *is* pag.74.l.4.r. *unctuous* pag.77.l.13. *VVhen* r. *Till* p.103.l.1. *dele* [*call*] p.140.l.16.r. *moving* p.146.l.3.r *certainely* l.13.r. *with* p.150 l.1.r. *principle* l.6.r. *noe*.p.151.l.14.r.*and our red* p.168.l.1.8.& 17.r. *Imbibitions* p.170.l.16.r. *leaves* p.200.l.15.r.*Philosophy* p.201.l.2.r.*Coyne* p.213.l.10.r. *Iudicum* p.215.l.14.r. *amerous* p.220.l.8.30.r. *Ragounce*.pag.223.l.29.r.*Tawre ythe* pag.224.l.12.r.*Three* p.226.l.1.r.*recomaund* p.227.l.16.r.*umeth might* p.228.l.12.r.*VVere* l.24.r. *friend* p.229.l.2.r.*couthe* p.230.l.10.r.*nil* p 234.l.18.r. *papere* l.28.r. *crude* pag.235.l.1.r.*Ascention* l.2.r.*fixe* p.240 l.17.r.*rave* p.240. *after* l.31.r. *Though it as great were as* Ninive p.241.l.7.r.*commune* l.9.r.*feinde* l.10.r.*begiled* p.242.l.16.r. *lene* l.18.r. *leneth* p.243.l.2.r. *fallen* l.24.r. *couthe* p.245.l.5.r. *three* l.15.r. *Christ* p.267.l.14.r. *After* l.15.r. *To* p.308.l.3.r. *wardes* p.309.l.1.r.*There* p.312.l.34.r. *an* p.317.l.16.r.*others* p.343.l.17.r.*exiguum* p.360.l.33.r. *If men* p.367.l.16.r. *Fier* p.383.l.24.r. *lyfe* p.416.l.2.r. *not* l.3.r.*Palace* l.5.r.*went* p.418.l.26.r.*solutive* p.423.l.20.r.*Redman* p.432.l.25.r. *mineralibus* p.448.l.29.r.*gratis* p.449.l.17.r.*knew* p.455.l.5.r. *omitting* p.458.l.2.r. *in his* p.459.l.18.r. *rythmicum* p.467.l.39.r. *dejected* p.465.l.13 r.*Vinculum* p.478.l.7.r.*after Charnock* l.25.*ns* r. *a* p.480.l.44.r.*unitatis*.

CPSIA information can be obtained at www.ICGtesting.com
Printed in the USA
LVOW10s0649270714

396213LV00002B/7/P